Cities, Citizens and Environmental Reform: Histories of Australian Town Planning Associations

Edited by Robert Freestone

SYDNEY UNIVERSITY PRESS

Published 2009 by Sydney University Press
SYDNEY UNIVERSITY PRESS
Fisher Library, University of Sydney
www.sup.usyd.edu.au

© Individual authors 2009
© Sydney University Press 2009

Reproduction and communication for other purposes
Except as permitted under the Act, no part of this edition may be reproduced, stored in a retrieval system, or communicated in any form or by any means without prior written permission. All requests for reproduction or communication should be made to Sydney University Press at the address below:
Sydney University Press
Fisher Library
University of Sydney NSW Australia 2006
Email: info@sup.usyd.edu.au

National Library of Australia Cataloguing-in-Publication entry

Title: Cities, citizens and environmental reform : histories of
           Australian town planning associations / editor, Robert Freestone.
ISBN: 9781920899356 (pbk.)
Notes: Includes index.
           Bibliography.
Subjects: City planning--Australia--History.
           Cities and towns--Australia--History.
Other Authors/Contributors:
           Freestone, Robert.
Dewey Number:
           307.12160994

Cover design by Miguel Yamin, University Publishing Service
Cover image: Melbourne's Post War Civic Center. Project by Percy Everett, Vice-President of the Victorian Town and Country Planning Association, from *Building*, April 1943.

Contents

List of figures v
List of tables x
Acknowledgements xi
List of contributors xii

Introduction: the historical role and significance of Australia's town planning associations 1
Robert Freestone

Part One: advancing the cause of town planning

1. Spreading the good news about town planning in Sydney 1913–34 27
   Robert Freestone and Margaret Park

2. Queensland's popular movement in planning 1914–30: socialism, regularity and profit 64
   Chris McConville

3. Town planning crusaders: urban reform in Melbourne during the progressive era 91
   Andrew May and Susan Reidy

4. 'Pedlers of new ideas': promoting town planning in South Australia 1914–24 120
   Christine Garnaut and Kerrie Round

5. Regenerating the people: town planning activism in Hobart 1916–39 148
   Stefan Petrow

6. 'Let our watchword be "order" and our beacon "beauty"': achieving town planning legislation in Western Australia 173
   Jenny Gregory

Part Two: critiquing proposals, plans and projects

7. 'The Kaleidoscope of Town Planning': planning advocacy in postwar South Australia 203
   Christine Garnaut and Kerrie Round

8. Visions of the city: town planning and community activism in postwar Perth 235
   Jenny Gregory

9. Democracy in action: public participation in planning in Hobart 1940–65 260
   Stefan Petrow

10. 'Wonderland': planning in a populist Queensland 1931–78 287
    Chris McConville

11. A new planning landscape for professional and community action in Sydney 1935–67 313
    Robert Freestone and Margaret Park

12. Dreams come true? Town planning ideals and realities in postwar Melbourne 342
    Susan Reidy and Andrew May

Conclusion: mixed fortunes, broadening agendas, and changing times 373
Robert Freestone

Index 381

List of figures

Figure 1.1: Sydney's Central Business District, 1915 28

Figure 1.2: George Taylor, founder of the Town Planning Association of NSW 30

Figure 1.3: Transforming the backyard into 'a veritable fairyland of brightness' 37

Figure 1.4: Civic Centre Scheme in Hyde Park, Sydney, c.1916 41

Figure 1.5: Catalogue of the NSW Association's 1913 town planning exhibition 43

Figure 1.6: Excursion of members to Culburra near Nowra, 1928 44

Figure 1.7: 'Town planners surveying Mud Flats and Mangrove Swamps at Concord', 1926 45

Figure 2.1: Aerial view of Brisbane, 1919 66

Figure 2.2: Breakfast Creek, Brisbane, 1929 67

Figure 2.3: Josephine Bedford, feminist playground and planning advocate, 1898 69

Figure 2.4: John Huxham: Queensland politician and QTPA President, 1916 71

Figure 2.5: Charles Chuter: public servant, local government reformer and supporter of planning 73

Figure 2.6: Advancing a metropolitan perspective: a 1928 plan from the Brisbane City Council's civic survey 81

Figure 2.7: Nambour: an early regional centre project of the QTPA, 1915 83

v

Figure 3.1:	Sir James Barrett in military uniform	92
Figure 3.2:	'Town Planning for Australia': from a flier for the 1914 town planning tour	97
Figure 3.3:	Charles Reade, Greater Melbourne Town Planning Scheme, from a glass lantern slide, c.1914	98
Figure 3.4:	J.B. Huggan	100
Figure 3.5:	Cover of the Town Planning Association's 1927 Annual Report	106
Figure 3.6:	Victoria Parade, Collingwood, c.1910	108
Figure 4.1:	Torrington George Ellery, c.1914	122
Figure 4.2:	Charles Reade, undated photograph	123
Figure 4.3:	Dr Ida Gertrude Halley, 1896	126
Figure 4.4:	SA Executive, First Town Planning and Housing Conference and Exhibition, 1917	128
Figure 4.5:	Lydia Longmore, c.1912	130
Figure 4.6:	West Terrace Children's Playground, 1917	131
Figure 4.7:	Mitcham Garden suburb, bird's eye view, 1917	136
Figure 5.1:	Rudolph Koch, leading town planning activist	151
Figure 5.2:	Reade's plan for an industrial area and garden suburb	152
Figure 5.3:	Low standard housing, Sackville Street, Wapping	160
Figure 5.4:	Franklin Square	163
Figure 5.5:	The opening of Princes Wharf Squares	164
Figure 5.6:	The opening of St David's Park	165

Figure 6.1:	W.E. Bold, Town Clerk of Perth 174
Figure 6.2:	Harold Boas, Chairman of the new Town Planning Commission, c.1928 177
Figure 6.3:	Bessie Rischbieth and Ethel Joyner, c.1919 180
Figure 6.4:	William Saw's vision for a greater percentage of parks throughout the city 182
Figure 6.5:	Mutilation of trees, Ord Street, West Perth, 1918 183
Figure 6.6:	Carl Klem's plan for civic improvements including the sinking of the railway 187
Figure 6.7:	Carl Klem (right) showing David Davidson the layout of the city the day after the latter's arrival in Perth, 1929 190
Figure 7.1:	'Re-planning Britain' exhibition, Adelaide 205
Figure 7.2:	Looking north from Victoria Square along King William Street, Adelaide 208
Figure 7.3:	'Can I make a suggestion?' 212
Figure 7.4:	David Higbed, c.1975 219
Figure 7.5:	'Of course we still have to iron out a few bumps' 220
Figure 7.6:	'The Future of the City of Adelaide' seminar papers, October 1973 222
Figure 8.1:	Barracks Defence Council sticker, c.1966 239
Figure 8.2:	St George's Terrace, Perth, 1954 242
Figure 8.3:	At the symposium organised by Professor Martyn Webb and the Civic Affairs Committee at the University of Western Australia, September 1972 244

Figure 8.4:	Members of the Civic Affairs Committee after the 1972 symposium at the University of Western Australia	245
Figure 8.5:	Conviviality marked City Vision gatherings	249
Figure 8.6:	The cover of City Vision's Manifesto, 1988	250
Figure 9.1:	Aerial view of central Hobart, c.1944	264
Figure 9.2:	John Arthur Turnbull, community planning advocate.	268
Figure 9.3:	Congestion in Elizabeth Street, Hobart, looking north	270
Figure 9.4:	Road through Franklin Square	271
Figure 9.5:	Car park fronting Bathurst Street	272
Figure 9.6:	The Brooker Highway looking south from Cleary's Gates c.1962	275
Figure 10.1:	Aerial view of Brisbane, 1936	288
Figure 10.2:	Victoria Street, Mackay in the 1930s	289
Figure 10.3:	Ian Wood, Mayor of Mackay (1930–33, 1943–52, 1967–70)	291
Figure 10.4:	Roma Street Markets, Brisbane, late 1930s	295
Figure 10.5:	Clem Jones, Brisbane Lord Mayor, 1967	297
Figure 10.6:	Trams in Adelaide Street, Brisbane, 1955	301
Figure 10.7:	Surfers Paradise, 1951	304
Figure 11.1:	Sydney's Central Business District, 1948	314
Figure 11.2:	Bertram Ford, President of the Town Planning Association from 1936–37	319

Figure 11.3: Proposed remodelling of Martin Place at Macquarie Street, late 1930s 323

Figure 11.4: Wartime meeting in a bomb shelter, 1941 326

Figure 11.5: Proposed civic centre at Bankstown, 1941 327

Figure 11.6: Proposed community centre at Collaroy, 1946 327

Figure 11.7: Bertram Ford in the Sydney Domain. He is addressing a public meeting demanding restoration of Sydney's GPO clock and tower, 1954 332

Figure 12.1: Cover of the TCPA's most successful publication, *National Parks Victoria Australia*, 1949 347

Figure 12.2: Professor Brian Lewis, 1966 353

Figure 12.3: Robert Gardner 354

Figure 12.4: Elevated view of Jolimont looking towards Melbourne, with proposed ring road indicated, 1963 355

Figure 12.5: Ruth Crow at Palm Sunday rally, Carlton Gardens, 19 March 1989 356

Figure 12.6: F19 freeway protest, 30 April 1977 359

Figure 12.7: South Australian Labor Premier Don Dunstan and federal Labor Minister Jim Cairns 361

List of tables

Table 1:	A brief contextual timeline of Australian planning history	5
Table 2:	Australia's town planning associations	9
Table 3:	The evolution of objectives of town planning associations	11
Table 1.1:	Office bearers in the Town Planning Association of NSW 1913–34	32
Table 1.2:	A select list of TPANSW deputations 1914–34	46
Table 1.3:	A select list of TPANSW lectures 1913–27	51
Table 7.1:	South Australian Town and Country Planning Association: public lectures and events 1964–69	214
Table 7.2:	South Australian Town and Country Planning Association: public lectures and meetings 1970s	217
Table 11.1:	A select list of TPANSW Deputations 1935–57	321
Table 12.1:	Publications by the TCPA 1942–87	349
Table 12.2:	Outline of the Town and Country Planning Association's 'Charter for planning' (1997)	363

Acknowledgements

The research for this book was made possible by an Australian Research Council Discovery Project grant (DP0771569) 2007–09 entitled 'Rediscovering historical contributions in environmental planning: Australia's Town Planning Associations'. The chief investigators were Professor Robert Freestone, Dr Christine Garnaut, Dr Stefan Petrow, Professor Jenny Gregory, Associate Professor Andrew May, and Dr Chris McConville. Early versions of various chapters were presented at four conferences: the 9th Urban History/Urban Planning History Conference at the University of the Sunshine Coast (February 2008), the 13th International Planning History Conference in Chicago (July 2008), the Australian Historical Association Biennial Conference at the University of Melbourne (July 2008), and the American Urban History Association Biennial Conference in Houston (November 2008). Productive discussion and constructive critique at all these meetings have helped shaped the contents of this book. In its writing, authors Christine Garnaut and Kerrie Round acknowledge the assistance of Brian Samuels, Stuart Hart, John Coulter, John Sibly and David Higbed in the preparation of chapter 7. Jenny Gregory acknowledges David Robinson and Ruth Morgan in assisting with archival research for chapter 6, and for chapter 8, the assistance of City Vision in allowing access to their archives and Ruth Morgan in undertaking archival research. Chris McConville acknowledges the substantial research for chapters 2 and 10 carried out by Sean O'Keeffe and Marie Lynch. Stefan Petrow thanks Dr Caroline Evans for her research assistance with chapters 5 and 9. Margaret Park prepared the index. The editor, authors and publisher collectively acknowledge the various individuals and institutions around Australia for supplying images and permissions for reproduction. Every effort has been made to locate the copyright holder of all images used.

List of contributors

Robert Freestone is Professor of Planning and Urban Development in the Faculty of the Built Environment at the University of New South Wales.

Christine Garnaut is Senior Research Fellow and Director, Architecture Museum in Art, Architecture and Design at the University of South Australia.

Jenny Gregory is Professor of History and Head of the School of Humanities at The University of Western Australia.

Andrew May is Associate Professor in Australian History in the School of Historical Studies at The University of Melbourne.

Chris McConville was a Senior Lecturer in the Faculty of Arts and Social Sciences at the University of the Sunshine Coast, and is now based in Melbourne.

Margaret Park has a PhD from UTS Sydney and is a public historian working mainly in Canberra and Sydney.

Stefan Petrow is a Senior Lecturer in the School of History and Classics, University of Tasmania.

Kerrie Round, a consultant historian and editor, is a research assistant, Centre for Regulation and Market Analysis in the School of Commerce at the University of South Australia.

Susan Reidy is a postgraduate student in Australian History in the School of Historical Studies at The University of Melbourne.

Introduction

The historical role and significance of Australia's town planning associations

Robert Freestone

Public participation in urban planning processes is now so entrenched that it is inconceivable that any study of policies, decisions and outcomes could be divorced from an appreciation of this broader community context. Involvement is expressed and transacted in many different ways including the now almost universal requirement to place planning proposals on public exhibition, through surveys gathering both opinions and activity data, charrettes involving stakeholders in the design process, and public meetings and hearings. Ever since Sherry Arnstein captured succinctly the idea of a ladder of participation in rungs from mere tokenism to citizen control in the late 1960s at a time when neighbourhood and environmental protest movements were on the rise worldwide, the political process has had to accommodate a greater degree of community intervention.[1] Just what type and degree depends on the scale, timing and complexity of the planning issue.[2] Checks and constraints constitute a counter trend as major and controversial developments are often re-routed from the full gaze of the public for determination by politicians, commissioners and judges. Even then there are protocols and accountabilities which open up the planning process to public scrutiny and input in a way inconceivable just a few decades ago.[3] Community contribution has certainly risen above a localised not-in-my-backyard NIMBYism to have increasingly more influence at the strategic level of goal formation and spatial visioning.

This is not all completely new. Our initial impression of participatory processes is still galvanised by the often confrontational urban social movements and environmental pressure groups in intervening in urban change in the post-World War II era, especially from the Vietnam War era in western countries.[4] An efflorescence of organisations arose to pursue localised and specialised agendas.[5] Collapse of the postwar consensus concerning bureaucratic planning 'in the public interest' caused the great surge towards more participatory frameworks internationally.[6] Allied to a marked rise in resident action group activity, the union-imposed green bans of the 1970s were a distinctively Australian contribution to this era of conflict.[7]

Yet there is a much longer history of community involvement in shaping or at least seeking to influence government plans and policies for cities and suburbs. Indeed, community activism has long been integral to the evolution of planning ideas and ideology. It has shaped diverse objectives and outcomes into community acceptability and political feasibility in big and little ways over many years. These contributions are frequently obscured by 'top down' history with its bureaucratic-technocratic orientation tending to enshrine official perspectives and a focus on plans, planners and planning institutions.[8] But other stories of inspiration, critique and contestation associated with actors outside the officially appointed commissions, executive committees, and advisory boards are equally noteworthy.[9] And when we look at the very birth of modern planning at the beginning of the 20th century some of the key initiatives came from outside government through improvement societies, civic associations and professional bodies calling for new possibilities for collective intervention in cities in the interests of health, economy and beauty.

This book is one set of stories in a 'pre-history' of community involvement in the development of Australian town planning from the early 20th century. They concern the town planning associations established in every Australian capital city between 1913–16 by citizens and professionals in the first wave of enthusiasm for modern town planning ideals. Their formation responded to challenging conditions in Australian cities in the early 1900s calling forth the need to explore innovative responses and new regulations. These groups do surface from time to time in accounts of planning activism, particularly in the 1910s and 1920s but their role and significance in Australian urban history have never been systematically documented and critically assessed.[10] Now for the first time, this collection assembles essays from leading researchers on each of the associations organised in Australia's six state capital cities. The authors consider how the associations' cutting edge contributions invented in the 1910s and early 1920s were sustained, reinvented or re-imagined within the different milieu for planning which developed from the 1930s into the post-World War II years.

The original town planning associations were not merely advocates for particular needs and projects although they took on a raft of specific issues in time. Their major cause was the very idea of town planning. This message was pitched to hostile property owners, apathetic business-people, an innocent public, and elected representatives who represented an array of community views in ways often watchful about the implications of new reforms on government expenditure and organisation. Unlike more specialised interest groups, the association agendas were broad brush. The archetypal organisation of this kind was the British Town and Country Planning Association. Founded by Ebenezer Howard in 1899 to promote his Garden City utopia, it evolved into and survives as an authoritative independent voice across the spectrum of environmental planning issues.[11] This prototype proved influential in Australia where British exemplars carried weight because of the historical origins of the nation.

To help set the scene for the chapters which follow, this introduction provides a national overview of early agendas and achievements. It highlights similarities and differences in the activities and longevity of the associations in the six Australian states. It surveys their formation, objectives, membership, and *modus operandi* in what was an unevenly paced metamorphosis from general advocacy of planning as a beneficent urban reform to more diverse agendas as members confronted the physical, social and redistributional impacts of planning in practice. Their longevity and resuscitation related to their relevance and adaptability to the changing political, institutional and professional contexts for urban planning in different states. Their eventual demise and renaissance at various times from the 1920s to the 1980s was forced by the reorientation of community organisation in planning action, although remarkably one body has hung on continuously since 1914. The overarching backdrop here is the broader evolution of urban planning in 20th-century Australia.

Development of planning in Australia

The evolution of modern urban planning as a force for shaping Australian cities has many parallels in other western nations, particularly the United Kingdom and the United States. The basic chronology is reasonably well established.[12] Table 1 provides a summary chronology encapsulating the main period covered by this book as a backdrop to specific events discussed. Responses to problems thrown up by rapid urbanisation at the end of the nineteenth century included both new public health legislation to regulate streets and buildings and utopian tracts promoting completely new communities. Incremental city improvements were pursued in hit-and-miss fashion. A more integrated and coordinated approach emerged in the early 1910s out of existing built environment professions such as architecture, engineering and surveying. A variety of innovations was tried including new statutes to enable local authorities to plan their territories in advance of settlement, formation of planning commissions to oversee preparation of comprehensive city plans, slum clearance schemes, powers and funds to acquire open spaces, and the building of planned communities.

Table 1: A brief contextual timeline of Australian planning history

1890	John Sulman, 'The laying out of towns', Australasian Association for the Advancement of Science Conference, Melbourne
1901	*Federation of colonies into states and formation of the Commonwealth*
1901	Congress of Engineers, Architects, Surveyors ... to discuss questions relating to the laying out and building of the federal capital
1909	Royal Commission for the improvement of the City of Sydney and its Suburbs
1912	Walter Burley Griffin declared winner of the international design competition for the federal capital of Australia
1914–18	*World War I*
1914	Charles Reade and William Davidge Town Planning Lecture Tour for the Garden Cities and Town Planning Association George Taylor, *Town Planning for Australia*, Building Limited William Bold, *Report on a Tour Round the World*, Perth City Council
1915	James Morrell, *Town Planning*, for Victorian Minister for Public Works
1917	First Australian Town Planning Conference and Exhibition, Adelaide
1918	Second Australian Town Planning Conference and Exhibition, Brisbane
1919	Vernon Memorial Lectures in Town Planning, University of Sydney
1920	South Australian town planning legislation
1921	John Sulman, *An Introduction to the Study of Town Planning in Australia*, NSW Government Printer
1928	Western Australian town planning legislation
1929–33	*The Great Depression*
1929	Melbourne Metropolitan Town Planning Commission, Report on General Development
1930	Report of the Metropolitan Town Planning Commission, Perth
1934	Town and Country Planning Institute of Australia (NSW)
1939–45	*World War II*
1944	Commonwealth Housing Commission, *Final Report* FO Barnett, WO Burt and F Heath, *We Must Go On*, The Book Depot
1944–45	*Town Planning Act*s for New South Wales, Victoria and Tasmania
1947	National Trust of Australia (NSW)

1948	*Report on the Planning Scheme for the County of Cumberland* (Sydney)
	National Lecture Tour by Sir Patrick Abercrombie
1949	First tertiary planning courses, South Australian Institute of Mines and the University of Sydney
1951	Alfred Brown and Howard Sherrard, *Town and Country Planning*, Melbourne University Press
	Formation of the (Royal) Australian Planning Institute
1954	Melbourne Metropolitan Planning Scheme
1955	Report from the Select Committee appointed to inquire into and report upon the development of Canberra
	Establishment of National Capital Development Commission
	Plan for the Metropolitan Region, Perth and Fremantle
1962–72	***Australian involvement in the Vietnam War***
1962	Report on the Metropolitan Area of Adelaide
1966	Australian Institute of Political Science, Australian Cities: Chaos or Planned Growth Conference
1967	Australian Institute of Urban Studies
1968	Sydney Region Outline Plan
1970	Hugh Stretton, *Ideas for Australian Cities*
1971	Coalition of Resident Action Groups, Sydney
1971–74	Green Bans
1972	Federal Department of Urban and Regional Development
1974	Report of the National Estate
1975	Leonie Sandercock, *Cities for Sale*
1988	Darling Harbour redevelopment, Sydney
1989	Abolition of the National Capital Development Commission
1991–96	Building Better Cities program
1991	Melbourne Docklands
	First Australian urban/planning history conference, University of New South Wales
1995	Australian Model Code for Residential Development
1996	Patrick Troy, *The Perils of Urban Consolidation*
1998	Save Our Suburbs, Melbourne
	Development Assessment Forum
2001	***The new millennium***
2001	Australian Council for the New Urbanism

2002	Reorganisation of the Royal Australian Planning Institute into the Planning Institute of Australia (NSW)
2003	Local Government and Planning Ministers Council
2005	House of Representatives Standing Committee inquiry on Environment and Heritage Inquiry into Sustainable Cities
2006	Productivity Commission Inquiry into Conservation of Historic Places
2008	Major Cities Unit, Commonwealth Department of Infrastructure, Transport, Regional Development and Local Government

From a protracted period of experimentation and voluntary advocacy came the institutionalisation of planning controls at different tiers of government, mainly after World War II. In the wake of enthusiasm for postwar reconstruction, the state finally acknowledged the necessity of regulation in the interests of economic, social and environmental health. Sanctioned by state legislatures, a new administrative machinery of government branches, departments and authorities codified collective goals and regulations as a framework for the development of comprehensive planning schemes by local authorities. Tension between state and local interests, occasional interventions by the federal government, and calls for simplification of controls were entrenched as part of the planning landscape. The latter have increased in frequency as the market-critical welfarist model of the 1940s mirrored a similar global trajectory towards (and now beyond) a more market-sensitive neo-liberalism paradigm of urban governance.

The distinctiveness of the Australian experience is rooted in the framework of a federal system of government with strong and competing states, weak local authorities, capital city dominance, a small population, modest-sized economy, and the early dominance of British conceptual and legal precedents in responding to urban issues. A heavy dose of pragmatism ruled city development, with the demands of capitalism pre-eminent. Different waves of enlightened approaches were felt. In the early 1900s the British garden city movement with its roots in housing and land reform had a major impact in tidying up existing suburbanisation trends into new model house-and-garden suburbs. By the 1920s the cutting edge was comprehensive city planning with a strong bias towards American city functional thought, but the legislative innovations arriving belatedly at a national scale in the 1940s followed British town and country planning precepts based largely around municipal land use control. American-style environmental policy reforms enter the scene in the 1960s.

Town planning associations played a vital role in the emergence and articulation of a bona fide town planning movement in the years immediately preceding World War I. City and state governments had begun to explore and tentatively experiment with town planning concepts, influenced both by overseas developments and the inspiration of the idea of a new federal capital city planned for the Commonwealth. Town planning associations provided an independent focus for activity separate from the professional institutes who were also awakening to the fresh possibilities of planning. This new discourse was played out primarily in the six capital cities where the associations were headquartered, but there were also ephemeral town planning associations in regional centres in the 1920s–30s including Launceston (Tasmania), Geelong (Victoria) and Newcastle (NSW).

The variable lifespans of the state associations can be organised into four main eras spanning the 1910s to the present day (Table 2). World War II is the fundamental divide. The nature of the post-World War II organisations which functioned against a backdrop of town planning legislation generally differed from their pioneering predecessors who had sought to achieve that very goal. The bodies in Brisbane and Adelaide were connected in name only to the initial organisations in these cities. In Hobart and Perth, a continuity is more apparent into new associations sharing the more expansive agendas of the earlier ones. While the Sydney body was virtually a one-man band from the 1940s, its Melbourne counterpart has endured as a community organisation, enjoying bursts of high profile and credibility in the 1970s and early 1990s.

Table 2: Australia's town planning associations

	Origins 1900s–1910s	Core period of activity 1910s–1930s	Twilight and successor groups 1940s–1960s	Ongoing 1960s–present
Town Planning Association of New South Wales	Formed in Sydney, October 1913	Active through 1920s–30s, particularly in propaganda work	Last annual report in 1962	
Town Planning Association of Queensland/Town and Country Planning Association	Formed in Brisbane, September 1914	Reformed in 1922–23, but inactive by late 1930s	Short-lived revival 1957–62 as TCPA but supplanted by development and ratepayer associations	
Victoria Town Planning and Parks Association/Town Planning Association of Victoria/Town and Country Planning Association	Formed in Melbourne, October 1914	Restructured in 1918 as TPAV	New constitution from 1941 as TCPA	Active body in urban affairs, planning and transport issues to present day
South Australian Town Planning and Improvement Society/Town Planning and Housing Association/ Town and Country Planning Association	Formed in Adelaide in March 1915	Reformed in 1916 as SAT-PHA, but dissolved in 1924	Idea revived as TCPA (1964–85)	

	Origins 1900s–1910s	Core period of activity 1910s–1930s	Twilight and successor groups 1940s–1960s	Ongoing 1960s–present
Southern Tasmanian Town Planning Association/ Southern Tasmanian Town Planning and Central Progress Association (STTPA)	Formed in Hobart, April 1915	Suspended in 1919; reformed in 1922; lapsed 1926; officially disbanded in 1939	Some continuity of effort in the Citizens Advisory Town Planning Committee (1948–58) and Council of Hobart Progress Associations (1944 to date)	
Town Planning Association of Western Australia (TPAWA)	Formed in Perth, March 1916	Active campaigning until formation of a Town Planning Institute in 1931	1953 plan to revive failed; continuity of purpose into groups like City Vision (1987 to date)	

Formation and objectives

The objectives of the town planning associations moved with the times as sampled through the decades in Table 3. For example, in 1914 the primary objective of the Victorian Association aimed to give 'the town a bit of the country and the country a bit of the town'. In the 1930s its slogan was 'Beautiful Cities for Beautiful Living'. In the 1940s the mission was 'to encourage an appreciation in the community of the need for properly guiding and shaping the growth of our towns and country centres in such as way as to ensure good living, working and recreational conditions'.[13] By the 1990s it was the principles of ecologically sustainable development.

Table 3: The evolution of objectives of town planning associations

Sydney, 1913
- To promote Town Planning on the principles enunciated by recognised authorities in respect of:
  - Badly arranged sections of older cities and towns
  - Suburban development of cities and towns
  - New garden cities, towns and settlement areas
- The improvement of:
  - Civic architecture, planning of streets and other highways
  - Housing, sanitation and other services
  - Environment of residential and manufacturing areas
- To collect and disseminate information as to the above
- The education of public opinion by:
  - Advocating the Establishment, at the University of Sydney, of a Chair of Architecture and Town Planning
  - Lectures, publication of reports, holding of exhibitions and such other means as the council may approve
- To urge effective administration under existing powers, and to advocate any additional out the objects of the Association.

Adelaide, 1915
- To take steps necessary, political and educational, to secure better housing of the people
- To secure proper designing of unoccupied land in the vicinity of city and suburbs, and any land on which the erection of cities and towns is contemplated
- To secure permanent reservations in the county for public use, and the protection of native fauna and flora
- To obtain and preserve parks, public playgrounds, and open spaces for the people
- To do all things in conjunction with the foregoing which will lead to the provision of healthy and reasonable surroundings of people during work and leisure
- To collect and [disseminate] information as to above

- To arrange lectures, publication of reports, holding of exhibitions, and such other means as the council may approve
- To urge effective administration under existing powers, and to advocate any additional legislation required to assist the carrying out of the objects of the Association.

Perth, 1929

The Town Planning Association of Western Australia aims at remedying the defects of the past, and providing for the future growth of our towns in an orderly, sane, economic, healthful and beautiful manner.

Adelaide, 1964
- To promote civic planning and design
- To secure adequate open spaces to meet present and future needs
- To conserve areas and features of unique beauty and interest
- To use planning as a means towards creating the most desirable living conditions for all
- To secure legislation that will facilitate sound and progressive development.

Melbourne, 2009
- To promote the application of principles of ecological sustainability to existing and new settlements and urban regeneration
- To encourage the practice of environmental planning
- To advocate the establishment of an effective strategic planning framework
- To motivate, educate and inspire popular support for environmental planning
- To arrange public lectures, demonstrations, exhibitions, conferences seminars, and meetings in support of the objectives of the Association and to pay for the costs and expenses of these from the funds of the Association
- To establish and support, and to aid in the establishment and support of, any other associations formed for all or any of the objectives of this Association
- To do anything which is legal and incidental or conducive to achieving any or all of the above objectives.

Sources: Constitution of the Town Planning Association of New South Wales (1913); Town Planning and Housing 12 April 1915; An Outline of Town Planning (TPAWA, 1929); www.tcpa.org.au

In the 1910s, recognition of the need for more farsighted pre-planning and day-to-day management of Australian cities reflected the global rise to prominence of the town planning movement. The leaders of the planning movement in Australia had direct ties with the British and American town planning fraternity and many of them travelled abroad on fact-finding tours. Australia's highly urbanised society ensured a prominent engagement with city planning concerns and in professional, government and media circles a recurrent set of issues was evident. These included the need for better housing and slum clearance; better health and sanitation; provision of open space, parks, recreation areas, and playgrounds; more community facilities; widening of streets; and protests about the alienation of public land. The answer was not more ad hoc interventions in the colonial tradition but comprehensive and forward-looking town planning in the form of new legislation and regulations. The focus was on the capital cities but planning reforms were also relevant to regional centres and country towns, especially in Queensland which had the most decentralised urban population of any state. The originality, appeal (and, to some critics, the threat) of the town planning movement lay in its ability to integrate diverse reform interests already in the air (housing, subdivision, parks etc) into a rhetoric of 'bird's eye view' coordination.

Federation injected a sense of optimistic nationalism into the town planning movement leading up to and into World War I. The siting, design and construction of the new federal capital as enshrined by the Australian Constitution of 1901 became both an issue in its own right and a touchstone of reform for architects, engineers, surveyors and some politicians. The 1911–12 design competition won by Chicago landscape architect Walter Burley Griffin captured international attention. The first Town Planning Association in NSW was strongly inspired by the federal capital project. George Taylor (Secretary) and John Sulman (President) strongly propagated the view that a truly planned national capital would place Australia in a prominent position on the world's stage of international politics and trade. Some of its membership envisaged the Sydney-based association as an Australian Town Planning Association, but due to early differences and styles, they settled on a state association with the hope that a national body would eventually follow.[14] Meanwhile, they set about encouraging other states to follow suit. An additional catalyst in several states was the lecture tour organised to educate the community about planning under the auspices of the British Garden Cities and Town Planning Association in 1914 by William Davidge and Charles Reade right at the outbreak of World War I, but with Reade continuing into 1915.[15]

The town planning associations had a communality of goals influenced both by the pioneering Sydney body and the template for action provided by Charles Reade in his town planning lectures. They campaigned on wide fronts of legislative enactment and reform, policy innovation, community education, and environmental improvements of diverse kinds. Their primary concerns focused on the health, efficiency, and beauty of cities. Public health was a foundational concept but one which expanded into broader notions of social wellbeing. Efficiency denoted the better functional and economic organisation of cities as sites of production and consumption. Beauty in the built environment was primarily seen as by-product of artistically fulfilling the other objectives. The emphases attached to these three goals varied. Early on, environmentalist ideology prevailed with the impassioned belief that improved surroundings directly improved the quality of people and their lives. Women members in particular promoted provision of children's playgrounds in several states. By the 1930s there was a strong orientation to planning for cities as economic growth machines, especially in NSW and Queensland, an ideological stance which intensified in the post-World War II years. The most distinctive positive departures from the foundational platform of slum abolition, improvement and beautification schemes, and the talisman of legislative reform, were conservation themes. Calls for the preservation of flora and fauna and the constitution of national parks featured in the agendas of the Victorian, South Australian and Western Australian bodies, partly reflecting the eclectic interests which had assembled for the first time under the town planning banner.

At their most influential, mostly in the early 1910s and 1920s, the town planning associations represented an unprecedented unified civic spirit demonstrating the power of informed community opinion determined to make a positive difference to the orderly processes of urban development on various fronts: changing government thinking, getting new legislation passed, modifying urban designs, and signposting better societal choices. Their marginalisation in public affairs, in most states from the late 1920s, came when established goals and approaches proved either redundant or irrelevant at the dawn of professional planning and with the emergence of new issue-specific organisations eroding their constituencies.

Membership

The town planning associations were all voluntary organisations. They brought together, certainly in their early years, virtually all the prominent town planning advocates in the respective capital cities – a veritable who's who of leading urban reformers. Architects, engineers and surveyors were the most prominent built environment professionals represented. Local, state and federal politicians, businessmen, and medical practitioners were also key contributors. These individuals dominated the executives and councils which directed their activities but members were also drawn from the wider community with relatives of the executive members frequently conscripted. Local authorities were encouraged to join as affiliate members in most states.

The founding members came predominantly from the middle-upper classes. The majority were male but women came to play a vital role in many activities and help shape the agenda towards social and children's issues, albeit sometimes after internal agitations for a greater voice. It is difficult to ascertain membership numbers; records are sketchy and they fluctuated in accordance with national prosperity and preoccupations. The most visible core of each association was a council of some 20 to 25 people, with a president, usually one or more vice-presidents, an honorary secretary and a treasurer. At its peak anywhere, state membership appears to have been around a couple of hundred. All associations complained when membership numbers dwindled due to wartime and economic recession, and all were regularly involved in membership drives, fundraising, and seeking donations. In the grimmest times as they faced extinction, numbers declined to a mere handful, a good indicator that membership numbers were the main predictor of vitality and profile.

Membership of the associations became skewed to particular constituencies. Queensland's dominant early figures were from the state government arena. A conservative strain in NSW and Tasmania reflected a significant appeal to businessmen and property owners. The mix of political alliances came and went depending on the interests, activities, reputation and methods of the association. Their status was invariably elevated when a leading public figure was actively associated, for example Lord Mayor Frank Stapley in Melbourne and state government minister John D. Fitzgerald in Sydney. The West Australian body was closely aligned with the City Council because of the prominence of long-serving Town Clerk William Bold. The South Australian association oriented its activities to the state government not only as the peak legislative body but also because of a city council hostile to town planning and housing reform. As the associations approached periodic catharses, generally the biggest names had either passed away or redirected their energies to other community and professional reform agendas.

Activities

The most conspicuous activities were educational: spreading the word and raising awareness through lectures and publications, newspaper articles, radio broadcasts, and exhibitions. All the town planning associations lobbied long and hard for new legislation and specific projects via personal deputations and written submissions to state governments and local authorities. Projects included central city redevelopment, beautification schemes, civic centres, new open spaces, and sundry improvement and landscape schemes. Members wrote letters to papers, articles for popular magazines, technical journals and the press, and produced copy for general, council and annual general meetings, reports of which often appeared in the local media. Members were often prevailed upon to advise councils, the general public, businesses, and government. Before being displaced by professional bodies, they were not infrequently called upon to nominate representatives to government boards and inquiries as well as carry out site inspections.

Diverse publications were used to promote town planning. As principals of a technical publishing company, George and Florence Taylor in Sydney were well placed to exploit print propaganda. Their various journals from the 1910s to the 1940s regularly carried news of monthly and annual meetings: the flagship journal *Building* in the 1910s, *Commonwealth Home* in the 1920s, *Harmony* in the 1930s, and *Construction* in the 1940s. The Taylors' short-lived national planning journal called *Town Planning and Housing* in 1915–16 captured their idea of 'linking up' the various state bodies in the quixotic quest for some sort of national body. Before 1920 they also published a number of small monographs on both broader goals such as 'The town planner and his mission', and more specialist topics such as co-partnership housing. The South Australian association ambitiously launched its own journal, the *Light Journal of Town Planning and Housing* in 1920. It only lasted one issue but scored a notable coup in reproducing a special message from Ebenezer Howard. Its successor body in the 1970s printed widely circulated newsletters. Notes on the activities of the associations were also carried in various architectural, building and local government journals as well as metropolitan daily newspapers. Activities of the Brisbane body were regularly covered by the *Architectural and Building Journal of*

Queensland, and for a brief time in the early 1960s the journal *Planner* was a co-production between the revived Town and Country Planning Association and the Brisbane Division of the Australian Planning Institute. In the 1930s both the Sydney and Melbourne associations produced series of annual reports, but these enjoyed only limited circulation. The output of the Victorian body from the 1940s was formidable – a succession of publications on town planning needs, its own journal *Plan News Review* (from 1964), later *Space* (1973–91), and then a web-based presence to the present day (www.tcpa.org.au). It is these sources alongside surviving archival records and contemporary newspaper articles which have underpinned the research for this book, although the availability of research material is uneven and the authors have had to assemble information from diverse sources.

Achievements

Just what was directly achieved from all this activity in different cities over many decades? Dennis Hardy's ultimate assessment of the contributions of the British Town and Country Planning Association – as high-profile and influential as it would appear to be with a heritage linked to the very beginnings of the modern town planning movement – is restrained. The Association emerges from his two volume history as a key actor but not necessarily the 'star' performer over time.[16] This conclusion reflects the complexities of longitudinal research in disentangling interwoven spheres and threads of influence, difficulties in assessing outcomes from an evolving set of generalist objectives, and the fact that planning is always unfinished business and constantly being reinvented. It is similarly difficult to assess the achievements of the Australian bodies.

Although not averse to casting themselves in the role, the town planning associations were not heroic lone guns but rather took their place within a web of governance concerned with the direction and control of urban development that involved diverse actors and stakeholders. Hence, when they pursued a cause they were usually not alone. Indeed, the *modus operandi* of some associations was to develop cooperative measures with other organisations to achieve goals. In the 1920s, the Hobart association developed strong linkages with local authorities and progress associations, a nexus maintained in the re-organisation of the town planning movement there after World War II.

The early associations had ambitious goals which could never be comprehensively realised and there were numerous campaigns with which they were identified – be they for comprehensive planning legislation or children's playgrounds – that proved unsuccessful. This situation exemplifies yet again one recurrent theme in Australian city planning – 'failure'.[17] Nevertheless, for as long as they remained credible organisations in the eyes of government and the community, the associations made undeniable contributions in promoting public awareness of and interest in town planning issues. It is impossible to recount how the town planning movement took shape in Australia from the 1910s to at least the 1940s without reference to their formation, activities and membership.

Most of the successes were modest and piecemeal, and the influence of the associations in shaping the tangible outcomes of particular planning, design and development projects was often a finessing one. Before World War II, the two campaigns identified with town planning associations with the most positive and substantial outcomes were arguably in Adelaide and Perth. In Adelaide, the association actively campaigned from 1916 for planning legislation as a framework for more orderly metropolitan and country town development. This complemented the efforts of the state government's main planning adviser Charles Reade who skilfully worked with it as an independent basis of support. The campaign culminated in passage of the *Town Planning and Development Act* in 1920. Although limited in its provisions, it was the first general planning statute of its kind in Australia. In Perth, the association with critical input from William Bold and William Saw drafted and redrafted numerous town planning bills for consideration by the WA government. When the *Town Planning and Development Act* eventually came into operation in 1929 it was the first genuine legislation to empower comprehensive planning by local authorities for any Australian state. It is perhaps not coincidental that both the Adelaide and Perth bodies were largely spent forces after these breakthroughs and soon folded. Intriguingly, the associations in other states unable to bask in at least the reflected glow of legislative reform remained alive, battling on with a comparable 'big win' still something to strive for.

Longevity is an achievement in its own right, indicating a continuing contribution to public discourse on planning matters. By that criterion the NSW body might seem outstandingly successful in surviving from 1913 to 1967. But for over 30 of the final years it was headed by a minor Sydney architect Bertram Ford whose style was far from cooperative or progressive. If anything it came to stand for anti-planning and in 1945 actually became a strong critic of the restrictive provisions in NSW's first proper planning act, something for which it had seemingly toiled for decades. By contrast, the Melbourne association remained a genuinely vital force in the postwar period. Affiliated with the British 'parent' organisation, it moved beyond its earlier history associated with prominent medical man and social reformer Sir James Barrett to maintain a niche as a respected commentator on planning matters, forum for debate, and clearinghouse of information. It found itself well placed to ride the rising tide of interest in urban affairs in Australia in the 1970s. Its profile today has diminished with many other non-governmental voices being heard in Melbourne on planning issues which became thoroughly politicised through a series of far-reaching local government 'reforms' in the 1980s.[18] But the TCPAV remains a contributor to public debate, and one of its most recent governmental submissions was on climate change.

Structure of this book

The core of the book comprises twelve chapters by the individual authors who have collaborated on this project. While sharing common objectives and concerns, all tell singular stories reflecting the distinctive urban reform cultures of six Australian capital cities over nearly a century, the different disciplinary perspectives of the authors, and the uneven and occasionally scarce resource material available for their task. Each chapter is a case study of a particular association during the eras which organise the book into two main parts. The first set of six chapters deals with the NSW, Queensland, Victorian, South Australian, Tasmanian and Western Australian associations in this order of their formation through their halcyon days from the 1910s and into the 1920s and 1930s. During these years, they constituted the vanguard of the propagandist campaign aimed at state and local government to implement town planning legislation and other reforms. The Great Depression followed closely by World War II represented a watershed for planning, thoroughly changing the political climate from scepticism and apathy to at least grudging acceptance that planning had or may have a crucial function to play for the modern state. The transformation was paralleled by the professionalisation of planning as it moved away from its community roots along with a greater fragmentation and specialisation of grassroot voices. Each of the chapters in the second set explore how the town planning associations in each state coped with these trends and in most cases were literally or effectively reinvented for challenging new environments. They are organised in the chronology of the demise of the original association formed at the genesis of the modern town planning movement in Australia. The subsequent fortunes and stories traced into post-World War II Australia are remarkably diverse but all point in some way to periodic sea-changes in the community's approach to social and environmental action through the 1940s, 1960s, 1980s and 1990s in particular. The emergent forms of engagement nevertheless owe something to the pioneering spirit of the town planning associations.

Town planning associations were important players in promoting the idea of town planning in Australia and shaping the planning agenda of the modern state from the early 20th century. Their relevance in complementing more official and professionally-oriented planning histories lies in highlighting the positive historical and evolving role of the community in determining and critiquing city planning policies and programs – something that continues today in many different guises. In their own right, the town planning associations obviously enjoyed fluctuating fortunes in their lifetimes. Their progress was shaped as much by internal fractions as external forces, with critical factors in their longevity being reinvention of their membership and rationales as planning progressively became more institutionalised and bureaucratised. These considerations are explored further in the conclusion to this book.

References

[1] Sherry Arnstein, 'A ladder of citizen participation', *Journal of the American Institute of Planners*, 35 (1969): 216–24.

[2] Les Robinson, 'Public outrage and public trust', Keynote address to Waste and Recycle Conference, Perth, Western Australia (October 2002), 3–4.

[3] Robert Zehner and Nancy Marshall, 'Community participation: to be involved or not to be involved – is that the question?', in *Planning Australia: An Overview of Urban and Regional Planning* ed. Susan Thompson (Melbourne: Cambridge University Press, 2007), 247–262.

[4] Chris Pickvance, 'From urban social movements to urban movements', *International Journal of Urban and Regional Research*, 27 (2003): 102–09.

[5] Manuel Castells, *The city and the grassroots* (London: Edward Arnold, 1983).

[6] Michael James Miller, *The representation of place: urban planning and protest in France and Great Britain, 1950-1980* (Aldershot: Ashgate, 2003).

[7] Zula Nittim, The Coalition of Resident Action Groups, in *Twentieth century Sydney: studies of urban and social history* ed. Jill Roe (Sydney: Hale and Iremonger, 1980), 231–47; and Richard Roddewig, *Green bans: the birth of Australian environmental politics* (Sydney: Hale & Iremonger, 1978).

[8] Leonie Sandercock, Rewriting planning history: official and insurgent stories, in her *Cosmopolis 2: mongrel cities* (London: Continuum, 2003), 37–58.

9. Stephen V. Ward, *Planning the twentieth century city: the advanced capitalist world* (Chichester: John Wiley, 2002).
10. Robert Freestone, Christine Garnaut and Alan Hutchings, 'A bibliographic guide to recent literature in Australian planning history', *Planning History*, 41(1), (2003): 21-34.
11. Dennis Hardy, *From garden cities to new towns* (London: E & FN Spon, 1991a); and Dennis Hardy, *From new towns to green politics* (London: E & FN Spon, 1991b).
12. These two paragraphs are adapted from Robert Freestone, *Designing Australian cities: culture, commerce and the city beautiful, 1900-1930* (Sydney: UNSW Press, 2007), Chapter 1.
13. Town and Country Planning Association, *Let's plan* (Melbourne: TCPA, 1945), 11.
14. Robert Freestone and Margaret Park, 'The limits to nationalism: moves toward an Australian Town Planning Association 1913-1917', *Australian Historical Studies*, 40 (March 2009): 32-46.
15. Robert Freestone, 'An imperial aspect: the Australasian Town Planning Tour of 1914-15', *Australian Journal of Politics and History*, 44 (1998): 159-76.
16. Hardy, *From garden cities to new towns*, 313.
17. Leonie Sandercock, *Cities for sale: property, politics and urban planning in Australia* (Melbourne: Melbourne University Press, 1975).
18. Miles Lewis, *Suburban backlash: the battle for the world's most liveable city* (Melbourne: Bloomings Books, 1999).

Part One
Advancing the cause of town planning

1
Spreading the good news about town planning in Sydney 1913–34

Robert Freestone and Margaret Park

The early history of the Town Planning Association of New South Wales (TPANSW) marks a distinctive phase in the development of town planning in Sydney. Private citizens, operating independently of government, were able to help mould understandings and shape solutions to the contemporary problems of the day. This chapter examines the first two decades of Australia's first town planning association. It sheds light on its main activities, concentrating on the nature and efficacy of the propaganda efforts which were its central raison d'être. The abrupt cessation of a vigorous lecture series and changes in leadership from the mid-1920s were the bellwether for its declining profile and status despite continuing activity through World War II and beyond.

Setting the scene

Accompanying the optimism at the dawn of the 20th century and the bold experiment of Federation, the early 1900s saw a sea-changing increase in concern for issues of urban development and civic improvement. Cries for legislative reform in all Australian cities were matched nationally by the push for a new federal capital to provide a modern and iconic exemplar of modern city development. This was a time of growing worldwide interest in town planning. Knowledge of new forms and processes of city-making overseas had a catalytic impact on local urban reformers.[1]

Sydney, as the oldest and largest Australian city, faced more challenges than its sister capitals (Figure 1.1). It had spread outwards and recently upwards in all directions in an unplanned fashion. It had experienced the birth of slumdom, the horrors of bubonic plague, the shame of poor sanitation, loss of open space, worsening traffic and port congestion, and ill-coordinated government responses at local and state level. The planning advocate and left-of-centre politician J.D. Fitzgerald lamented an uncoordinated metropolitan muddle whose present government structures were 'ripe for the scrap-heap'.[2]

Figure 1.1: Sydney's Central Business District, 1915. Source: *Town Planning and Housing*, May 1915

Improving the metropolis 'was no easy task', as Peter Spearritt recounts in *Sydney's Century*, and most of the impetus came from 'the pre-war reform movement'.[3] Early expressions were scattered demolitions of inner-city slum housing stock and the development of new garden suburbs. The 1909 *Royal commission into the improvement of the city and its suburbs* backed such measures and established the basis of a stop-start program of street widenings, infrastructure improvement, and minor beautification schemes. A nascent reform movement sought coordination of such interventions into a broader discourse of town planning from the 1910s. The much-needed harbour crossing allied to city and suburban railway development assumed centre stage and preparations were in full swing when the Depression hit, lasting into the mid-1930s. The flat building and housing boom of the early 1920s came to an abrupt end as a result. The fluctuating fortunes of the Town Planning Association through its first two decades are set against this backdrop.

Formation and membership

The professionals who identified with the concept of modern town planning in the early 20th century were drawn mainly from the ranks of progressive architects, engineers and surveyors. The prominent architect, John Sulman, for example, had been at the forefront of propaganda efforts since the 1890s. The growing interest in town planning was reflected in coverage in professional journals, trade magazines, and newspapers through the 1910s. A key organ was the trade journal *Building*, the brainchild of George Taylor and his architect-wife Florence. George was an astute businessman and journalist whose interests were wide reaching and eclectic (Figure 1.2). With the redoubtable Florence alongside, they were prolific and persistent stalwarts for modernisation and technical progress, albeit with a conservative stance. As the momentum for town planning grew in the face of government inaction, in late 1913 George Taylor took his agenda to a higher level by mooting formation of a town planning association which could open 'up wonderful possibilities for the uplifting of Australia'.[4]

Taylor's idea sparked immediate interest. G. Sydney Jones, President of the Institute of Architects of NSW expressed his support for linking planning to architecture whilst introducing a talk by Walter Burley Griffin, who had recently arrived to advise the Commonwealth Government

Figure 1.2: George Taylor, founder of the Town Planning Association of NSW. Source: J.M. Giles, *Some chapters in the life of George Augustine Taylor* (1957)

on the federal capital. Richard Stanton, developer of the garden suburb of Haberfield was similarly positive: 'If a Town Planning Association were established in Australia, its work would educate the people up to the benefits of town planning, and through the people they could get at the local governing bodies'.[5]

On 17 October 1913 George Taylor organised a well-attended public meeting in the Sydney Town Hall, drawing both curious and committed representatives of the professions, some state parliamentarians, local councillors, and the public at large. Initially proposed as a national body, all present eventually agreed that they should concern themselves with the state of planning affairs in New South Wales, and more especially Sydney, which would keep the Association fully occupied. This formal inauguration was presided over by the former government architect, Walter Liberty Vernon. News of the meeting and reports of discussions and motions were featured in the *Sydney Morning Herald* the following day. Sulman was quoted as saying that:

> The towns in Australia had grown up without any relationship between the component parts. It was time they began to make an effort to fall into line with countries that sought to develop their cities on scientific and artistic lines.[6]

Forming a committee to ensure the successful establishment of the Association was paramount. It was agreed that it would meet and report back within a month.[7] Committee members included Sulman, Vernon, Taylor, Griffin, Jones and Fitzgerald along with Professor Robert Irvine, author of a report on workers' housing in Europe and America for the NSW government, and architect J. Burcham Clamp. The committee set to work enthusiastically and by 17 November members reported that they had drafted a constitution, formed a council of office bearers, and established a raft of specialist committees. The basic organisational framework set in place endured for decades (Table 1.1). Sulman was duly elected foundation president, Fitzgerald and Irvine as vice-presidents, and the industrious Taylor was ensconced as honorary secretary. Architects dominated the Council, with members proudly carrying their part-time military rank, for example: Colonel Walter L. Vernon, Lieutenant-Colonel Alfred Spain, and Major F. Ernest Stowe.[8] The metaphor is compelling: war had been declared on unhealthy, inefficient and ugly cities.

Table 1.1: Office bearers in the Town Planning Association of NSW 1913–34

Date	President	Vice-President	Hon. Secretary
1913	John Sulman	J.D. Fitzgerald Prof R. Irvine	George A. Taylor
1914	John Sulman	J.D. Fitzgerald Prof R. Irvine	George A. Taylor
1915	John Sulman	J.D. Fitzgerald Prof R. Irvine	George A. Taylor
1916	John Sulman	George A. Taylor Richard Stanton	W. Scott Griffiths (replaced by W.D. Cowdery)
1917	John Sulman	George A. Taylor Richard Stanton	W.D. Cowdery
1918	John Sulman	George A. Taylor J.J.C. Bradfield	W.D. Cowdery (replaced by Reg E. Reid)
1919	John Sulman	George A. Taylor J.J.C. Bradfield	Reg E. Reid
1920	John Sulman	George A. Taylor James Nangle	Reg E. Reid
1921	John Sulman	Henry F. Halloran G. Sydney Jones	E. Anderson
1922	John Sulman	Justice Milner Stephen Col Alfred Spain	Geoffrey Sawyer
1923	John Sulman	Dr Grace Boelke Dr J.S. Purdy Sir Charles Rosenthal	Miss Allen Miss Salter (also E. Anderson)
1924	John Sulman	Col R.M.S. Wells Col T.H. Kelly Dr Mary Booth	Miss Salter

Date	President	Vice-President	Hon. Secretary
1925	John Sulman Dr J.S. Purdy (elected March 1925)	Dr J.S. Purdy Miss Grace Scobie Col Alfred Spain	Norman Weekes
1926	Col Alfred Spain (elected November 1926)	J.J.C. Bradfield (elected August 1926) Dr Mary Booth D.L. Davidson	Florence M. Taylor
1927	Col Alfred Spain	Henry F. Halloran (replaced Bradfield October 1927)	Florence M. Taylor
1928	Col Alfred Spain D.L. Davidson (elected March 1928)	Henry F. Halloran Sir Charles Rosenthal Dr Mary Booth	Florence M. Taylor
1929	D.L. Davidson T.E. Rofe (elected April 1929)	Aubrey Halloran David G. Stead D. Bennet Dobson Mrs Norman Lowe A.E. Rudder Roland Cook	Florence M. Taylor
1930	Arthur J. Small (elected March 1930)	Henry F. Halloran Justice Milner Stephen D. Bennet Dobson Col R.M.S. Wells Mrs Norman Lowe Roland Cook	Florence M. Taylor
1931–32	Arthur J. Small	Justice Milner Stephen Prof E.G. Waterhouse Dr Mary Booth Aubrey Halloran David G. Stead J.D. Walker	Bertram W. Ford

Date	President	Vice-President	Hon. Secretary
1932–33	Arthur J. Small	Justice Milner Stephen Prof E.G. Waterhouse Hon Lionel T. Courtenay A. Pixley David G. Stead J.D. Walker	Bertram W. Ford
1933–34	A.J. Brown (to 31 May 1934) David G. Stead (from 31 May 1934)	Justice Milner Stephen Arthur J. Small Hon Lionel T. Courtenay A. Pixley David G. Stead J.D. Walker	Bertram W. Ford
1934–35	David G. Stead (to 9 August 1934) Bertram W. Ford (from 9 August 1934)	Justice Milner Stephen Arthur J. Small Hon L.T. Courtenay A. Pixley J.J. Cranitch J.D. Walker	F.A. Faviell

The Association assumed an instant credibility in civic and government circles with its high profile executive. Ordinary membership quickly attracted interest from citizens concerned with the state of the city and was open to all for a subscription fee of 10/6 per annum. Nevertheless, such an annual fee would have limited the type of subscriber to the professional classes as the basic living wage introduced by the Commonwealth Court of Conciliation and Arbitration in 1907, and not appreciably increasing over the ensuing decade, was only £2/2/- per week.[9] A special report prepared in 1916 by Honorary Secretary Walter Scott Griffiths provides the most detailed membership breakdown. The total number of members was probably near a peak at around 230. Not unexpectedly, over half resided in affluent and elite suburbs. They were of an educated class who fitted easily into high society and lived physically and emotionally distant from the ills they sought to rectify. The eastern harbourside suburb of Woollahra had the most members at 33. Mosman, Ku-ring-gai, North Sydney, Randwick, Burwood and Lane Cove were also well represented. Remarkably, about half the membership was female. The Florence Taylor factor was undoubtedly infectious. She wrote screeds of articles in a dedicated 'Home Building Section' in *Building* articulating women's interests as primarily in the realm of healthy cities, urban design and the domestic front under the slogan 'Men make houses but women make homes'.[10] A special women's section was inaugurated but quickly collapsed amid personal acrimony between Florence and Marion Mahony Griffin (architect and wife of Walter Burley Griffin) over issues of 'womanliness' and autonomy.[11] The importance of women in the general ranks was never reflected in the official office bearers, with no women elected to Council before 1920 and Dr Grace Boelke recorded as the Association's first woman vice-president some ten years after the Association's formation.

The Association's mission

The formation of the TPANSW enabled Sulman, Fitzgerald, Taylor and other members to consolidate their views into a lobby group with some substance and clout. Philosophically, their views aligned with environmentalist logic of bringing better health and joy into community living through physical design (Figure 1.3). They promoted slum clearance and redevelopment, the planning of new suburbs, improvements in traffic and road arrangements, and the greening and dressing up of urban places. A metropolitan plan was an early aim of the TPANSW and George Taylor sought subscriptions to the cause, but it was not vigorously pursued and jostled with sundry other problems on the Association's agenda.[12] The Association's numerous causes were unified by a proselytising mission to instil a willingness in the community, other professional organisations, and government to cooperate and bring about change to ensure a modern and dynamic 20th-century Australia.

In his message associated with the publication of TPANSW's Constitution, Sulman passionately summed up the foundational objectives:

> The Town Planning Association of New South Wales aims at remedying the grievous defects which have grown up unchecked in our midst and providing for the future growth of our towns in an orderly, sane, economic, healthful and beautiful manner. I appeal, therefore, to every citizen, without distinction of sex, class or creed, to join in this good work. It is essentially one that pays for itself by securing better conditions for carrying on the business of life, and at the same time lifts the whole people a stage higher in the upward progress of humanity.[13]

Fundamental to delivering town planning results was the introduction of a properly framed and viable town planning act. While the TPANSW seemed initially prepared to work through adaptation of existing regulations, the idea of new legislation to enable local authorities to plan for their areas consistent with broader metropolitan or statewide policies became a mantra into the 1930s. Arthur J. Small's call for a 'town planning authority' in 1933 was accompanied by a typical lament: 'Despite repeated representations … to many governments, the State of NSW is still without a *Town Planning Act*.'[14] There were several close calls in parliamentary debates, notably in 1919 when David Hall, the Minister for Housing, put forward a bill providing for a town planning board to oversee the development of all cities and towns across the state. This lapsed and Fitzgerald's new local government legislation passed the same year was to provide de facto planning control through residential district proclamations and other ordinances controlling amenity through to the mid-1940s.[15] A combination of conservative governments and forces hostile to more regulations and any curtailment of private property rights always won the day.[16] Consequently, NSW persistently lagged behind other states where new town planning acts were enacted, notably South Australia (1920) and Western Australia (1929).[17]

HOW A BACKYARD WAS REMODELLED.

Figure 1.3: Transforming the backyard into 'a veritable fairyland of brightness'. Source: *Town Planning and Housing*, September 1915

Other causes were far narrower. The perceived lack of order and beauty in the city's streetscapes was one of the Association's particular bugbears. In spite of health regulations and sales restrictions adopted by the City Council in 1915, the control of barrowmen (street peddlers) on busy city streets proved to be complex and unsatisfactory.[18] Not necessarily a lone voice within the TPANSW in his campaign, Taylor insistently pleaded for complete removal of 'gutter shops' on several grounds: as dilapidated and ramshackled eyesores, as impediments to vehicle and pedestrian traffic, and as unfair competition to rate paying shopkeepers.[19]

While frequently adopting stances critical of government, the Association itself was fundamentally conservative. This rather paradoxical and self-limiting positioning reflected George and Florence Taylor's pro-business orientation. Even with the polite and politic Sulman holding court as president, hard-line stances on various matters were frequent. There were few sacred cows and some of the early targets – like the pathbreaking state housing suburb of Dacey Gardens (1912) – relate directly to the Taylors' right-wing ideology. The Taylors retreated from backing anything smacking of 'big government'; the 'greater Sydney' reforms pursued by Jack Fitzgerald were not enthusiastically pursued. Inevitably, there were skirmishes with those who did not share their planning and design opinions like Fitzgerald, Charles Reade (seen as a foreigner and too pro-regulationist) and Walter Burley Griffin (eventually dismissed as a dreamy do-gooder). Bloodletting in the Association's own ranks was not unknown; more genuinely liberal reformers like Fitzgerald and Irvine were periodically estranged.[20]

The TPANSW was very selective in partnering with other bodies in reform causes. A request from the Australian Forestry League seeking affiliation with the TPANSW in the early 1920s was refused as it 'would not benefit the [Association] in any way'.[21] However, open space presented more mutual concerns. From its first meeting in 1913, the Parks and Playground Committee boasted an ambitious agenda. Diligently, it was to 'report on street tree planting' and where 'additional parks, reserves, or playgrounds' were required.[22] As the first legitimate 'offshoot' of the TPANSW in the early 1930s, the Parks and Playground Movement (PPM) targeted these issues more robustly.[23] It worked primarily towards increasing the amount of city and suburban parklands while also protesting further alienation of parks and reserves threatened by both public and private development.[24] TPANSW member Charles Bean, journalist and official war historian, was a prominent PPM figure.[25]

The range of Association activities

In attempting to affect physical, attitudinal and legal reforms, the TPANSW was active on many fronts. It exchanged correspondence with municipal councils and government departments on countless local matters, prepared submissions, undertook deputations in regard to town planning legislation and specific planning projects, gave numerous public lectures, organised fieldtrips for members, proffered practical advice to councils, published pamphlets, instituted competitions for school children, and nominated representatives to official advisory committees.

From the outset, propaganda was one of the cornerstones of the TPANSW's raison d'être. The Constitution confirmed an educative role involving 'the education of public opinion' by firstly 'advocating the establishment, at Sydney University, of a Chair of Architecture and Town Planning' as well as providing 'lectures, publication of reports [and] holding of exhibitions'.[26] Members debated whether it should be a 'militant' association or a 'theorising' body. The views of John Sulman prevailed: 'I think we should strive to educate from the beginning. Education is the best example. Militancy could follow'.[27] George Taylor reiterated the overall emphasis on community education as a major focus by stating:

> [It] is agreed that the primary necessity is to present the doctrine of town planning, and so, by degrees, and occasional example, educate the people into a due appreciation of its merits, and make them realise that it actually is an essential acquisition to our national evolution.[28]

The initial methods used by the TPANSW to spread the good news about town planning were wide in scope and time demanding. Much energy was thrown into planning and preparing monthly lectures, luncheons and other events with guest speakers on topical planning matters. The TPANSW's publicity committee had initial responsibility for arranging lectures, meetings, discussions, exhibitions and media liaison. The first committee comprised Fitzgerald, Irvine, and Jones alongside Alderman Milner Stephen, architect James Nangle, and William Williamson.[29]

The Association was criticised for inaction from early in its lifetime. A report in the *Bulletin* in 1914 complained that the Association 'doesn't do any real town planning but just hangs around Sydney', which in any case can 'no longer be planned – only patched'.[30] Lord Mayor Sir Allen Taylor remarked that the TPANSW was 'too much thunder and too little work'. *The Salon* (Journal of the Institute of Architects) concurred in

1915: 'we fail to know what the Town Planning Association has done, excepting in the entertaining line and in that they are "past masters" in luncheons and afternoon teas'.[31] In reply, a combative George Taylor lacerated *The Salon* as a journal that 'never sees. If it ever did, it might see itself as others see it. Then, most likely, there would be a sudden suicide'.[32] Such vitriolic language was used frequently in Taylor's editorials, especially when criticism was directed at the TPANSW.

The major contribution undoubtedly came in the form of words rather than actual deeds and either orally, in print or over the airwaves. In his annual report for 1926, President Dr J.S. Purdy recounted:

> It was recently said that the Town Planning Association does nothing but talk. This is true except it also writes – no less than 2,000 letters were sent out by our energetic Hon. Secretary, Mrs Taylor. As a matter of fact, the main function of the Association is to promulgate propaganda, to emphasise the necessity of showing some foresight in the development of towns, so as to secure adequate provision for carrying on industry with as little interference as possible with the natural scenic beauty of the area and above all, the satisfactory housing of the people, provision of parks, playgrounds and other amenities.[33]

Anxious to get its message across about the cultivation of a town planning ideal, the Association appealed to the young and the inquisitive minds of primary and high school children. By doing so it believed it would be encouraging youth to better understand the conditions which existed and the methods available to enact change. Funds were provided both by individual members of the TPANSW and by the Association as a whole to conduct competitions with prizes as incentives to participate. George Taylor's generous prize donation of £2/2/0 for an essay on 'the city beautiful' was one of the first reported initiatives.[34] In the 1920s, school essay prizes were held annually and featured a different topic each year; in 1922, for example, children were invited to prepare an essay on the 'principles of town and district improvement'.[35]

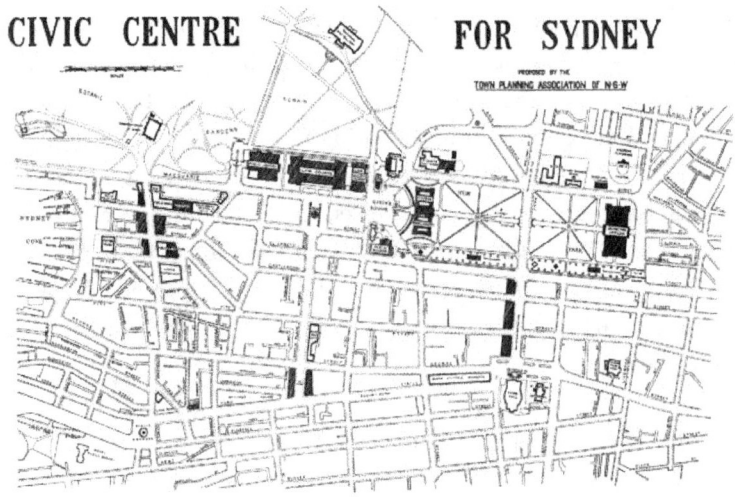

Figure 1.4: Civic Centre Scheme in Hyde Park, Sydney, c.1916. Source: John Sulman, *An introduction to the study of town planning in Australia* (1921)

An early publicity initiative was the mounting of an exhibition of photographs and plans to relay the possibilities of town planning. Organised by George Taylor, it was held at the Royal Art Society in November 1913, barely a month after the inaugural meeting at the Town Hall.[36] The exhibition featured contemporary architectural schemes, town plans and engineering works including the work of several of the founding members of the Association. Prominent were sketches of the new Sydney suburb of Rosebery by John Sulman for the Town Planning Company of Australia, J.J.C. Bradfield's design for the proposed Sydney Harbour Bridge, and Walter and Marion Griffin's Canberra designs plus illustrations of some of Griffin's American work. Also on display were images of the improvement schemes which arose out of the Royal Commission for the Improvement of the City of Sydney and its Suburbs (1909). Other Australian architects' works were also showcased.[37] Following on, a city plan exhibition was proposed for mid-1915.[38] Displays were assembled for the national planning conferences held in Adelaide in 1917 and Brisbane in 1918. In Adelaide the Association exhibited plans and drawings of its new civic centre proposal in Hyde Park (Figure 1.4).[39]

The Taylor's publishing and printing empire ensured a constant outpouring of articles and editorials in their various journals as well as other publications. Pages and pages of talks, lectures, addresses and papers given from 1913 up until the late 1920s, either in full or abstracted, featured in *Building, Commonwealth Home* and *Property Owner*. It was not uncommon to find the exact article represented in two or sometimes all of these journals.

The catalogue of the 1913 town planning exhibition was the first major publication and typical of the Taylors' publishing enterprise (Figure 1.5). It contained accounts of the speeches given at the exhibition's opening. The necessity for the formation of the new association was explained in detail by Taylor and taking advantage of previous copy from *Building*, women and town planning were not omitted. Side by side with exhortations to join the good fight to nation build via town planning were advertisements for a variety of business and trades. This business aspect of the Taylors' operations permeated the activities of the early TPANSW.[40]

A series of four small pamphlets was a highlight of 1914. The first was a general treatise by Fitzgerald whose experience in the field of local government and town planning was well established by the time the Association formed.[41] George Taylor's *The town planner and his mission* was first read to the Institute of Local Government Engineers' Conference in Melbourne in November 1913. It promulgated his stance on the virtues of town planning in the physical, mental and emotional development of humankind; the contribution seemed progressive but frequently veered to an uncompromisingly patriotic and free enterprise position drifting towards a proto-fascism.[42] 'Whatever uplifts mankind by making a virile race with purity of body and soul is surely a religion worthy of adherents from all creeds. And that is the mission of the Town

Planner', he wrote.⁴³ Robert Irvine's contribution was more reflective and critical in its advocacy of a housing and town planning act 'to provide a comprehensive code of laws laying down a broad policy'.⁴⁴ Sulman's pamphlet on co-partnership housing commended a strategy midway between government and private housing approaches following the British garden suburb model of tenant partnership societies.⁴⁵

Figure 1.5: Catalogue of the NSW Association's 1913 town planning exhibition. Courtesy Mitchell Library.

Complementing the magazine articles and the special monographs were other initiatives. Taylor's unabated enthusiasm led to the lively but short-lived *Town Planning and Housing* journal between 1914 and 1915, initially as a supplement in *Building*. It featured reports not only on the Sydney scene but the 'splendid achievements' of town planning associations in other states.⁴⁶ Taylor's blend of nationalism and environmentalism was also captured in his two books: *Town planning for Australia* (1915) and *Town planning with common-sense* (1918). The latter advocated appointment of specialist commissions without which 'town planning will ever remain either a channel for wasting money on impractical schemes, or simply a theme for essays and debates between theorists'.[47]

Figure 1.6: Excursion of members to Culburra near Nowra, 1928.
Source: *Commonwealth Home*, 1 December 1928

The Association's excursions, mainly in the 1920s, were not only a means of disseminating the town planning message, but also demonstrated to its membership the vast array of planning needs awaiting attention. In 1926, for example, there was a well-publicised tree-planting ceremony in Canberra involving 21 members. And in 1928 a similar-sized party travelled to inspect the estates of businessmen-surveyor Henry Halloran, one of their own, in the Shoalhaven District on the NSW south coast (Figure 1.6). The party not only discussed the virtues of town planning and the nature of subdividing land but also took advantage of ample social opportunities provided over luncheons and dinners.[48]

From time to time, the Association would proffer or be called upon for specific advice about matters such as the design of parks, community facilities and street improvements (Figure 1.7). A.J. Small claimed that the Association was both 'willing and competent to advise on such matters, possessing within its membership all the skilled opinion necessary for the purpose'.[49] As early as 1915 the Association deemed itself to be an adviser to all councils and shires in Sydney. George Taylor proposed that 'district committees' be formed to investigate matters of town planning relevance and report back to the TPANSW council.[50] However, without sufficient response from members, John Sulman admitted that the concept was doomed, and over-optimistically 'looked to a time after the war' to re-group.[51]

Figure 1.7: 'Town planners surveying Mud Flats and Mangrove Swamps at Concord', 1926. Source: *Commonwealth Home*, 1 July 1926

Lobbying government

The standard technique for interest groups seeking to impress their opinions on politicians and garner broader community support was the public delegation. Although the Association singularly organised such deputations drawing on the skills and knowledge of its own members, there were also joint efforts on sundry causes with like-minded bodies, including the Institute of Architects (NSW). Within six months of its formation in November 1913, the TPANSW was calling on various state ministers for lands, works, roads, local government and even the Premier. Many more were to follow into the 1930s (a sampling of these from sources available is provided in Table 1.2). Of course, not all met with an enthusiastic response, but these events were usually reported in the press of the day and engendered at least some degree of community attention.

Table 1.2: A select list of TPANSW deputations 1914–34

Year	Issue	Representation
1914	Full TPANSW council deputation to Minister on a *Town Planning Act* and Building Act for Sydney and Suburbs, a grant of £200 towards Davidge-Reade lecture tour, improvement to housing conditions and the establishment of a chair of Architecture and Town Planning at Sydney University	Minister for Public Works
1916	TPANSW's scheme for developing radial roads to southern suburbs; cooperation from relevant councils obtained	Minister for Local Government
1916	Widening of South Head Road and reclamation of Rose Bay. Joint deputation from the TPANSW Council and Woollahra Council	Minister for Local Government
1917	Discussion of the inauguration of National Good Roads Convention to oversee proper road-building and highway development (first Convention held in 1918; attended by Sulman and Taylor)	Acting Premier
1918	Greater Sydney Bill: a nine-point platform was put to the Premier requesting that the Nationalist government should seize the opportunity to 'settle this question in wartime, before the return of the soldiers in order to show them that while they were fighting we were looking after the welfare of future generations'	Premier

Year	Issue	Representation
1918	Eradication of slums: a joint deputation included TPANSW, Health Society of NSW, Benevolent Society, Women's Christian Temperance Union, Woman's National Association Club, Council for Civic and Moral Advancement, Workers' Educational Association for Prevention & Cure of Consumption	Lord Mayor – Sydney City Council
1918	Town Planning Bill: a joint deputation of town planners, surveyors, architects and engineers. Premier promised 'in reply ... that he would place the question of a Town Planning Bill before the Cabinet, with a view to passing it in the following session'	Premier
1919	Town Planning Policy: Premier announced support for town planning in reply to a deputation by TPANSW, Institutes of Architects, Surveyors, Electrical Engineers and Engineers. Advised that first instalment awaited confirmation as Local Government Amending Bill	Premier
1919	Design of War Memorials: John Sulman present as President of Art Gallery of NSW and TPANSW. Professor Wilkinson and G. Sydney Jones spoke on artistic design of Soldiers' War Memorials	Minister for Local Government
1919	Lithgow Housing: proposed garden suburb adjoining the 'small arms factory' at Lithgow	Minister for Repatriation
1919	Moore Street Extension: a joint deputation included TPANSW, Institute of Architects (instigated deputation), Master Builders and others. Sought a commission of experts to help re-plan Sydney	Town Clerk – Sydney City Council
1919	George Street Widening: a joint deputation representing the Open Air Spaces Movement and included the TPANSW, Institute of Architects, Housewives' Association and Master Carriers' Association. Urged consideration of overall Sydney re-planning	Lord Mayor – Sydney City Council

Year	Issue	Representation
1920	Central Square traffic congestion. TPANSW concerned about danger between Tram Waiting Shed and Railway on one side and the Tram Stop and George Street on the other. Suggested four subways be built	Lord Mayor – Sydney City Council
1921	City improvements: Sulman, Dr Boelke and T.H. Kelly raised several issues including slums and rehousing, playgrounds, street widenings and city improvement schemes. Lord Mayor commented that he 'acknowledges the great help that the TPA has been to those who desired to make Sydney something that it should be'	Lord Mayor – Sydney City Council
1921	Town Planning and Greater Sydney Bills: deputation urged the advisability of introducing these Bills (but George Taylor spoke against the deputation on Greater Sydney Bill at that time)	Minister for Local Government
1921	Road between Sydney and Newcastle: the Northern Roads Association called for delegates to attend deputation (Halloran attended)	Minister for Local Government
1921	Destruction of street trees in city and suburbs: TPANSW invited by Institute of Architects to attend delegation (Sulman, Halloran and Spain attended)	NSW Government
1921	Town Planning issues (12 presented) – seven TPANSW members attended deputation for the eradication of slum areas, provision of playgrounds, Martin Place extensions and Elizabeth Street widening. Meeting reported on in the daily press.	Lord Mayor – Sydney City Council
1922	Town Planning Bill: Holman Government carried Bill to second reading. TPANSW recommended a deputation to Premier to ask that the bill be introduced in coming session	Premier Holman
1922	Middle Harbour: deputation and inspection – promise of reserve land	Minister for Lands

Year	Issue	Representation
1922	Burwood Council: new road near public school. Sulman attended opening of the road	Commissioner for Railways
1923	Resumption of Kissing Point: deputation requested by the Putney Progress Association. Sulman replied in the affirmative and action was endorsed	NSW Government
1926	Berala Station right of way: Mr Davidson appointed to represent TPANSW in a deputation to the Premier to secure a small portion of land for access	Premier
1929	Circular Quay station: deputation from representatives of TPANSW, MLAs, Northern Suburbs Councils, NRMA, and Noise Abatement Society in support of retention of Quay site for Circular Quay Station	Acting Premier
1929	Parks and Playgrounds: joint deputation with representatives from TPANSW in conjunction with the Parks and Playground Movement, Australian Forest League, NSW Lawn Tennis Association and NSW Cricket Association to increase land devoted to parks and preservation of existing parks and reserves	Minister for Lands
1929	Circular Quay station: large deputation arranged by TPANSW urged adoption of Bradfield's scheme for Circular Quay	Premier
c1932	Residue land at Milsons Point (former Dorman Long bridge construction workshops). A deputation organised by TPANSW and supported by North Sydney Council to seek Government approval to vest this land in the Council	Minister for Public Works
c1933	Trolley buses in Macleay Street, Kings Cross: deputation advised that the wrong route had been proposed	Commissioner for Road Transport
c1934	Chinamans Beach, Middle Harbour: TPANSW concerned about unregulated growth and the need for an overriding town planning commission	Minister for Lands

Main sources: TPANSW *Minutes* and *Annual Reports*, *Building* and Sydney City Archives.

The Association wound its way to the City Council to present its position and concerns on numerous matters to the Lord Mayor of Sydney. Covering issues of street widening and extensions, road works, and sundry city improvement and beautification schemes, these deputations were frequent agenda items at council meetings. Early in 1921 members raised their concerns over the perceived dangers of traffic and pedestrian congestion at Railway Square in the CBD. After moving to mount a deputation, the Lord Mayor was approached and a period of waiting for a reply ensued. This time the Association scored a bonus as the Lord Mayor, Alderman William Lambert, agreed to discuss a whole suite of topics. During the hour and a half meeting on 29 May 1921, each member spoke on their own special concern. Dr Boelke opened with slum eradication and provision for play areas for children in densely populated residential areas and President Sulman summed up with references to numerous city improvements from road tunnels to a site for a National War Memorial. The Lord Mayor politely extended his appreciation for the Association's many ideas, but frustratingly reminded the deputation that there was no overall plan let alone sufficient funds to carry out such works.[52]

Hitting the lecture circuit

Public presentations and a monthly lecture series were central to winning hearts and minds to the town planning cause and demonstrating its practical benefits. There was a slow start to gaining public attendance at the monthly public lectures, but the Association pressed on and utilised the professional expertise of its leading members who delivered numerous lantern slide shows often with insights and information gained from overseas visits.[53] The Association invited visiting interstate or international town planning officials and dignitaries to speak at formal luncheons and meetings whenever it could. It also held regular 'conversaziones' stimulating discussions amongst themselves and related professionals.[54] By 1921 it could claim that 'the chief means of making its influence felt and enlightening the public has been by monthly discussions and lectures which have been well attended'.[55]

The effort undertaken in the preparation and organisation of these events would have occupied a great deal of members' time. Up until the late 1920s there was an estimated five public lectures per annum. The select list of lectures presented between 1913 and 1927 from the sources available listed in Table 1.3 demonstrates the breadth of themes and topics prepared by the Association's membership. As president from 1913 to 1925, the semi-retired but untiring Sulman led the way by presenting numerous lectures at luncheons and conferences. Other notable spruikers included Fitzgerald, Irvine, and the Taylors. From accounts of the lectures, it appears they were serious events usually accompanied either by lantern slides and/or maps and plans of the topic at hand. Precise attendance figures are elusive. Published references to numbers attending events were usually reported as 'well-attended' but even lectures attracting 'meager' attendance 'were of much value' for their intrinsic merit.[56] Generally, reports of the monthly lectures depicted highly successful events with a diverse range of topics focusing on the benefits of town planning and its significance to all aspects of community life including building and design, economics, public health and social reforms.

Table 1.3: A select list of TPANSW lectures 1913–27

Year	Lecture	Speaker	Venue
1913	Town Planning and Civic Ideals	Walter Burley Griffin	Sydney Town Hall Vestibule, 13 October
1914	The Planning of Sydney – Past, Present and Future	John Sulman	British Association for the Advancement of Science, Sydney
1914	Town Planning and the Workers	J.D. Fitzgerald	British Association for the Advancement of Science, Sydney

Year	Lecture	Speaker	Venue
1914	Town Planning as a National Investment	J.D. Fitzgerald	British Association for the Advancement of Science, Sydney
1914	The Past and Future Government of Sydney	J.D. Fitzgerald	Sydney Chamber of Commerce
1914	Town Planning for Australia	George A. Taylor	Local Government Engineers
1914	City of the Future	George A. Taylor	Master Builders Association
1915	Tree Culture	J.H. Maiden	Royal Society's House – TPANSW Hall
1915	Federal Capital	John Sulman	Brisbane Town Hall, Queensland TPA
1915	A *Town Planning Act* for NSW	John Sulman	Liberal Debating Club
1915	My Visit to America with lantern slides	Major F.E. Stowe	Builders' Exchange Conversazione
1915	Town Planning and Hygienic Building Construction	George A. Taylor	Victorian Master Builders Association
1915	Street Planning, with Relation to Traction	W. De Putron	Local Government Engineers' Conference
1915	Town Planning – Daceyville and Councils and Town Planning	John Sulman	TPANSW – Royal Society Hall
1916	Canberra with lantern slides	W. Scott Griffiths	TPANSW – Royal Society Hall
1916	Greater Sydney	J.D. Fitzgerald	TPANSW – Royal Society Hall, June
1916	Conversazione	J.D. Fitzgerald	TPANSW – Royal Society Hall, August
1916	My American Experiences	William Williamson	TPANSW – Royal Society Hall, September
1916	The Relation of Architecture to Town Planning	G. Sydney Jones	TPANSW – Royal Society Hall, September

Year	Lecture	Speaker	Venue
1916	The Planning of Subdivisions	John Sulman	TPANSW – Royal Society Hall, October
1916	Where People Live and How They Travel	J.J.C. Bradfield	TPANSW – Royal Society Hall. November
1917	Do We Want Town Planning?	Prof R.F. Irvine	Lindfield Progress Association
1917	Town Planning Association of NSW – plans and progress	John Sulman	Victorian and Tasmanian Town Planning Associations
1917	Town Planning and Housing	George A. Taylor	Master Builders Association
1918	Town Planning	John Sulman	TPANSW – Royal Society Hall, November (attended by State Governor)
1919	Town Planning, Public Health and National Development	J.D. Fitzgerald	Local Government Engineers' Conference
1919	Town Planning and National Prosperity	John Sulman	Local Government Engineers' Conference
1919	The Apprentice	James Nangle	Master Builders' Association
1920	The Widths of Roads	Henry Halloran	TPANSW – Assembly Hall, Education Department, April
1920	Local Government Association and Town Planning	George A. Taylor	TPANSW – Assembly Hall, Education Department, September
1920	Town Planning and Health	Lt-Col [Dr] J.S. Purdy	TPANSW – Assembly Hall, Education Department, October
1920	Housing of the People	Lt-Col [Dr] J.S. Purdy	Pleasant Sunday Afternoon Association
1921	Principles of Town Planning	John Sulman	TPANSW – Assembly Hall, Education Department, January

Year	Lecture	Speaker	Venue
1921	New Towns for Old	J.D. Fitzgerald	TPANSW – Assembly Hall, Education Department, March
1921	Eradication of Slums	Dr Grace Boelke and Miss Grace Scobie	TPANSW – Assembly Hall, Education Department
1921	The Modern School (in relation to town planning)	Dr Harvey Sutton	TPANSW – Assembly Hall, Education Department
1921	Grouping of Public Buildings	G. Sydney Jones	TPANSW – Assembly Hall, Education Department
1921	The Location of Railway Towns	Henry Halloran	TPANSW – Assembly Hall, Education Department
1922	The Aesthetics of Town Planning	Prof. Wilkinson	TPANSW – Assembly Hall, Education Department, July
1922	Trees and Plants suitable for Town Planning purposes	T.H. Kelly	TPANSW – Assembly Hall, Education Department, August
1922	Country Homes and Their Comfort	Florence M. Taylor	Conference of Country Women
1922	Open Air Spaces	Dr Mary Booth	Ashfield, Auburn, North Sydney and Waverley
1923	Town Planning Impressions Abroad	Ald Milner Stephen	East Sydney Technical College
1924	Architecture – Australian dwellings	Florence M. Taylor	British Empire Exhibition – London
1924	Civic Architecture	Norman Weekes	TPANSW – Assembly Hall, Education Department
1925	Town Planning and Prosperity	George A. Taylor	Radio 2BL Broadcast
1925	Town Planning and Women's Work	Florence M. Taylor	Radio 2BL Broadcast

Year	Lecture	Speaker	Venue
1925	Women and Town Planning	Florence M. Taylor	Radio 2BL Broadcast
1925	The New Sydney	J.J.C. Bradfield	Sydney City Council – luncheon, July
1927	Town Planning and Recreation	D.L. Davidson	Fairfield Chamber of Commerce
1927	Sydney Regional Plan and the Northern Suburbs	D.L. Davidson	Manly Master Builders Association
1927	Town Planning and Housing	D.L. Davidson	Eastern Suburbs Master Builders Association
1927	Town Planning for Local Improvements	D.L. Davidson	Manly Methodist Guild

Main sources: TPANSW *Minutes* and *Annual Reports; Building*.

The lecture series and associated educational initiatives were maintained throughout World War I. Although the Association regularly expressed its respect and admiration for those in action overseas and the national commitment to fighting for the Empire, it believed wholeheartedly that its efforts in fostering town planning on the homefront was also in the best interest of the nation when it came time for resettlement in peacetime.[57]

Members did not confine themselves to lecturing in Sydney. By early 1915 they were propagandising in regional centres like Newcastle, Katoomba, Bathurst, Lithgow and Wollongong. By lecturing in the suburbs and country NSW, the TPANSW was not only fulfilling its educational role and fostering understanding about what town planning meant, but seeding the possibility of establishing branch associations. Few were, as noted in Sulman's first presidential report, but a Newcastle Betterment Board emerged to be officially affiliated with the TPANSW.[58]

The TPANSW leadership actively promoted town planning ideas in numerous roles. Officer bearers were invited to offer guest lectures to other professional societies and associations, such as the Local Government Engineers' Association, the Master Builders' Association, and the Health Society. Walter Liberty Vernon's death in 1914 sparked the idea for a commemorative series of lectures. The TPANSW was at the centre of fund-raising efforts and Sulman eventually presented the first Vernon Memorial Lectures at the University of Sydney in 1919.[59] A tangible outcome was his authoritative book *An introduction to the study of town planning in Australia* (1921). The TPANSW also actively offered lectures to progress associations, local councils and the state government. Sulman's offer in 1915 to present a 'lantern lecture' to both houses of parliament on 'Practical Town Planning' was accepted with Fitzgerald, then a Member of the Legislative Council, to provide a complementary account of its 'sociological aspects'.[60]

In the mid-1920s TPANSW members also took advantage of the new communication medium of radio to inform 2BL radio audiences on issues of town planning through occasional weekly radio chats. In 1925 Florence Taylor broadcast on 'Women and Town Planning'. She urged listeners to avoid 'reverting to the uglification of Sydney ... let the women of Sydney and of New South Wales open a campaign of looking for and enjoying beauty'. Anticipating future ecological concerns, she spoke on the importance of 'water conservation for country towns and the planting of much needed trees'.[61]

Changes from the late 1920s

All these activities of the Association were constantly intertwined. But from the mid-1920s – and not coincidentally the resignation of Sulman as president in late 1925 – the Association's efforts and standing could not match its original commitment and output. At its annual meeting in November 1927, the decision was made to discontinue the monthly public lecture series, even though the Association reported that its meetings were still attracting 'about 20 people each'.

There are different explanations for the demise of the lecture program. Poor attendance figures were blamed, along with the flagging ability of the general public's 'mental effort ... to follow'.[62] A dwindling enthusiasm on the part of the executive for organising such events would also have been a factor. To sustain such an ambitious program of events and activities was difficult for a proudly voluntary association, especially in the face of seemingly limited impact on the decisions of governments. Other factors came into play. While an inveterate doer to the end, George Taylor had a flourishing printing and publishing business which demanded more of his attention, and the Association felt the blow when its guiding light and founder member died early in 1928. Special editions of the journals of Building Limited celebrated his life and times with numerous testimonies. 'Whatever Mr. Taylor touched he uplifted: and all those who have benefited by his influence mourn his great loss to the community.'[63]

The Depression affected every section of society and the TPANSW was no exception. Its focus narrowed noticeably as attendance at meetings dropped off. It became more affiliated with pursuing particular issues rather than promoting broader community enlightenment. Perhaps leading members believed that they had got the message out about town planning and now preferred to defend their own pet projects and pass critical commentary on others' proposals. The Association with the Taylors at the helm did not mind making enemies, even when this seemed counter-productive to the town planning cause. There were major disagreements with other parties and notably the state government when controlled by Labor administrations. The hatred for Jack Lang (Labor Premier from 1925 to 1927 and 1930 to 1932) maintained a conservative rage that undoubtedly detracted from the TPANSW's original social reform objectives.[64]

The standing of the Association was also impacted by changes in leadership. The TPANSW faced a particularly difficult year in 1934, coincidentally the year of John Sulman's death. A.J. Small's two presidential terms were followed by three presidents in the one year – Alfred J. Brown held office until May and David G. Stead lasted less than three more months before former honorary secretary Bertram W. Ford assumed office. This instability had a disruptive impact on the membership and was reflective of wider instability in the governance of planning in Sydney at that time, in particular the rise of a rival professional planning body.

The TPANSW had had the field to itself for many years. Holding onto its self-anointed role as Sydney's town planning authority, it had little time for upstart bodies such as the Sydney Regional Plan Convention (SRPC), formed in the early 1920s to press for a comprehensive development plan for Sydney and its environs.[65] Henry Halloran, Alfred Spain and John Sulman nonetheless represented the Association on its council and various committees.[66] However, discontent soon grew over the Convention's professional rather than participatory direction. While casting aspersions on some SRPC members as having emphatically 'as little idea of town planning as of common sense', George Taylor stressed that the TPANSW was the better choice as it has 'kept the public alive' in regard to the greater town planning movement.[67] Florence Taylor was equally adamant that the SRPC offered members 'little or nothing ... to do', unlike the TPANSW wherein 'every member is useful in that he or she constitutes so much "backing" to the council that appears to do all the work'.[68]

While the SRPC was seen off, the formation of the Town and Country Planning Institute of Australia in 1934 proved a more damaging competitor and a watershed in the life and fortunes of the TPANSW. Alfred Brown's resignation from the presidency of the TPANSW to take up the same position in the new Institute represented a broader shift away from a narrow, idiosyncratic and often compromised anti-socialist paradigm of 'city improvement' toward a more informed approach to planning policy informed by best practice overseas. The TPANSW may have kept the town planning dream alive but from the late 1920s and certainly from the early 1930s, its ageing and declining membership no longer could represent mainstream professional or indeed community concerns.

Conclusion

The Town Planning Association of New South Wales proved to be a highly energetic, motivated organisation from its inception in 1913 through to the early 1920s. This was its heyday, when members socialised and networked with other professional organisations forming an influential force for propagating their ideas and ideals. Its prodigious educational and promotional activities kick-started and maintained the momentum of the town planning movement in Sydney for many years. In this sense, the TPANSW achieved a number of its key goals as written in its Constitution in regard to promotion, education and dissemination of information. By the 1920s the Association was a voice which stood mainly for 'town betterment' schemes to instil a sense of 'civic pride' with concerns for improving streetscapes, adding fixtures and eradicating existing 'ugliness'.[69]

Notwithstanding the energy and commitment the Association applied to its ideals, it faced criticism from the beginning. Its critics often accused it of too much talk and not enough action. While clearly able to widely communicate its views and schemes through literature, lectures, and lobbying, tangible and direct practical outcomes of the Association's lobbying are less obvious. While the NSW government (and J.D. Fitzgerald specifically as a reformist Minister of Local Government) appointed a Town Planning Advisory Board in 1919, it backed off from any town planning legislation or metropolitan planning scheme. Few of the Association's interventionist projects were realised but its advocacy of tree planting apparently produced dividends. In 1926 the Association claimed that it was responsible for the planting of 156,000 trees this year in NSW 'for park shelter and street beautification purposes'.[70]

In 1934 President David Stead bemoaned the fact that the Association's work was an 'uphill fight', a reference to the continued rejection or ignoring of its many campaigns.[71] But the larger issue by then was the Association's loss of standing as representative of progressive town planning thought in Sydney. Although a much diminished force, the Association continued its business as usual. In fact, it is that dullish regularity and lack of evolutionary change that no doubt resulted in the organisation steadily leaching its credibility through the years. The longevity of the TPANSW into the 1930s was nonetheless a significant achievement in itself. Even more extraordinarily, the organisation which George Taylor formed in 1913 continued to remain active for nearly another three decades.

References

[1] Stephen V. Ward, *Planning the twentieth-century city: the advanced capitalist world* (Chichester: John Wiley, 2002).

[2] J.D. Fitzgerald, *The metropolitan problems of Sydney*, A Lecture before the National Debating Club (August 1918), 12.

[3] Peter Spearritt, *Sydney's century* (Sydney: UNSW Press, 2000), 29.

[4] *Building* (11 October 1913): 44.

[5] *Building* (11 October 1913): 50.

[6] 'Town Planning – new association' in *Sydney Morning Herald*, Sydney (18 October 1913): 19.

[7] *Building* (November 1913): 89.

[8] Town Planning Association of NSW (TPANSW), *Constitution* (Sydney, 1913), 2; and 'Town planning section', *Building* (February 1915): 65.

[9] Marjorie Barnard, *A history of Australia* (Sydney: Angus & Robertson, 1978), 603–04.

[10] *Building* (12 March 1914): 101.

[11] Robert Freestone and Bronwyn Hanna, *Florence Taylor's hats: designing, building and editing Sydney* (Sydney: Halstead Press, 2007), 147–49.

[12] TPANSW Papers, MSS 209, Folder: November and December 1917, Mitchell Library, State Library of New South Wales (SLNSW).

[13] TPANSW, Constitution, 8.

[14] TPANSW, Annual Report, 1933–34, 3.

[15] F.A. Larcombe, *The advancement of local government in New South Wales 1906 to the present* (Sydney: Sydney University Press, 1978), 267–68.

[16] Leonie Sandercock, *Cities for sale: property, politics and urban planning in Australia* (Melbourne: Melbourne University Press, 1975).

[17] *Commonwealth Home* (1 March 1929): 53.

[18] *Town Clerk Annual Reports* 1917, City of Sydney Council Archives: 195–97.

[19] *Property Owner* (23 February 1923), 9.

[20] Sandercock, 26.

[21] TPANSW, *Minutes of Council Meeting* (14 November 1923), MSS 4420, Mitchell Library (SLNSW).

[22] TPANSW, *Constitution: committees and their functions* (November 1913): 2.

[23] TPANSW, *Annual Report* (1931–32): 7–8.

[24] Chris Cunneen, 'Hands off the parks! The provision of parks and playgrounds', in *Twentieth century Sydney* ed. Jill Roe (Sydney: Hale and Iremonger, 1980), 105–19; Parks and Playground Movement of NSW, *Circular* – Agenda Items for 21 June 1939 and correspondence, in Mitchell Library (SLNSW), MLQ 352.706/11938–1940.

[25] TPANSW, *Annual Report*, 7–8.

[26] Town Planning Association of NSW, *Constitution*, 5.

[27] 'Report of the first meeting of the provisional committee of TPANSW' in *Local Government Journal of Australasia/Construction*, Sydney, (3 November 1913): 5.

[28] *Town Planning and Housing* (April 1915): 2.

[29] Town Planning Association of NSW, *Constitution*, 3.

[30] 'New Town Planning and Old Traditions', *Bulletin* (2 February 1914): 7.

[31] *The Salon* (April 1915): 99.

[32] *Town Planning and Housing* (28 June 1915): 8.

[33] TPANSW, *Annual Report*, 1926, 4.

[34] TPANSW, *Minutes* 1919–24, monthly meeting, 14 December 1921.

[35] *Building* (12 April 1922): 51.

[36] *Town planning display under the auspices of the Town Planning Association of NSW* (Sydney: Building Limited, 1913), 1.

[37] *Town Planning Display*, 37–61.

[38] *Town Planning and Housing* (May 1915): 17.

[39] TPANSW Papers, MSS 209, Folder: September 1917, Mitchell Library (SLNSW).

[40] *Town Planning Display*: 13–27.

[41] *Building* (12 February 1914): 66.

[42] Michael Roe, *Nine Australian progressives: vitalism in bourgeois social thought 1890-1960* (Brisbane: University of Queensland Press, 1984).
[43] George A. Taylor, *The town planner and his mission* (Sydney: TPANSW, 1914), 12 and *Building* (12 November 1913): 61-64.
[44] Robert Irvine, *Town planning: what it means and what it demands* (Sydney: TPANSW, 1914), 10.
[45] John Sulman, *Co-partnership housing* (Sydney: TPANSW, 1914), 7.
[46] *Town Planning and Housing* (Sydney: Building Ltd, 1914 -15).
[47] George A. Taylor, *Town planning with common-sense* (Sydney: Building Ltd, 1918), 31.
[48] *Commonwealth Home* (1 December 1928): 29.
[49] TPANSW, *Annual Report*, 1933-34, 3.
[50] *Building* (12 June 1915).
[51] TPANSW, *Annual Report*, 1917; *John Sulman's notes* 1913-25, Mitchell Library.
[52] TPANSW, *Minutes* 1919-24 (ML MSS 4420) and *Town Clerk Annual Reports* 1922, City of Sydney, Archives.
[53] 'Town Planning Section', *Building* (February 1915): 68.
[54] *Building* (12 March 1917): 86.
[55] 'Town Planning in Australia', *Building* (March 1921): 82.
[56] 'Australian town planning – what is being done in N.S.W.', *Building* (March 1917): 86.
[57] *Building* (March 1917): 86.
[58] John Sulman, 'First presidential report to N.S.W. Town Planning Association' in *Building* (February 1915): 68.
[59] *Property Owner* (16 June 1919): 5.
[60] John Sulman, 'First presidential report', 68.
[61] 'Women and town planning', *Commonwealth Home* (31 July 1925):18-19.
[62] 'Annual Report of Town Planning Association of NSW', *Building*, (April 1928): 79 and *Commonwealth Home* (10 July 1925): 22.
[63] 'The policy of the late George A Taylor and the commonwealth home' in *Commonwealth Home* (1 February 1928): 3.
[64] 'Around Australia', *Building* (January 1927): 41 and (May 1932): 37 and *Australian dictionary of biography Online* at www.adbonline.anu.edu.au.
[65] Robert Freestone, 'The Sydney regional plan convention: an experiment in metropolitan planning 1921-1924', *Australian Journal of Politics and History*, 34 (1988): 345-58.

[66] *The First Annual Report and Financial Statement of the Sydney Regional Plan Convention*, Sydney, 11 October 1923; *The Second Annual Report and Financial Statement of the Sydney Regional Plan Convention*, Sydney, 4 November 1924 and *Sydney Regional Plan Convention – inauguration, progress and objectives*, Sydney, 1925.

[67] *Property Owner* (October 1923): 5.

[68] *Property Owner* (March 1924): 8.

[69] 'Town Betterment Schemes', *Building* (September 1927): 87–89.

[70] 'Improving architectural design – town planners take action', *Building* (August 1926): 64a.

[71] TPANSW, *Annual Report*, 1933–34, 3.

2
Queensland's popular movement in planning 1914–30: socialism, regularity and profit

Chris McConville

'The Town Planning Movement is making fine progress in Queensland, that is, for a place so passively resistant to innovation'. With this comment, the journal *Building* in March 1915 welcomed the reformation of the Queensland Town Planning Association. For in its almost accidental amalgam of health campaigns, moralising crusades and preference for deurbanised gardenesque landscaping, the early town planning movement seemed entirely malleable, posing little danger to a place 'passively resistant to innovation'. Perhaps this fluidity explains planning's initial success in Queensland, where the reformist state government hosted a major town planning conference in 1918 and in the following decade a new Greater Brisbane City Council could claim that it was the first civic body in Australia to have established a town planning department.[1] The Queensland Town Planning Association remained a far more prominent community voice than the pioneers of the movement could have hoped for. And yet by 1930, the Association's malleability hastened a decline. In Brisbane it transformed into little more than a supportive voice to Brisbane property owners. The most promising opportunities for shaping land use through planning now appeared in coastal regions to the north of the capital.

In exploring Queensland's popular response to town planning after 1914 it is possible to trace the overriding influence of the Queensland Labor government's unique version of 'state socialism'. The subsequent influence of the Queensland Town Planning Association (hereafter QTPA) during the 1920s can be seen most directly in the shaping of the

Greater Brisbane City Council. A more fertile arena for town planning and community influence on the urban environment then appeared in small townships such as Nambour and Noosa rather than in Brisbane. This chapter is an attempt to unearth these abstracted forces and to trace transitions in the QTPA from 1914 to 1930.

The first planners

The popular movement for town planning in Queensland emerged from a promotional tour by Charles Reade and William Davidge in 1914.[2] Davidge's lecture in the Albert Hall, Brisbane, dealt with the 'economic and aesthetic aspects of town planning' and warned of dangers in Brisbane's rapid growth rate, in particular its 'higgeldy-piggeldy' stilt housing and generous height limit of 120 ft.[3] The meeting was presided over by C.M. Jenkinson, Mayor of Brisbane, who listened to Davidge's claims that his city's failure to control building heights had created an 'insidious danger (in) the encroachment of buildings on reserves'. Reade followed Davidge and lectured at City Hall, Stanley Street, South Brisbane on 'Garden Cities v. Australian Slums and Suburbs'.[4] E.C. Barton presided over Reade's lecture. A small subtropical town like Brisbane had little in common with the European garden cities familiar to the town planning lecturers and perhaps the city ought to have been understood on its own merits rather than condemned for its unique and rambling townscape. Nonetheless it sounded as if neither Reade nor Davidge had much to say in favour of the urban form of Brisbane (Figure 2.1). Reade deplored the manner in which small houses were clustered together despite the vast spaces of Queensland. A drive around Brisbane revealed to him that property owners 'beautified' their land by cutting down trees. 'Surely in a country like this a wealth of trees and foliage would be protection against the tropical sun', he mused.[5] Davidge divided the town planning challenge into three areas: land, buildings and transit, in none of which Brisbane seemed a success.[6]

Figure 2.1: Aerial view of Brisbane, 1919. Source: John Oxley Library, State Library of Queensland, 199519

These lectures enthused listeners sufficiently for Barton to move, and Alderman Russell (Mayor of Hamilton) to support, the formation of a town planning association. The gathering endorsed this motion and a representative committee was drawn together for a fledgling Queensland Town Planning Association.[7] Further meetings in April and May were focused on the need for more metropolitan parks.[8] By July 1915 the QTPA had an executive in place. It had sparked curiosity and even enthusiasm amongst local government aldermen, members of state parliament from the left and the right, as well as the medical and engineering professions.[9] The new QTPA council soon extended an invitation to planning advocates such as John Sulman to visit Brisbane.

The QTPA was intent on providing more parks for the city.[10] Schemes were proposed for low-lying lands along Breakfast Creek, where residents were more interested in boat moorings rather than landscaping but where creek banks could be converted to parkland (Figure 2.2).

Planning advocates saw the creek as a starting point for a network of parks along creek and river valleys throughout the city.[11] Association members proposed a state-wide Town Planning Commission to the Premier whilst initiating sustained criticism of the South Brisbane Council, a body, which they claimed, was destroying the beauty of the river banks. They attacked the council as an organisation obsessed by money rather than soul.[12]

Figure 2.2: Breakfast Creek, Brisbane, 1929. Source: John Oxley Library, State Library of Queensland, 185372

The Association also initiated a long-running campaign to diminish the significance of railways in urban transportation. Members commended the plan of R.A. McInnis (the most persistently enthusiastic advocate of town planning over more than two decades) for a contour road around the river bend at New Farm. McInnis, like others in the new Association, was actively involved in the Royal Automobile Club of Queensland and road plans always seemed to take priority over rail in the QTPA's 'transit' discussions. They particularly sought to reconstruct the road network around the South Brisbane rail terminal – to benefit motorists rather than rail travellers. Alongside concerns for parks, aesthetics and transit the new Association frequently returned to problems of public health.

Health, socialism and the city

Although women were powerful advocates for town planning and related public health reforms in Brisbane, the QTPA rejected a proposal for a women's section.[13] In so doing it probably robbed itself of town planning's most determined advocates. In Queensland as elsewhere, pioneer planners remained enmeshed in problems of public health and the group most active in seeking to healthily manage urban space was the feminised Children's Playground Association.[14] Playgrounds were designed for several inner Brisbane areas, Fortitude Valley and Ithaca being the best known. Whilst the women interested in children's health were no doubt prepared to support campaigns for green belts and civic squares, their goals remained more immediate, concerned with converting small inner city open space into planned and ordered playgrounds with educational buildings attached. Josephine Bedford, along with other women interested in structured children's play, participated in planning conferences and warned about the dangers to children in inner Brisbane. The Association's Ithaca playground design was promoted at the 1918 Brisbane town planning conference.[15] Such playgrounds, and education for working-class children, drew less enthusiasm from road builders and civic designers, so that over time Bedford and other women did seem to have grown uneasy about their more ambitious male colleagues and to have at least partly withdrawn from QTPA activities.

Figure 2.3: Josephine Bedford, feminist playground and planning advocate, 1898. Source: John Oxley Library, State Library of Queensland, 177525

As an ideology, town planning appealed most directly to a broad range of socially-conscious professional men and women; the women often directly connected to the medical profession as was the case with Josephine Bedford (Figure 2.3) whilst the men by and large were drawn from surveying, engineering and related professions.[16] An exception to this divide was T.A. Price, one of the more vocal of the state's enthusiasts for town planning (and certainly the most prominent Queensland participant at the Adelaide conference) who straddled both fields, as a qualified provincial doctor and architect. Price was also an early supporter of the national parks movement.[17] Like others shaping the direction of the QTPA he took an active role in local government, as Mayor of Toowoomba. Price's interest in the public health benefits of planning stemmed from his battle against the mosquitoes of the Darling Downs, a campaign commenced before World War I. He had become mayor after running as an independent against both Nationalists and Labor in 1918 (the first year of the Greater Toowoomba council and after he had served as deputy mayor for four years). Price had however been lobbying for pest and vermin controls for nearly a decade. Tom Price was eventually dubbed the 'mosquito king' and set up a Rat and Mosquito Board, replanned the city's water supply, and sent out inspectors to fine those who failed to adopt the new standards. When the state government began seeking out a site for a planned and modern industrial suburb, Price emerged as one of the most active promoters of the planned industrial suburb of Darra.[18]

Such public health campaigns and the town planning which they spawned, owed much to a distinctive ideology: Queensland's very own version of 'state socialism'. After June 1915, advocates for healthy cities and for an aesthetically pleasing urban form, found a ready welcome for their ideas in state parliament and the Queensland public service.[19] Leading identities in an ideologically assured Australian Labor Party – in power in Queensland from 1915 – and their most trusted civil service administrators – drove support for town planning ventures. It was no accident that one of the largest bodies of delegates at the 1918 conference was drawn from the unionised public servants of Queensland. In promoting town planning the Labor Party saw an experimental movement trying to create new ways of dealing with material forms. Like public health advocates, they too were intent on improving living conditions in working-class suburbs and amongst the poorest families.

Like town planning advocates, they wanted to raise the quality of the state's housing stock. A few of the town planners, Price amongst them, could see sense in Labor's plans for regional industrial centres. Such common ground however could easily be destabilised. Labor's materialism was tied fundamentally to a redistribution of wealth and power. The embryonic planning movement devoted itself to a systematic and efficient urban remodelling, for which wealth redistribution eventually proved inessential.

Figure 2.4: John Huxham: Queensland politician and QTPA President, 1916. Source: John Oxley Library, State Library of Queensland, 68242

Gathered in the Town Planning Association, local aldermen, surveyors, architects and engineers liked to think of themselves as a voluntary network of professional and public-spirited citizens. In reality their movement had become a creature of the state, and in particular of three prominent men: Premier T.J. Ryan, who gave a political voice to planning ideals, Home Secretary John Huxham (Figure 2.4), who saw planning as a practical aid to his health and housing projects, and Charles Chuter, a career public servant who had risen through the system and understood planning as vital to any restructure of local government and redistribution of wealth in Queensland. Together they gave impetus to the 1918 Brisbane planning conference and to the revived QTPA of the 1920s. Of the three, Charles Chuter (Figure 2.5) remained the most influential and stands as one of those committed civil servants, often overlooked by historians, critical to the character of Australian life in the first half of the 20th century.

After the 1915 state election, the Labor government, led by union lawyer Ryan, had seen in 'town planning' one key to a broader integration in planned management, defined loosely as 'state socialism' or 'state enterprises'.[20] For Ryan, town planning offered a relatively uncontroversial instrument for a redistributive politics which could encompass workers' housing schemes, collectivised farmland, state-run sugar mills and heavy industry, and state-managed retail trading in fresh fruit, meat and fish.[21] Ryan and Huxham brought town planning into this ambitious project and Chuter, by then a senior official in Huxham's department, became honorary director of the 1918 conference. Huxham was president of the QTPA in 1916. In this role he routinely restated Ryan's dictum about the 'scientific' integration which town planning could bring to disparate reforming projects.[22]

The state government's donation of £300 to fund the conference and exhibition had effectively removed control of the QTPA from the hands of Barton and fellow town planning enthusiasts. Initially the Brisbane conference was supposed to give a stage to town planning pioneers. As it came under state political control it turned into a showcase for social and urban reform, programs now being embarked upon across a number of state government ministries, but especially in the Home Secretary's Department.[23] It was Chuter, later promoted to Assistant Under-Secretary to Huxham, who corresponded with Charles Reade, organiser of the earlier national conference in Adelaide.[24] This transition in authority, from collegial professionals, to ideologically inspired state officials, was acknowledged by Reade, who wrote to Chuter in March 1918 congratulating the Queensland government for placing the conference under its patronage.[25] Chuter organised press coverage and promoted the notion of town planning to rural councils.

Figure 2.5: Charles Chuter: public servant, local government reformer and supporter of planning. Source: John Oxley Library, State Library of Queensland, 54328

In later, similar efforts, Chuter had the willing support of the new Queensland Governor (1920–25), Sir Matthew Nathan, who adopted an improvement in outback ('western') housing as his favoured project and spoke frequently at QTPA gatherings. The QTPA also attracted that unrelenting Roman Catholic builder, Archbishop James Duhig, who regularly attended the Association's meetings, proposed novel solutions to Brisbane's sewerage difficulties, and on his tours through suburbs and the bush routinely chided his clergy for not taking sufficient interest in the planning opportunities of their parishes.[26] Town planning thus provided a meeting place for Queensland's occasionally disloyal Irish Catholic communities, for the British Crown's representative in the state, and for radical socialists with no sympathy for the monarchy, albeit somewhat more for Christianity.

Chuter and Huxham saw the 1918 town planning exhibition as an ideal opportunity to promote welfarist projects such as their plans for a Queensland Workers Dwelling Board. Chuter wrote to Reade not long before the exhibition opened, explaining that in order to promote the need for better housing, 'I have asked a man here to dig up (photographs) of the worst places he can'.[27] The conference itself he advertised through a 'boosting campaign', with 'hoardings' at railway stations and in June an appeal to editors of all major newspapers for cooperation and 'kind assistance'.[28] Free excursion trains ran from some country towns to the exhibition and Chuter pestered local government mayors across the state to either attend or to send delegations. Some, like the delegation from Rockhampton, did go away enthused and in several of the larger towns returning delegates took ideas about better planning back home with them.

Whilst Chuter and Huxham doubted the interest of several cabinet ministers in town planning, they did have the support of Ryan and perhaps to a lesser extent his treasurer and later premier, Ted Theodore. To Ryan, the central importance of town planning lay not so much in what it could achieve for Brisbane, but in the role of good regional planning in halting any drift to the city. Plans for a state-run iron and steel industry in north Queensland (with Bowen the preferred site) were deliberately promoted so as to minimise the possibility of slum housing (such as

Queenslanders perceived in inner Melbourne and Sydney) from enveloping older riverside locales in Brisbane. In a message to the Adelaide conference, Ryan proposed that the main role of planners was 'improvement of country roads and rendering the rural more attractive ... the undesirable congestion of population in great cities is often largely due to unsatisfactory conditions of life and labour in country places'.[29]

In opening the Brisbane conference, the Premier again drew a link between what he saw as the aesthetic and civic mission of town planning and the need to maintain small farmers on the land, reduce population drift to the coast, and provide better housing and roads beyond Brisbane itself. Ryan and some local government delegates, R.A. Bulcock from the Shire of Landsborough for example, also hoped that town planning would enable profitable and orderly soldier settlement schemes.[30] In similar vein to Ryan, Bulcock argued that through planning in the bush and provincial centres, Brisbane could best use its majestic riverside location and grow in a manner which might forestall the great evil of the modern city – the slum.[31]

Ryan also spoke lyrically of his visit to Washington DC with its 'broad straight tree-lined avenues, the multiplicity of exquisite parks and gardens and the grandeur of the architecture of both public buildings and private dwellings'.[32] To Queensland Labor, these constituted the more decorative and so dispensable aspects of town planning. Aesthetic values, which they acknowledged as critical to the wellbeing of workers and their families, could be best introduced to cities through properly planned industrial estates. At the 1918 conference, and in subsequent programs for regional processing plants, Labor idealists drew on garden city models, which they sought to apply to quotidian urban forms and so render them fair, healthy and comfortable.

No doubt these grand prospects came as welcome respite for Ryan who, through the war years, had to battle opponents both from the left, inspired by the Bolshevik Revolution, and on the right, who felt threatened by his theories of 'state socialism' and his closeness to Irish revolutionaries and prominence in the anti-conscription movement. His speech set the tone for several of the discussions at the 1918 gathering. Papers ranged from detailed consideration of the cross-river problem in Brisbane, a project dear to the interest of McInnis, to the need for boulevards, and better public buildings. Playgrounds, parks and sewerage in Brisbane figured in exhibits and conference papers as did schemes for low-cost housing and planned rural settlements. Alongside these offerings, one paper extolled the superior virtues of modern art, and a cubist exhibition accompanied the convention!

City planning and 'regularity'

If the 1918 gathering drew on concerns about health, welfare, redistribution and fair access to housing, the QTPA as it emerged after 1922 seemed neither idealistic nor egalitarian. Instead it concentrated on introducing a symmetrical and mechanistic ordering to urban space, and to Brisbane in particular. The principles of town planning as set out by Davidge in 1914 – the remodelling of land, buildings and transit – did roughly cover the themes discussed by the QTPA after 1922. Whilst members retained a deep concern for improvements in public health (sewers were regularly seen as a problem), they seemed less confident about any scheme for wealth redistribution, subsidised workers housing or industrial estates along garden city lines. Instead they emphasised solutions to problems of transit in motor travel and new roads, the creation of parkland, and zoning and building codes. Not surprisingly then, improving the built environment of Queensland was emerging as a task for the engineer rather than the health campaigner or trade union activist.

The QTPA had lost momentum after 1918 and was restructured in 1922–23. At a meeting in the city council chambers, again with Barton in the chair, McInnis spoke about the progress of the QTPA – of which he could find little. To McInnis the crude death rates of Brisbane demonstrated how much the city needed planning in public health.[33] But for all of the QTPA's lectures and lobbying, members could point to few material results for almost a decade of hard work. They had not done much for 'practical town planning'. To McInnis this meant fast river transport, district 'co-ordination' (zoning) and a central planning body.[34]

When it met again in 1923, members were still discussing playgrounds, the hygienic value of trees, and other aspects of public health.[35] Archbishop Duhig continued to promote the need for a unique sewerage system for Brisbane. The Association battled public indifference to planning through newspaper articles, a lecture series and regular radio broadcasts in Brisbane. At the same time, any enthusiasm for the welfare of the working class and small farmers had clearly waned. Engineers and surveyors chafed against further abstracted idealism or an expanded educative program. They wanted instead to lay out streets and allotments with system and order. In 1918, Professor R.W.H. Hawken of the University of Queensland had delivered a paper at the conference calling for a broad-scale 'remodelling of towns'.[36] After 1923 remodelling came to mean regular block sizes and building heights, greater width for city roads, regular river ferries and better access to the centre of Brisbane. Areas were to be set aside exclusively as industrial zones, with special attention paid to the Eagle Farm-Pinkenba area.[37] The QTPA was looking to regularity and remodelling rather than redistribution and education as governing principles.[38]

Perhaps the major change amongst QTPA priorities sprang from their focus on Brisbane rather than the bush. By 1924, Charles Chuter's long-term project for larger metropolitan governments with expanded planning powers was drawing to a successful conclusion.[39] The *City of Brisbane Act 1924* (known during its progress through parliament as 'Mr Chuter's Bill') established a Greater Brisbane City Council. For more than a decade, Chuter had insisted that only the broadest urban boundaries would give Brisbane the rate base to improve health, transport and infrastructure services. All the while he worked on the amalgamations (or 'greaterisations' as they were called), Chuter remained an active member of the QTPA. The new metropolis-wide management of Brisbane seemed an ideal opportunity, for Chuter, McInnis and other members, to put town planning principles into practice.

As might be expected the QTPA 'rejoiced' at the birth of a new Brisbane City Council with powers in town planning.[40] William J. Earle was appointed Brisbane Town Planner and the Council seemed ready to embark on a systematic survey of land use. Yet in drawing their focus back onto the capital city, the QTPA turned planning into a scheme for efficient management, as the Association was reduced to one amongst a range of parties sniping at the new Brisbane council's planning.

As the novelty of planning itself dulled, the QTPA struggled to define exactly what it meant by planning. In 1922 members welcomed the first garden city design for a Brisbane suburb at Coronation Park (with a contoured street lay-out designed by McInnis) as a resounding achievement. The QTPA formed a part of the group invited to visit the new estate (1000 allotments over 240 acres) by the Coronation Park Company. The QTPA routinely proposed new parklands within the city. Members supported the Queensland Art Society in its deputation seeking a National Art Gallery in Brisbane and they took up the cause of preservation of woodland at Currumbin and on Springbrook Plateau, which they saw as a site for an ex-urban sanatorium along garden city lines.[41] Yet such localised triumphs were not enough to establish planning as the overarching principle of state development. Price spoke defensively in 1924 asking 'What is town planning?' and answering 'It is not a special brand of lunacy and it does not waste money it saves money'.[42] The savings were to be achieved, Price told delegates to the annual general meeting that year, through the twin 'essentials of town planning – communication and zoning'.[43]

No doubt prototype garden suburbs remained a fine achievement, yet what the Association saw as the critical task of traffic management remained unresolved. The QTPA identified traffic problems at Brisbane's North Quay and Five Ways in Woolloongabba and led deputations to successive mayors of Brisbane demanding road improvements here and elsewhere. In this they generally found support from William Earle and some elected figures. Their more pragmatic approach to planning seemed also to have won other allies. J.J. Cavanagh told one meeting of the QTPA that 'so-called hard-headed business men have a fashion of twitting Town Planners as Dreamers'. In the success of Coronation Park and in the drive for better roads, Cavanagh thought that the QTPA had demonstrated that planners were not dreamers but instead qualified as 'practical people'.

In grasping for the practicalities of urban life, the QTPA concentrated on regularity in urban form – a regularity to be obtained through zoning or 'districting', in conjunction with an efficient road system. Almost all of these discussions of roads and zoning stressed the problems of Brisbane rather than the wider urban network of Queensland. In the capital, this prized regularity was to be achieved by a uniform block size and by strict regulation of building height as well as built form. The problem of communication, as defined by Price, was to be resolved by a systematic and standardised network of arterial roads around Brisbane. With the formation of the Greater Brisbane Council and the planners' desire to zone the capital and expand its roads, any planning possibilities in provincial Queensland receded rapidly from view.

By the mid-point of the decade then, members of the QTPA were indeed well on their way to disproving any reputation as 'dreamers'. They now promoted a mundane functionality in widened roads, building heights and subdivision.

Property rights and planning

It did not take long for the adventure of a Greater Brisbane to disappoint planning enthusiasts. The QTPA had placed great faith in this new civic entity and whilst members felt some concern at the confusion of strictly administrative responsibilities with political ones, Greater Brisbane and not the state as a whole seemed the most promising site for planning.[44]

For its part the new Brisbane council was quick to make clear that it viewed the QTPA as an advisory group, with no legal role in planning decisions. Mayor Jolly told a deputation of the QTPA that he would be 'glad of the co-operation of the Association in an advisory capacity only'.[45] Jolly did promise to bring the concerns of the QTPA before council but insisted that he could not delegate authority to an outside body such as the independent town planning commission proposed by the delegation.[46] And although the council's appointment of a town planner certainly pleased the Association, it may well have noted with concern that two of the most active QTPA members, Ray Nowland and R.A. McInnis, were interviewed for the position and rejected.[47]

Looking back over their successes in 1928, the QTPA listed a range of projects, from redesigned intersections in the city, to the South Brisbane War Memorial Park, flood prevention works on the Brisbane River, conversion of St Helena from a prison into a 'public pleasure resort', and similar plans for Mt Tambourine and Springbrook Plateau.[48] The Association had at the same time, failed to convince Brisbane City Council to complete its detailed civic survey (Figure 2.6) or to produce a development plan.

As the QTPA's disillusion with Greater Brisbane grew, the town planning movement very quickly became an ally of commerce and property owners. The Association had always had some involvement from major Brisbane commercial figures: T.C. Beirne, for example, who lectured members on urban life in the United States. For such city merchants, a resolution to traffic congestion was imperative and through 1926 and 1927 the QTPA continued to take part in deputations to the mayor, seeking a restructure of Brisbane's main roads, an interest aided no doubt by McInnis' role as spokesman for the traffic committee of the Royal Automobile Club of Queensland.[49] As an extension of their concerns about the 'cross-river problem', the QTPA tried once more to alter traffic arrangements around the South Brisbane railway terminal – and met with a stiff rejection from the Queensland Railway Commissioners.[50]

Figure 2.6: Advancing a metropolitan perspective: a 1928 plan from the Brisbane City Council's civic survey. Source: Fryer Library, University of Queensland, Map G9004.B67.S63.1928, C57 1928

In 1929 the QTPA returned to familiar issues of water supply and sewerage, estate design and housing. By then the sponsors of the 1918 gathering had gone. Ryan was drawn into federal Labor pre-selection, before he died suddenly in 1921. Chuter moved from managing local government reformation to restructuring the state's hospital system. Huxham had spent several years in London as Queensland Agent-General, and on his return to Brisbane in 1929 took little part in public life. In that year Hannibal King a director of the Bank of Australasia became President of the QTPA, an indication of the Association's increased dependence on the world of the 'so-called hard-headed business men'.

Where a few years earlier the Association had pushed Greater Brisbane to develop a zoning scheme prior to a building survey, the QTPA now rejected any such attempt. In opposing the city's zoning scheme, the QTPA found itself linked to a broad property owning and investing alliance, which included Chambers of Commerce, the Chamber of Manufacturers, the Real Estate Institute, the Master Builders Association, Merchants Association, and the Property Owners Protection Association. Their major project in 1930 was 'opposing the attitude of the Brisbane City Council towards the recognised principles of town planning'. 'True town planning' it was now claimed ought not 'impose a costly scheme of public works or unduly restrict personal liberty'. Town planning had thus completed its journey from public health, wealth redistribution and social welfare to enhancing capital gains in real estate.[51] Brisbane's attempted move to zoned districts meant that businesses could be forced to relocate with no compensation and uncompensated restrictions on use drew the ire of the Combined Committee on Rezoning of which the QTPA was a key member.[52]

Beyond Brisbane

With its focus on Brisbane and its direct involvement in the campaigns of property owners and chambers of commerce to sabotage a zoning scheme, the QTPA had only an intermittent influence on the broader directions of town planning in provincial Queensland, as evidenced in town planning proposals for coastal localities to the north of Brisbane.

Rockhampton became one of the first provincial towns to take an interest in the possibilities of town planning. No sooner had the Brisbane town planning conference closed than Chuter and Price were on their way up the coast to visit. Chuter listened to complaints about the water supply, whilst promoting a 'Greater Rockhampton' as the best solution for local infrastructure problems. Price lectured on town planning principles and managed to raise some interest from Rockhampton, Livingston and Fitzroy councillors.[53] Neither he nor Chuter seemed able to convince the civic leaders of North Rockhampton, who remained staunch opponents of any municipal amalgamation and by extension of town planning. The Mayor of Rockhampton however seemed supportive. 'Everything which goes to make life pleasant must be studied in city planning', Mayor C.O. Gough informed his council.[54] He went on to explain the need for narrowed streets and more kerbside street planting, buildings in concrete rather than timber, and houses sited in line with garden city principles.

Figure 2.7: Nambour: an early regional centre project of the QTPA, 1915. Source: John Oxley Library, State Library of Queensland, 61961

Nambour, a sugar town on the main northern rail line between Rockhampton and Brisbane, also showed interest in planning (Figure 2.7). In 1916 the Nambour Progress Association had sought membership of the QTPA.[55] Along with other provincial newspapers, the Nambour *Chronicle*, edited by A.W. Thynne, a great planning supporter, provided space for publicity surrounding the 1918 conference (much of it sounding as if it was written by Chuter himself). However Maroochy Shire (then centred on Nambour) turned down the opportunity to send delegates to the conference claiming that a youthful Nambour needed no planning.[56] By 1921 and despite such indifference, a Development Association had commenced in Nambour (the association being a small group of men who met over a cup of tea once a week) and put forward planning proposals 'to prevent the place developing into another Woolloomooloo or Chinatown'.[57]

On a 1923 visit, John Huxham reassured such local business people that the state government would provide assistance for town planning in Nambour. His new local government act came into force in January 1924 granting wide discretionary powers to councils like Maroochy. Within a few days of this act's passing, a fire had burnt out the centre of Nambour.[58] McInnis and others in the QTPA now urged that the town be rebuilt along proper planned lines with uniform block sizes, a series of laneways, and with all construction in concrete.[59] Within a few months, the Shire had rejected schemes for a new planned town centre. In 1929 further fire damage and a new town hall brought renewed impetus to plans for a civic centre and town square. This time, Earle came up from Brisbane and 'an elaborate system of gardens, rockeries, car parking and pedestrian walkways was designed'.[60] Only part of the plan was ever completed. The gardens died, rockeries collapsed in a subtropical downpour, and Maroochy Council moved to flatten the project for a car park.[61]

When rebuffed in Nambour, the QTPA was able to turn to the neighbouring Shire of Noosa. McInnis and Colonel Corrigan (a Queensland state manager for T.M. Burke and member of the QTPA) presented their ideas for Noosa (in what is now Sunshine Beach) to the Shire Council. They explained that Burke's firm had at great expense contour-planned and zoned the entire township, preserving where possible the 'many natural beauties of the land'. Burke's company had already designed the contour-planned Glenlyon Estate in Brisbane's Ashgrove as an experimental garden suburb.[62] In Noosa they laid out small blocks and planned public amenities ranging from beachside kiosks to a wide entrance boulevard. They banned random shop locations and asymmetrical house siting. When completed they expected that 'there was not the slightest doubt that [the township] would be developed with all its original characteristics and beauty'.[63] The QTPA shared its enthusiasm and when the estate-township opened in 1929 the Association proclaimed Noosa as the 'first town in Queensland to be planned and zoned in advance of settlement and marks an epoch in the history of town planning in Queensland'.[64] In this shire 'unequalled in the world for its surfing beaches and other picturesque and varied qualities', a town plan had been adopted, so as to function efficiently, preserve scenic views and maintain easy access to the beach.[65]

Bridgeworks impressed local councillors as much as the township itself and the Weyba Bridge opening drew 700 cars. Planes landed on the beach.[66] Noosa councillor W.I. Ferguson had first imagined an entire town unified by the vision of a private developer and had approached Corrigan with the idea in 1926.[67] Corrigan for his part pointed out that from the official opening onwards the success of the venture lay in local hands and could no longer be guided solely by an interstate developer. Charles Chuter also spoke noting that in Australia 'no finer piece of town planning had been introduced' and R.M. Wilson, president of the QTPA, reminded his audience that the Noosa scheme was only possible through the close cooperation between Burke's company and the QTPA. By working closely with this expert body, he remarked, towns elsewhere in Queensland could enjoy the benefits of good planning.[68]

Conclusion

The history of the QTPA between 1915 and 1930 can be read as a narrative of drift from the high idealism of social redistribution towards partnership with the real estate industry. Whilst planning advocates and state civil servants could find common ground in seeking better public health measures, the pioneer planners struggled with notions of centralised, state-controlled marketing of food or subsidised and worker-owned housing, just as civil servants and Laborist councillors may have been slow to accept the need for contour-aligned roadways. But the visions of planning's popular movement could be made to mesh effectively with redistributive social policy, especially where both were dependent on the successes of Chuter's 'greaterisations'. The mid-decade interest in orderly urbanism and regular geometric design placed urban form above social relations. Once detached from social goals, the QTPA's concern for zoning seemed in many ways the undoing of the Association. It was transformed by the end of the decade into a relatively minor player in campaigns to defend property rights against such municipal zoning – Noosa's success excepted – an unwarranted narrowing for an organisation once backed by the ALP, Queensland's premier, the state governor and the Irish Catholic prelate of Brisbane.

References

[1] W.A. Jolly, *The inauguration of Greater Brisbane* (Brisbane: Watson Ferguson and Co, 1928).
[2] Annabel Lloyd, *Timeline, key dates, and events in the development of town planning in Brisbane, 1882–1992* (Brisbane: Brisbane City Council, 2006), 3.
[3] Brisbane *Daily Mail*, 9 September 1914.
[4] Brisbane *Daily Mail*, 7 September 1914.
[5] Brisbane *Courier*, 10 September 1914.
[6] Brisbane *Courier*, 11 September 1914.
[7] Brisbane *Courier*, 12 September 1914.
[8] *Building* (June 1915): 94–95.
[9] The QTPA executive of 1915 was President: the Mayor of Brisbane, G. Down; Vice-Presidents: J. Allen MLA, A.A. Spowers; Councillors: D. Taylor Dr E. Calpin, F.J. Charlton, W.F. Finlayson, M.J. Kirwan MLA, E.J. Manchester, L.L. Powell, H.M. Russell, H.D. Macrossan MLA; Treasurer: Alderman G.L. Duff, Alderman C.M. Jenkinson; Secretary: E. Barton; Assistant Secretary: W. Smyth.
[10] *Town Planning and Housing Review*, 12 April 1915.
[11] Ibid.
[12] Ibid.

[13] *Building* (June 1915): 94.
[14] George Taylor, *Town planning with common sense* (Sydney: Building Limited, 1918), 9.
[15] Children's Model Playground, Town of Ithaca, exhibition catalogue, *Proceedings of the Second Australian Town Planning Conference and Exhibition, Brisbane Queensland, 30th July to 6th August 1918* (Brisbane: Queensland Government Printer 1919), vol. 2, 58–59.
[16] See Miss Josephine Bedford, *Evidence, Minutes of Evidence, Royal Commission on Health*, Commonwealth of Australia, 1925, 970–73; Julia Gatley, 'For King and empire: Australian women and nascent town planning', *Planning Perspectives*, 20 (2005): 121–45.
[17] See Drew Hutton and Libby Connors, *A history of the Australian environment movement* (Melbourne: Cambridge University Press, 1999), 85; and 'Dr Tom Price', Toowoomba City Council website (December 2008), www.toowoomba.qld.gov.au/index.php?option=com_content&task=view&id=114&Itemid=384.
[18] Toowoomba *Chronicle*, 20 February 1918, 5 February 1918; R.S. Marriott, *This is the story of Toowoomba's first hundred years, 1860–1960* (Toowoomba: Toowoomba City Council, 1960), 17–18.
[19] Shawn Sherlock, '"Good-bye the state's progress": State enterprises and Labor's plan for a North Queensland steel industry', *Labour History*, 90 (May 2006): 68–72.
[20] Queensland Government, *Socialism at Work* (Brisbane: Queensland Government Printer, 1918).
[21] Auditor General of Queensland, *Report on State Enterprises*, 1918–19. See also D.J. Murphy, 'The establishment of state enterprises in Queensland, 1915–1918', *Labour History*, 14 (May 1968): 13–23; Ross Laurie, 'State enterprises in Queensland 1915–1929: a case study of pragmatic idealism', *Journal of the Royal Historical Society of Queensland*, 19 (2006): 82–90; and Ross Laurie, 'Cheap meat to the people: the Queensland Government Butcher Shops', *Proceedings of the Eighth National Labour History Conference* (Brisbane: Australian Society for Labour History, 2003), 196–200. It is hard to find any sense that redistributive policies were extended to Queensland's Aboriginal population although several government departments did seem interested in extending village settlement ideas to aboriginal communities such as that on Palm Island.
[22] Correspondence, Town planning documents, Home Secretary's Department, Queensland, col/190 Items id 17994,5,6, State Archives of Queensland. On

Huxham see *Australian dictionary of biography* (Melbourne: Melbourne University Press, 1983), 9, 419–20.

[23] Edward G. Theodore, *Summary of various administrative actions of the Labor government in Queensland during 1918* (Brisbane: Queensland Government Printer, 1919).

[24] Charles Chuter to Charles Reade, Item ID 17994, 5, 6 Col/190. State Archives of Queensland. For Chuter's biography see *Australian dictionary of biography*, online edition, 2006. Sighted November 2008. www.adb.online.anu.au/biogs/A130469b.htm.

[25] Reade to Chuter, 26 March 1918, 17994, 5,6 Col/190, State Archives Queensland.

[26] T.P. Boland, *James Duhig* (Brisbane: University of Queensland Press, 1986), 260.

[27] Chuter to Reade 24 May 1918, State Archives of Queensland.

[28] Chuter Correspondence to Garlick, Under-Secretary Local Government Department, NSW, 27 June 1918, 25 May 1918, State Archives of Queensland.

[29] *Proceedings of the Second Australian Town Planning Conference and Exhibition*, Brisbane 30 July to 6 August 1918 (Brisbane: Queensland Government Printer, 1919), 30.

[30] See Nambour *Chronicle*, 9 August 1918.

[31] *Proceedings of the Second Town Planning Conference*, 2, 22.

[32] Ryan, *Proceedings of the Second Town Planning Conference*, 2, 22.

[33] *Daily Standard*, 30 June 1922.

[34] *Daily Standard*, 30 June 1922.

[35] *The Architecture and Building Journal of Queensland* (hereafter *ABJQ*), 2 (7 January 1924): 30A.

[36] F.W.R. Hawken, 'The work of the municipal engineer in relation to town planning'. *Proceedings of the Second Town Planning Conference*, 2, 125.

[37] *ABJQ*, 7 August 1925.

[38] *ABJQ*, 7 August: 13–14; 7 September 1923: 13–15; 7 December: 65–68.

[39] J.R. Cole, *Shaping a city: Greater Brisbane 1925–1985* (Brisbane: William Brooks, 1984).

[40] *ABJQ*, 10 November 1925. William Earle was appointed as Brisbane's Town Planner, November 1925. Sir Matthew Nathan resigned as patron the same month.

[41] *ABJQ*, 10 September 1926, 10 September 1926.

[42] *ABJQ*, 8 September 1924, 26–27.

[43] *ABJQ* 7 September 1924, 13–15.

[44] On the confusion of politics with administration see Doug Tucker, 'Changing practices and conceptions of the executive function in urban government: the Greater Brisbane experience', *Australian Journal of Public Administration*, 53(4), (December 1994): 508–18. To the dismay of planning advocates the mayor of Brisbane assumed the executive functions of today's CEOs.

[45] *Reports and proceedings of the Municipal Council of the City of Brisbane during the year 1925* (Brisbane: H. Pole and Co, 1926), 25.

[46] *Proceedings of the City of Brisbane during 1925*, 25.

[47] On McInnis see Stefan Petrow, 'Planning pioneer: R.A. McInnis and town planning in Queensland 1922–1944', *Royal Historical Society of Queensland Journal*, 16(7), (August 1997): 285–98. Nowland went on to lecture in town planning in the engineering faculty at the University of Queensland between 1937 and 1946 and to design several significant public buildings during the 1930s. See *Time and Place*, 13, (Autumn 2006): 4–7.

[48] 'The Town Planning Association of Queensland' typescript, Brisbane City Archives.

[49] *ABJQ*, 10 Sept 1927.

[50] Nowland and McInnis, 'The cross river problem'. *Proceedings of the Second Town Planning Conference*.

[51] *ABJQ*, 11 August 1930: 20A.

[52] *ABJQ*, 11 August 1930, and Town Planning Association of Queensland, *Seventh Annual Report, year ending 30 June 1929*.

[53] Rockhampton *Morning Bulletin*, 25 September 1918.

[54] Rockhampton *Morning Bulletin*, 18 September 1918.

[55] Nambour *Chronicle*, 11 February 1916.

[56] Nambour *Chronicle*, 26 July 1918.

[57] Nambour *Chronicle*, 16 December 1921.

[58] On Nambour and Maroochy Shire generally see Helen Gregory, *Making Maroochy: a history of the land, the people and the shire* (Brisbane: Boolarong, 1991), Chapters 8–10.

[59] Nambour *Chronicle*, 18 January 1924.

[60] Gregory, 124.

[61] Ibid.

[62] Burke had commenced work on the Glenlyon estate in Ashgrove from the early 1920s.

[63] Nambour *Chronicle*, 17 May 1929.

[64] *ABJQ*, 10 August 1929: 38B.
[65] Denise Edwards, *Country and coast: a history of the development of the Noosa shire* (Noosa: Shire of Noosa, 2001).
[66] Gympie *Times*, 21 October 1929.
[67] Ibid.
[68] Ibid.

3
Town planning crusaders: urban reform in Melbourne during the progressive era

Andrew May and Susan Reidy

Victoria's growing enthusiasm by the early years of the 20th century for town planning initiatives, housing and land developments, one metropolitan governing body, and the garden city movement, has been well documented.[1] Concerns about city and suburban improvement – slum clearance, architectural controls on city buildings, pollution, zoning, the alienation of public parklands – spilled over into the new century and coalesced around an increasingly internationalised town planning movement.[2] In this chapter we concentrate on those particular events and individuals which catalysed the formation of the Victorian Town Planning and Parks Association (VTPPA) in 1914, and its sphere of influence and activity in the first decade and a half of its operation. The Australasian Town Planning Tour's lectures were not the exclusive catalyst for the VTPPA, and this chapter highlights its unusual make-up arising from two pre-existing lobby groups, the involvement of a number of passionate individuals and its influence on the Metropolitan Town Planning Commission. Its formation might be linked both to a crescendo of public interest in town planning, but perhaps also to more intricate lineages of concern for social reform and the urban environment.

The local context

In 1910, the Melbourne *Argus* published an article about the newly reserved national park at Wilson's Promontory. Its author, Dr James Barrett, was joint honorary secretary (with Baldwin Spencer) of the National Parks Association, and was later to become the founding President of the VTPPA:

> The movement for the creation of national parks represents something much more than sentiment. It is a part of that great educational movement ... which aims at redirecting men's attention to the earth beneath them ... those who are so educated will be much more likely to form sane and just views of human relationships.[3]

Figure 3.1: Sir James Barrett in military uniform. Source: University of Melbourne Archives, UMA/I/1836

The indomitable James Barrett (1862–1945) was an ophthalmologist and academic by profession, and a 'practical visionary' by inclination (Figure 3.1). He was born in South Melbourne and from the late 1880s he kept up an enduring correspondence with the Melbourne press on issues of public interest. Barrett was a professional technocrat, and Melbourne's 'busiest committeeman'.[4] He brought to bear his core ideologies about the importance of education, environment, physical and social health, and scientific rationalism, on a host of topics from decimalisation to pure milk.[5]

Barrett gave his first public town planning lecture in Melbourne in 1911, and in 1912 travelled overseas on a fact-finding tour to Canada, the USA, Great Britain, Germany and India. On his return, he shared what he had learned in a series of illustrated lectures to several groups, among them the Anti-Slum Committee and the Trades Hall Council. The lecture (for it was really one, repeated), illustrated with limelight views of model towns such as the world's first garden city, Letchworth, and variously titled 'Garden city planning' or 'Garden cities and housing', covered the American playgrounds movement, adult fitness and recreation, garden cities and the town planning movement. Barrett spoke of the 'wretched effects' of overcrowding in towns overseas and of the measures adopted in the provision of playgrounds and housing, noting that something should be done in Australia 'before it was too late'.[6] He also used his overseas experience in his contribution to the Victorian government's 1913 Joint Committee on Housing, where, in his answers to 81 questions, he explicitly articulated town planning ideals. He expounded on his civic ideologies in the magazine *Home and Garden Beautiful*, alongside articles on the cultivation of roses and the servantless house:

> One hopes that Australia will rise to the occasion and produce garden cities and suburbs of its own, with suitable recreation centres, parks, beaches, and other places of outdoor enjoyment, and will fully recognise the extensive social and civil development which can be produced through their agency.[7]

Barrett's character as a scientist and his interest in the environment reveal an amateur but nonetheless ardent passion, which he shared with other concerned citizens, for the preservation of open spaces for everyone, whether located in the city or country. While the national park enthusiasts were not the only supporters of ideas about rational control over human treatment of the environment (local architects were avidly reading overseas ideas on the topic), Barrett's writing at the time signalled rising public expression of those ideas in Victoria.

The international context

This concept of a rational approach to controlling the world's burgeoning metropolises sat behind the Australian town planning movement in the first 20 years of the 20th century. But it was preceded by decades of interest in the shaping of cities, at home and internationally. Any notion that developments in Australian town planning are always linked to 'the delayed arrival of international fashions',[8] might suggest that it was all one-way traffic, and that the tyranny of distance mitigated against intricate networks of information and intelligence. Ewen and Hebbert, while Eurocentric in focus, have characterised the networked municipality as a creature of the 20th century, and that any earlier connections were 'ad hoc' and 'individual'.[9] But at the level of municipal government, it is clear that there was a great early interchange of ideas about city government and the municipal ideal. Quite robust networks of exchange were well established in Melbourne's case, and increasingly over the latter half of the nineteenth century a deliberate attempt was being made to subscribe to an organised municipal network via general correspondence, exchanges of model by-laws, and international tours of municipal officers.[10]

This period of increased internationalisation and codification of networks and technologies of governance saw the formation of many professional bodies concerned with city affairs such as the Permanent Road Congresses International Association (1909). In Australia, bodies such as the Municipal Association of Victoria (formed 1879) and the VTPPA, reflected a burgeoning international consciousness about the efficiency and quality of life of the modern city.

Municipalities across the British Empire and beyond relied upon organs such as the *Municipal Journal* for information on the latest developments and best practice in city affairs. It had regular columns on housing, town planning, water supply, roads, street cleansing and sewerage disposal. It made an implicit connection between transforming the urban environment and moral improvement. As John Griffiths has noted, ideas flowed freely across the municipal world, and not simply from metropolis to periphery.[11] Percy Russell (President of the Municipal Association of Victoria)[12] and William Bold (Perth Town Clerk) were interviewed while on visits to Britain, the latter noting his particular interest in town planning and the agitation in Western Australia for a town planning bill and the creation of a Greater Perth Council.[13]

Speakers from Melbourne participated prominently at the 1914 Imperial Health Conference in London, organised by the Victoria League. James Barrett's paper on town planning developments in Sydney and Melbourne noted the lack of open space in new suburban subdivisions and encroachments on many of Melbourne's parks and reserves. He supported the provision of playgrounds, public control over subdivisions to mitigate the spread of slum housing, and a down-fences policy. Mrs Wrigley spoke on 'Free kindergartens' and Dr A.T. Wood on 'The Talbot milk supply'. Dr Jean Greig, and Barrett's sister, Dr Edith Barrett (two other founding members of the VTPPA), gave papers on child welfare and the bush nursing service.[14]

Formation of the Victorian Town Planning and Parks Association

In May 1914, the *Argus* published a feature article on the 'The city beautiful: town planning successes' about British town planning achievements and ideas, lavishly illustrated with four photographs and two diagrams at a time when newspapers carried few editorial illustrations.[15] By the time the Australasian Town Planning Tour's town planning experts, William Davidge and Charles Reade, arrived in Australia to give their lectures,

Melbourne was already well versed in the preoccupations of contemporary town planning discourse.

Davidge was Surveyor, Architect and Engineer for the London County Council and Reade, a former Auckland journalist and Assistant Secretary of the Garden Cities and Town Planning Association, was the chief organiser of the tour.[16] When Reade wrote to the City of Melbourne Town Clerk in November 1912 on the initiative, he noted, 'One of our most active assistants in Melbourne is Dr Barrett, of the University, with whom I have been in personal touch in London.'[17] Sir Ralph Neville, President of the Garden Cities and Town Planning Association, had written to the Lord Mayor of Melbourne in January 1914 soliciting municipal support for the tour, which was being explicitly organised 'in the hope of arousing public spirit in favour of Town Planning legislation adapted to the particular needs and conditions of Australian municipal life.'[18] The British Housing, Town Planning Etc Act (1909) had enabled local authorities to develop municipal planning schemes infused with new town planning ideologies.

The Victorian leg of the tour was sponsored under the auspices of the University of Melbourne Extension Board and the Housing Crusade Committee. Municipal contributions included free use of halls and lanterns for slides. In February 1914, Arthur Pearson, President of the Minimum Allotment, Anti-Slum and Housing Crusade Committee (MAASHCC), wrote to Melbourne's Lord Mayor requesting that the city support the tour, both by lobbying the Victorian Premier for financial aid and providing free use of the Town Hall.[19] Barrett chaired two public meetings in May to raise the £270 needed to underwrite the tour. He personally contributed £10. In effect, these preliminary meetings of a core interest group were a recapitulation of existing interests which animated this class of people, as well as a springboard for the genesis of the VTPPA.[20]

Town-Planning for Australia

A Study in Contrasts

Figure 3.2: 'Town-Planning for Australia': from a flier for the 1914 town planning tour. Source: City of Melbourne, Town Clerk's Correspondence Files, 1914/3133, 19 May 1914

Beginning with a lecture at the Melbourne Town Hall, the Victorian tour commenced on 22 September 1914 and involved 25 lectures on town planning (with a particular focus on greater powers for municipalities, an anti-slum message, and better transport to outer suburbs), accompanied by selections from a thousand lantern slides and plans (Figure 3.2). Reade tried to adapt best practice ideas to local conditions, and sketched what for the time was a visionary new metropolitan form for Melbourne in the garden city tradition (Figure 3.3). Attendances varied,[21] but on Monday 5 October, 400 attended Reade's lecture at the

Melbourne Town Hall, which was immediately followed by a public meeting—over which Barrett presided—which agreed to establish a local town planning 'league' to lobby for the 'scientific regulation' of the town-planning system: 'Underlying the whole thing was the theory of providing beautiful, healthful surroundings for the people in their homes as well as at other times.' An interim committee was established and it developed a draft constitution and an interim set of 'objects' or terms of reference.[22]

Figure 3.3: Charles Reade, Greater Melbourne Town Planning Scheme, from a glass lantern slide, c.1914. Source: State Library of Victoria, Accession Number: H91.90/53 Image Number: b13995

The first general meeting of the VTPPA was held at Melbourne Town Hall on 26 October 1914, at which a committee was elected and the interim objects adopted. While an alternative set of objects to the ones drafted by the interim committee had been published in the *Argus* (and are sometimes cited as the official objectives)[23] – and which included the charming and often repeated object, 'To give the town a bit of the country and the country a bit of the town' – the VTPPA's Constitution, dated

30 October 1914, confirms that the interim committee's objectives were those adopted by the new Association. These indicated the newly formed Association's active and serious intent around five main issues: better housing, the 'pre-design of unoccupied land', the reservation of parks and playgrounds, protection of native fauna and flora, and generally the 'provision of healthy and reasonable surroundings of people during work or leisure'.[24]

Under the Association's joint patronage of the Australian Governor-General and the Victorian Governor and their wives, Barrett presided over an executive which included Honorary Treasurer J.T. Raw, architect H.W. Tompkins, and Dr John Smythe (Principal of the Training College), as well as former office bearers from the MAASHCC – Vice-President Arthur Pearson (ex-President), and Honorary Secretary John Huggan (ex-Honorary Secretary) (Figure 3.4). The 30 members of the VTPPA Council included: Professor Richard Berry (University of Melbourne anatomist); Dr John Leach (naturalist, teacher, a founder of the Gould League of Bird Lovers); Dr Jean Greig (Education Department medical officer, active in child welfare, one of the founders of the School Medical Service); surveyor Saxil Tuxen; educationist Charles Richard Long; Morris Mondle Phillips (lawyer, member of the University Extension Board); Maurice Blackburn MLA (lawyer, politician, pacifist, defender of civil liberties); Edward Rigby (solicitor, Hawthorn City Councillor, Anglican synod member); Frederic William Eggleston (lawyer, Caulfield City councillor); and Dr Edith Barrett (medical practitioner, humanitarian, foundation member of the National Council of Women in Victoria).

The new VTPPA absorbed two existing organisations, the National Parks Association (founded 1908) and the MAASHCC.[25] While Grubb noted that this was a marriage of convenience, centred around the pivotal role of Barrett, it led to a hybrid set of objectives that mirrored the values of the two bodies.[26] The Town Planning Tour had catalysed

Figure 3.4: J.B. Huggan. Source: *Town Planning and Housing*, August 1915

existing concerns among an educated middle-class reformist elite for progressive urban renewal. The movement for national park reservation in Victoria was supported by, amongst others, various champions of tourism, nature conservation, and the protection of indigenous flora and fauna. But as Mirams argues, it was also based on a profoundly moral vision, buttressed by particular ideologies of natural efficiency, utilitarianism, race, scientific planning and eugenics, and drawing on vitalist and modernist discourses that had spawned a range of urban 'improvement' campaigns in Britain and North America from the 1890s. It is not at all surprising that as a principal architect of the movement for national parks, Barrett was concerned that the relationship between the moral malaise of urban life and the rejuvenating properties of nature should be intimately linked to a progressive urban agenda.[27]

Town planning preoccupations with social health and national efficiency took root in Melbourne's fertile social reform culture, that, having moved away from its former models of charity and philanthropy, underpinned the community of interest that united Melbourne's social elite.[28] In moral terms, town planning was seen as more than just a scientific approach to the social problems of city and society; it was also a new 'crusade'.[29] Its *mode d'emploi* was breathtakingly simple – 'Bad houses produce bad people'[30] – a mantra of environmental determinism that would have disturbing ramifications for some inner-city communities in later decades. Suburbs such as Fitzroy were characterised as blighted by physical and moral decay by 1890s philanthropists and 1930s modernists alike, justifying middle-class reformist interventions into the lives of working-class and immigrant communities.[31] By 1914 there was 'a new breed of scientific slum reformers equipped … with eugenic theory and social statistics'.[32] Among them, Barrett was a leading light. Alongside C.E.W. Bean (who had called in 1907 for the remaking of Australian cities as more healthy environments),[33] Barrett has been characterised by Davison as one of the leading 'prophets of urban degeneration'.[34] Circulated in Melbourne, a 1914 poster of the Town Planning Association of NSW, 'An appeal to nationalism', quite explicitly articulated the connections between racial purity, nationalism, and scientific methodologies:

> In a country of Australia's magnificent distances, where there is nothing to justify congestion of any description, fresh air and commodious living conditions should be a national heritage … Provision can be made for the chief attributes to healthy settlement, and the foundations of a virile race laid. But … where there is no recognised standard, no aesthetic or practical ideal, uniformity of action toward an accepted ideal is impossible. The Town-Planning Association is thus the direct response to an urgent want. It supplies the means of vitalising into the one

concentrated effort the spasmodic 'reform movements' that were at intervals made in various quarters … As a Big Australian you should, therefore, join the Town-Planning Association.[35]

The VTPPA 1914–16

Where it has previously been thought that the VTPPA went into a kind of abeyance because of Barrett's overseas service in World War I,[36] recently located VTPPA's Council Minutes (1913–18) make it clear the Association was active and thriving until late 1916.[37] Despite his absence, Barrett remained as President, while other Council members shared the chair at meetings. A program of fact-finding and proselytising was established, annual reports were published, and the Association's activities were regularly reported in the newspapers.

With the absorption of the MAASHCC into the VTPPA, Honorary Secretary John Huggan transferred his minute-taking skills to the new body, and it is strange to see the minutes of the two groups written in the same style of language and elegant hand, as though the ideals of the MAASHCC were somehow flowing through his pen into the future of the VTPPA, as indeed they were to do.[38] Although it might be assumed that the VTPPA's abiding passion for the preservation, protection or creation of parks, playgrounds and country picnic grounds – which it saw as necessary places of amenity for otherwise deprived urbanites – had derived primarily from the National Parks Association (NPA), surprisingly, this view was also held by the MAASHCC. The NPA was talking about the need for more parks for Melbourne's masses as early as 1912, when it wrote to the Minister for Lands, making a case for 'open spaces and ample foliage in Melbourne', because they would provide beauty, 'recreation and rest'. It suggested that all of Melbourne's parkland and playgrounds should be identified and that ten per cent of municipal land should be dedicated to recreational reserves (not including sports grounds).[39] And unexpectedly, the MAASHCC championed a statistical model in the form of a chart that, for a given year, recorded the overall area of each municipality, the area devoted to parkland and its percentage of the whole. The VTPPA would use this chart in its annual reports to record municipal parkland failures and rare successes. These organisations were in part responding to a wider context of community concerns about the state of the city's open spaces and the desire that they be presentable and 'beautified', at a time of municipal inaction, when many reserves were being degraded by their use as rubbish tips, for sand mining, animal grazing and other iniquities.[40]

One of the VTPPA's first acts was to seek affiliations with Melbourne's progress associations, and by December 1914 several progress associations were lining up for lectures (Barrett left his slide collection with Huggan for just this purpose). By February 1915, the VTPPA was formally registered with the Garden Cities and Town Planning Association of London and had set up communication with other town planning associations in Australia. In early 1915, Huggan wrote to 70 Victorian local councils commenting on the new *Local Government Act* and encouraging them to exercise their new powers to effect change.[41] In the same year the VTPPA championed a scheme (promoted also by the *Age*) to convert Yarra River land into a national park through the suburbs of Hawthorn, Kew, Camberwell and Heidelberg, which would require significant purchases of land. And the Association persuaded the *Herald* to publish its latest statistics on municipal reserves and playgrounds.[42]

The newspapers regularly reported the VTPPA's opinions, covering diverse topics such as the *Commonwealth Year Book*'s inaccurate statistics on reserve areas, the lack of government attention to housing, its congratulations to Caulfield Council for creating the Hopetoun Gardens in Elsternwick and filling it with native plants, and to the Minister for Public Works on upholding minimum allotment sizes. The Association commented on the location of planned railway stations and pushed for town planning legislation.[43] In December 1915, Edward Rigby's lecture to the Chelsea Progress Association on 'Town Planning of Garden Cities' was published in full by the local paper.[44] The VTPPA's 1915 Annual

Report printed statistics on parks and reserves that revealed 'the bad condition of all the outer suburbs as regards reserves' and registered the members' disgust at the state of public reserves. It also reported that 'Melbourne is very badly equipped with playgrounds' and that children must play in the streets in inner suburbs, but noted that the Guild of Play was managing two city playgrounds in Carlton and South Melbourne.[45]

The first annual general meeting in October 1915 re-elected Barrett as President and, tellingly, added a new object to the constitution – 'To secure Town Planning Legislation'.[46] A circular was sent to more than 100 Victorian local councils encouraging them to change their building regulations, and articulating in some detail the improvements that could be made to the quality of residential land and housing by attention to minimum allotment sizes, street widths, and the lighting and ventilation of houses.[47] The Association castigated the Minister of Lands for deciding to sell foreshore land in Brighton. However, this high period of activity could not last through the war years, and at the 1916 annual general meeting in October, regret was expressed that 'only about 20 members' were present.[48]

1917–20

In 1917, the Association's public profile dropped, as did its membership. The minutes record a succession of attempted resignations from the Council, but it continued to meet once a month even though its activities had shrunk to a trickle of correspondence to local councils and government ministers. It worried about 'fellmongeries on the Yarra', how to turn a 'quarry-hole into a fern-gully', tramway parks and building regulations. But changes were coming. And what happened next tends to suggest that vigorous discussions had taken place at the VTPPA's exhibition stand at the 1917 Adelaide Town Planning Conference between the nine VTPPA delegates (the largest contingent of any state association)[49] and the more extensive Victorian contingent of municipal, government and professional delegates. These included Frank Stapley and George

Ellery from the Melbourne City Council and representatives from Ballarat, Bendigo and Geelong. Ellery and Edward Rigby also presented a paper on 'The future of Australian cities'.[50]

At its February 1918 meeting (with Rigby in the chair) the VTPPA Council resolved to form a new association on 7 March and to 'amalgamate with Architects etc'. A new constitution in draft form was circulated to members. A letter sent to professional associations was explicit about the proposed changes: to create a 'strong and active Town Planning Association in Victoria' by uniting the VTPPA with the 'Vic Executive and Delegates' to the first Australian Town Planning Conference and 'members of the Professional Societies such as Architects, Engineers, Surveyors, Medical, Law and Commerce'.[51]

A new name, Town Planning Association of Victoria (TPAV), was also proposed, as was a potential letter to Barrett (still President), thanking him for the use of his rooms and slides. The national parks contingent was nowhere to be seen (although they would re-emerge). It was time for City of Melbourne Lord Mayor Frank Stapley to step onto the larger town planning stage. He became President of the newly constituted TPAV, and the Association's focus would shift more specifically to the pursuit of town planning legislation.

Now it seemed the original constituency of legal, medical and educational professionals had, in the words of the *Argus*, undergone 'a strong leavening of professional knowledge'.[52] The new, 25 member Council was more clearly drawn from the ranks of municipal professionals, comprising eight local councillors, five architects, two educationists, seven engineers and surveyors, and three medicos. There was now also representation from the regional cities of Geelong, Bendigo and Ballarat. City of Melbourne officials dominated as office bearers, including Frank Stapley as President, and Town Clerk George Ellery as one of five vice-presidents.[53] By the time of the second Town Planning Conference in Brisbane in 1918, a number of the sixteen TPAV delegates in attendance professed multiple allegiances, as personified by Stapley: Lord Mayor of Melbourne, Commissioner of the Melbourne and Metropolitan Board of Works, and Vice-President of the Royal Victorian Institute of Architects. He addressed the conference on the need for proper housing 'from a national and racial standpoint'.[54]

Figure 3.5: Cover of the Town Planning Association's 1927 Annual Report

At the 1919 Victorian Town Planning Conference in Ballarat, TPAV President Stapley introduced Lieutenant-Colonel Sir James Barrett as 'one of the foremost experts of the Town Planning movement'. Barrett presented a paper on 'What town planning really is', stressing the need for 'civic conscience' in developing concerted mass action on issues of urban amenity, and calling for the creation of a central expert board to adjudicate on municipal planning issues.[55] After receiving a vote of thanks for his address, Barrett again entreated his audience to 'see that something definite is done ... there has been quite enough talking, and the Government should be induced to deal with this question quickly and on approved lines'.[56]

Quite enough talking: the 1920s

In 1922, state government finally acted decisively by passing legislation to establish the Metropolitan Town Planning Commission (MTPC) with the aim of producing a comprehensive metropolitan plan. This followed a great push from Stapley, who became the MTPC's Chairman, and the Melbourne City Council (among others), growing out of fears about the metropolis expanding uncontrollably and the existing confusion of regulatory bodies.[57] The MTPC ran from 1923 to 1930 as an advisory body comprising members from municipal councils, professional interests and infrastructure organisations.

This left the TPAV to set its own agenda. The first thing it did was to research and publish a lengthy booklet, *Suggestions for the improvement of the City of Melbourne*, presented to the MTPC in December 1923, after it had been leaked to the newspapers (which made much of it).[58] The TPAV expressed its 'opinion' and recommendations on 22 topics representing both the TPAV's pet causes and the MTPC's agenda, among them, an agricultural belt, outer park ring, 'civic centre', garden suburb, subdivisional plans, reserve area in municipalities, health resorts and recreation areas for Melbourne, supervised children's playgrounds, zoning, roads, 'bottle-necks', Greater Melbourne, and others.[59]

Throughout the 1920s the TPAV was a vigorous organisation with a solid public profile. It developed a slogan – 'Beautiful cities for beautiful living' – and was able to focus on particular enthusiasms. It ran a program of lectures and radio broadcasts (as did the MTPC), which were part of what it referred to as 'propaganda' for the cause. And while each TPAV Annual Report carried comment on all the current and fashionable town planning topics, its continuing passion lay with parks and reserves, to which it devoted much attention (Figure 3.5). This reflected the power of the National Parks Section within the TPAV; it sometimes held its own public meetings, such as one in 1921 about native flora and fauna.[60]

Figure 3.6: Victoria Parade, Collingwood, c.1910, showing cable trams on north side and tree-lined area in the centre of the avenue where new tram lines would be located, despite James Barrett's protests. Source: State Library of Victoria, Accession Number: H35249/41, Image Number: a03941

Roads and traffic were left to the MTPC, unless they clashed with the TPAV's favourite concerns. While its annual reports throughout the

1920s reflected the Association's engagement with the wider town planning agenda, and reported for its members on activities interstate and overseas, for the most part the TPAV confined its activism to protecting existing parklands from encroachment, a topic also dear to the newspapers. Park 'filching' was a popular headline and park 'nibbling' was a constant refrain in the TPAV's rhetoric. The Association opposed the potential alienation of land from the inner city Yarra Park, threatened by plans to expand the rail yards and the Melbourne Cricket Ground, and the MTPC's plans to create a new road to relieve peak hour city traffic congestion. The enlarged rail yards, enormous Melbourne Cricket Ground and Brunton Avenue attest to the TPAV's failure to influence the situation.[61]

The Association also failed in a more volatile struggle to prevent the Victoria Parade tram lines being moved from the roadway to the wide, tree-lined median strip (Figure 3.6). The parties involved included the Tramways Board, an ambivalent Collingwood Council, the Melbourne City Council and the MTPC, the latter two supporting the change because they worried about motor traffic increases. Barrett fought in the press to retain the green median strip so Collingwood's apparently underprivileged children would not have to play in the streets. When that was ignored, he argued to save the trees. The debate played out in the newspapers, sometimes to the point of irrationality. Eventually the Botanic Gardens was persuaded to declare the trees too sick to survive. Despite protests from Barrett lambasting this notion, the Melbourne Council killed off the controversy by uprooting the trees. That the TPAV again failed to influence bureaucrats is evident today as the tram makes its unimpeded way along Victoria Parade's median strip under a new canopy of elms while the motor traffic jams up in the roadways on either side.

Another scenario unfolded on Melbourne's outskirts. With the MTPC's focus on the inner city, and despite its own predictions about Melbourne's future growth, the official body had little time for town planning issues affecting the edges of the metropolis that would, in time, inevitably come within the boundaries of the greater metropolitan area. The TPAV was aware that the Dandenong Police Paddock was the 'only large reserve' beyond the city's south-eastern fringe and under threat of being sold off by the state government. Originally established as headquarters for a native police corps, the Dandenong Police Paddock in the 1920s covered about 1700 acres (688 ha) and was used as a horse stud by the Victorian police. So began a period of advocacy throughout the 1920s for what the Association's National Park Section referred to as 'health resorts and recreation areas for Melbourne',[62] and it used the Police Paddock to set its own agenda about these areas. It looked with envy on what it claimed was Sydney's 70,000 acres of 'picnicking grounds',[63] writing:

> As cities grow, the people instinctively long for room in which to stretch themselves and come again into contact with nature, as large reserves in the vicinity of the city become requisite for the mass of the people, particularly at holiday time. No adequate provision has been made near Melbourne for anything of the kind.[64]

The National Parks Section sought support from the Field Naturalists Club in 1926,[65] and in October 1928 organised a delegation that visited the Minister for Lands, with representatives from 'many councils, Progress Associations, Field Naturalists, Forest League, and Wattle League'. It gave the Minister 'many and weighty reasons why none of this land should be sold'.[66] Success was assured when most of the Paddock became a public reserve in 1931. Now managed by Parks Victoria, it is 490 ha and a site of significance for its Aboriginal heritage and indigenous flora.

At the end of this period, the TPAV's 1929 Annual Report reveals that Barrett was still President, with Stapley, Campbell, Rigby, Wharington and Henderson as vice-presidents. The Council, now much smaller, even with the addition of artist Arthur Streeton (also a committed member of the Forest League), still included some founding members (Greig,

Tuxen, et al.) and was made up of the same kind of middle-class activist citizens with which the Association had begun.

Business as usual: the 1930s

Once the Metropolitan Town Planning Commission's report was with the Victorian government, and town planning legislation eagerly anticipated, it was business as usual for the Victorian Town Planning Association under the leadership of its founding President Sir James Barrett and a number of long-standing Council members. Prominent issues for the TPAV in the 1930s included the lack of parks and reserves in outer and emerging suburbs, traffic congestion and lack of uniform regulations, protection of existing public reserves, the creation of nature reserves, calls for a 'national trust' to protect foreshores, zoning, ribbon development, state road improvements, tree planting, and support for the establishment of low-cost housing at Fisherman's Bend near Port Melbourne. The Association continued to lobby for national parks, and its annual reports from 1931 until the 1950s displayed 'including The National Parks Association' on their covers. In 1937 the TPAV's National Parks Section successfully persuaded the Victorian government to agree to reserve land for national parks at Wyperfeld, Badger Creek and Cumberland.[67]

An active Geelong Branch flourished for a few years. Liaising closely with other volunteer organisations, the Geelong municipal authority and the newly created Country Roads Board, TPAV members laboured on roadside and riverbank beautification and restoration projects. They planted thousands of trees in the district, for example along the Melbourne-Geelong Road. The branch even provided wildlife: a 'flock of swans' (black and white) were prepared in 1932 for 'placing' on the Barwon River's south bank.[68] The branch closed in 1941.

From its inception, the TPAV had cultivated a close relationship with local government and in the 1930s and 1940s this link was emphasised with the inclusion, on the title page of the *Australian Municipal Journal*, of the statement 'the official organ of the Victorian Town Planning Association', and occasional articles in its pages.[69] The TPAV kept a close eye on 'municipal doings'. One outcome was an emerging interest in civic centres and town hall precincts as well as growing concern about the infiltration of factories and flats into what were regarded as residential areas with flats looked on as problematic even towards the end of the decade.[70]

By 1936 a town planning act was considered an 'urgent necessity' and the Association was actively lobbying the state government ('Victoria is one of the few places in the civilized world that has not a properly constituted Town Planning Authority').[71] It felt that the issues which should be encompassed by legislation were suburban development, zoning and traffic, and a 'uniform code of building laws'.[72] Generally, considerable faith was expressed in the ideal of centralised planning as the solution to all problems; but conservative opposition would still obstruct the development of unified town planning legislation.[73] Planning in the first three decades of the 20th century has been characterised as a cyclical process tied very much to economic conditions (expansion encouraged through periods of growth, social welfare in times of hardship). Planning action 'was more dependent on the state of politics and suffered accordingly, both from the short-term instability of Victorian politics and from the more enduring inbuilt rural and conservative bias of its political institutions'.[74]

As it had done in the 1920s, the TPAV used site inspections as a way of generating opinion, followed by a report, which could then be used as the foundation to arrange a delegation to visit and hopefully influence the appropriate government minister, the Premier or local councils.[75] Slum abolition and housing concerned the TPAV well into the 1950s. As Sandercock has argued, conservative middle-class reformist ideals about urban planning – in particular the environmental determinism of slum clearance – were heavily influenced by British thought and practice.[76] The Housing Commission of Victoria had been established by the Victorian government on the back of a public campaign spearheaded by Methodist layman Oswald Barnett arguing for housing reform. Barnett and a number of other social workers had made their views known in the Report of the Housing Investigation and Slum Abolition Board, which had recorded the effects of the Depression on inner-city social and material life.[77] The formation of the Commission was welcomed in 1937, particularly as it sought the advice of the TPAV on questions such as affordable housing.[78]

In 1939, the TPAV, for the first time, introduced municipal membership of its Council: eleven representative members joined (from Brunswick, Coburg, Essendon, Fitzroy, Hawthorn, Heidelberg, Malvern, Northcote, Broadmeadows, Mornington and Werribee). This representation would grow to 21 by 1944. In the absence of town planning legislation, this suggests that the TPAV had decided to push the state government hard and was using a relationship with local government to this end. It celebrated its success in getting some town planning clauses into the new Reclamation and Housing Act.[79] One other effect of municipal membership was the introduction of more formal procedures and the TPAV minutes reflect a shift from a chatty and more informal style of record-keeping to an increasingly bureaucratic tone with a growing number of motions put through the chair. And more change was afoot.

Conclusion

This chapter has detailed the origins of the TPAV, and its activities and preoccupations into the 1930s, and in so doing has made more complex the simplistic but oft-repeated claim that British garden city ideals first landed on Australian shores in 1914 in the persons of Davidge and Reade.[80] Had the town-planning caravan not passed through Melbourne, middle-class social reformers and the growing cohort of architects, engineers and surveyors alike would likely have continued the trajectory that had already been mobilised around class and professional communities of interest, with their concerns for environmental reform rooted in late-nineteenth-century anxieties about urban and moral decay. The origins of the TPAV exemplify Melbourne's intricate networks of social reform culture in the first decades of the 20th century. As Davison again reminds us, the particular ideologies of nascent professional middle-class interests can help to explain the nature of their reform ideologies, and perhaps also the restraints on their achievement.[81] As Mirams has also demonstrated in relation to James Barrett's role in the national parks movement, determining the contours of influence of progressive ideals is as much about charting individuals and their influence as it is mapping larger movements and campaigns.[82] By the time Barrett had re-engaged with the town planning movement in Melbourne after his wartime absence, the core objectives of the ginger group that he had fostered were already being subsumed by a broader and more expert group of civic practitioners. The creation of the MTPC in 1922 set the trajectory of comprehensive town planning on a more even keel (though its practical successes were muted by the onset of the Depression and political indecision). Into the 1930s, the role of the TPAV was characterised by its ability to act as a voice for specific aspects of town planning idealism. But while popular with the press and community groups and successful in influencing public opinion, it was generally unable to change public events. This dichotomy would characterise the Association through the war years and beyond.

References

[1] Max Grubb, 'A history of town planning in Victoria 1910–1944' (MTRP thesis, University of Melbourne, 1976); Robert Freestone, *Model communities: the Garden City movement in Australia* (Melbourne: Nelson, 1989); Robert Freestone, *Designing Australian cities: culture, commerce and the city beautiful, 1900–1930* (Sydney: UNSW Press, 2007; David Dunstan, *Governing the metropolis: politics, technology and social change in a Victorian city: Melbourne, 1850–1891* (Melbourne: Melbourne University Press, 1984); David Nichols, 'Leading lights: the promotion of garden suburb plans and planners in interwar

Australia' (PhD thesis, Deakin University, 2001); Miles Lewis, *Melbourne: the city's history and development*, (Melbourne: City of Melbourne, 1995).
2. Robert Freestone, 'City planning', in *The encyclopedia of Melbourne*, eds. Andrew Brown-May and Shurlee Swain (Melbourne: Cambridge University Press, 2005), 139.
3. *Argus*, 26 February 1910, 6.
4. Graeme Davison, 'The city bred child and urban reform in Melbourne 1900-1914' in *Social process and the city*, ed. Peter Williams (Sydney: George Allen and Unwin, 1983), 148, 150. See also 'Our busiest citizen. Sir James Barrett's public activities', *Herald* 11 April 1924 in Public Record Office of Victoria (hereafter PROV) VPRS 10281/PO/19.
5. See Stephen Murray-Smith, 'Barrett, Sir James William (1862-1945)', *Australian dictionary of biography* (Melbourne: Melbourne University Press, 1979), 7, 186-89. Murray-Smith characterises Barrett as at times mean, dogmatic and ruthless, but always 'guided by the vision of civic virtue'.
6. *Argus*, 4 April 1913, 15; 5 April 1913, 20; 10 May 1913, 20; 14 June 1913, 21; 29 August 1913, 15.
7. 'Garden cities and town planning', *Home and Garden Beautiful* (August 1913): 57-58.
8. Graeme Davison, 'Melbournes that might have been: three dreams of the future city' in *Melbourne centre stage: the corporation of Melbourne 1842-1992*, eds. Graeme Davison and Andrew May, special issue of the *Victorian Historical Journal*, in association with City of Melbourne, 1992, 169.
9. Shane Ewen and Michael Hebbert, 'European cities in a networked world during the long 20th century', *Environment and Planning C: Government and Policy*, 25(3), (2007): 327-40.
10. Andrew Brown-May, 'In the precincts of the global city: the transnational network of municipal affairs in Melbourne, Australia' in *Another global city: historical explorations into the transnational municipal moment 1850-2000*, eds. Pierre-Yves Saunier and Shane Ewen (New York: Palgrave Macmillan, 2008), 19-34.
11. John Griffths, 'Communicating civic ideals in the British world: *The Municipal Journal* 1893-1939', paper presented to the British World Conference, Bristol, July 2007.
12. *The Municipal Journal*, 17 October 1913, 1355-56.
13. *The Municipal Journal*, 28 November 1913, 1543. See also 21 November 1913, 1511; 6 February 1914, 155.

[14] *Argus*, 22 June 1914, 6.
[15] *Argus*, 2 May 1914, 10.
[16] Robert Freestone, 'An imperial aspect: the Australasian town planning tour of 1914-15', *Australian Journal of Politics and History,* 44(2), (1998): 159-76.
[17] Charles Reade to John Clayton, London, 25 November 1912, Melbourne City Council, Town Clerk Correspondence Files 1913, No. 34, PROV, VPRS 3183/P1.
[18] PROV, VPRS 3183/P1, Unit 185, 1914, No. 757, Ralph Neville to the Lord Mayor of Melbourne, 1 January 1914.
[19] A. Pearson to the Lord Mayor, City of Melbourne, 19 February 1914, PROV, VPRS 3183/P1, Unit 185, 1914, No. 1168.
[20] *Argus*, 15 May 1914, 10; 13 October 1914, 10. See also circular letter on the subject of 'Australasian town planning tour: proposed lantern lectures by British experts', James W. Barrett, M.M. Phillips and J.B. Huggan to The Mayor and Councillors, City of Melbourne, 15 May 1914, PROV VPRS 3183/P1, Unit 185, 1914, No. 3133.
[21] *The Independent*, Melbourne, 26 September 1914; 'Town planning for Victoria', *Building* (January 1915): 97, cited in Freestone, 'An imperial aspect', 167.
[22] *Argus,* 6 October 1914, 4; 22 October 1914, 9.
[23] Grubb accepts interim objectives (p. 32, quoting the *Age* 27 October 1914); and Freestone accepts the alternative set (Model Communities, 71, quoting the *Argus* 27 October 1914).
[24] Victorian Town Planning and Parks Association (hereafter VTPPA) Constitution leaflet, 30 October 1914, VTPPA Council Minutes Book, in Town and Country Planning Association (hereafter TCPA) papers, 93/7, University of Melbourne Archives.
[25] *Argus*, 27 October 1914, 10.
[26] Grubb, 32.
[27] Sarah Mirams, '"For their moral health": James Barrett, urban progressive ideas and national park reservation in Victoria', *Australian Historical Studies* 120 (2002): 249-66. See also Davison, 'The city bred child'; Michael Roe, *Nine Australian progressives: vitalism in bourgeois social thought 1890-1960* (Brisbane: University of Queensland Press, 1984), including chapter on James Barrett.
[28] See Shurlee Swain, 'Voluntarism' in Brown-May and Swain, 754.
[29] 'Town-planning crusade', *Argus* 21 September 1914, 12.
[30] *Argus* 2 May 1914.

[31] See for example A.K. Birch, 'Framing Fitzroy: contesting and (de)constructing place and identity in a Melbourne suburb' (PhD thesis, University of Melbourne, 2003); Chris McConville, 'From "criminal" class to "underworld"' in *The outcasts of Melbourne: essays in social history*, eds. Graeme Davison, David Dunstan and Chris McConville (Sydney: Allen and Unwin, 1985), 69–90.

[32] Graeme Davison and David Dunstan, 'This moral pandemonium – images of low life', in *The outcasts of Melbourne*, 29–57.

[33] *Sydney Morning Herald*, 8 June 1907, quoted in Davison, 'The city bred child', 147.

[34] Davison, 'The city bred child', 146.

[35] 'Town Planning for Australia', leaflet in Melbourne City Council, Town Clerk Correspondence Files, PROV, VPRS 3183/P1, Unit 185, 1914.

[36] Expressions of this view include Grubb, 30.

[37] 'Town Planning Association Victoria (hereafter TPAV), Council Minutes Book, 1915 to 1918', in TCPA papers, University of Melbourne Archives, No. 93/7, Box 1.

[38] Minutes of MAASHCC and TPAV, in TCPA papers, No. 93/7, University of Melbourne Archives.

[39] Printed letter, National Parks Association to Minister for Lands, 1912, in James Barrett Papers, National Parks box, University of Melbourne Archives; *Argus* 4 April 1912.

[40] See, for example Williamstown and Albert Park, *Argus*, 30 August 1913, 9 and 25 July 1913, 13.

[41] *Age*, 19 February 1915.

[42] *Age*, 9 and 19 April 1915; *Herald*, 18 May 1915.

[43] *Age*, 9 April 1915, 16 March, 15 April, 6 July 1916; *Herald*, 1 June 1916.

[44] *Seaford News*, 11 December 1915, 2.

[45] TPAV, Annual Report 1915, interleaved in TPAV, Council Minutes Book 1915–18, TCPA papers, Box 1. 'Skinners' in South Melbourne is still operated as a managed playground in 2007.

[46] Minutes, Annual General Meeting, 28 October 1915, in TPAV, Council Minutes Book 1915–18, TCPA papers.

[47] *Argus*, 29 June 1916, 8.

[48] Minutes, Annual General Meeting, 28 October 1916, in TPAV, Council Minutes Book 1915–18, TCPA papers. The small number of members present is put down to 'the referendum campaign'.

⁴⁹ Edward Rigby (Vice-President, also representing Hawthorn City), John Huggan (Hon. Secretary), S.C. Brittingham, J. Edmund Burke, William Gates, E.W. Prior, C.E. Ogden, Saxil Tuxen, Percy E. Everett.

⁵⁰ *First Australian Town Planning and Housing Conference and Exhibition, Adelaide, October 17th to 24th, 1917, Official Volume of Proceedings*, Adelaide, 1917.

⁵¹ TPAV, Minutes 27 February 1918, and printed letter interleaved, dated 23 February 1918. in TPAV, Council Minutes Book 1915–18, TCPA papers.

⁵² *Argus*, 19 March, 1918, 4.

⁵³ *Argus*, 19 March 1918, 4; 29 June 1918, 18.

⁵⁴ *Second Australian Town Planning Conference and Exhibition, Brisbane, 30th July to 6th August, 1918, Volume of Proceedings*, Brisbane, 1918.

⁵⁵ *First Victorian Town Planning Conference and Exhibition, Ballarat, 13th, 14th and 15th November, 1919, Official Volume of Proceedings*, Ballarat, 1919.

⁵⁶ 'First Victorian Town Planning Conference, 28.

⁵⁷ Robert Freestone and Max Grubb, 'The Metropolitan Town Planning Commission 1922–30' in *Journal of Australian Studies,* 57 (1998): 129.

⁵⁸ See for example *Herald*, 'The vision of a great and happy city', 23 November 1923.

⁵⁹ TPAV, *Suggestions for the improvement of the City of Melbourne, and of the metropolitan area, presented to the Metropolitan Town Planning Commission, 1923* (Melbourne, 1923).

⁶⁰ For example, 25 May 1921, leaflet advertising a public meeting on native flora and fauna, in James Barrett Papers, National Parks box.

⁶¹ *Herald*, 25 March 1924, 30 September 1926; *Argus*, 15 April 1924, 7 June 1927; Barrett letter to the *Age*, 2 June 1927; TPAV 1927 Annual Report, 'Nibbling at parks'.

⁶² *Suggestions for the improvement …*, 8.

⁶³ TPAV, Annual Report 1923, 3.

⁶⁴ *Suggestions for the Improvement …*, 8.

⁶⁵ *Age*, 13 July 1926.

⁶⁶ TPAV, Annual Report 1928, 4.

⁶⁷ TCPA, Annual Report 1937, 9.

⁶⁸ TCPA, Annual Report 1931 and 1932.

⁶⁹ See, for example, 'Town Planning Association Annual Meeting', *Australian Municipal Journal*, 21(466), (15 August 1941): 56.

[70] See Seamus O'Hanlon, *Together apart: boarding house, hostel and flat life in prewar Melbourne* (Melbourne: Australian Scholarly Publishing, 2002).
[71] TCPA, Annual Report 1936, 3.
[72] TCPA, Annual Report 1936, 4.
[73] J.B. McLoughlin, *Shaping Melbourne's future?: town planning, the state and civil society* (Melbourne: Cambridge University Press, 1992), 24–34; Toni Logan, *Urban and regional planning in Victoria* (Melbourne: Shillington House, 1981), 6.
[74] Leonie Sandercock, *Property, politics and urban planning: a history of Australian city planning, 1890-1990* (New Brunswick: Transaction Publishers, 1990), 118.
[75] See, for example, a site visit to the Dandenong Police Paddock, followed by a delegation to the Premier. TCPA Council Minutes 24 March 1938, TPAV Papers, State Library Victoria Manuscripts MS13473.
[76] Sandercock, 69–70.
[77] Renate Howe (ed.), *New houses for old: fifty years of public housing in Victoria, 1938-1988* (Melbourne: Ministry of Housing and Construction, 1988).
[78] TCPA, Annual Report 1937, 5.
[79] TCPA, Annual Report 1938–39, 2.
[80] See for example Davison, 'Melbournes that might have been', 169.
[81] Davison, 'The city bred child', 153.
[82] Mirams, 266.

4
'Pedlers of new ideas': promoting town planning in South Australia 1914–24

Christine Garnaut and Kerrie Round

Among Australia's colonial capitals, Adelaide is renowned as a city laid out by William Light on the 'Grand Model'.[1] However, despite its celebrated plan, by the early years of the 20th century the effects of decades of laissez-faire development and inadequate legislative control had taken its toll on Adelaide's physical growth and appearance and it faced many of the problems of its unplanned counterparts.[2] Yet, a number of politicians and community leaders did not see the need for improvement, claiming Adelaide as the 'Garden City of the South',[3] and smugly announcing that 'as residents of really the only first-class city beautiful in Australia … they had a duty as missionaries to other parts to convert them to some of their ideals'.[4] Others were more attuned to the problems of the day and alive to opportunities for, and approaches to, achieving environmental reform. A number collaborated formally and this chapter investigates one such alliance, the South Australian Town Planning and Housing Association (SATPHA) which was active between 1914 and 1924.

Early initiatives towards control of development and town planning legislation

The first call for legislation to control urban development in South Australia was made a mere thirteen years after settlement. Journalist and newspaper owner John Stephens ended a lecture that he gave in 1849 on the dire state of Adelaide by perceptively forecasting that 'we must also have a Building Act calculated to ensure the health of the inhabitants, the proper alignment of streets, [and] the removal of impediments and nuisances'.[5] A further appeal in 1879 for legislation to control the city's development led to minor, mostly inadequate, reforms.

After Federation in 1901 the state government gradually accepted the need to curb the excesses of developers and the indiscriminate spread of the suburbs. In 1911 it introduced a Building Bill that it hoped would lead to Adelaide being a healthier and more wholesome place to live.[6] The endeavour proved ineffective so Frank W. Young, Commissioner of Crown Lands, with the help of Victor Ryan, Director of the Intelligence and Tourist Bureau, arranged a meeting of all municipal bodies in Adelaide. Several months later, in July 1913, municipal representatives formed a committee to draft town planning legislation for the state.[7] The government intended to put a Town Planning Bill before Parliament in 1914.[8]

Others outside of the political arena also wished to introduce regulations to improve residential areas. The Rev. J. Ernest James of the Manthorpe Memorial Congregational Church, Unley, used his sermons to promote the need for open spaces in the suburbs, primarily to improve the health of the inhabitants. In 1912 he led a deputation to remind the Unley Corporation of the 'ever-increasing need for parks and public reserves'[9] and subsequently the Unley Branch of the Australian Natives' Association pledged to support the Corporation 'in its efforts to secure open spaces for the recreation of the citizens'.[10]

Well-known social reformer Canon Charles Hornabrook delivered a series of lectures in 1913 on housing problems in the city and the suburbs and urged the passing of a town planning bill 'so that townships might be founded upon the most modern lines'.[11] At a service commemorating the founding of the Corporation of the City of Unley, he exhorted the councillors to 'think out means by which every part of the city and suburbs would be made fit to live in both for the present and for the future.' He argued that 'The work of the councils was sacred and [that] it was the duty of every Christian citizen to take an interest in the Town Planning Bill' then under consideration.[12]

Figure 4.1: Torrington George Ellery, c.1914. Source: SLSA: B7965. Image courtesy of the State Library of South Australia

Adelaide City Council (ACC), too, had had its town planning proponents. Torrington George Ellery (Figure 4.1), Town Clerk from 1899, was an ardent disciple and bemoaned the slow development of a 'city sense' in Australian capital cities.[13] He was particularly conscious of the shortcomings in the suburbs – too few ovals and sports grounds – and was an early advocate for the provision of open space in suburban environments. Acknowledging that Adelaide's residents had many reasons to be proud of their city, Ellery was not among those blind to the faults of Light's plan and insisted that 'we should not allow ourselves to be lulled into a sense of complacent self-satisfaction'.[14]

The ACC supported the proposed lecture tour by the London-based Garden Cities and Town Planning Association (GCTPA).[15] Councillors enthusiastically received Charles Reade (Figure 4.2) when he passed through in April 1914 to finalise tour arrangements. The mayor, A.A. Simpson, held that 'in Adelaide they had been a little too self-satisfied with what they had'. They could fully acknowledge 'Colonel Light's ability as a surveyor and still admit that if he were alive to-day there was hardly a thing about Adelaide that he would not have altered'.[16]

Figure 4.2: Charles Reade, undated photograph. Source: Christine Garnaut collection

While the initial publicity for the tour lauded William Davidge as the principal lecturer, he returned to England on the advent of World War I leaving Reade to lecture alone. But even before his lectures began Reade lost the support of many of the city councillors. His opinion that Adelaide's '"cast-iron" and monotonous' grid system 'was not so satisfactory as the systems now generally adopted' raised the ire of Alderman Cohen, who asked what improvements could possibly be made to Adelaide 'with its magnificent parks and gardens'.[17] Cohen was further incensed when he found that, instead of 'enlightening us in regard to garden cities in England and prominent cities in Europe', one of Reade's lectures was to be on 'Garden cities versus Adelaide slums and suburbs'.[18]

Canon Hornabrook leapt to Reade's defence, urging the council to 'take heed and profit' from the lectures.[19] Reade himself said:

> It is the very fact that a number of people are convinced that "Adelaide is the garden city of Australia, and that it is one of the cleanest cities in the world", which compels missionaries like myself in favour of better housing and living conditions to deal with Adelaide as it is in order to convince people that there are opportunities for improvement here just as there are in Melbourne, Sydney, and Brisbane.[20]

At the end of the Australasian Town Planning Tour, the Vaughan Labor government was anxious to move ahead with its stalled Town Planning Bill. Reade wangled an appointment as Town Planning Adviser in South Australia with the express task of finalising the bill and engaging in a number of practical town planning projects.

A town planning association emerges

Davidge and Reade's tour was the catalyst that united all those calling for town planning legislation in South Australia. The prominent architects, municipal councillors, public servants, businessmen and civic reformers, several of whom were women, who assembled in the Mayor's Reception Room at Adelaide Town Hall in April 1914 to hear about the forthcoming lecture series formed a general committee to oversee the Adelaide program.[21] Then, in March 1915, South Australian Institute of Architects

(SAIA) President Henry Ernest Fuller convened a meeting to put in train the formation of a local town planning association to carry on the work commenced by the tour committee.

A key participant in the 1915 meeting and later first president of the association was William Sowden, editor of the *Register* newspaper and Chairman of the Board of Governors of the Public Library. Another was explorer William Wilkinson, who suggested adding 'Improvement' to the association's title because of the 'defacement of the natural beauties of the country' through a proliferation of advertising hoardings, 'tin shanties' and other inappropriate buildings in urban and country areas.[22] Wilkinson's recommendation was accepted and the South Australian Town Planning and Improvement Society was duly inaugurated. Reflecting the impact of a growing movement calling for the end-of-war provision of houses for soldiers and their families, the Society changed its name in 1916 to the South Australian Town Planning and Housing Association.

An impressive array of citizens, including members of Parliament, men of religion, industrialists, senior public servants, architects, legal practitioners and other professionals constituted the original membership led by Sowden. Most were also active in other professional and civic groups. In addition to the president, office bearers included five vice-presidents: the Hons. J. Lewis MLC and F.S. Wallis MLC; Dr Gertrude Halley (Figure 4.3), one of Australia's first female doctors active locally in women's and children's health; solicitor Henry Uffindell; and Wilkinson. SAIA President Fuller was honorary secretary and treasurer. The committee comprised the Right Rev. Dr Nutter Thomas (Bishop of Adelaide); the earlier crusaders Canon Hornabrook, the Rev. James, Ryan and Ellery; industrialist and Mayor of Norwood Henry J. Holden; architects Albert Selmar Conrad and Alfred Barham Black; Mrs A.H. (Jeanne) Young; Canon Hornabrook's daughter Annie; Amy Tomkinson, a member of the Justices Association; the Hon. J.H. Vaughan MLC and his brother Crawford Vaughan MP; J.H. Clonston; G.A. Webb; E.B. Grundey KC; W. Ward; architect Thomas Smeaton MP and S.E. Yelland.

Figure 4.3: Dr Ida Gertrude Halley, 1896. Source: SLSA: B40799. Image courtesy of the State Library of South Australia

The SATPHA adopted a Constitution and set down a number of broad objectives intended largely to secure the improvement of residential, work and leisure surroundings.[23] Members were hoping to draw in allied organisations to assist their cause, including the Park Lands League that had formed in 1903 to advocate for the protection of the distinctive belt of parklands surrounding the city,[24] and associations for the preservation of open spaces in the suburbs and development of children's playgrounds. However, the Association's immediate goal was passage of town planning legislation and to that end it pledged to actively urge the government to reintroduce its shelved Town Planning Bill.

At the foundation gathering Sowden conceded that the ongoing war was likely to restrict the SATPHA's work but that, nevertheless, it would be able to prepare a campaign for the future. His prediction proved accurate as the group took time to find its feet.[25] Nevertheless, in the first year, three municipal corporations, three district councils and 48 individuals joined. Members took part in a successful deputation to the state government to request a recreation ground in the eastern suburb of St Peters but failed in their collaboration with Unley Council and Unley High School to secure Kyre Oval, a prominent open space adjacent to the school, as a recreation ground for students and the local community.[26] However, members were pleased with popular interest in the Association's display at the 1916 Child Welfare Exhibition, which 'being attended largely by the right class of people' they believed should be 'followed by satisfactory results in the matter of the welfare of children, especially as regarded housing and general environment'.[27]

A new leader and a more active association

When solicitor Henry Uffindell succeeded Sowden as SATPHA President at the 1916 Annual General Meeting and several new members replaced a number of the original cohort, the Association became more active. In 1918 Reade accepted the permanent position of Government Town Planner and the SATPHA became the first town planning association nationally to have such an official with whom to work.

A critical focus of the SATPHA was to support Reade and the passage of the proposed Town Planning and Housing Bill. But the bill was a major and a contentious matter. The local press supported the legislation, the *Daily Herald* calling it 'one of the finest and best reformative measures that has ever been presented to the South Australian Parliament' and urging 'every Labor councillor and all ratepayers in different suburban areas' to defeat those who would 'squash' it.[28] In a leader the *Register* proclaimed that the bill represented a reform that it had long advocated and which was 'much overdue'.[29] A committee comprising members of metropolitan councils hoped that the measure would proceed quickly.[30] But the Institute of Surveyors and many ACC councillors vehemently opposed it. At times the opposition became personal, with much invective against

Reade. One councillor claimed that 'the organizer of the townplanning movement had been in Adelaide for two years planning to make a job of some kind for himself',[31] and others never forgave Reade for suggesting that Adelaide had slums.[32]

Figure 4.4: SA Executive, First Town Planning and Housing Conference and Exhibition, 1917. *Official Volume of Proceedings First Town Planning and Housing Conference and Exhibition*, (Adelaide: Vardon & Sons Ltd, 1918)

In a letter to the *Register* in September 1916, Uffindell made the SATPHA's position clear. He strongly protested:

> against the attitude and decision of the City Council both in regard to the Bill and to the townplanner … [T]o treat an important reform, and the gentleman whose valuable services are being requisitioned in the attempt to provide such reform, in the cavalier-like fashion [is] neither dignified nor worthy of that august assemblage.[33]

But the opposition succeeded and the bill stalled in the Legislative Assembly and then lapsed at the end of 1916.

Meanwhile, the SATPHA turned to its educative role. It sponsored talks on town planning, including lectures by Reade. In 1917 most of the Association's attention was devoted to helping the Government Town Planner and committee member Victor Ryan prepare for the First Australian Town Planning and Housing Conference and Exhibition which was held in Adelaide that October (Figure 4.4). The event was a significant moment for town planning advocates nationally and attracted about 250 delegates who included members of the federal and state governments, the Governor-General and the state vice-regal representatives, representatives of city and municipal councils of all states, and professionals in fields such as architecture, surveying, health and education. Exhibitions, films, field trips and social activities augmented the program of speakers.

Uffindell was Chairman of the South Australian Committee for the conference. A subcommittee of that group, including solid SATPHA representation, formed to oversee the design and construction of a model children's playground as one of the exhibits. The children's playground movement was then strong internationally and two female Association members, Halley and infant school teacher Lydia Longmore (Figure 4.5), were prime movers behind the Adelaide project. Designed to 'teach tiny tots how to play, for they have to learn that art, just as any other branch of knowledge',[34] the playground was used over the week by 2000 children who attended in school groups and took part in folk dancing, maypole drill, kindergarten games, sport and gymnastics. At the conclusion of the conference the playground equipment and a portion of the profits were handed over to the SATPHA for a proposed playground in the West Park Lands (Figure 4.6).

The SATPHA realised the danger of being seen as simply an enthusiast for playgrounds so to set the record straight, it included a detailed policy statement in the conference proceedings delineating the separate roles of town planning and of children's playgrounds – 'they are two distinct things'.[35] Despite its caveat, playgrounds remained a major item on the Association's agenda and following the conference it formed several subcommittees to report on the suitability of government land for playground sites in various suburbs.³⁶

In addition to practical organisational support, the SATPHA contributed to the program of the 1917 Conference through a paper presented

Figure 4.5: Lydia Longmore, c.1912. Source: SLSA: B63020/56. Image courtesy of the State Library of South Australia

by Albert Conrad on 'Town Planning: Adelaide and the Metropolitan Area'. Uffindell's influence was clear in securing not only Conrad's involvement but also in defining his topic; he commenced his presentation with the words 'The President of our Association … has asked me to consider the town planning possibilities of the city and suburbs, and to make some suggestions in regard to their improvement'.³⁷ Association members Tomkinson, Halley, Hornabrook and Longmore constituted four of the nine female conference delegates.

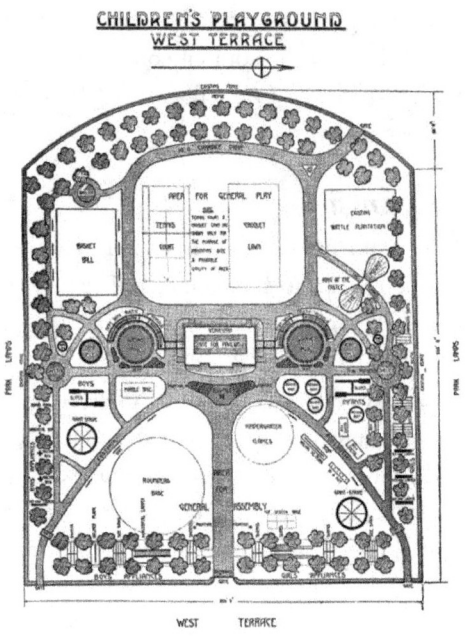

Figure 4.6: West Terrace Children's Playground, 1917. Charles Reade, *Planning and development of towns and cities in South Australia* (Adelaide: Government Printer, 1919)

Following its major involvement in the 1917 conference, the following year the SATPHA participated less conspicuously in the Second Town Planning and Housing Conference held in Brisbane. Three of the four government delegates, Reade, Ryan and Francis McNamara, Inspector-General of the State Bank, were all Association members.[38] Uffindell, too, was present.[39] None was a speaker, although the Hon. Henry Barwell, Attorney-General and Minister in Charge of Town Planning, delivered a paper about the proposed Mitcham Garden Suburb, a concept that the

SATPHA ardently supported. Initially the ACC was reluctant to be involved in the Brisbane conference. One councillor viewed the town planning conferences as 'an annual jaunt to the Australian capitals' while Lord Mayor Isaacs thought it 'a waste of money to send anyone to Brisbane, because the objects of the council could be gained if Parliament passed the Building Bill'.[40] The Council relented, however, and sent the Town Clerk, H.P. Beaver.

Interwar reorganisation

The signing of the Armistice in November 1918 allowed governments and the people to focus on peacetime pursuits. The SATPHA determined that the time was right to increase its profile. To attract a wider membership, it reformed its structure in 1919, maintaining its executive but introducing a council of 50 individuals representing all sections of the community. Uffindell remained chairman and much of the same committee continued, but there was a greater representation from local government, including the ACC.[41] Despite this, the ACC was one of two municipal councils that declined to formally affiliate with the reorganised Association.[42]

Uffindell and colleagues were appalled at the Council's ongoing endeavours to remain aloof not only from the Association but also from the town planning movement generally:

> It is little short of farcical that those who profess to reverence the name and work of Col. Light – the pioneer townplanner, to whom this city owes everything – who once a year hand round a loving cup in memory of a great man, should refuse support and encouragement for a movement which aims directly to secure the logical continuation of his great and lasting work.[43]

Few members of the Council even bothered to attend a service organised by the SATPHA to commemorate the eightieth anniversary of William Light's death. As Reade reported:

[T]he ceremony on Sunday last ... was a great success. It had to be arranged in the face of prejudice and hostility from the city and other folk, who seem as benighted as ever. The struggle for townplanning in this state makes heavy going but notwithstanding Adelaide's noted "culture" we are beginning to break in upon the walls of deeply rooted prejudice and civic nefariousness.[44]

Getting down to business: promoting town planning legislation

The achievement of town planning legislation remained the reorganised SATPHA's main goal. It strongly supported the Government Town Planner's and his allies' moves to introduce a Town Planning and Development Bill, and in August 1919 it issued a manifesto emphasising the urgent need for both a Town Planning and Development Act and an updated Building Act.[45] It organised a deputation comprising representatives of local councils and professional and other bodies to object to the government's decision to introduce temporary legislation in the form of an amendment to the Real Property Act.[46] Unfortunately, even though Barwell, a convert and 'zealous champion' of the movement,[47] introduced the Town Planning and Development Bill, its debate was delayed and the government passed the unwanted interim measure.[48]

Controversy over the Town Planning and Development Bill intensified during 1920. A joint committee of architects, surveyors and land brokers strongly objected to control of town planning being placed solely in the hands of a single person, in particular if this person was Reade, who was not a qualified architect, engineer or surveyor. A.J. Blakeway, honorary secretary of the South Australian Institute of Surveyors, was especially vehement on what he and others perceived as Reade's town planning frills:

> Wherever possible, in the designs which appear in the Town Planner's report, streets are curved. From experience, surveyors know what a curse they will become to landowners and munici-

pal bodies in the years to come ... Surely our legislators can see the whole business is absurd.[49]

Uffindell immediately countered that:

> certain surveyors, lacking any special training or experience in town planning, are actuated less by public welfare than antiquated ideas, personal animus and purblind prejudice. Mr A.J. Blakeway ... certainly has neither right nor justice on his side in seeking to cloud the issues concerning the Town Planning Bill by indulging his own personal feelings in misleading and garbled statements that in any modern country where town planning operates would probably be laughed out of existence.[50]

The SATPHA continued to lobby for the legislation and to support Reade, who was now on its committee, using the press, public petitions and deputations to government to exert pressure for the bill's passage. In particular, the Association considered that the objectors were unjustifiably attempting 'to secure a central controlling board, in part representative of their own profession [and] to prejudice the Legislative Council against the effect of the bill, and the distinctive professional qualifications and capacity of the town planner'.[51]

Eventually Barwell managed to shepherd through the legislation, the first of its kind in Australia. It was the last measure to be approved by the Legislative Council before its December 1920 recess, 'secured at the eleventh hour after strenuous effort and hard fighting'.[52] The resulting Act was in an extremely emasculated form – indeed, it was described as 'the covers of an Act'.[53] It made permanent the Town Planning Department and the position of Government Town Planner but their powers were limited largely to the planning of new suburbs and rural towns and the control of subdivision.[54]

The SATPHA could claim the achievement of what had become, by 1919, its central objective. The ACC too got its wish and the City of Adelaide was exempt from the provisions of the act. Uffindell, with a touch of irony, hoped that 'time and experience ... will assuredly, with an intelligent body like the City Council, induce this body to eventually realize that it is not only to their interests, but to the interests of the community at large ... to avail themselves of the beneficent reform'.[55]

Addressing broader SATPHA aims

During its campaign for town planning legislation the SATPHA also turned to related matters. It publicised new metropolitan and rural developments laid out on modern – garden city – principles by the Town Planning Department,[56] and was a strong advocate for the *Garden Suburb Act 1919*. This Act laid the groundwork for what was initially named the Mitcham Garden Suburb (Figure 4.7), but which the Association proposed should be called the William Light Garden Suburb (it was in fact named Colonel Light Gardens).[57] Furthering the Association's educative aims, it organised a showing at the Adelaide Town Hall of the film *Modern British war towns and town planning in Great Britain*, which had been presented to the Department of Town Planning by British industrialist Lord Leverhulme.[58]

A crucial decision of the more mature SATPHA was the proposal to attract more publicity for its causes by producing a regular publication. A consequent goal was to raise its membership to 160 to fund *The Light Journal of Town Planning and Housing*.[59] The first issue was launched in 1920 with great fanfare. The journal was intended to 'fill a definite gap in civic life' and provide 'the detailed publicity that the Association's more ardent champions ... desire'.[60] In addition to a descriptive list of fifteen aims and objectives, particulars of the Association's activities filled many pages. Successes and failures were raised and discussed at great length, as were the benefits of town planning to urban, industrial and economic life. Throughout, however, was a lament about lack of money and facilities, in particular in its appeal for funds for publicity and education, and for developing the proposed children's playground in the West Park Lands.[61]

Figure 4.7: Mitcham Garden suburb, bird's eye view, 1917. Source: Colonel Light Gardens Historical Society

Despite dreams of a monthly, indeed even fortnightly, periodical,[62] only one issue of *The Light Journal* appeared. However, for a time starting in May 1923 the local journal, *The Builder incorporating the Town Planning & Local Government Journal,* contained a quarterly supplement headed 'Official Organ of the South Australian Town Planning and Housing Association'. This section carried articles on town planning and housing reform in Britain, children's playgrounds, descriptions of local initiatives, and across three issues, a series on 'Practical and scientific planning of towns and cities' by the then Government Town Planner, Walter Scott Griffiths.[63]

The SATPHA's final years

The SATPHA predicted correctly that the need for its work would increase after the passage of the *Town Planning and Development Act*.[64] In 1922 it worked with allied professional bodies to submit a report on the long-delayed Building Bill.[65] In July that year Uffindell also responded to further criticisms of the town planning legislation and calls to vest control of the act in the Surveyor-General's Department.[66] Surveyor J.H.

Packard questioned whether Uffindell was 'strictly in order in writing as President', being 'under the impression [the TPA] had become defunct'. He claimed to have been appointed as a representative of the Institute of Surveyors several years before but never to have been invited to a single meeting.[67]

The 1924 Annual Report published in *The Builder* suggested that membership was healthy at 166 individuals, although only two municipalities still belonged. In the preceding year the executive had led a deputation objecting to moves by the ACC to widen Adelaide's major cultural boulevard, North Terrace.[68] This unsuccessful representation was seemingly the last gasp of the Association as a vital force. H.C. Richards replaced Uffindell as chairman at the Annual General Meeting (AGM) on 5 June 1924.[69] Uffindell's reasons for not seeking reappointment are unrecorded. With his departure the Association lost a long-standing and pivotal member. No further reports of activities of the SATPHA were published after 1924, and it appears that it dissolved following the June AGM.

Reflections on the demise of the SATPHA

One person seldom keeps an organisation afloat, but often one person can enthuse others and the loss of key leaders certainly debilitated the SATPHA. Henry Uffindell was the last of the inaugural committee and with him gone there was no one with the necessary passion and vision to energise existing members or to attract new ones. Others who made fundamental contributions included Torrington George Ellery, an early casualty who was appointed Melbourne's Town Clerk from 1915. He was the strongest proponent of town planning within the ACC, and the only Association member in a position to temper the moves of those within the Council with vested interests, both individually as property owners and corporately as defenders of the power of local government.

Others left the SATPHA when their particular areas of interest dropped off the Association's agenda. One was children's playgrounds. In its initial enthusiasm, in 1915 the Association had asked the ACC to provide sites for playgrounds on the West, South and East Park Lands.[70] Despite its commitment and advocacy, the playgrounds failed to materialise. In 1921 the SATPHA relinquished any hope of establishing even one,[71] and Gertrude Halley and Lydia Longmore turned their attention elsewhere.[72] After the 1917 conference, Victor Ryan, too, was overtaken by other interests. But by far the most damaging loss was Charles Reade, who accepted a secondment as town planner to the Federated Malay States and departed from the state after the successful passage of the *Town Planning and Development Act* in 1920. Others followed in the role, but none could match his vision, magnetism or drive.

Diminishing support for the SATPHA from some of the local press also played a part in the Association's demise. William Sowden left the *Register* in 1922 but the paper had already been affected by the views of Sydney-based journalist George Taylor who, with his wife Florence, was a leading light of the Town Planning Association of NSW.[73] George Taylor criticised Reade's regulationist approach to town planning reform.[74] A *Register* editorial in 1920, at the time when town planning legislation was grinding its way through the Legislative Council, pulled no punches:

> its chief advocates in South Australia are so zealous and persistent, that there is a real danger of Parliament being induced to enact legislation, which, because of its autocratic extremism, would prove mischievous and lead to a reaction against a worthy and desirable aim.[75]

By association, the SATPHA was also under fire. The constant and prolonged opposition of land brokers, surveyors and architects also seriously undermined the SATPHA cause. While always professing general support for reform, they invariably objected to the specifics of proposed legislation. Packard's comments on the Town Planning and Development Bill typified their view: 'I am strictly in favour of reform … but … can only characterise the provisions of the bill as townplanning run mad'.[76] A deputation of surveyors and land brokers and auctioneers told the government that the bill was 'unworkable'; they also aired their objections publicly in the press.[77]

Opposition to the legislation continued even after the 1920 Act was enforced. The Surveyors' Institute expressed the view that town planning was part of the surveying profession and should be under its control.[78] The SATPHA was drawn into the fight, defending the legislation but ultimately bearing the brunt of the Institute's spleen:

> From reading the report of the Townplanning Association one would think that Adelaide and suburbs were one huge slum. These would-be saviours of mankind cannot be cornered into admitting that there are many parts of the suburbs well and truly planned ... Townplanning, according to some exponents of the art in Adelaide, consists of distorting and twisting a township into all shapes.[79]

Political will was fundamental to the success of the SATPHA's objectives and when the will foundered so too did the Association. By arranging for his government to purchase land for a model garden suburb, Labor Attorney-General Howard Vaughan not only put town planning on the political agenda but also invigorated the early town planning movement.[80] From then, however, the state wavered in its attitude to town planning, depending on which party was in power. Liberal premier Henry Barwell was its fiercest advocate but when his government was removed in early 1924 the new Labor Ministry made no specific provision for town planning.[81] Eventually, in 1929, the persistent professional criticism of town planning legislation had permanent effect when the 1920 Act was repealed and replaced by the even weaker *Town Planning Act*.[82]

Motivations for promoting town planning

What motivated the eclectic band of civilians and politicians who involved themselves in promoting town planning in South Australia and joined or supported the SATPHA? A suite of individual convictions can be canvassed although in some cases it is difficult to determine specific motives. For example, there seems nothing special in the background or interests of J. Howard Vaughan who as Attorney-General introduced the 1916 Town Planning Bill and who was later the Hon. Organising Director of the SATPHA. While an advocate of Labor and trade union causes, he showed no other interest in civic affairs.[83] On the other hand, Henry Barwell, from the opposite side of politics, was an early convert to the town planning cause, a staunch supporter of Reade and a champion of the Town Planning and Development Bill.[84] Like Reade he 'acknowledged the value of far-sightedness and the need for a comprehensive legislative approach. He was confident, outspoken and persistent, qualities that made him an ideal ally'.[85] Victor Ryan's interest may have been simply *ex officio*: as Director of the Intelligence and Tourist Bureau, he was responsible for promoting the beauties of the state.

Civic pride and nationalism were to the fore for some. As editor of the *Register* from 1899 to 1922, William Sowden campaigned for Federation and state rights. He was on the committees of numerous government, patriotic and civic groups and was a strong advocate of the natural environment, but ultimately baulked at serious new controls on development.[86] Industrialist Henry Holden also contributed substantially to civic life, working in municipal and state governments, judicial affairs, education, religious affairs and charity.[87]

Henry Uffindell's motives, too, were related to a wish to improve civic amenities and early on he grasped 'the social and economic values of the town planners' mission'.[88] Born in suburban Norwood, he served his articles in the mid-north of the state and then moved to the Yorke Peninsula where he practised for 25 years. In addition to environmental interests he was on the Moonta Council for seven years (and mayor for two). He set up practice in Adelaide around 1909, where town planning was not his only interest: he was also a member of the Poetry Society, the Dual Club, and the South Australian branch of the Australian Forest League.

Other 'faddists'[89] were more directly focused on the benefits of town planning. Torrington George Ellery, whose interest was linked with his involvement in the greater cities movement, believed that town planning would improve public health and sanitation, and that combining the ACC with the metropolitan bodies would improve the services and reduce the expenses of local government, allowing them to institute further reforms for their residents.[90] Working in the slums of London had convinced the Rev. James of the need for fresh air to prevent thousands of slum dwellers dying from the ravages of fever.[91] Canon Hornabrook was also concerned with the lives of the poor and was instrumental in establishing an Anglican mission in Adelaide.[92]

The women involved in the SATPHA were equally civic minded. Lydia Longmore, Gertrude Halley and Annie Hornabrook were the daughters of clergymen. In 1917 Longmore was appointed the first female inspector of infant schools. In 1918 she was instrumental in introducing correspondence lessons for outback and isolated children and in 1920 helped form associations of infant teachers and their charges' mothers. Halley was prominent in women's health in Victoria, Tasmania and New South Wales before coming to South Australia in 1913 to establish the first medical branch for the Education Department. She chaired the League of Loyal Women,[93] and she and Longmore were committee members of the National Council of Women and active in the Women's Non-Party Political Association.[94] Hornabrook was the principal of the School for Mothers in Wright Street, Adelaide. She supported her father's work and used her position to highlight overcrowded inner-city conditions.[95] With Dr Helen Mayo and Harriet Stirling she established the Babies' Hospital Association to care for babies too young to be admitted to the Adelaide Children's Hospital.[96]

Hornabrook, Halley and also Amy Tomkinson were members of the South Australian Branch of the British Science Guild, and Hornabrook and Tomkinson belonged to the Women's Non-Party Political Association. Members of that association were at the forefront of the establishment of the Local Government Women's Association (LGWA) and the Electoral Reform Society. In 1916, with LGWA support, Hornabrook and Tomkinson became the first women to nominate for local government in South Australia when they stood as candidates for the Adelaide City Council.[97] These women's close involvement in local politics and their intimate connections with a number of reform groups were critical in helping the SATPHA establish an early introduction into a wider political and citizen reform network. However, mirroring the impact of the departure of key male leaders, the vibrancy and impact of the Association decreased once its female members took up opportunities elsewhere.

Conclusion

In a message of support for the SATPHA and its objectives, Mayor of Unley, W.H. Langham, wrote in *The Light Journal* that:

> Like all pedlers [sic] of new ideas, the town planners have had to give battle to prejudice, indifference and selfishness. In civic life nothing is more difficult to overcome. The average citizen is deeply immersed in his own affairs, and has never been aroused to think and care for the corporate welfare of his own city.[98]

For a short time the SATPHA challenged the citizens of Adelaide to appraise realistically the physical condition of their city and to work actively towards its improvement. They were, in fact, urging residents to develop a civic consciousness and to collectively contribute to the greater good of the capital and to the future development of its suburban and rural areas along modern town planning lines. At first a group of loosely aligned members, the SATPHA galvanised formally after the Australasian Town Planning Tour of 1914–15. Swayed by the tour's message and enthused by the prospect of widespread benefits from town planning generally and town planning legislation in particular, they initiated and promoted a range of activities to advance the town planning cause.

Led by individuals prominent in public life, who cannily drew in others from strategic political and civic groups, the SATPHA became a leading community voice, enunciating new ideas on civic welfare and improvement generally. Despite increasing opposition to town planning legislation, the Association persisted in supporting that founding objective through to its achievement. However, although it could claim to have aroused public interest in its work, as Langham presciently penned, 'prejudice and indifference' eventually took hold. Following the SATPHA's passing it would be a further 40 years before a civilian-based group again took up the town planning cause in South Australia.

References

[1] Robert Home, *Of planting and planning: the making of British colonial cities* (London: E&FN Spon, 1997), 9.

[2] Christine Garnaut, 'Towards metropolitan organization: town planning and the Garden City idea', in *The Australian metropolis: a planning history,* ed. Stephen Hamnett and Robert Freestone (Sydney: Allen and Unwin, 2000), 46–64.

[3] *Observer*, 1 August 1914.

[4] *Register*, 8 April 1914.

[5] *Register*, 8 April 1921.

[6] *Advertiser*, 23 April 1914.

[7] Draft of a circular re town planning to the Commissioner of Crown Lands, 1 February 1913, State Records of South Australia (hereafter SRSA) GRG 35/1/1913/157.

[8] *The Salon*, June 1914, 693.

[9] 43rd Annual Report, Mayor's Report, 30 November 1913, 18, Archives of the City of Unley.

[10] 43rd Annual Report, Mayor's Report, 30 November 1913, 19, Archives of the City of Unley.

[11] *Register*, 28 May 1913.

[12] *Advertiser*, n.d.

[13] Adelaide City Council, Annual Report 1911, 47, Adelaide City Council Archives (hereafter ACC).

[14] Adelaide City Council, Annual Report 1912, 67, ACC.

[15] Mayor's Minute, Adelaide City Council, Annual Report 1913, 5, ACC.

16. *Advertiser*, 23 April 1914.
17. *Advertiser*, 23 April 1914.
18. *The Salon*, November 1914, 167.
19. *The Salon*, November 1914, 169.
20. *The Salon*, November 1914, 170.
21. Robert Freestone, 'An imperial aspect: the Australasian Town Planning Tour of 1914–15', *Australian Journal of Politics and History*, 44(2), (1998), 159–76.
22. *Register*, 21 January 1915.
23. *Town Planning and Housing Review*, 12 April 1915, 15.
24. Peter Morton, *After light: a history of the City of Adelaide and its council, 1878–1928* (Adelaide: Wakefield Press, 1997), 155.
25. *Town Planning and Housing Review*, May 1916, 8.
26. *Town Planning and Housing Review*, May 1916, 8–9.
27. *Register*, 10 May 1917, 9.
28. *Daily Herald*, 13 September 1916.
29. *Register*, 23 August 1916.
30. *Advertiser*, 7 October 1916.
31. *Register*, 12 September 1916.
32. *Advertiser*, 2 September 1916.
33. *Register*, 12 September 1916.
34. *Register*, 15 October 1917; Official Programme of the First Australian Town Planning and Housing Conference and Exhibition, Adelaide (South Australia), 21.
35. 'Children's playgrounds in South Australia'. A Statement of Policy by the South Australian Town Planning Association, *Official Volume of Proceedings of the First Australian Town Planning and Housing Conference and Exhibition* (Adelaide: Vardon & Sons Ltd, 1918), 159.
36. *Register*, 10 May 1917.
37. Albert S. Conrad, 'Town planning: Adelaide and the metropolitan area', *Official*, 88.
38. Town Planning File, Personal, Town Clerk, undated unsourced newspaper clipping, ACC.
39. *Daily Mail*, 4 August 1918.
40. Town Planning File, Personal, Town Clerk, undated unsourced newspaper clipping, ACC.
41. *Register*, 30 April 1919; Town Clerk's Department, Dkt 2713/16, File No. 2, ACC.

[42] *Register*, 23 August 1919; Town Clerk's Department, Dkt 2713, File No. 2, ACC.
[43] *Register*, 6 August 1919.
[44] Letter from Charles Reade to J.D. Fitzgerald, 17 October 1919, SRSA: GRG73/63 Miscellaneous Letters 1919 July–December.
[45] *Register*, 19 August 1919.
[46] *The Light Journal of Town Planning and Housing*, 1(1), (June 1920), 13.
[47] Henry N. Barwell, 'Town Planning'. An address delivered to the Members of the SA Town Planning and Housing Association at the Annual Meeting on Tuesday, 29 April, 1919.
[48] *The Light Journal*, 12.
[49] *Advertiser*, 10 September 1920.
[50] *Daily Herald*, 11 September 1920.
[51] *Daily Herald*, 22 October 1920.
[52] *Observer*, 30 April 1920.
[53] *Register*, 30 November 1920.
[54] Alan Hutchings, 'The inter-war years', in *The Australian Metropolis*, 67–68.
[55] *Observer*, 30 April 1921.
[56] *The Light Journal*, 11.
[57] *The Light Journal*, 13; Christine Garnaut, *Colonel Light Gardens: model garden suburb* (Sydney, Crossing Press, 2006[1999]), 58.
[58] Town Clerk's Department, Dkt 2713/16, File No. 2, ACC.
[59] Town Clerk's Department, Dkt 2713/16, File No. 2, ACC.
[60] *The Light Journal*, 1.
[61] *The Light Journal*, 15.
[62] Charles Reade to J. Sulman, 11 December 1919. Miscellaneous Letters 1920, SRSA: GRG73/63.
[63] See, for example, *The Builder*, 1 June 1923, 1 August 1923, 20 October 1923.
[64] *The Light Journal*, 2.
[65] *The Builder*, 31 March 1923, 4.
[66] *Register*, 15 July 1922.
[67] *Register*, 17 July 1922.
[68] Town Clerk's File, 49; The Town Planning Association of South Australia, Annual Report for the Year, 1923–24, ACC.
[69] *Register*, 6 June 1924.
[70] Town Clerk's Annual Report, 1916, 29, ACC.
[71] Town Clerk's Annual Report, 1921. Dkt 2713/16 File No. 2, ACC.

[72] Julia Gatley, 'A scandalous affair?: women at the First Australian Town Planning & Housing Conference & Exhibition, Adelaide, 1917' in *Formulation fabrication: the architecture of history*. Proceedings of the 17th Annual Conference of SAHANZ, Victoria University of Wellington, Wellington, New Zealand, 13–17 (November 2000), 9.

[73] Robert Freestone and Bronwyn Hanna, *Florence Taylor's hats: designing, building and editing Sydney* (Sydney: Halstead Press, 2008).

[74] John Tregenza, 'Reade, Charles Compton (1880–1933), *Australian dictionary of biography* (Melbourne, Melbourne University Press, 2000), 11, 340–42.

[75] *Register*, 2 November 1920.

[76] *Register*, 2 October 1919.

[77] See, for example, *Register*, 28 September 1919; 1 November 1919; 6 September 1920.

[78] *Register*, 10 July 1922.

[79] *Register*, 3 May 1921.

[80] *The Light Journal*, 15.

[81] *Advertiser*, 17 April 1924.

[82] Hutchings, 68.

[83] G. Grainger, 'Vaughan, Crawford (1874–1947)', *Australian dictionary of biography* (Melbourne: Melbourne University Press, 1990), 12, 313–15.

[84] Maryanne McGill, 'Barwell, Sir Henry Newman (1877–1959)', *Australian dictionary of biography* (Melbourne: Melbourne University Press, 1979), 7, 200–02.

[85] Christine Garnaut 'Model and Maker: Colonel Light Gardens and Charles Reade' (PhD thesis, University of South Australia, 1997), 58.

[86] Carl Bridge, 'Sowden, Sir William John (1858–1943)', *Australian dictionary of biography* (Melbourne: Melbourne University Press, 1990), 12, 24–25.

[87] Joan Hancock and Eric Richards, 'Holden, Henry James (1859–1926)', *Australian dictionary of biography*, (Melbourne: Melbourne University Press, 1983), 9, 330–32.

[88] *The Builder*, 24 February 1923.

[89] For example, *Advertiser*, 12 September 1916.

[90] Robert Thornton, 'Ellery, Torrington George (1872–1923)', *Australian dictionary of biography* (Melbourne: Melbourne University Press, 2005), Supplementary Volume, 115–16.

[91] *Daily Herald*, n.d.

5
Regenerating the people: town planning activism in Hobart 1916–39

Stefan Petrow

Throughout the nineteenth century the interests of property owners were paramount in Hobart, the capital city of Tasmania. As the municipal franchise was heavily weighted in their favour, property owners dominated the Hobart City Council, which allowed them to pursue their own interests including building shoddy housing and cramming as many houses as they could on their land. The Council also showed little interest in providing and maintaining parks and reserves for the people, or in beautifying the landscape by planting trees and flower beds. The outcome was to detract from and not enhance the beauty of the landscape. Greed and indifference overshadowed aesthetic and health concerns. Attitudes slowly changed after 1900 when businessmen with a social conscience were elected to the Council and adopted a forward-looking approach to city governance.[1] According to the *Tasmanian News*, aldermen were galvanised by the federation of the Australian colonies. They expected federation to increase competition between cities for people and industry and Hobart would lose out if the city was not 'run upon up-to-date lines'.[2] Garden city and city beautiful ideas became popular in Australia and influenced municipal reformers in Hobart.[3]

Formed in 1915, the Southern Tasmanian Town Planning Association (STTPA) was the key body in publicising town planning ideals and projects until 1926. It attempted to secure town planning legislation, better housing and roads, and more parks and playgrounds for children. The association had the greatest success in beautifying Hobart rather than in improving urban housing and town planning legislation was not passed. Aldermen were willing to beautify the city because aesthetic improvements were not a heavy drain on limited funds and promised to increase revenue by attracting tourists. Altering the urban environment by slum clearance and removal of insanitary housing was less appealing because it required interference with the rights of landowners and would be a much heavier charge on municipal finances. This chapter will begin by considering the formation and aims of the STTPA and then examine its attempts to secure town planning legislation, improved housing and roads, and more parks, reserves and playgrounds.

Formation and aims

As in other states, town planners were inspired by the Australian Town Planning Lecture Tour of Charles Reade and William Davidge. The lecturers visited Hobart in March 1915 at the invitation of the Tasmanian Institute of Architects.[4] Reade was pivotal in spreading the town planning gospel throughout Australia and his 'personal magnetism' worked its magic in Hobart.[5] Commenting on Hobart's 'natural advantages' and 'scenic wealth', Reade declared that town planning was essential to retain these features and make Hobart 'one of the most attractive cities in the Southern Pacific'.[6] His first public lecture in Hobart on 18 March highlighted developments in Germany and England and explained the principles of town planning.[7] The meeting, attended mainly by middle-class professionals, passed a motion by respected architect and urban activist, Rudolph Koch (Figure 5.1), to establish a branch of the Town Planning Association in Hobart. A northern branch was established in Launceston in April 1915, but the two bodies seem to have had no contact.[8]

Reade gave further lectures in April 1915 on 'The message of garden cities and town planning' and 'Town planning: its application to Hobart'.[9] According to the *Mercury*, the city's main newspaper, the lectures evoked regret that Hobart had not been 'laid out with some systematic attempt to make the best of its natural beauties and to house the people with more attention to their health and comfort'. The imperative was 'to improve what we have and to provide that the future growth will be on better lines'. Nothing would change unless the people of Hobart developed 'an intense civic patriotism and a desire for beautiful surroundings'. The conservative *Mercury* urged the town planning movement to give precedence to aesthetic concerns over social reform in the coming years. But the *Daily Post*, organ of the Labor Party, wanted social reform to be pre-eminent. It condemned landowners and speculators for subdividing land and building poor quality houses on small blocks and the 'landlord'-dominated Legislative Council and City Council for not restraining them.[10] This created a city that was 'ugly, squalid, architecturally a heap of bricks shovelled about by commercialism, with rights of way that climb impossible hills and water fronts ruined'. The *Daily Post* was criticised by vested interests for attacking landlords and politicising town planning, but the newspaper pointed out that Hobart remained unplanned because of 'political and economic causes' and therefore 'the cure is political and economic'.

The *Daily Post* believed that town planning could only succeed if public control over land was tightened. This was unlikely in Hobart while the City Council protected the needs of landowners. The *Daily Post* therefore supported Reade's proposal to establish an independent town planning authority with wide powers 'to organise the future development [of Hobart] on scientific lines'.[11] Town planning was necessary, not for 'aesthetic' reasons, but for the social benefits of better housing in garden suburbs, where crime, alcoholism, immorality and infant mortality would be eliminated.[12] Old buildings should be removed, not for being 'unsightly' but for being 'insanitary'. Playgrounds and reserves were necessary as 'lungs' for the health of the young, not just to beautify the city. The *Daily Post* told private investors that town planning was 'a good investment': it was possible to 'beautify and improve' Hobart while making 'a reasonable profit'.[13] Thus aesthetic and social benefits were expected of town planning in Hobart.

Figure 5.1: Rudolph Koch, leading town planning activist. Source: *Tasmanian Mail*, 21 March 1928

Taking advice from Reade, the STTPA aimed to remodel Hobart; to prepare a plan for future growth, including the provision of more playgrounds and reserves; and to improve architecture and housing.[14] These broad aims would be pursued by educating the public on the need for town planning, by persuading local authorities to use their existing powers, and by seeking new town planning legislation. In October 1915 Reade in a special lecture bolstered by lantern illustrations told both Houses of Parliament that town planning legislation 'could be adopted irrespective of party politics'.[15] The STTPA presented itself as a non-political party organisation and wanted to attract a wide cross-section of the community. V.W.O. Barker, Labor member for Denison, moved at one meeting that the association 'encourage the idea of co-operative or public ownership of town building land', but the motion was defeated. Koch explained that such an objective would undermine the Association's neutrality and alienate the 'shrewd' businessmen members of the association, who were 'by no means favourable to Labor views'.[16]

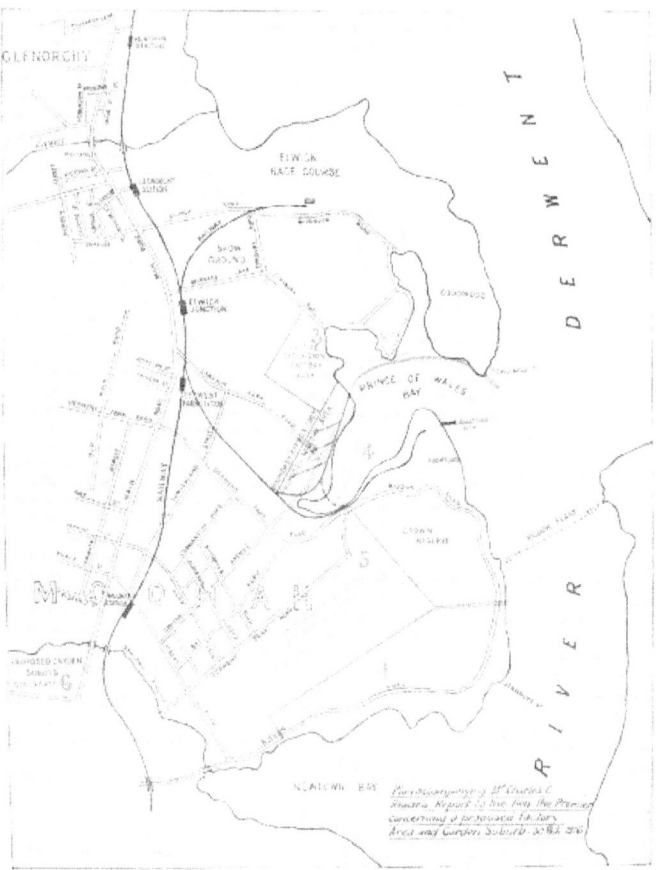

Figure 5.2: Reade's plan for an industrial area and garden suburb.
Source: *Journals and Printed Papers of Parliament* (*Tasmania*), 75, (1916–17), paper 19

STTPA members regularly wrote articles on town planning for both daily newspapers. The *Daily Post* started a column, compiled by the Secretary of the STTPA, H.D. Flannagan, called 'Town planning notes', which highlighted national and international developments.[17] In 1916, receiving a subsidy from the Labor government, Reade returned to deliver further lectures. One lecture claimed that Hobart had 'originally' been laid out on town planning lines, but those principles had been neglected by the City Council.[18] Flannagan interviewed prominent citizens and the *Daily Post* published their views on the benefits of town planning. By July 1916 STTPA membership had reached 187 and support for town planning was growing.[19] The *Mercury* received favourable comment from clergymen, municipalities, merchants and professional men.[20] Members included leading Labor figures like Premier John Earle, who believed that town planning could contribute to 'the regeneration of the people', and President of the Worker's Political League L.F. Giblin.[21] Earle commissioned Reade to draft a town planning bill based on the 1909 Town Planning and Housing Act of Great Britain, but lost office in April 1916 before the bill could be submitted to Parliament.[22] Reade also prepared a government report on a proposed industrial area and garden suburb for Crown land between Prince of Wales and New Town Bays on the Derwent River (Figure 5.2).[23]

Town planning legislation

The STTPA pinned its hopes on the passing of town planning legislation, with a strong central body to coordinate planning in the Greater Hobart area and greater powers being given to local authorities. As Secretary Flannagan argued, after 'the wastage created by the war, nothing legislative can be more urgent or justifiable' than town planning legislation, which will 'remedy such tragic faults in our civic life' and improve 'health, morals and citizenship'.[24] A major stumbling block was the Lee Nationalist government, which showed less interest in town planning than its predecessor. It initially denied the existence of Reade's report on the proposed garden suburb and negotiated secretly with the Electrolytic Zinc Company to build a factory and nothing more on the same site.[25] Reade's report was only released after the government reached an agreement with the Zinc Company, which refused to contemplate the alternative site of North-West Bay about twelve miles south of Hobart, where a noxious trade area had been mooted. The STTPA and the Labor opposition condemned the disfigurement of the 'beautiful' Derwent site by 'the possible future smoky atmosphere of factorydom', and exerted pressure on the Zinc Company to ensure 'the scientific planning of the factories' and to develop part of the land as a garden suburb.[26]

More ominously, Lee omitted reference to Reade's town planning bill in the Governor's speech to open Parliament. The STTPA warned Lee that as more local industries were established to take advantage of the recently developed hydroelectric power, as the port developed and as immigration increased after the war, 'the increase in population will be immense'.[27] Without a city plan for the next 20 years, Hobart would 'suffer an aesthetic, economic and hygienic cost, which will be unredeemable except at very great cost'. Many municipalities and 'other public and semi-public bodies' passed resolutions in support of the bill.[28] In October 1916 Lee told the STTPA that, after a town planning bill before the South Australian Parliament had been passed, he would examine it closely and assess if it was appropriate for Tasmania.[29] Flannagan commented that political divisions caused by the conscription referenda during wartime diverted attention from reforms like town planning.[30]

The South Australian bill did not pass, but in August 1917, after further STTPA representations, Lee asked the Engineer-in-Chief of Public Works, Thomas Fowler, to comment on Reade's draft bill.[31] Fowler felt that it was 'not suited for Tasmanian conditions'. Although it was desirable to control the planning of towns, Fowler opposed Reade's 'elaborate and costly' recommendation to establish town planning boards for Hobart and Launceston and a government housing board with separate staffs. Fowler thought town planning should be the responsibility of local councils. This convinced Lee that the proposals were 'too far in advance of public opinion' and that the power of local authorities would make it politically damaging to create 'a new authority with controlling powers over municipalities'.[32] Contrary to the STTPA's view that town planning was 'a doubly necessary corrective of the ravages of war against life, health and refinement', the Lee government regarded town planning as 'a luxury' and shelved Reade's bill.[33]

The STTPA decided to make Reade's bill as widely known and acceptable as possible and to meet with all municipalities to remove 'doubts and misconceptions' that town planning was 'experimental' or was 'admirable only in theory'.[34] The growth of cities must not be left to 'the vagaries of land speculators and others; but must be planned and developed by technical experts' according to the principles of 'scientific planning'. In March 1918 the STTPA formed a committee to suggest amendments, consisting of architects Koch and Bruce Stewart, a solicitor Gilbert Johnstone, a public servant from the Department of Public Works W.R. Nimmo, and Councillor F.M. Young of New Town, a municipality adjoining Hobart. The committee based their amendments on principles endorsed by the Australian Town Planning Conference held in Adelaide in 1917 and attended by Koch, Stewart and the Assistant Secretary for Lands, W.N. Hurst.[35] The main amendment gave responsibility for implementing legislation to local authorities, working with a Town Planning Commission or Commissioner 'acting in an advisory capacity'. The bill granted new powers to local authorities for the 'efficient control of sub-divisions' by stipulating 'the minimum sizes of allotments, the minimum distance between houses and the provision of a reasonable proportion of open spaces in every subdivision of large dimensions'. Although the STTPA had substantially met his major objections, Lee remained unpersuaded that town planning was necessary and did not introduce new legislation.

The Association might have progressed further if it had managed to win the support of the Hobart City Council, but this body also showed little interest in town planning. In March 1919 the STTPA, together with the Institute of Architects and Master Builders Association, professional bodies with an interest in town planning, proposed that no new dwelling built in the suburbs or outside the city business section 'should occupy more than two-thirds of an allotment, or … have a yard space of not less than 600 square feet'.[36] Aldermen dismissed this proposal as 'a town planning theory' and intolerable interference with 'the liberty of the subject', which meant the right of property owners to use their land as they wished. Such entrenched conservative views disillusioned the STTPA and interest in town planning began to decline. Membership dropped to 70 in December 1918 and its work, like all 'movements in the general interest of the city', was 'borne by a few men, who subscribe money and much time, thought and effort'.[37] The last straw was the failure of aldermen to assist the STTPA to prepare 'a plan of the entire city area within a five mile radius of the General Post Office', which would deal with 'purely practical possibilities of improvement and expansion'.[38] In late 1919 the STTPA suspended its activities because, wrote Koch, 'no substantial reforms could be effected … without increased powers being given to the municipalities of the State' and the City Council did not seem to want those powers.[39]

The STTPA was revived in August 1922 when an early member, J.C. McPhee, became Chief Secretary in John Hayes' Nationalist government. McPhee 'pledged' himself to introduce a town planning bill, but it must 'not clash too much with vested interests' or be 'anything too expensive'.[40] Impetus for revival came from the September 1922 decision of the City Council to recognise 'the valuable assistance rendered by the various progress associations' and other associations seeking 'the general improvement of Greater Hobart' and to ask those bodies to report on the needs of their localities.[41] This sign of greater openness by aldermen to outside ideas encouraged town planning advocates and on 4 October their organisation was officially re-established and renamed the Southern Tasmanian Town Planning and Central Progress Association. The change of name was designed to broaden the base of the town planning movement by affiliating with the progress associations that had been formed in all parts of Greater Hobart including Battery Point, Bellerive, Glenorchy, Golf Links, Moonah, Nelson, New Town, North Hobart, Queenborough, Risdon Road, South Hobart and West Hobart.[42] Other affiliates included the Australian Natives Association, the Druids, the Women's Health Association, the Child Welfare Association, the Chamber of Commerce, the Master Builders Association and the Institutes of Architects and Engineers.

The aims of the reconstituted body reflected the eclectic interests of affiliates: 'the promotion of a civic spirit'; 'the improvement of civic architecture, housing and sanitation'; 'the encouragement of the provision of attractive homes at moderate rentals'; and the 'preservation and improvement of existing parks, reserves or playgrounds'.[43] This powerful alignment of pressure groups strengthened the town planning movement and linked it more directly with municipal and urban reform. Significantly, the Mayor of Hobart, Alderman J.A. McKenzie, a builder, became President of the STTPA.[44] For McKenzie, town planning 'did not mean pulling down' the city and 're-erecting it at enormous cost but ... effecting improvements whenever an opportunity occurred'. He expected the STTPA to assist aldermen with suggestions for 'the city's development' and encourage residents to take 'a proper pride in their city'.[45] He singled out control of subdivisions and zoning of areas as important reforms.

More effective legislation remained the key plank. The STTPA drafted new legislation based on the South Australian *Town Planning and Development Act 1920* and adapted to Tasmanian conditions.[46] The draft bill created a Central Advisory Board comprised of architects, engineers, builders and members of associations like the STTPA, who would advise the Minister for Lands and the Government Town Planner. The Government Town Planner would 'plan and design all works on Crown land, such as new towns or extensions'. He would have 'power of final approval' over all subdivisions passed by councils and could compel councils to pass by-laws on town planning lines, although the STTPA executive was divided over whether compulsory clauses would jeopardise the bill's chances.

The bill was presented to McPhee in April 1923.[47] He acknowledged that, as 'a large section of the community' supported town planning, it 'strengthened both his hands and those of the government'. As promised, McPhee submitted the town planning bill but, before it reached the Second Reading stage, his government lost office to the Labor Party led by Joseph Lyons.[48] Town planning was less prominent in the Labor Party in 1923 than it had been a decade earlier. The Lyons government was preoccupied with the disastrous state of State finances and its increasingly tense relations with the Legislative Council.[49]

As Vice-President of the STTPA, McPhee assumed responsibility for generating support for his bill in the Assembly. In December 1924 he moved 'That in the opinion of this House the effective town planning of urban and rural districts is desirable and that Ministers be instructed to bring in a bill to give effect to it'.[50] McPhee argued that Hobart urgently needed town planning because the roads and streets had been built for 'the slow moving traffic' of the past and not for the 'much faster' vehicles of the present, and that public health would be improved by 'the elimination of slums'. Chief Secretary J.A. Guy accepted 'the general principle' that town planning was needed, but thought it would be difficult to gain consensus on the details of new legislation. Already in conflict with the landowners in the Legislative Council, the Labor government knew that contentious legislation proposing to interfere with property rights would be opposed. McPhee's motion was passed near the end of the session, but it was too late to bring in a bill. The Labor government promised to bring in legislation in the next session, but relations with the Legislative Council worsened and nothing appeared. Koch lamented that they had not got 'the ear of the Government' and McKenzie wished that a town planner had been appointed as those employed by the Victorian and South Australian governments had done much 'practical work' in guiding future

[92] *Observer*, 12 January 1918; www.samemory.sa.gov.au/site/page.cfm?u=125&c=1761, accessed 5 July 2007.
[93] Constitution of the League of Loyal Women, 1915, SLSA: SRG 684/1 vol. 1; www.womenaustralia.info/biogs/AWE0988b.htm, accessed 16 July 2007.
[94] Elizabeth Kwan, 'Longmore, Lydia (1874–1967)', *Australian dictionary of biography* (Melbourne: Melbourne University Press, 1986), 10, 140–41; Elizabeth Kwan, 'Halley, Ida Gertrude Margaret (1867–1939)', *Australian dictionary of biography* (Melbourne: Melbourne University Press, 1983), 9, 170–71.
[95] *Register*, 17 September 1913.
[96] N. Hicks and H.N. Mayo, 'Private medicine and public health', unpublished paper, Department of Community Medicine, University of Adelaide, 1986.
[97] www.samemory.sa.gov.au/site/page.cfm?u=125&c=1761, accessed 5 July 2007.
[98] *The Light Journal*, 7.

growth.⁵¹ Throughout the 1920s and 1930s the Labor Party's municipal platform proposed a system of town planning with provision for roads and reserves, but this aim was not pursued with any vigour.⁵²

The failure to secure comprehensive town planning legislation was mainly due to the refusal by landowners, property owners and others to accept any strategic government intervention in the urban development process. This was reinforced by the refusal of the Hobart City Council to transfer this power to an independent commission or commissioner. The STTPA had failed to secure what Davidge called 'the driving force necessary to obtain' legislation from any groundswell of public opinion.⁵³ Hence no attempt was made to introduce town planning legislation again before 1939. Let us see what the STTPA achieved in other areas, beginning with housing and roads.

Housing and roads

In 1915 STTPA Secretary H.D. Flannagan asserted that his organisation put 'the welfare of the oppressed slum dwellers and the less affluent workers before all other considerations'.⁵⁴ It wanted to improve the quality of worker housing and lower the cost of rents by five shillings. STTPA members had been shocked by Reade's claims that housing conditions in Hobart were as bad as those in Sydney and London.⁵⁵ Much of what was achieved in the provision of better housing by government and private investors was not directly attributable to the STTPA, but showed that town planning made some advances in Hobart. The Earle Labor government built seven workingmen's cottages with space for flowers and gardens between 1914 and 1916.⁵⁶ After the war the state government, under the *Homes Act 1919*, and the federal government, under the War Service Homes scheme, built houses in Hobart, which were more sanitary than many workingmen's homes. The City Council built six houses for its employees and eight houses for 'indigent' people. Demand inevitably far exceeded supply after the war, especially for the classes town planners had hoped to serve. The STTPA council reluctantly agreed with

William Cadbury, from the well-known confectionary firm, who told a council meeting in April 1923 that 'the Housing Problem must be solved before they could go very far with town planning'.[57] The STTPA urged the government and the City Council to do more, even to build tenements if necessary, but lack of funds held back large-scale projects until the mid-1930s.[58]

Enduring in isolation, a cottage of solid stone in the Sackville Street vicinity of Hobart's "Wapping" area.

Figure 5.3: Low standard housing, Sackville Street, Wapping. Source: *Tasmanian Mail*, 30 November 1933

More directly drawing upon town principles were the estates developed by private investors. Some STTPA members had 'either influence or interests' in various subdivisions.[59] For example, Gilbert Johnstone had connections with the Co-operative Estates Ltd, which developed the Newlands estate off Augusta Road in the suburb of Lenah Valley in 1918. It was 'most artistically laid out with garden reserves' by P.D. Marshall, 'the landscape expert' and STTPA member. The STTPA praised attempts, not altogether successful, to create garden suburbs in the 1920s by the Zinc Company at Lutana and by Cadbury's at Claremont.[60]

The removal of the numerous insanitary 'architectural atrocities of the past' also fell short of town planning ideals.[61] Aldermen ordered the demolition of some hovels which were beyond repair, but hesitated to go further because poor residents of insanitary housing, unable to pay high rents, would be forced to share houses: health and morals would suffer from overcrowding. Slum removal was attempted once by the City Council, when Wapping near the Hobart wharf was demolished.[62] The Council expected handsome profits from the sale of land for commercial purposes, and made no attempt to rehouse the residents or beautify the area (Figure 5.3).

In one respect the STTPA won municipal approval. Koch had long argued that more space needed to be provided around dwellings and, while waiting for town planning legislation to be passed, drafted new by-laws for the *Hobart Building Act 1923*, which were accepted by the City Council 'with scarcely an alteration'.[63] Koch laid down that land in the middle zone of inner suburbs should have 45 feet frontage and 80 feet depth as 'a minimum' and for the outer zone of suburbs where land was plentiful 50 feet frontage and 100 feet depth, which if implemented would do away with 'slum areas'. Koch knew much more could be done, pointing out in December 1924 that building acts in the 'suburban cities of Melbourne' were 'framed far in advance' of Hobart's.[64]

The STTPA also became concerned about the failure of the City Council to plan for the city's future road needs for residents and businesses alike. One member, William Baillie, complained in September 1923 about the 'congested entrances' into the city and noted that 'the motor traffic on roads is replacing the work done by railways and will continue to do so'.[65] Poorly constructed roads and streets could not cope with heavy motor traffic. More worryingly, new subdivisions in the adjoining suburbs of Sandy Bay and Mount Nelson were being rapidly developed without provision for an arterial road.[66] The STTPA urged the Council to build a high level road on the slopes of Mount Nelson, to widen congested thoroughfares such as Macquarie and Elizabeth Streets, and to prepare 'a complete plan of the road system' of the Greater Hobart area.

This was broadened in 1925 to the call for 'a Civic and Regional Survey of the City of Hobart and environs', which would be essential to 'economic development'.[67] The survey could be undertaken by a commission similar to the Melbourne Metropolitan Town Planning Commission. Encouragingly, the City Council had already combined with the adjoining Glenorchy Municipal Council to prepare a survey plan of 'a new road' from Rosetta to New Town Bay on the western banks of the River Derwent where many acres of land would be subdivided in the future.[68] The Council also began spending substantial amounts of money on road widening, but the task was large.

Parks, reserves and playgrounds

The small change to housing conditions showed that the social reform side of town planning had made limited gains by 1926. The provision and beautification of parks and reserves, persistently advocated by the STTPA, saw greater advances.[69] Park beautification was one way to improve the aesthetic appearance of the city. Most of Hobart's parks and reserves had been terribly neglected until 1913 when the City Council began to levy a rate of not more than one penny in the pound on reserves.[70] In February 1915 the Council appointed L.J. Lipscombe as Superintendent of Reserves. Lipscombe was known throughout the Commonwealth for his horticultural expertise.[71] Within two years, Parliament Reserve, Barrack Square, Long Beach, and Garden Crescent Reserves had all been cleaned up and flowers and shrubs planted. Work had also begun on the university grounds in the Domain, Arthur's Circus in Battery Point, and in Upper Goulburn Street, West Hobart. These successes prompted demands by town planning advocates and others that the City Council assume control of the Queen's Domain from a government appointed committee, and this occurred in January 1918.[72] Once the beautification of the Domain had progressed, support grew to place other neglected government reserves in Lipscombe's care, especially historic Franklin Square. Lipscombe started work on Franklin Square in late 1922 and by August 1923 it began looking like 'a beauty spot'.[73] In 1924 control was formally vested in the Council (Figure 5.4).

Another improvement, suggested by the architectural members of the STTPA, illustrated the opposition faced by town planning enthusiasts. In 1916 the STTPA, inspired by a plan drawn up at Governor Arthur's direction in 1835 and modified by one of its members Bruce Stewart, urged the City Council to beautify with trees, grass and flower beds allotments between Princes Wharf and Castray Esplanade in front of the warehouses on Salamanca Place.[74] Gilbert Johnstone thought the beautified area would give tourists 'a good impression on arriving at the port', 'add to the lungs of the city', and provide 'playing places' for children. In September the government vested its part of the land in the City Council.

Figure 5.4: Franklin Square. Source: Tasmanian Archives and Heritage Office, State Library of Tasmania, PH 30-1-8875

The other part was leased for timber stacking to the Marine Board, which refused to forgo commercially valuable land for beautification. The Master Warden, Thomas Murdoch, was an early STTPA council member, but withdrew, accusing it of making irresponsible suggestions costing fellow citizens much expense.

A Princes Wharf Improvement Association, growing out of the STTPA, was formed in 1918 to secure public support.[75] In June 1918 a petition by leading businessmen supported beautification. Minister of Lands John Hayes declared that 'Though they all wished to beautify the city, when commerce and beauty came into conflict, the former must take precedence'. He urged the businessmen to withdraw their petition. The *Daily Post* praised the businessmen and the Princes Wharf Square Improvement Association for fighting 'for the people and the people's rights, one of which is beauty, space and air'.[76] The *Daily Post* predicted that 'We will have no town planning in Hobart without trouble, and this is the beginning of it – and the first real test'. The businessmen stood firm and the government declared the Princes Wharf Squares a reserve. The City Council agreed to convert the blocks into gardens if the public raised the money. The Princes Wharf Association did and by March 1919 half a block had been 'completely metamorphosed' by Lipscombe (Figure 5.5).[77]

Figure 5.5: The opening of Princes Wharf Squares. Source: *Tasmanian Mail*, 13 March 1919

There was some disagreement over the quality of Lipscombe's work. In March 1923 the *World* newspaper thought that the work of the Municipal Reserves Department met with 'the unqualified approval of citizen's generally'.[78] The parks and reserves of Hobart were now 'things of beauty and a joy to everyone'. One member of the STTPA, P.D. Marshall, disagreed that some of the reserves were 'beautiful' and deprecated 'the lack of good taste' which was 'growing more and more evident in the Reserves Committees of the last decade'.[79] He expected more from the large amount of money spent.

Figure 5.6: The opening of St David's Park. Source: *Tasmanian Mail*, 17 November 1926

While there was debate over the value of the City Council's work on reserves, its attitude to parks certainly deserved criticism. Despite the City Health Officer Dr Gregory Sprott's view that Hobart was 'worse off than any other capital city in the way of open spaces and playgrounds for children', in 1915 aldermen rejected a proposal emanating from the STTPA that one and three-quarter acres of the Wapping site in front of the new railway station be used for reserves because the land was too commercially valuable and the Domain was nearby.[80] Although Alderman Nettlefold thought the idea farsighted, Alderman Lord described the scheme, which involved widening a number of streets to provide easier access to the station and the port and buying businesses for demolition at an estimated cost of between £100,000 and £250,000, as 'too gigantic' while Alderman Meagher dubbed it as too 'theoretical'.

The Council also refused to take over the unsightly disused cemeteries that scarred the landscape and turn them into parks.[81] Disused cemeteries symbolised for some critics the city's backward approach to environmental improvement, revealing it as 'a City of the Dead, incapable of real progress … dominated by the dead hand of the Bad Old Past'.[82] In 1916 the STTPA, in its initial guise, pushed hard for municipal control of disused cemeteries and against the Vacuum Oil Company or any other business erecting buildings on the land.[83] President Gilbert Johnstone wanted the land turned into 'pleasant, open spaces for rest and recreation' for citizens and 'ornaments and attractions to tourists'. Obstacles to municipal control were the uncertain legal position of the titles and the possibility of paying compensation to the various trustees. A public meeting convened by the STTPA voted for municipal control and against compensation.[84]

The City Council negotiated with the trustees of St David's, the largest cemetery near the city centre, but compensation proved a stumbling block. In May 1919, after hearing that the Repatriation Department wanted to build a temporary structure on part of St David's, almost 1000 citizens petitioned aldermen to act.[85] The trustees succumbed to public pressure, agreeing to hand over the land provided the Council paid some compensation and converted the cemetery into 'a place for quiet recreation and an ornament to the city' but not a playground. Parliament sanctioned the agreement and the Council paid £12,000 in compensation and renovation.[86] By 1926 Lipscombe had converted St David's from 'an eyesore into one of the city's most beautiful parks' (Figure 5.6).

The Council gave priority to park beautification over the provision of children's playgrounds, another illustration that the aesthetic side of town planning was more popular than the social in Hobart. In 1917 an STTPA subcommittee on children's playgrounds envisaged publicly equipped playgrounds visited by municipal playmistresses, who would 'direct and stimulate the children in exercises conducive to their amusement and physical well-being'.[87] The Council built recreation grounds in some suburbs but only one playground in Murray Street.[88] Another STTPA campaign in 1924 failed to secure more playgrounds, but this campaign was taken up by the Children's Playground Association in March 1926.[89] The Children's Playground Association, comprised of representatives of progress associations, and the Hobart Rotary Club sought, with municipal help, to acquire, conduct and improve children's playgrounds in all suburbs.[90] This was an example of how some of the STTPA's broad agenda was taken up by narrower campaigning bodies.

The STTPA in decline

In the mid-1920s other campaigns competed with the STTPA for public attention and members and town planning faded from public debate. One competitor was the American-inspired 'Clean up, paint up, and keep it up' Campaign initiated by H.E. Trousselot, Superintendent of the Fire Brigade, in 1924.[91] In part the campaign was designed to clean and beautify Hobart before the tourist season began. Shop windows were dressed up, houses and shops were repainted and repaired, and vacant blocks and backyards were cleared of rubbish. Citizens realised that 'We may not be able at present to remodel our town, but we can certainly brighten it up, make it more attractive and a far nicer place to live in'.[92] The STTPA fully supported the campaign.[93] In February 1924 a Rotary Club was formed in Hobart and members of the STTPA joined it.[94] Of the many ways Rotarians offered service to the community, the provision of open spaces and playgrounds and the planting of trees and shrubs particularly echoed the aims of the STTPA. From December 1926 businessmen boosters also formed the Hobart Development League to trumpet Hobart as a tourist, sporting and industrial centre and unrivalled port.[95] Some members were also prominent in the STTPA, including McPhee and Koch.

After 1926 the STTPA continued as an association, with McKenzie as President, but held no meetings until 1936 when an attempt to revive it failed. When McKenzie died in 1939, the association finally folded.[96] Progress associations, which had been officially registered at the Town Clerk's office from November 1924, continued to raise some town planning concerns for their local areas to 1939.[97] These concerns included the beautification of their districts, more recreation grounds and improved footpaths, but the associations lacked the city-wide vision that had characterised the STTPA and were satisfied with local, incremental improvements. From 1929 to 1946 Koch was Building Surveyor on the Hobart City Council and in the 1930s, which saw record building construction, did his best to enforce the *Hobart Building Act 1923* he had helped draft, but many areas required 'demolition and reconstruction' on the eve of World War II.[98]

Conclusion

While the STTPA did not achieve all that it intended, it persistently brought town planning ideas to public prominence. The STTPA included among its members politicians and aldermen who pushed the cause in Parliament and in the City Council. Newspapers helped publicise their town planning ideas. Public support began to decline when it appeared that town planning would serve the interests of businessmen and speculators and enhance the professional standing of architects more than benefit urban residents. Decline was reinforced by the failure of the STTPA to achieve many of the objectives of its broad agenda. It sought social and aesthetic changes in Hobart, but in practice aesthetic improvements were easier to achieve because fewer vested interests were threatened by city beautification. Parks and reserves were beautified and disused cemeteries gradually disappeared. The other major change to the urban environment was the demolition of Wapping, but nothing imaginative was done with the site and insanitary housing was still too common. Both state and local governments were not prepared to override the interests of property owners by passing new town planning legislation. Therefore, the STTPA campaign failed fundamentally to change or shape the urban environment, but its members deserve recognition as pioneering grassroots urban activists and educationalists.

References

[1] Stefan Petrow, *Sanatorium of the south? public health and politics in Hobart and Launceston 1875-1914* (Hobart: Tasmanian Historical Research Association, 1995), ch.6.

[2] *Tasmanian News*, 9 January 1901.

[3] Robert Freestone, *Model communities: the Garden City movement in Australia* (Melbourne: Nelson, 1989) and *Designing Australia's cities: culture, commerce and the city beautiful, 1900-1930* (Sydney: UNSW Press, 2007).

[4] Robert Freestone, 'An imperial aspect: the Australasian Town Planning Tour of 1914-15', *Australian Journal of Politics and History*, 44(2), (June 1998): 159-76; *Tasmanian Institute of Architects Minute Book*, 15 June 1914, RAIA (Tasmanian Chapter), Hobart; *Mercury*, 19 March 1915.

[5] Southern Tasmanian Town Planning Association (hereafter STTPA) Annual General Meeting, 11 August 1925, Non State (hereafter NS) 612, Archives Office of Tasmania Hobart (hereafter AOTH).

[6] *Daily Post*, 1 March 1915.

[7] *Mercury*, 19 March 1915.

[8] *Examiner*, 20 April 1915.

[9] *Mercury*, 9, 15 April 1915.

[10] *Daily Post*, 9, 12, 13 April 1915.

[11] *Daily Post*, 9, 12, 13 April 1915.

[12] *Daily Post*, 7 December 1915.

[13] *Daily Post*, 30 April 1915.

[14] *Mercury*, 29 April, 20 September, 6 October 1915.

[15] *Mercury*, 15 October 1915.

[16] *Mercury*, 29 April 1915; *Daily Post*, 30 April 1915.

[17] For example see *Daily Post*, 24 April 1916.

[18] *Mercury*, 31 March 1916.

[19] *Mercury*, 21 July, 15 September 1916.

[20] *Mercury*, 15 September 1916.

[21] *Daily Post*, 19 May 1915, 6 January 1916; *Mercury*, 28 June 1916.

[22] *Mercury*, 21, 24 July 1916.
[23] *Journals and Printed Papers of the Parliament of Tasmania* (hereafter JPPPT), 1916-17, vol. 75, Paper 19, Report by CC Reade on Garden Area and Industrial Suburb for Hobart.
[24] *Mercury*, 21 July 1916.
[25] *Daily Post*, 15, 17 July, 4 August 1916.
[26] *Daily Post*, 13, 14 July 1916, letters by Flannagan, 8 August 1916.
[27] *Mercury*, 24 July 1916.
[28] *Mercury*, 6 September 1916.
[29] *Mercury*, 5 October 1916.
[30] *Mercury*, 21 February 1917, article by Flannagan.
[31] Memo, by Thomas Fowler, 9 August 1917, Premier's Department (hereafter PD) correspondence 1/305/34, AOTH.
[32] *World*, 12 July 1919, letter by Koch.
[33] *Mercury*, 1 September 1917.
[34] Stewart to Premier, 25 January 1918, PD 1/316/34, AOTH; *Mercury*, 5 March 1918.
[35] *Mercury*, 6 December 1918; Chief Secretary's Department correspondence 22/231/38/13, AOTH.
[36] *Mercury*, 31 March 1919, letter by Koch.
[37] *Mercury*, 23 March 1918, letter by Koch.
[38] *Mercury*, 14 November 1919.
[39] *Mercury*, 19 August 1922.
[40] *Mercury*, 19 August, 5 October 1922.
[41] *Mercury*, 19 September 1922.
[42] STTPA, List of Members and Councillors 1922-24 (Hobart: *The Association*, 1924).
[43] *Mercury*, 30 November 1922.
[44] *Mercury*, 22 February 1923; STTPA Council Meeting, 2 February 1923, NS 612, AOTH.
[45] *Mercury*, 5 October 1922.
[46] STTPA Council Meeting, 2 February 1923, NS 612, AOTH.
[47] *Mercury*, 18 April 1923.
[48] *Mercury*, 16 August 1923.
[49] Michael Denholm. 'A study of achievement: the Lyons Labor government, 1923-28 and the career of Joseph Lyons', (BA Hons thesis, University of Tasmania, 1973), 21-24, 44.

50 *Mercury*, 12 December 1924.
51 *Mercury*, 12 August 1925.
52 Labor Party conferences 1926, 1927 and 1934, NS 603/1/35-37, AOTH.
53 W.R. Davidge, 'Town-planning in Australia and New Zealand', *Garden Cities and Town Planning*, 14 (1924): 126.
54 *Daily Post*, 14 September 1915, letter by Flannagan.
55 *Mercury*, 1 October 1919, letter by Rushton.
56 Stefan Petrow, 'Hovels in Hobart: the quality and supply of working class housing, 1880-1942', *Tasmanian Historical Research Association Papers and Proceedings*, 39(4), (December 1992): 170-75.
57 STTPA Council Meeting, 11 April 1923, NS 612, AOTH.
58 STTPA Council Meeting, 9 May 1923, NS 612, AOTH; Petrow 1992, 175.
59 *Mercury*, 23 March 1918, letter by Koch.
60 STTPA Council Meeting, 9 May 1923, NS 612, AOTH; Freestone, Model Communities.
61 *World*, 20 March 1919; Petrow 1992.
62 *Wapping History Group, Down Wapping: Hobart's vanished wapping and old wharf districts* (Hobart: Blubber Head Press, 1988), 143-7; *Mercury*, 23 October 1923, 9 June 1915.
63 STTPA Annual General Meeting, 11 August 1925, NS 612, AOTH.
64 *Mercury*, 6 December 1924, letter by Koch.
65 *Mercury*, 6 September 1923, letter by Baillie.
66 STTPA Council Meetings, 5 March, 13 August 1924, NS 612, AOTH; *Mercury*, 26 March, 18 August 1924.
67 STTPA Council Meeting, 24 March 1925, NS 612, AOTH.
68 STTPA, Annual General Meeting, 15 August 1923; Council Meetings, 21 April, 11 August 1925, NS 612, AOTH.
69 *Mercury*, 23 March 1918, letter by Koch.
70 *Mercury*, 4 March 1913.
71 *Mercury*, 12 June, 14 August, 28 November 1916, 22 July 1929.
72 *Mercury*, 23 January, 5 August, 10 December 1918.
73 *Mercury*, 31 October 1922, 10 August 1923, 23 February 1924.
74 *Mercury*, 20 July, 12 August, 12 September 1916; *Daily Post*, 12 August 1916.
75 *Mercury*, 7 June, 6 December 1918.
76 *Daily Post*, 24 June 1918.
77 *World*, 4 November 1918; *Mercury*, 11 March 1919.
78 *World*, 14 March 1923.

[79] *Mercury*, 12 March, 9 July 1923, letters by P.D. Marshall.
[80] *Mercury*, 9 June 1915; *Daily Post*, 9, 10 June 1915; *Wapping History Group, Down Wapping*, 143–47.
[81] Stefan Petrow, 'God's Neglected Acres: A History of Cemeteries in Tasmania 1803–1990', *Public History Review*, 2 (1993): 144–67.
[82] *Daily Post*, 13 November 1915.
[83] *Mercury*, 11 May, 12 July, 22 September, 7 December 1916, 8 March 1917.
[84] *Mercury*, 24 May 1916.
[85] *Mercury*, 31 May, 3, 5 June 1919.
[86] JPPPT, 1924–25, vol. 91, Paper 29, St George's Burial Ground Hobart Disposal Bill 1924 (Private): Report of Select Committee with Evidence, pp. 39–40; *Mercury*, 3 May 1927, 22 July 1929.
[87] *Mercury*, 8 March 1917.
[88] *Mercury*, 23 May 1923.
[89] STTPA Council Meeting, 9 July 1924, NS 612, AOTH.
[90] *Mercury*, 26 March, 29 April 1926.
[91] The News, 25 August, 11 September 1924; *Mercury*, 12, 23 July 1924.
[92] *Mercury*, 12 July 1924.
[93] STTPA Council Meetings, 9 July, 13 August 1924, NS 612, AOTH.
[94] *Mercury*, 9 October 1924; Hobart Rotary Club Minutes, 1924–34, NS 1103/1–4, AOTH.
[95] *Mercury*, 16 December 1926, 9 February 1927.
[96] *Mercury*, 21 August 1939; *Walch's Tasmanian almanac 1939*, 324; STTPA meeting, 17 February 1936, NS 612, AOTH.
[97] *Mercury*, 25 November 1924; STTPA council meeting, 24 March 1925, NS 612, AOTH.
[98] In 1936 Koch complained that parts of the 1923 amendment had been 'disregarded or overlooked', Koch to Town Clerk, 28 October 1936, Hobart City Council, correspondence Relating to Parliament, Building Act file, MCC 16/37, AOTH; *Mercury*, 4 March 1940.

6
'Let our watchword be "order" and our beacon "beauty"': achieving town planning legislation in Western Australia

Jenny Gregory

In the parliamentary debate preceding the enactment of town planning legislation in Western Australia, credit was given to:

> the members of the Town Planning Association who, while acting in a purely voluntary way, have laboured most earnestly in striving to achieve the betterment of conditions under which we live. Though few in numbers, they have combated apathy and ignorance ... to arouse interest ... in a scheme of approved town planning and to create a civic conscience ... [F]uture generations will look back with feelings of gratitude towards those who first recognised the wisdom of cultivating civic beauty.[1]

This chapter examines the development of town planning in Perth from the earliest years of the 20th century to the enactment of town planning legislation in 1928 and the eventual demise of the Town Planning Association of Western Australia (TPAWA) that had brought it into existence. It builds on the research of earlier writers, though none has fully explored the activities of the TPAWA.[2] The work of the TPAWA was directed toward the enactment of legislation, and to achieve this end it promoted the cause in a variety of ways. It raised public understanding of the need for town planning through lectures and articles, lobbied government departments on specific issues, advised on the improved positioning of street trees and services, urged the creation of parks and playgrounds, and argued for the creation of a civic heart and street widening in the city.

Figure 6.1: W.E. Bold, Town Clerk of Perth. Source: *The Australasian*, 3 October 1903, courtesy Battye Library

Laying the foundations

The need for town planning must be seen in the context of the Western Australian gold rushes of the 1890s. People flooded into Western Australia and between 1890 and 1901 the population of Perth quadrupled to 70,700 and then almost doubled again to 111,400 in 1911. It took time for civic infrastructure to be set in place to cope with such rapid urbanisation. Tent cities had sprung up on the banks of the Swan River to provide shelter for those en route to the rushes, water and sewerage supplies were inadequate or nonexistent, typhoid raged, and public authorities struggled to provide services. The state government, dominated by Sir John Forrest until his departure to the federal scene, set in place a massive program of public works. But at the city level there was little long term planning and the Perth City Council Chamber was said to be 'a place of squalid controversy and a forum for irrational attacks upon struggling staff'.[3]

Western Australia's boom of the 1890s paralleled the depression on Australia's east coast and, as well as gold seekers, an influx of professionals looked for opportunities in Perth. Indeed few of the key individuals that promoted town planning in Perth were born in the state and of the four men who played central roles through the life of the TPAWA – W.E. Bold, W.A. Saw, Harold Boas and Carl Klem – only one was native-born.[4]

Appointed Town Clerk of Perth in 1900, Lancashire-born W.E. 'Billie' Bold (1873–1953) was the central personality (Figure 6.1). Described as a 'toffy-nosed young spark' in his first years with the City, he wore a top hat and morning coat with a stiff, high-collared shirt, and his manner was formal, even unbending. Council matters were in disarray when he was appointed but Bold soon showed the breadth of vision and organisational strengths that would mark his 47-year tenure. Influenced by knowledge of Birmingham's urban reforms of the 1870s, and aiming to increase the efficiency of the city council, Bold was a strong advocate of both municipal socialism and the greater city movement.[5] In 1911 he prepared a town planning report for Perth and two of his proposals – a civic heart for the city and the sinking of the railway – have continued to resonate to the present. There was then little sense of a coherent civic focus in Perth with the main public buildings scattered along the city's major street, St George's Terrace. Bold's proposed solution was to sink the railway, which constrained northwards expansion, and develop a civic centre on a new site to the north.[6] Despite extensive newspaper coverage of these ideas, and the support of the Council, which called for a Royal Commission into Perth's planning in 1913, the proposal sank into oblivion.[7] Nevertheless the level and standard of debate on the governance and future of the city had soared, and in 1914 the Council sent Bold to Europe and the United States to investigate town planning.[8] During his absence Charles Reade, organiser of an Australasian Town Planning tour, visited Perth giving six free illustrated lectures funded by the Council and the state government.[9] These lectures, plus Bold's report on his tour, stimulated further public interest, setting the stage for the emergence of a Town Planning Association, with the Mayor commenting:

> It is not too much to express a hope, if not a determination, that we, with all our advantages, should do all we can to improve our City, and if we cannot excel we should at least attempt to equal other cities in the direction of improvement and advancement ... We are far behind in the work of attaining to the "City Beautiful" or the "City Perfect".[10]

William Saw (1860–1949) was one of those who took up the cause. Born in Perth, and originally a surveyor taking part in several of Sir John Forrest's expeditions, he was Director of Plans and Surveys and Assistant Registrar of Titles from 1893 to 1921. He had also been a local government councillor and an executive member of the state Institute of Surveyors. His brother Dr Athelstan Saw was a member of the WA Legislative Council from 1915 and Chancellor of the University from 1922. William Saw was a pivotal figure in the town planning movement as the first President of the TPAWA, holding that position from 1916 until 1928.[11]

Harold Boas (1883–1980), the third of the major early advocates of town planning in Perth, became honorary secretary of the TPAWA at its foundation (Figure 6.2). He was from a prominent Adelaide Jewish family, and after completing his indentures as an architect, had arrived in Perth in 1905, joining a well-established architectural firm, which became Oldham, Boas and Ednie-Brown. In 1914 he became a Perth City Councillor, a position he held for 20 years. He was also involved in conservative politics, serving on the Executive of the Liberal League of WA before World War I, actively working against the spread of communism during the interwar years, and after World War II campaigning against the Labor Party. He was active in the Jewish community, and had a keen interest in international affairs.[12] Boas was a power house within the town planning movement with strong views, a robust sense of self-worth, and extensive personal networks.

Figure 6.2: Harold Boas, Chairman of the new Town Planning Commission, c.1928. Source: courtesy Battye Library, 1327A

The fourth major advocate for town planning in Perth was Carl Klem (1883–?), who succeeded Boas as Secretary of the TPAWA in 1919. Also from South Australia, he had arrived in Western Australia in 1902. After a period working in the Titles Office, in 1911 he established a practice as a surveyor draughtsman with his brother-in-law surveyor Percy Hope.

177

They designed a number of suburban estates using elements of the garden city concept (including Dalkeith Estate, Victoria Park Station Estate, Mt Lawley No. 3 Estate, Floreat Park and City Beach).[13]

Building on the impact of Bold's report and Reade's visit as well as increasing public interest, the TPAWA was formed on 31 March 1916 at a meeting held in the Perth Town Hall. There were 45 men in attendance, representing local government authorities, the state government, the Chamber of Commerce, and a number of professional and cognate organisations. Bold was initially the driving force having, according to Boas, 'done all the preliminary organising work'.[14] Those present constituted the foundation members of the TPAWA. A council of 20 was elected, with the then Mayor of Perth, Frank Rea, as President. There were five vice-presidents: Bold, Saw, George Temple Poole, Fred Brockman (Surveyor General), and W.B. Hardwick. Boas was elected Honorary Secretary and James D. Sanders, ex-President of the Builders and Contractors Association, became Honorary Treasurer. In total the Council included at least eight architects (Michael Cavanagh, W.J. Forbes, W.A. Nelson, A.R.L. Wright, Boas, Hardwick, Poole, Sanders), three surveyor/draughtsmen (G.M. Nunn, L. Steffanoni and Saw), two engineers (E.H. Gliddon, Professor A. Tomlinson), and six builders (S.B. Alexander, M.L. Lloyd, R.H.B. Downes, W.B. Shaw, R.P. Vincent and J.T. Franklin (the latter two serving terms as lord mayors), as well as Dr Atkinson (Commissioner of Public Health) and politicians R.T. Robinson (Attorney-General) and J.D. Connolly (Member for Perth).[15]

The constitution of the TPAWA drew from the NSW association, Harold Boas writing to the NSWTPA to request copies of their reports. Contact was also maintained with other town planning associations. In 1916 Boas represented both the WA and the SA associations at a Sydney meeting held to discuss setting up a federal council and, although that idea lapsed, he kept in close contact with the TPANSW particularly on planning for the federal capital.[16] The cordiality of relations is well exemplified by a TPANSW resolution, moved by George Taylor, congratulating Boas on 'his patriotic action in sacrificing all his private interests' when he went to the front.[17]

Within less than twelve months of its establishment the TPAWA had attracted 130 individual members and a 'fair proportion' of affiliated local government associations and other public bodies.[18] Over time the TPAWA formed alliances with like-minded organisations, including the Kindergarten Union, the Parents and Teachers Association, the Women's Service Guilds and the National Council of Women.

Although only comparatively small numbers of women were involved in the TPAWA, their influence was disproportionate to their number, for these were well-connected and well-travelled women of considerable drive. All were closely involved in the Women's Service Guilds of WA.[19] Most well known was Edith Cowan (1861–1932), descendant of early Swan River settlers, who had long championed social welfare and women's rights and in 1921 was elected to the West Australian legislature, thus becoming the nation's first female member of parliament.[20] Next was Bessie Rischbieth (1874–1967), Adelaide-born wife of a wealthy wool merchant and a prominent feminist both nationally and internationally (Figure 6.3). Remembered as a woman of indomitable spirit, the driving forces in her life were social reform and the status of women.[21] The title 'Mrs Poole' in the minutes of the TPAWA reveals little of the vivacious and forthright young wife of foundation member George Temple Poole: South Australia-born Daisy Rossi (1879–1974) was a renowned wildflower artist who had studied in Paris and London and was noted for the salons she held for artists, writers and men and women of affairs.[22] Less well travelled, but equally influential were Ethel Joyner (1873–1952), a foundation member of the Kindergarten Union (WA), the Girl Guides in WA and founder of the Little Citizens' League (Figure 6.3); and Ettie Hooton (1875–1960), born in country NSW, inaugural secretary of the WA Parents' and Citizens' Association and an active member of the Australian Labor Federation.[23]

Figure 6.3: Bessie Rischbieth and Ethel Joyner, c.1919. Source: Kindergarten Association of Western Australia Collection, courtesy State Library of WA

Four subcommittees were formed by the nascent TPAWA: Legislative, Publicity, Planning and Vigilance. The latter was an early warning group to report on diverse concerns such as proposed subdivisions, traffic routes, and other public works, disfigurement by 'sky-signs', posters and hoardings, proposed destruction of natural beauty, street planting, and improvement of parks and playgrounds.[24] But the major thrust was the development of town planning legislation and convincing government to put a town planning bill to parliament, a long and frustrating campaign over more than two decades.

Promoting the cause

Publicity was important in spreading the message of town planning and members regularly wrote articles and presented illustrated lectures, most of which were reported in the press. In 1916, for example, Bold addressed the Workers' Educational Association at the university reporting on his tour overseas and promoting Kansas City as an example of a city that 'had been converted from a commonplace town to a veritable paradise' within 20 years through laying out of parks and boulevards. Boas wrote an article for the *West Australian*, peppered with quotable quotations to explain the aims of town planning, including Thomas Mawson's 'it is not the attempt to pull down your city and rebuild it at ruinous expense' and Daniel Burnham's memorable refrain: 'let our watchword be "order" and our beacon "beauty"'. Other members of the TPAWA used business and personal trips interstate and overseas to gather information which they then presented in local public forums. Bessie Rischbieth and Edith Cowan, for example, returning from overseas gave illustrated lectures on Welwyn Garden City and the buildings of Washington DC respectively.[25] In terms of concrete results, gains from the continued promotion of town planning were promising. Perth City Council began to consult the TPAWA on the development of the City Endowment Lands Estate and, in 1921, the university accepted the TPAWA's recommendations for the establishment of a lecture series for engineering students, utilising printed lectures by John Sulman President of the TPANSW, as a text.[26]

There was considerable discussion of detailed planning and surveying issues within the TPAWA. In 1919, for example, members bemoaned the passing of a new *Road and Municipalities Act* that had numerous anomalies detrimental to good planning. They discussed the financial gain to be made from rejecting 'the old checker board system of subdivision', and were gratified that this was gradually being recognised by the Lands Department, local authorities, land agents and private owners of

Fig. 18.

Percentage of park area to city area. The districts showing the smallest are those which have been subdivided by private owners.

Figure 6.4: William Saw's vision for a greater percentage of parks throughout the city. Source: WA Saw, 'Some aspects of town planning', paper read to the Royal Society of Western Australia, 19 November 1918

land. Provision of open space was a concern (Figure 6.4), and the TPAWA also called for at least five per cent of land area to be dedicated as public open space in new subdivisions. In the same year the Surveyor General was congratulated in getting government consent for the declaration of a magnificent frontage of riverside land at Dalkeith as A class reserve. They drew attention to the importance of rounding street corners, lobbied the Minister for Railways for the establishment of an Advisory Board on tramway extension, and suggested that a betterment system be set up under which landowners who benefited financially from tramway extensions pay half the increase in their land value to the government.²⁷

Figure 6.5: Mutilation of trees, Ord Street, West Perth, 1918. Source: WA Saw, 'Some aspects of town planning', paper read to the Royal Society of Western Australia, 19 November 1918

There was also considerable concern about the mutilation of street trees by lopping (Figure 6.5). This was carried out to keep branches clear of electricity and telephone wires. The TPAWA gave advice to local government authorities, the Telephone Department and the Electricity Supply Department regarding the most economical and aesthetically appropriate way to position street trees and power and telephone poles, suggesting that the services should be erected in right-of-ways behind houses.²⁸

In 1925 representatives of the TPAWA attended a Conference of Public Gardeners. There was considerable discussion about the most suitable positions for street trees and the relationship of street trees and light poles, with recognition that some trees obscured street lighting, causing 'much uneasiness and trepidation to lone pedestrians, especially women and children at night'.[29] Joyner and Saw were TPAWA delegates at another conference of Public Gardeners in 1926. The same issues were aired, but this time a plan for the ideal layout of a residential street was drawn up, showing the optimum width of roads and footpaths, and the position of trees and light poles. It was sent to most local government authorities in the state, with a list of the most suitable species of street trees.[30]

One of the major foci of the TPAWA's activities was the impact of inadequate town planning on children. In 1919 Saw delivered a paper to a Child Welfare Conference in Perth drawing attention to the slums of Fremantle and Perth and the lack of parks and children's playgrounds.[31] The TPAWA then established a Joint Playground Committee with the Kindergarten Union and the Parents and Teachers Association in 1921 with Saw as Chair and Rischbieth as Secretary. As a result playground equipment was installed in parks by several organisations and in some schools. This, plus the beautification of school grounds through the establishment of lawns, gardens and the planting of trees, was said to have transformed children at one school from problem students to some of the brightest.[32] The Committee also approached the Minister for Lands and received a sympathetic response to its request that ten acres, rather than the current five, be set aside for new school sites. It then wrote to the Perth City Council seeking a long-term approach, suggesting that the Council levy between a farthing and a penny in the pound to establish and maintain Children's Playgrounds. 'A person paying rent at £60 pa rated at the farthing would pay 1/3 pa, not a very large sum to assist in laying the foundation of good citizenship' they argued, but to no avail.[33]

The city beautiful movement had a significant impact on the thinking of the TPAWA, which had some success in lobbying efforts to improve the appearance of the city in the early 1920s. These ranged from arguing successfully to have the surrounds of railway stations beautified by landscaping, complaining about government departments hiring out prominent sites for advertising and campaigning for the suppression of hoardings, to protesting a proposal to encourage the building of factories between St George's Terrace and the river.[34]

In the prosperous mid- to late-1920s, Perth came under considerable development pressure and efforts to promote town planning were stepped up. In 1927 the *West Australian* carried an article promoting the ideas of the city beautiful movement. 'Experts', including Bold and Klem, forecast a future when Perth would be 'a city of stately buildings and graceful boulevards, with a majestic civic centre, underground railways, and electric barges on the Swan'.[35] The TPAWA was encouraged by the growth in 'civic conscience'. This partly related to the state's coming centenary in 1929 but also to the enactment of greater local government powers for Perth and Fremantle in 1925. The Perth City Council had begun a program of civic improvement. A highway was being built to the City's Endowment Lands at City Beach and sand hills were being levelled for a 'new sea-side resort'. The Public Gardens Board was beautifying Perth's river frontages. A new causeway across the Swan River was on the drawing board and, using the new powers of the Swan River Improvement Scheme, there were moves to align it with Adelaide and St George's Terraces to create a vista from Parliament House to the other side of the river.[36]

The subject of street widening in the city appeared in the TPAWA's discussions from 1920. For many years Perth's narrow streets had exercised the minds of town planners who dreamed of wide tree-lined boulevards. The issue came to the fore when the federal government acquired land for the construction of federal buildings. The demolition of existing buildings provided an excellent opportunity to beautify the city centre. The TPAWA, with the support of a raft of other organisations, petitioned the Commonwealth to preserve 'the whole of the cleared area lying eastward of the new Post Office'.[37] Drawing on a village green version of a European piazza, it proposed that the area become 'an ornamental setting, a green oasis of grass and shade in the heart of the city ... a "place" for public enjoyment and refreshment in the midst of urban aridity'.[38] The Commonwealth's response was mean. The street, by then named Forrest Place, was widened to 90 feet, 60 feet less than requested, leaving an unsatisfactory legacy for the future. The Commonwealth land also fronted Murray and Wellington Streets and, on these frontages, the federal government planned to set back the buildings by fifteen feet. The TPAWA called on Perth City Council to compel adjacent owners to do likewise, but compensation was the stumbling block.[39] The idea of sinking the railway in order to extend Forrest Place northwards as Bold had suggested in 1911 and for which Klem had prepared a plan in 1927 was not taken up (Figure 6.6).

The passage of two acts – *City of Perth Act 1925* and *Fremantle Municipal Act 1925* – had the potential to make a difference. For the first time these councils had the power to declare new streets, widen existing streets, colonnade streets and fix building lines. Perth City Council came up with an ambitious proposal to extend Forrest Place right through the city to St George's Terrace. They held a referendum of ratepayers, but only 8472, of approximately 30,000 ratepayers, bothered voting. Of these, 6546 voted 'no'. The TPAWA despaired, warning that increasing land costs would make redevelopment even more difficult in the future.[40]

Towards legislation

Throughout these years, work had also proceeded on the drafting of a town planning bill, based largely on the Canadian Town Planning Bill that was in turn based on the British Town Planning Act. With Bold playing a central role, it had first been presented to Premier Wilson in 1917, but the government collapsed and interest stagnated.[41] The TPAWA Legislative Sub Committee continued working on the bill. Boas and Bold pushed for schedules from the *South Australian Act* to be added, for the title of the proposed act to be changed to the Town Planning and Development Act, and for a deputation to the new Premier.[42]

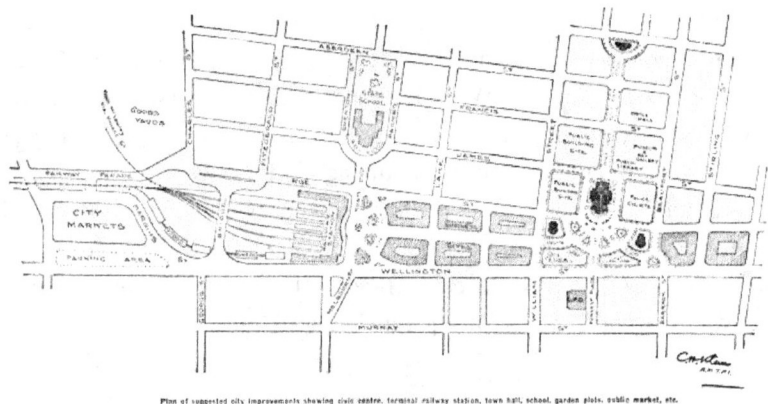

Figure 6.6: Carl Klem's plan for civic improvements including the sinking of the railway. Source: *West Australian*, 9 September 1927, courtesy Battye Library

In due course, a 34-member TPAWA deputation met with Premier Sir James Mitchell on 1 July 1921 to press for the introduction of new legislation. They represented 'practically every public body in Perth', 'ladies' making up a large proportion of the deputation. Saw, as President of the TPAWA, was the spokesman advising the Premier that the bill was based on progressive legislation in Australia, Canada and India and was intended to control 'the future laying out of all urban, suburban and rural lands'. Poole followed up saying that 'the public conscience had been awakened to the necessity for a town planning act'. Bessie Rischbieth, on that occasion representing the Women's Service guilds, then spoke of the need for town planning legislation to provide adequate parks and playgrounds. While the Premier appeared sympathetic, envisaging hundreds of new towns being laid out throughout the state, he did nothing more than promise to consider the proposal and to introduce a bill to Parliament 'as early as possible'.[43] The bill was sent to the Parliamentary Draftsman but there it languished.[44]

In 1923 another deputation met with Premier Mitchell, pressing the point that, despite the agreement of three premiers, the bill had been pigeonholed.[45] The TPAWA continued to gather support for the bill, with the Metropolitan Local Government Association, representing 22 local government authorities, endorsing it with only two minor additions. But, although the new government appeared favourably disposed towards planning, the bill was again shelved in 1925. During the following year, the TPAWA was exasperated to learn that the New Zealand government had passed town planning legislation:

> For ten successive years your Council has had to report the failure of the Government in power to recognise the importance of Town Planning to the community, and the necessity for a *Town Planning Act*, and this year is no exception. Premiers come and go, and while in Office make Town Planners verbal promises, but do not honour them. However, the day must surely come when a Premier possessed of "more wisdom and understanding" than his predecessors, will recognise the folly of further procrastination.[46]

Meanwhile, there had been moves to develop a town plan that would encompass the whole of the metropolitan area. In 1925 the Perth City Council had appointed a subcommittee to consider a Civic Development Scheme, inviting Saw as President of the TPAWA to attend. It was decided that it should cover the complete metropolitan area and a deputation met with the Minister for Works to urge the appointment of a Commission to prepare the scheme. Nothing happened initially despite urging from Perth City Council and the TPAWA. In 1927, however, a bill to establish a Metropolitan Town Planning Commission, based on Victorian legislation, was introduced and passed by both Houses of Parliament without the delays that had delayed the passage of the general planning legislation. At the time the TPAWA was not impressed; 'a grievous error' had been made, the work of a Town Planning Commission is 'futile, a waste of time and money, unless a *Town Planning Act* gives the local Authorities the power to carry out, if they approve, the recommendations and suggestions of the Town Planning Commission'. The experience of Melbourne was cited as a prime example. The Town Planning Commission established there in 1923, and a model for the Perth body, had reportedly still to deliver practical outcomes; 'the same haphazard growth is still going on, creating further problems to solve'.[47]

Three prominent members of the TPAWA – Boas, Saw and Klem – nonetheless accepted appointments as Commissioners of the new Town Planning Commission in April 1928, with Boas as Chairman. There were fifteen members in all (eight representing the Perth City Council, three from other metropolitan local government authorities, three government representatives and the Perth City Council Engineer), all appointed on an honorary basis.[48] The purpose of the Commission directly mirrored the Melbourne body: to report on 'the present condition and tendencies of urban development in the Metropolitan area' and to recommend 'better guidance and control of such development and other [related] varying broad and more detailed matters'.[49] In its three-year life the Commission took evidence on the problems affecting town planning in the metropolitan area and Boas, like Bold a decade earlier, toured Britain, Europe, the United States and North America to investigate town planning and to attend the Conference of the International Federation for Housing and Town Planning in Rome.[50] The Commission's report was submitted to the government at the end of 1930.

The passage of the Town Planning Bill was more tortuous. Although it began wending its way through the parliament at the same time as the bill to establish the Metropolitan Town Planning Commission, it had already been redrafted six times over a twelve-year period and brought before four premiers before going up for its first reading in November 1927. It languished, while attention switched to the bill for the Commission, and was referred to a Select Committee in October 1928.[51] After a month it came back to the parliament to be met by the comment that a new clause must have been 'drafted by an expert clown'. After some further adjustment and the reading of a letter of support from Boas as

Figure 6.7: Carl Klem (right) showing David Davidson the layout of the city the day after the latter's arrival in Perth, 1929. Source: courtesy Battye Library

Chairman of the new Metropolitan Town Planning Commission, the bill was finally passed in December 1928.[52]

In July 1929 the government appointed Sydney planner and former TPANSW President David L. Davidson (Figure 6.7) to the position of Town Planner and in December established a Town Planning Board to advise the Minister for Town Planning on all matters relating to the new *Town Planning Act*. Davidson became Chairman of the Board and the other members were J.M. Tait (Principal Government Architect), J.B. Hawkins (a building contractor), and Saw. The Chairman was paid a salary and members were paid fees. The Board had the responsibility for all land subdivision in the state and became the authority for preparing government town planning schemes.

Little was achieved as a result of either the report of the Commission or the work of the Board – depression, changes in government, lack of interest from both state and local government, and then the outbreak of World War II meant that little action was taken. Boas was probably correct in his belief that the publicity generated by the report helped to bring 'the need for effective modern Town Planning' to the fore and 'paved the way for intensive activity' after the war.[53] Nevertheless there would be bridges to mend before effective town planning could take place.

Changing relationships

In 1931 the City Council established its first Town Planning Committee, comprising Boas and Klem (who had then both completed their work as Commissioners), Bold (still the Town Clerk) and the City Engineer, with Saw, now a Town Planning Board member, attending as an advisor. It was appointed 'to prepare a plan of development of the City' and report on recommendations made by Bold in a new report on a town planning scheme for the City. Bold, Boas and Klem had been working on town planning issues for years and here was their chance to implement their ideas in the city, which at that time stretched beyond the central business district to include suburban residential and industrial areas to the east and a huge swathe of largely undeveloped bushland west to the ocean. The fact that the Town Planning Commissioner would also be working on these issues on a broader scale, and that demarcation lines should be developed, did not seem to occur to them. They set to work in developing parameters for the position of the railway system, considered a key question on which all other features of the plan would depend, instituted ward studies in preparation for the development of sectional street improvement schemes throughout the city, worked on dividing the city into residential, commercial and industrial zones, and establishing building alignment by laws. They decided that ten per cent of the total area of the city should be devoted to open spaces, as Saw had argued years before, and began a program of street tree planting.[54]

Presaging future complications and a dampener to their ambitions, was a message from Davidson, now known as Town Planning Commissioner, advising that 'he would be prepared to furnish a statement in writing as to the lines upon which *he considered* a town planning scheme for the City should be prepared'.[55] One of the problems was that Davidson took a utilitarian approach to planning and wanted to improve basic infrastructure and create stronger building controls, while Bold's long held vision, on which the report was based, was to create a 'city beautiful'.[56]

Relations between the Council Committee and Davidson soon broke down. Davidson, on reading the Committee's interim report, believed that Council was encroaching on the Town Planning Board's powers and wrote to them accordingly. Boas 'strongly resented the tone of [Davidson's] letters', proposing that 'drastic action should be taken in the matter to prevent the Commissioner from indulging in correspondence of a similar nature in the future'. But tempers cooled.[57] In 1933 Davidson attended several of the committee's meetings to discuss the general principles of zoning. The discussion turned to lowering the railway, a key plank in any city beautiful ideal, but Davidson said that it would be too costly, arguing (misguidedly in the light of hindsight) that 'the railway was in the proper position and that the area between the railway and the river would be sufficient for business, commercial and shopping purposes for the next 100 years'.[58]

What of the TPAWA during these years? Its activities had continued at a slower pace during the depression. It began a campaign to develop branch associations with local government authorities throughout the state, mounted an exhibition, and committee members gave public lectures, but economic conditions were beginning to bite. Saw had retired after fourteen years as TPAWA President and in 1930 printed annual reports ceased and some committee members resigned, including Klem who had taken over from Saw as President.[59] There was also considerable disagreement among its members as to its future goals and, as Boas described it, 'a conflict of temperaments and personalities'.[60]

In 1931 a Town Planning Institute (TPI) was established to continue the work of the TPAWA, which was winding down. Its 39 foundation members comprised architects, surveyors and engineers, as well as Davidson and Bold. The indefatigable Boas was its first President and, like him, other members of its executive had also been active in the TPAWA. Essentially the Institute saw itself mainly as a watchdog for it specifically aimed 'to observe the operations of the *Town Planning Act*' and 'to secure amendments' if necessary. It differed from the TPA in several respects. It had more in common with professional organisations, in that it represented the views of the three professional occupations most closely involved in town planning and there was only one woman in its membership. While in the forefront of the move toward the professionalisation of planning nationally, the initiative could not be sustained and in 1936 according to Boas' memoirs, 'disrupting influences ... killed all enthusiasm of its members and the Institute ceased to exist'.[61]

Some seven years after the enactment of Western Australia's pioneering town planning legislation, its inadequacies had become clear and disagreements between the City and the Town Planning Board were frequent. In 1935, for example, the City's Town Planning Committee submitted a Zoning Scheme to the Board, but they disagreed on whether zoning should be implemented by scheme or by by-law and it was abandoned.[62] Boas, as Chairman of a committee set up to prepare a town planning scheme for the City of Perth, had pointed to its 'experimental nature'.[63] The key issue preventing local government authorities from establishing town planning schemes, as provided for under the legislation, revolved around the likelihood that building and land owners would sue local governments for compensation if they instituted a scheme that adversely impacted on their property. Hence the City of Perth, amongst other local government authorities, baulked at establishing a town planning scheme and instead tried to achieve improvement in a piecemeal fashion by creating by-laws and regulations.[64]

But the City lost credibility when its shortcomings were well and truly aired in a sensational 1938 parliamentary Royal Commission into its administration.[65] Tom Stannage has suggested that Bold, 'in pursuing his City Beautiful ideals … had become a little careless in his administration of the central city'.[66] But witness statements to the Commission revealed a serious political challenge to the City through an attack on Boas (then Chair of the City's Town Planning Committee, and ex Chairman of the Town Planning Commission) by Davidson (the Town Planning Commissioner). He alleged that Boas had used his influence to get plans that did not meet Council by-laws approved by the City Council. Davidson, reputed by public servants to be 'secretive and choleric' and judged by Geoffrey Bolton to be 'a forceful administrator handicapped by a cranky temperament'[67] was not circumspect in his opinions, telling the Royal Commission of a serious altercation between him and Boas accompanied by 'expletives' and a threat of violence. Boas said that he was 'the victim of dour Scotch hate'. If there was a winner in the whole sorry affair it was Boas, as there was insufficient evidence to support the suggestions of corruption. If there was a loser it was Davidson, for the town planning and council lobby generally supported Boas. But detailed coverage of evidence in the local newspapers clearly indicates that the politics of town planning were the talk of the town and, that the City's reputation had been tarnished.

The core of the Royal Commission's nineteen detailed recommendations was more stringent building and health by-laws.[68] By the time the Commission reported the City of Perth had already prepared a comprehensive set of draft building by-laws but it lacked the power to promulgate them and the Commission recommended that the *Municipal Corporations Act 1906*, be amended to address this. But the City continued to delay developing a town planning scheme, instead relying on haphazard amendments to its by-laws. Underlying this was continuing legal advice that the City would be liable for 'claims for injurious affection' if a town planning scheme was introduced.[69]

Conclusion

For nearly fifteen years, the TPAWA had been the leading citizens' body in the town planning movement in Perth. In pursuing Burnham's maxim 'Let our watchword be "order" and our beacon "beauty"', the TPAWA had publicised the aims of the town planning movement, drawing attention to exemplars overseas, and created a widespread appetite for town planning in Perth. Its members believed that 'order' would surely flow from legislation. They had also mobilised other interest groups who believed that, through beautification, town planning would be a panacea for many social ills. While the depression dampened their activity, ironically it was largely the passage of town planning legislation – the Association's raison d'être – that spelt the TPAWA's demise. Coupled with this the impact of a state planning commissioner motivated by a different political imperative and believing that real social improvements could only be made through more utilitarian means than those held high by Perth's old planning guard, disturbed the equilibrium. The TPAWA disbanded in 1933. The locus of planning discourse in Perth had shifted from local to state government, but this did not occur without considerable difficulty. The transformation in power relations between city and state that had resulted from the introduction of town planning legislation would continue to be a source of antagonism well into the future.

References

[1] Western Australia Votes and Proceedings (hereafter WAV&P), Second Reading Town Planning and Development, Chief Secretary Hon. J.M. Drew, 11 December 1928; and Hon. J. Nicholson, 14 December 1928.

[2] See R.K. Clark, 'The city beautiful: promise and reality', *The Architect*, 10(2), (June 1969): 40–44; R.K. Clark, 'The Garden City movement and Western Australia', *The Architect*, 10(4), (December 1969): 25–32; C.T. Stannage, People of Perth (Perth: Perth City Council, 1979); Martyn J. Webb, 'Urban expansion,

town improvement and the beginning of town planning in metropolitan Perth', in *Western Landscapes*, ed. Joseph Gentilli (Nedlands: UWA Press, 1979), 359-82; Jenny Gregory, 'The manufacture of middle class suburbia' (PhD thesis, University of Western Australia, 1989); Phil McManus and Oren Yiftachel, 'Early metropolitan planning in Perth, Western Australia', *Planning History*, 13(3), (1991): 5-8; David Hedgcock and Oren Yiftachel (Eds.), *Urban and regional planning in Western Australia: historical and critical perspectives* (Perth: Paradigm Press, 1992); Barrie Melotte, 'Planning in the Perth metropolitan region 1900-1970', in *The twentieth century urban planning experience: proceedings of the Eighth International Planning History Society Conference and Fourth Australian Planning/Urban History Conference*, ed. R. Freestone (Sydney, 1998), 610-15; Geoffrey Bolton and Jenny Gregory, Claremont: A History (Nedlands: University of Western Australia Press, 1999); Stephen Hamnett and Robert Freestone, *The Australian metropolis: a planning history* (Sydney: Allen & Unwin, 2000); Robert Freestone and David Nichols, A 'Particularly Happy' Arrangement?: Idealism, Pragmatism and the Enclosed Open Spaces of Perth Garden Suburbs', *Limina*, 7 (2001): 65-81; Robert Freestone, *Designing Australia's cities: culture, commerce and the city beautiful, 1900-1930* (Sydney: UNSW Press, 2007).

[3] R.E. Robinson, 'W.E. Bold OBE' (MA thesis, Politics, University of Western Australia, 1970), 39.

[4] Harold Boas, 'Evolution of town planning in Western Australia', paper read before the Fourth Australian Planning Congress, 3 September 1956, 7, J.S. Battye Library of WA History (hereafter BL).

[5] W.E. Bold, 'Lecture on municipal socialism' reported in *Morning Herald*, 27 August 1906, Bold Scrapbook 1897-1913, BL; see also Tom Stannage, 'Bold, William Ernest (1873-1953)' *Australian dictionary of biography* (Melbourne: Melbourne University Press, 1979), 7, 335-36.

[6] W.E. Bold, 'Perth improvement', 6 November 1911, BL; see also Freestone, *Designing Australia's cities,* 156-58.

[7] Perth City Council (hereafter PCC), Minutes, 23 June 1913; *West Australian*, 19 July 1913.

[8] *Sunday Times*, 29 January 1914.

[9] Boas, 'Evolution …', 4; and PCC, Minutes, 2 and 16 March 1914.

[10] PCC, Minutes, 15 February 1915.

[11] J.S. Battye (ed.), *The cyclopedia of Western* (Adelaide: Hussey & Gillingham for the Cyclopedia Co., 1912-13) 481-82; Boas, 'Evolution …', 7.

[12] Max Poole, 'Boas, Harold (1883-1980)', *Australian dictionary of biography* (Melbourne: Melbourne University Press, 1993) 13, 207-08.

[13] Clark, 'The Garden City movement and Western Australia', fn 14; J.G. Wilson, 'Mr C.H. Klem, town planning progress', in *Western Australia's centenary 1829-1929* (Perth: Historic Press, 1929), 356.

[14] Boas, 'Evolution …', 5. See also Freestone and Nichols, 65-81.

[15] Town Planning Association of Western Australia (hereafter TPAWA), minutes, inaugural meeting, 31 March 1916, BL 641A/1 MN16; see also Ray Oldham, 'Poole, George Thomas Temple (1856-1934), *Australian dictionary of biography* (Melbourne: Melbourne University Press, 1988), 11, 257-58; Clive Moore, 'Robinson, Robert Thomson (1867-1926), *Australian dictionary of biography* (Melbourne: Melbourne University Press, 1988), 11, 426-27; J.S. Battye, 'James Douglas Sanders', *The cyclopedia of Western Australia* (Adelaide: Hussey & Gillingham, 1912), 659.

[16] See Robert Freestone and Margaret Park, 'The limits to nationalism: moves toward an Australian Town Planning Association, 1913-1917', *Australian Historical Studies*, 40(1), (March 2009), 32-46.

[17] TPAWA Constitution, TPAWA Minutes, 31 March 1916, BL 641A/1 MN16; and Boas to Town Planning Association of New South Wales (TPANSW), letter, 14 June 1916, and SA Town Planning and Improvement Association to TPANSW, letter, 9 Oct 1916, Folder E, July 1916, TPANSW Papers 1916-18, ML MSS 209; and Minutes of Meeting, 11 October, Folder H, 1916; TPANSW Minutes, 13 December 1916, Envelope Dec 1916.

[18] TPAWA Annual Report (TPAWA AR), 1917.

[19] See also Dianne Davidson, *Women on the warpath: feminists of the first wave* (Nedlands: UWA Press, 1997).

[20] Margaret Brown, 'Cowan, Edith Dircksey (1861-1932)', *Australian dictionary of biography* (Melbourne: Melbourne University Press, 1981), 8, 123-24.

[21] Nancy Lutton, 'Rischbieth, Bessie Mabel (1874-1967)', *Australian dictionary of biography* (Melbourne: Melbourne University Press, 1988), 11, 394-96.

[22] Dorothy Erickson, 'Rossi, Daisy Mary (1879-1974)', *Australian dictionary of biography* (Melbourne: Melbourne University Press, 2005), Supplementary Vol., 345-46.

[23] Michal Bosworth, 'Hooton, Harriet (Ettie) (1875-1960)', *Australian dictionary of biography*, (Melbourne: Melbourne University Press, 1996), 14, 488-89.

[24] Boas, 'Evolution …', 5.

[25] TPAWA ARs, 1924 and 1925.

[26] Newspaper cuttings, c. 4 June 1916 with TPAWA Minutes, 31 March 1916; TPAWA ARs, 1919-28.
[27] TPAWA AR, 1919 and 1920.
[28] TPAWA ARs, 1919 and 1920.
[29] TPAWA AR, 1925.
[30] TPAWA AR, 1926.
[31] *West Australian*, 14 November 1919.
[32] Meeting of Children's Playground Sub Committee, TPAWA, 18 May 1922; *West Australian*, 19 June 1922.
[33] TPAWA AR, 1921, 1922, 1923.
[34] TPAWA AR, 1921.
[35] *West Australian*, 28 July 1928, in Klem Scrapbook, BL PR Stack, PR 1389-C/16.
[36] TPAWA ARs, 1927, 1928-29.
[37] Joint Committee of TPA and kindred bodies, 31 January 1923.
[38] *West Australian*, n.d. c. Jan 1923.
[39] TPAWA AR, 1922. See also Freestone, *Designing Australia's cities*, 182-86.
[40] TPAWA AR, 1925, 1926 and 1927.
[41] Newspaper cuttings, 4 June c.1916 with minute papers, 31 March 1916, TPAWA Minutes, 1916-24, BL 641A/1 MN16.
[42] TPAWA Legislative Sub Committee meeting, 8 September 1920, with TPAWA Minutes
[43] *West Australian*, 2 July 1921.
[44] TPAWA AR, 1921.
[45] *West Australian*, 17 July 1924.
[46] TPAWA AR, 1926.
[47] TPAWA AR, 1927.
[48] TPAWA AR, 1928.
[49] Boas, 'Evolution …', 2.
[50] TPAWA ARs, 1928-29.
[51] Town Planning and Development Bill, first reading 16 November 1927, second reading 22 November 1927 the same day as the second reading of the Metropolitan Town Planning Commission Bill. WAV&P, 16 November and 22 November 1927.
[52] WAV&P, 11 December 1928.
[53] Boas, 'Evolution …', 2-3.
[54] PCC Town Planning Committee (hereafter PCCTPC), Minutes, 11 and 18 September, 2, 23, 30 October 1931, 11 September 1931, 27 May 1932.

[55] PCCTPC, 13 November 1931.
[56] Freestone, *Designing Australia's cities*, 79.
[57] PCCTPC, 5 August, 2 September, 14 October 1932.
[58] PCCTPC, 19 May 1933.
[59] TPAWA AR, 1930.
[60] Boas, 'Evolution …', 5.
[61] Ibid.
[62] Boas, 'Evolution …', 8.
[63] Boas, 'Report on a City of Perth Town Planning Scheme', City of Perth, 1 March 1935, 4.
[64] See PCCTPC, 5 June 1947; Lord Mayor's Annual Report, PCC, 1946–47.
[65] Report of the Royal Commission appointed to inquire into the Administration of the Municipal Council of the City of Perth, 1938.
[66] Stannage, 'Bold'.
[67] G.C. Bolton, 'Davidson, David Lomas (1893–1952)', *Australian dictionary of biography*, (Melbourne: Melbourne University Press, 1993), 13, 578.
[68] Report of the Royal Commission.
[69] PCC minutes, 27 May 1938; PCCTPC minutes, 8 February 1940 and 21 January 1941.

Part Two
Critiquing proposals, plans and projects

7
'The kaleidoscope of town planning': planning advocacy in postwar South Australia

Christine Garnaut and Kerrie Round

The South Australian Town Planning and Housing Association (SATPHA) had formed in 1914 primarily to support the endeavours of the state's Government Town Planner Charles Reade but its demise in 1924 was followed by a lengthy period of inertia. Persistent professional criticism of the *Town Planning and Development Act* introduced in 1920 won out and that legislation was repealed in 1929. Its replacement, the *Town Planning Act*, negated most of the efforts of the preceding 15 years; it dealt only, and in an elementary way, with the control of subdivision of land. Thus, from the beginning of the 1930s, South Australia had neither effective legislation nor a vigilant group of involved citizens to monitor development. This chapter explores community and professional efforts in support of town planning through the 1940s to 1960s as background to the formation in 1964 of the Town and Country Planning Association (T&CPA), South Australia's second community-based planning advocacy group. Additionally, it surveys the T&CPA's activities and achievements prior to its dissolution in the mid-1980s.

Returning town planning to the community and political agenda

Despite the absence of a formal organisation to promote town planning in the development of South Australia, some key individuals and organisations were vitally concerned about town planning matters at the end of

World War II. One person in particular, William C.D. Veale, assistant city engineer and surveyor with the Adelaide City Council (ACC) from 1923 and Town Clerk for nineteen years from 1947, had a deep interest.[1] Other professionals shared his disquiet over South Australia's lack of regard for planning in the interwar years and in 1947 the Royal Australian Institute of Architects (RAIA) charged two local architects, Dean W. Berry and Jack Cheesman, with the responsibility of forming a professional town planning body.[2] Veale's credentials and interest in town planning made him the logical choice to assist them. The Town Planning Institute of South Australia (TPISA) was inaugurated in April 1948 with Veale as its founding president.

In its first year the TPISA collaborated with the Commonwealth and state governments and the British Council in organising the South Australian leg of a tour of Australia by Sir Patrick Abercrombie, Professor of Town Planning at University College London and principal author of the County of London Plan (1943), a replanning scheme for London.[3] Abercrombie's itinerary was covered by the local press and his observations on mistakes that Adelaide had made in town planning were keenly reported. His views elaborated upon comments made by another British planner, Clough Williams-Ellis, who had been in Adelaide the previous year. Williams-Ellis described Adelaide's 'sprawling unplanned suburbs' and the lack of adherence to its plan as 'a tragedy'.[4] Media reporting of such overseas expert opinion, together with events like the exhibition 'Re-planning Britain' (Figure 7.1) that was held in conjunction with the Abercrombie tour, assisted in bringing town planning into sharper focus for South Australians.

A significant local outcome of the Abercrombie tour was the introduction of a professional course in planning at the South Australian School of Mines and Industries. Responding to advice from Abercrombie, the TPISA initiated discussions with the School of Mines through its Council member, architect Gavin Walkley, who lectured in architecture at the School. As a consequence the School introduced a Graduate Diploma in Town Planning from February 1949.[5] Association president Veale regarded it as one of the TPISA's 'greatest [early] achievements'.[6]

Figure 7.1: 'Re-planning Britain' exhibition, Adelaide. Source: *The Advertiser* 23 April 1949. Reproduced with permission *The Advertiser*

In the wake of the local success of Abercrombie's visit, in 1950, members of the TPISA persuaded the daily newspaper, *The Advertiser*, to sponsor Professor Denis Winston, Foundation Professor of Town and Country Planning at the University of Sydney, to deliver a series of public lectures in Adelaide. His presentations received substantial press coverage. Winston reinforced Abercrombie's comments and reiterated the need for appropriate town planning measures. As F.W. Symons, Town Clerk of the suburban council of St Peters and a part-time lecturer in town planning at the School of Mines, explained:

> Unless the work of local governing authorities and Government and State bodies responsible for housing, transport and essential services is properly co-ordinated and related to a master plan, the haphazard development of Adelaide will continue as it has in Sydney and Melbourne.[7]

Although the TPISA's main focus was the implementation of effective town planning legislation, its efforts through 1948 had been unsuccessful.[8] Spurred on by the positive response to Winston's lectures, it tried again and in August 1950 organised a deputation of leaders of professional, municipal and community bodies including the Municipal Association, Federal Institute of Architects, Harbors Board and National Fitness Council to meet with Premier Thomas Playford. Deputation members requested that an honorary committee be formed to investigate and report on a new Town Planning Act and on the development and coordinated planning of new areas.[9] The normally parsimonious Playford agreed to the suggestion, which was subsequently approved by Cabinet. The ten-member committee included Veale, C.R. Sutton, President of the Municipal Association and Harold Chalkan Day, who had been a draughtsman in the state's first Town Planning Department and Government Town Planner since 1929. Its key recommendation was the establishment of a planning authority led by a qualified planner.[10]

Meanwhile other concerned individuals were promoting, and educating the public about, town planning. For example, during 1948, architect Andrew Benko and engineer Rex Lloyd presented 24 lectures at the University of Adelaide on the history of, and contemporary issues in, town planning; these were subsequently published as the monograph *Replanning our towns and countryside* (1949).[11] Through the first half of the 1950s South Australian newspapers frequently published citizens' calls for a master plan for Adelaide to provide a vision for the city's future development and to avoid the perils of urban sprawl and traffic congestion increasingly evident elsewhere in Australia. Editorials supported the master plan approach.[12]

Commentators considered that Adelaide had rested too long on its laurels as a planned capital. A strongly worded *Advertiser* editorial referred to statements by A.N. Kemsley, a member of Victoria's Town and Country Planning Board, who argued that Adelaide was 'the most beautiful in the Commonwealth' but 'the "most moribund" of all the Australian capitals' with regard to town planning. Indeed he accused South Australians of 'living on Light's vision for more than a century without doing anything to extend it'[13] (Figure 7.2). But still the government did not act and more than one year later a newspaper columnist lamented:

> The City of Adelaide commemorates this year a strange – and not particularly proud – Jubilee. For 1954 marks the 25th anniversary of the original *Town Planning Act* of 1929. For 25 years, the Government and Parliament of South Australia have explicitly acknowledged the validity of the principle of proper town planning. Yet in all that time, not one worthwhile practical step towards the creation of a master plan for Greater Adelaide, a plan which would last for at least 50 years, has been taken.[14]

Perhaps the persistence and nature of media comment as well as the honorary committee's efforts had an influence on Playford, who had long opposed the formulation of a town plan. He held that 'Adelaide had been planned as a city many years ago and all that could be done now was street widening and other alterations, except with recreation reserves and other safeguards to ensure that the city's growth was not haphazard'.[15] Although he told the 1954 Town Planning Institute Congress in Adelaide that he would not consider town planning until his program for industrialisation was complete,[16] he later supported the preparation of a master plan. Significantly, in 1954, he introduced a bill to amend the *Town Planning Act*.[17]

Figure 7.2: Looking north from Victoria Square along King William Street, Adelaide. Early 1950s photograph. Source: Architecture Museum, University of South Australia, Smith collection S317/7/24

After much acrimony and 'heated scenes in parliament', the bill passed in November 1955.[18] '[U]nique for its brevity and simplicity',[19] it was completely inadequate. Like the 1929 Act, it dealt primarily with the control of land subdivision and did not regulate land use or control growth.[20] It focused only on the metropolitan area, ignoring country regions. One positive, though, was the provision for a Town Planning Committee to prepare a plan to develop the Adelaide metropolitan area. The inaugural Committee chair, Harold Day, was replaced in 1957 by the new Government Town Planner, Stuart Hart. A qualified planner and engineer and a member of the Royal Town Planning Institute, Hart was recruited from Scotland expressly for the job.[21]

However, town planning adherents were not content to leave all the running to the Town Planning Committee. The Royal Geographical Society of South Australia arranged a seminar at which Rolf Jensen, Professor of Architecture at the University of Adelaide, emphasised the inadequacy of existing legislation. The National Council of Women determined to adopt town planning as a major policy.[22] Aware of the impact and consequences of suburban development, three district councils asked the government to amend the legislation to include their areas in the metropolitan master plan.[23] Attendees at a symposium on town planning and recreation held at the University of Adelaide unanimously supported the reservation of a minimum of 3000 acres on the fringes of the metropolitan area to prevent them from being overrun by housing.[24] Hart, who spoke at the symposium, emphasised his committee's advisory role but expressed his concern that the state would go on '"muddling through" and make an awful mess of both our obligation and our opportunity to see that Adelaide has enough reserves in sight for the day when it becomes a city of a million people'.[25]

Meantime the Town Planning Committee was undertaking its careful and extensive investigations into a range of subjects pertaining to the historical and future development of Adelaide and rural South Australia. Its comprehensive *Report on the Metropolitan Area of Adelaide* was tabled in Parliament on 24 October 1962. For almost a year the Report's proposals were neither implemented nor safeguarded: 'It may be months or years before the administration of town planning is properly organised and functioning', bemoaned a 1963 *Advertiser* editorial.[26]

A formal citizens' organisation emerges

During the years of advocacy and action towards raising the profile of town planning there had been a 'quiet "revolution"' and a 'gradual conversion' of a large number of South Australia's community leaders to town planning's ideals.[27] From 1962 the Australian Planning Institute (API), the National Fitness Council, Junior Chambers of Commerce (groups of local businessmen who aimed to protect and advance the professional, manufacturing and commercial interests of their district), the National Council of Women, and many other voluntary groups debated the subject in countless meetings and discussion groups.[28] The time seemed right for the formation of a representative organisation to promote the development of a legislatively backed master plan for Adelaide's metropolitan and rural areas, as well as the reservation of open spaces throughout the state.

Prompted by the release of the Town Planning Committee's report, talks by Albert Simpson, Director of the National Fitness Council, and a town planning study on the provision of a children's playground in its area, the Henley and Grange chamber of the South Australian Junior Chambers of Commerce began agitating for solutions to the lack of local reserves.[29] Don P. March, its president and the coordinator of its Open Spaces Project, led the charge and headed a deputation to the premier asking that the state government acquire more open space.[30] He then chaired the steering committee that, after months of research, developed the framework for what became the Town and Country Planning Association (T&CPA), a name that reflected the committee's admiration for its well-established British counterpart.[31]

In addition 'to bring[ing] together the sociologist, planner, architect and layman to assist the education of the public in matters of planning', the Association had civic improvement in mind since it aimed to 'help in the sensible development of our communities in order that the future habitations will be congenial to overall living'.[32] It also intended to be a vehicle for citizens to have their say on town planning matters,[33] and to 'help those who plan the development of our community to avoid follies which may be thoughtlessly committed in honest pursuit of progress'.[34]

The T&CPA was inaugurated on 26 August 1964, a date chosen to coincide with the API National Congress in Adelaide. The 200 members whom it attracted in its first year were a broad church embracing architects, engineers, sociologists, lawyers, clerics, economists, laymen and planners.

Inaugural business

The T&CPA's initial achievement was to produce an abridged version of the Town Planning Committee's 1962 report. Some 3000 copies were donated to libraries, local government officers and key citizens, with the remainder sold to the public.[35] During an extremely busy first year the Association also held public meetings on planning issues, arranged guest speakers, organised a members' discussion group, led a deputation to the newly elected Attorney-General Don Dunstan to learn his views on town planning procedures, attended joint meetings with the Architectural Research Group at the University of Adelaide, and approached the Adult Education section of the South Australian Education Department and the Workers' Education Association (WEA) requesting that it arrange courses on town planning and on the plan of Adelaide.[36] Not all of the early ventures were successful. Only 100 out of 2000 invitees attended a three-session symposium on 'Maintaining human values in a motorised community', with guest speaker Paul Ritter, Perth City Planner. Lunch-hour meetings for members were discontinued in 1965 because of poor attendances.[37]

The T&CPA took on the role of public advocacy in a major way. Even before its official inauguration, March wrote a letter objecting to *The Advertiser*'s assertion that the inadequacies in planning legislation were 'due to the apathy of the people and their so-called disinterest in the aesthetics of their environment', and promising that the Association was prepared to help 'those people with a sense of responsibility towards Adelaide's future and assist them to take a deep and active interest'.[38] It made one of the very few submissions on the 1962 Plan and its accompanying report.[39] Association members protested against or commented on such matters as the construction of steel pylons to carry electricity wires in the Little Para River valley to Adelaide's north, the siting of Adelaide's proposed Festival Theatre, the incorporation of the Adelaide City Council area into the control of the *Town Planning Act*, city parking stations, removal of coastal sand dunes, and housing development and quarrying on the Adelaide Hills' face, the capital's scenic backdrop.[40]

"Can I make a suggestion?"

Figure 7.3: 'Can I make a suggestion?' Source: *The Advertiser* 4 October 1967. Reproduced with permission Mrs Olga Atchison

Of foremost concern to the T&CPA was the passage of planning and development legislation to replace the existing Act and to establish a planning authority with responsibility for guiding the development of the city and its environs. The Association stressed the need for such a body to have powers 'not only of planning but also of implementation' and within those powers have planning control over such authorities as the Highways Department, Electricity Trust and also the *Building Act*'[41] (Figure

7.3). Not surprisingly, then, when the Town Planning and Development Bill was eventually introduced in early 1966 the Association described it as potentially 'the beginning of a new era for the state' and the moment when 'the kaleidoscope of town planning ... [was] well and truly shaken'.[42]

But the bill was not received as favourably in some quarters and a range of amendments was put to Parliament; the T&CPA perceived that these were forwarded either 'to improve ... [the] legislation or to nullify clauses which certain groups considered to be impractical or detrimental to certain interests'.[43] Alarmed in particular at the potential effect of proposed Legislative Council amendments including appointing representatives of groups such as the Real Estate Institute to the proposed planning authority, with the University of Adelaide's Department of Adult Education, directed by Jim Warburton, and the WEA, the T&CPA organised a public meeting in March 1967 to highlight and debate the amendments. Success followed the well-attended meeting as most of the amendments were defeated. The *Planning and Development Act* was passed on 13 April 1967 despite 'opposition, misrepresentation, exaggeration and chicanery'.[44] With the establishment of a State Planning Authority, 'the ability to guide the future development of South Australia, to remedy the errors of the past and to ameliorate the shortcomings of the present' was incorporated into legislation.[45] The T&CPA had lent significant support to the achievement of this long-sought reform.

Advancing the profile of planning

The T&CPA organised guest speakers from a variety of backgrounds to address its meetings through the 1960s. Politicians, architects, planners and civil servants lectured on a broad spectrum of topics, from the proposed planning legislation to planning overseas and recreation and leisure spaces (Table 7.1). Soon after the passage of the new planning act, the Association helped the Jaycees in Whyalla, a regional town on Spencer Gulf, to organise the seminar, 'Planning South Australia under the new *Planning & Development Act*.[46] Also in 1967 it participated in the symposium 'Outrage', organised by the South Australian Chapter of the RAIA and held in conjunction with a photographic exhibition entitled 'Australian outrage' that documented the results of 'unchecked despoliation of Australian cities'. A direct outcome of the symposium was moves towards the formation of the Civic Trust of South Australia (established 1969),[47] an endeavour assisted by several T&CPA members.

Table 7.1: South Australian Town and Country Planning Association: public lectures and events 1964–69

Date	Topic	Speaker/Co-coordinator
August 1964	Plan SA Now	Les Perrott Jnr, President, Victorian Division, API
October 1964	Blight on the City	Harry Parsons, Senior Lecturer Planning, SAIT
November 1964	The Adelaide sprawl – to be or not to be?	Not recorded
April 1965	The conversion of Rundle Street	Architectural Research Group, University of Adelaide
September 1965	Maintaining human values in a motorised community	Paul Ritter, Town Planner, Perth
October 1965	Why bother?	Lance Milne
February 1966	The Planning and Development Bill 1966	The Hon. D.A. Dunstan, Attorney-General
April 1966	On the Planning and Development Bill, 1966	Panel
June 1966	Commented on the problems to be overcome by the Planning and Development Bill, and replied to questions on the principles involved	Dr F.W. Ledgar, town planning expert, Melbourne
September 1966	Planning SA – a look back and a look forward	Stuart B. Hart, Government Town Planner, Chairman, SA Town Planning Committee

Date	Topic	Speaker/Co-coordinator
March 1967	Trees and landscape Beaches and foreshores Public transport Slum clearance and urban renewal	J. Symons, Highways Department of South Australia F.D.W. van Zyl, Faculty of Architecture and Town Planning, University of Adelaide P. Keal, Public Transport Planner, Municipal Tramways Trust P.B.G. Hall, Senior Planning Officer, State Planning Office
May 1967	Planning South Australia under the new Planning and Development Act	Whyalla Jaycees
May 1967	Planning and Development in South Australia under the new Act	The Hon. D.A. Dunstan, Attorney-General
July 1967	What does planning mean in other countries?	Neil F. Wallman, Planner, P.G. Pak Poy and Associates
November 1967	All dressed up and nowhere to go?	Albert Simpson, Director, National Fitness Council Noel Lothian, Director, Adelaide Botanic Gardens; Federal President, Australian Parks and Gardens Institute
November 1968	MATS and the future development of Adelaide	DAE
February 1969	The MATS plan – effect and alternatives	Dr John Coulter
November 1969	The scope for federal action in environmental planning	Chris J. Hurford MHR

*API: Australian Planning Institute; SAIT: South Australian Institute of Technology; DAE: Department of Adult Education, University of Adelaide
Source: *Plan SA* 1964–69

In recognition of its educative role, the T&CPA was allotted space in the exhibition 'Towards a Better Environment' which coincided with the

API's Jubilee Conference held in Adelaide in 1967.[48] The other principal organisations involved locally in introducing or furthering the town planning cause – the Municipal and Local Government Organisation, Jaycees of SA (Junior Chambers of Commerce), Mount Lofty Ranges Association, the National Trust, the National Fitness Council and the Australian Conservation Council – also participated.

Shifting directions

In parallel with organising talks, symposiums and exhibitions, T&CPA members maintained their advocacy and lobbying roles, writing to newspapers and meeting with the appropriate ministers on matters including Hills' face quarrying, sand-dune mining, natural scrub conservation, nature reserves and land subdivision.[49] While it had shown concern for the natural environment from its inauguration, and in its second newsletter held that 'Natural scenery is a heritage which must be preserved as a tranquiliser against our garish 20th Century environment',[50] the Association's initial motivation had been to secure effective town planning legislation and an overarching body to control indiscriminate development. With that objective secured and as its public lecture program through the 1970s indicates (Table 7.2), the focus gradually shifted from the built to the natural environment. Such a trend reflected the wider societal emphasis in the late 1960s and 1970s on nature conservation and increasing community concern 'about the loss of habitat ... and ... of spaciousness and solitude' in urban areas.[51]

After the passage of the 1967 Act, the T&CPA formed an 'active and enthusiastic' Natural Environment Subcommittee that took on an increasingly dominant role.[52] Its secretary, David Strahle, distributed the first South Australian Conservation Newsletter to conservation-oriented societies throughout the state. The publication covered various topics including protection of reserves, parks and flora, water catchment in the Mount Lofty Ranges, and development of a conservation strategy. With the Department of Adult Education and the Mount Lofty Ranges Association (MLRA), the T&CPA organised a seminar on the Adelaide Hills.[53] In 1969 the Natural Environment Subcommittee opened a Conservation Fighting Fund and in 1970 strengthened its support for the preservation of the Hills' face.[54]

Table 7.2: South Australian Town and Country Planning Association: public lectures and meetings 1970s

Date	Topic	Speaker/coordinator
August 1970	The population crisis – where we stand Tape recording of an address to the 'San Diego Open Forum' (Sierra Club, 2 November 1969)	Dr Paul Ehrlich, Professor of Biology, Stanford University, California
November 1970	Planning and Conservation	Geoff T. Virgo MP
November 1971	Famine, pestilence, war or what? Launch of the SA Division of ZPG	Paul Sharp, Vice President, ZPG
November 1972	A debate on important conservation issues	Norm Foster, MHR for Sturt Ian Wilson, LCL Candidate for Sturt, ZPG representative
November 1972	Future urban transportation	Dr Derrick Scrafton, Director General of Transport Prof. John Bockriss, Professor of Chemistry, Flinders University
December 1973	The philosophy of Monarto Practical aspects of the development of Monarto	The Hon. D.G. Hopgood, Minister Assisting the Premier A.W. Richardson, General Manager, Monarto
December 1973	Redcliffs petrochemical project	Speakers from ICI, Department of Environment and Conservation and Department of Industrial Development

Date	Topic	Speaker/coordinator
November 1974	Alternative technology and the politics of science	David Dixon, author
July 1975	The role of uranium	Sir Philip Baxter, Former Chairman, Australian Atomic Energy Commission Dr John Coulter, Medical Researcher, Conservationist
October 1975	The work of the ACF and current national conservation topics	Dr J.G. Moseley, Director, ACF
November 1978	Public involvement in private development	Stuart Hart, Former Chairman SA State Planning Authority

*ACF: Australian Conservation Foundation; ZPG: Zero Population Growth
Source: *Planning SA 1970-78*

An early manifestation of the T&CPA's refocusing on the environment was its various collaborations with the MLRA. Founded in 1965, this group had similar interests to the T&CPA but concentrated on planning and environmental matters in the Adelaide Hills region. In November 1969 the two bodies wrote a joint letter to the editor of *The Advertiser* on legislation relating to re-subdivision of land and in 1972 made a joint submission objecting to changes in local council planning regulations.[55] In 1974 they combined with the Department of Adult Education and the Australian Conservation Foundation to present a seminar on the Adelaide Hills.[56] Illustrating the extent of overlapping interests, Ron Caldicott, a scientist and active T&CPA member, was also on the MLRA executive in 1970 and that association's president from 1973 to 1975. His wife was MLRA secretary.[57]

Figure 7.4: David Higbed, c.1975. Source: David Higbed

Of course, town planning and conservation concerns frequently coincided. The T&CPA supported the state government's proposal to introduce deposits on bottles and cans and weighed into ongoing community battles against development in the Adelaide Hills. Other matters that aroused the Association's 'interest, approval, ire, criticism or action' included the conversion of Rundle Street, Adelaide's premier shopping street, into a mall; proposals to introduce a buffer zone around an area of scientific interest at Hallett Cove on the mid-south coast; and extensions to the Belair golf course adjacent to a major foothills reservation named National Park. But in a far more environmental vein, the T&CPA forwarded 'an authoritative case for the restriction of uranium use to physical and biomedical research and for medical use only' to the Australian Conservation Foundation.[58]

The Association promoted the work of local conservation organisations, including the Nature Conservation Society of South Australia (established 1963) and the Australian Conservation Foundation, and was among the thirteen conservation bodies that launched the Conservation Council of South Australia (CCSA) in February 1971.[59]

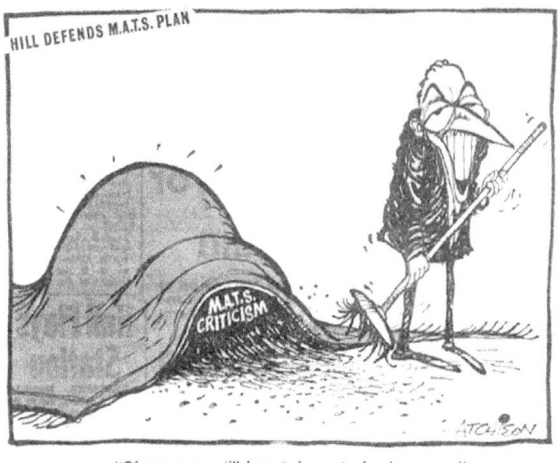

Figure 7.5: 'Of course we still have to iron out a few bumps …'. Source: *The Advertiser* 12 December 1969. Reproduced with permission Mrs Olga Atchison

The perils of population growth were a particular focus for John Coulter and his wife Brenda, David Higbed (Figure 7.4) and Ron Caldicott, who were among the T&CPA's most active members.[60] The Association held a joint meeting with Zero Population Growth in 1972 in which two parliamentarians conducted 'A debate on important conservation issues', and in 1973 the T&CPA made a submission to the National Population Inquiry.[61] Caldicott disagreed with Federal Immigration Minister Al

Grassby's statement 'that curbing Australia's population increase did not seem to warrant priority treatment' and in 1974 wrote to *The Advertiser* on overpopulation and lack of food and resources.[62]

Despite sharpening its conservation stance, the T&CPA's original objectives were not abandoned entirely. From 1968 it focused on the Metropolitan Adelaide Transportation Study (MATS) plan, applying to give evidence to the Metropolitan Transportation Committee on the plan's inadequacies to cope with noise and air pollution and to suggest alternative land-use patterns (Figure 7.5). Extraordinarily, the Association was refused permission to appear before the Committee because none of its concerns was considered relevant. It did, however, submit a lengthy critique—one of 966 received—in which it criticised the timidity of modifications to the *Planning and Development Act* because they did not go far enough. In 1973 it organised a seminar, 'The future of the City of Adelaide' (Figure 7.6), and participated in another on the inner suburbs.[63]

The direction of the monthly newsletter *Plan SA* (later *Planning SA*) definitely altered in the late 1960s as articles on environmental subjects such as the Normanville sand dunes and mining in the Flinders Ranges came to dominate. The change intensified from June 1970 when Caldicott became editor. Caldicott was appointed T&CPA Director of Research in mid-1970 and was the first full-time paid employee in any conservation group in Australia.[64] The position was funded by a benefactor's donation.[65]

Caldicott quickly earned his salary. In his first month he lodged an appeal on behalf of the Association against subdivision of land at Windy Point on the Hills' face; saw the editors of *The Advertiser* and the *News*; arranged to meet with the Labor Party's committee on the environment; and wrote to the Engineering and Water Supply Department (E&WS) on coalescing hills properties and to the premier about Commonwealth road funding.[66]

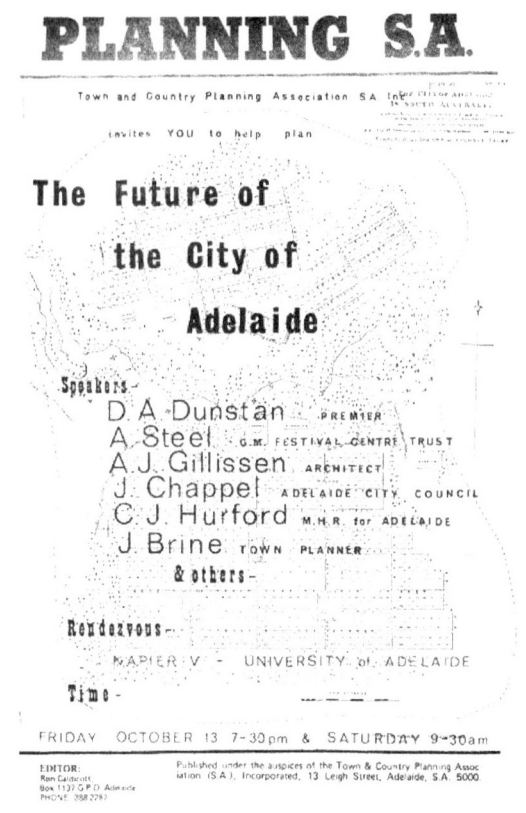

Figure 7.6: 'The future of the City of Adelaide' seminar papers, October 1973. Source: Architecture Museum, University of South Australia, S32S/1/2

The first editorial penned by Caldicott coincided with the T&CPA newsletter absorbing the South Australian Conservation Bulletin. He focused on the problems of industrial waste pollution at Lake Bonney in the state's south-east, and on national parks and wildlife. The issue promoted a forum organised by the South Australian Mountain Activities Federation on 'South Australia, chaos or conservation?' with T&CPA member David Strahle as one of the speakers. Under Caldicott the newsletter adopted a more strident and activist tone, with editorials decrying the effects of 'cancerous economic growth. Its greedy suckers have fastened onto the fabric of our society drawing the life-blood from our communities, creating crime, poverty, anonymity and destroying our precious natural environment'.[67]

Before assuming his paid role with the T&CPA, Caldicott, with then President Higbed and Natural Environment Subcommittee Chair Strahle, had written a number of provocative – in title and content – letters to the editor in the local press. Some of their shots were aimed at the work and composition of the State Planning Authority.[68] These were silenced when Caldicott accepted an appointment to the Authority from July 1971 (until 1979). He joined as a member with 'knowledge of conservation or aesthetics'[69] and was active on a number of its advisory committees.

While retaining some content relating to traditional town planning concerns such as the Adelaide parklands, planning within the City of Adelaide, local government boundaries, and the evolution of recent planning legislation, through the 1970s the newsletter devoted more and more space to environmental matters. Overpopulation, alternative means of transport and, increasingly, the perils of nuclear energy were regular topics. Finally, one member had had enough:

> The reason why I joined this association was that I was interested in town planning; yet, when I have a query or problem in this field I do not seem to be able to enlist the aid of the T&CPA. It seems to me that the T&CPA has become just another conservation organization. If this is the case, it should amalgamate with some other established conservation body. If not, please could this magazine be more orientated to practical planning matters?[70]

The member's plea was close to the heart of the newsletter's new editor Higbed. After lengthy debate the previous year he had succeeded in having the committee agree that 'With the exception of seminars already planned, the future public activities of the Association should involve a much greater emphasis on planning matters as related to the concerns of the SPA [State Planning Authority] and SPO [State Planning Office] and local councils'.[71] Nevertheless, Higbed was a realist. In a nutshell he encapsulated the history of the T&CPA's raison d'être and the rationale for its new course:

> [W]hen the Town and Country Planning Association was first formed, the issues confronting us were, if not uncomplicated, at least plainly seen. They related solely to the urban environment, the planning of the metropolitan area, and the building of a legislative base that would, eventually, enable the principles of enlightened planning to be applied to the whole of the State. But today the 'bricks and bitumen' part, important though it still is, is merely a fraction of the task that faces the concerned and thinking person. Beyond this are vastly greater issues that affect not the comfort, convenience and appearance of our immediate surroundings, but the whole social and economic fabric of our life.[72]

For a while the Association's newsletter did make some effort to highlight traditional town planning matters while not eschewing its environmental leanings. But by the beginning of 1980 the editor could be reached at the Conservation Centre and John Sibly, vice-president of the Nature Conservation Society, president of the CCSA and Caldicott's replacement on the State Planning Authority, was guest writer for an entire issue devoted to environmental matters.[73]

However, in the last issues of *Planning SA* the T&CPA's founding focus regained prominence, perhaps because Albert Simpson, one of its instigators and still Director of the National Fitness Council, became president. The Association proposed a permanent exhibition on town planning to be set up as a South Australian Jubilee 150 project and organised a public meeting on town planning for the future.[74]

But members' interest was clearly waning. Vacancies on the Council remained unfilled. The agenda for the meeting in June 1982 carried the desperate plea:

Would all members of Council please give ideas, or, better still, come up with names for new members of Council for consideration by the next meeting. If EVERYONE NEW was given a job to do, then we would have new members for Council, even if they are unwilling to assume Council membership straight away.[75]

The few remaining T&CPA members, probably now only council members, did not give up and in 1983 made submissions to the government on various reports. In addition to further submissions and attempts to change legislation on mining in national parks, in 1984 members organised seminars on 'The control of vegetation clearance' (with the Environmental Law Association), 'Recreation and planning in the '80s' and 'Parklands under siege?' (with the WEA). They also lobbied the government on amendments to the Planning Act.[76]

Some members became even more active on the CCSA: John Rolls, T&CPA council member since 1977 and long-time secretary, represented the Association, and Betty Fisher, who joined the T&CPA council in 1969, was elected CCSA vice-president in 1983. John Coulter, now a Democrat senator in the federal government, and John Sibly both stood for president of the CCSA that year, perhaps creating a tension that did not help the T&CPA. Any disagreement must have been overcome as in the following year (1984) Coulter was elected CCSA president and Sibly its vice-president.[77]

In 1985, as Rolls' last recorded report to the CCSA indicates, the T&CPA concerned itself with a mix of planning and conservation issues that included the Environmental Impact Statement for the Wasleys to Adelaide Gas Pipeline Looping Project; the Management Plan for the Coorong National Park; advertising hoardings on Commonwealth land; the Supplementary Development Plan for the Renmark Flood Zone; Native Vegetation Clearance Controls; and, in association with the Aurora Action Committee, development within the city of Adelaide. It held two public meetings.[78]

Due to a shortage of volunteers, *Planning SA* had been in abeyance for several months. Interestingly, its final issue was also November 1985, when it included details of the T&CPA's Annual General Meeting and called for volunteers to stand for the committee.[79] The absence of any indication that volunteers were forthcoming, or indeed of any further record of activities, suggests that this was its last gasp.

T&CPA achievements: reflections and observations

The 1960s in South Australia has been described as a decade 'when citizens found a voice [and] more than usual wrote to papers, while others looked for ways of joining forces with like-minded people by forming committees and societies. There was no end to new movements [which included] nature conservation, residents' and planning associations'.[80] The T&CPA fits squarely into this story. But its operations were clearly constrained.

From the start, the T&CPA was plagued with the usual problems of citizen action groups – too few members and a lack of support from those who did join. March found it 'impossible to delegate' his workload 'due to most members of Council not taking an interest in subcommittee work.' He stressed that: 'If we want the Association to function as a worthwhile community organisation, we must speak up and say what we are prepared to do'.[81] When the secretary resigned because of work commitments, no suitable replacement came forward.[82] Some members must have been unhappy with the leadership since March commented: 'Knowing that I cannot please everyone, I have done my best to make this Association a success'.[83] Prominent businessman and committee member Alan Hickinbotham offered a loan to 'temporarily subsidise an overdraft' to fund a secretary. The position was advertised but does not appear to have been filled.[84] Some of the Association's initial fire was dimmed when March resigned from the committee in mid-1967.

The Association was most active and perhaps most focused in its first years when it collaborated closely with Attorney-General Dunstan to ensure passage of the Planning and Development Bill through Parliament. The legislation was 'handicapped by its strong representation of vested interests'[85] from the private and the public sector. Consequently the T&CPA maintained a watching brief, criticising inadequacies of the *Town Planning Act* and perceived shortcomings in the operations of the State Planning Authority.

The T&CPA maintained a public profile. For example, in September 1973 Higbed, Caldicott and Coulter appeared as witnesses at the Royal Commission on Local Government, advocating the dissolution of state governments.[86] Also that month a large number of people responded to a call to 'Bike in for a better city', creating publicity for the re-introduction of bike tracks for metropolitan users. Some of these riders, including T&CPA stalwarts Sibly and Higbed, continued this campaign and helped to form the Bicycle Institute of South Australia.[87] The next year an *Advertiser* editorial praised the Association's views on the development and use of Adelaide's ring of parklands as being 'a sensible and imaginative set of proposals'.[88]

In time, the rise of groups with overlapping or competing interests deterred community participation in the T&CPA. For example, many of the architects who were involved initially with the Association redirected their effort to the Civic Trust, which formed in 1969. The Trust's objects were 'to encourage the creation of buildings, precincts, comprehensive developments and landscapes which our descendants could be proud of'. It hoped to attract 'designers, planners, non-specialists, and institutional members like local councils which administer planning laws and regulations', the very same groups that had joined the T&CPA. Jim Warburton, who had headed the University of Adelaide's Department of Continuing Education (previously the Department of Adult Education) since 1966, was also a committed Civic Trust member. Consequently Warburton's Department, until then a frequent co-convenor with the T&CPA, now arranged seminars on the built environment with the Trust, although it continued to cooperate with the T&CPA on the natural environment.

Town planning topics coordinated by the Department of Continuing Education and the Trust included residential design standards, the planning of tourist resorts, housing in South Australia, the built environment, street trees, protection of the parklands, and outdoor advertising, all original concerns of the T&CPA.[89]

At the same time, other actual and potential T&CPA members, including those who perhaps shared the view of the newsletter correspondent who had expressed frustration at the Association's dominant conservation focus, began to see more advantage in forming or belonging to organisations that were concerned directly with their own residential areas. Such residents' associations had been suggested by Professor Winston during his 1950 visit to Adelaide so that the city could 'protect its special character'.[90] Residents were slow to act, but in 1968, in response to the poor quality of local roads and problems with sewage, the Morialta Residents' Association formed.[91] A spate of such groups then emerged for broadly similar reasons: zoning and land use,[92] general concerns about planning[93] and the MATS Plan that proposed freeways through some Adelaide suburbs.[94]

While the Civic Trust and the residents associations attracted the ordinary members of the T&CPA, members of council were drawn to the CCSA, of which the T&CPA was a founding member. The purpose of this umbrella organisation was the conservation and protection of the environment.[95] Representatives from member groups were elected to the CCSA's executive committee, and the T&CPA certainly provided many of them.

The T&CPA emerged at a time when South Australia was on the cusp of new planning legislation and a new administrative approach to planning. The Association survived the lifetime of each and responded to the opportunities and challenges extended by both. Planning administration changes afoot federally and locally from 1976 affected and ultimately spelt the end of the State Planning Authority. The death knell came in 1979 when Labor was defeated by the Liberal Party, and David Tonkin became premier. As a consequence 'the planning system as expressed by the *Planning and Development Act*'[96] was rebuilt. Hart, who had stepped aside as Director of Planning in 1977, drafted new legislation. The *Planning Act 1982* 'created different administrative bodies to take over the role of the Authority'[97] and, effectively, gave local councils planning responsibilities. There had been considerable stability in the state's planning administration for about eight years after the 1967 Act was introduced but thereafter the climate was one of change and uncertainty. In this milieu it is not surprising that the T&CPA's focus and members strayed.

Conclusion

While all seemed in order in its early years when the T&CPA was being publicly commended and the Association itself expressed 'satisfaction at having achieved much',[98] its later contributions are less easy to define. It was certainly a mouthpiece for a seemingly small cohort and it assisted in bringing built and natural environment issues of contemporary relevance into the public eye. Like the earlier citizens planning advocacy group, SATPHA, the T&CPA endeavoured to arouse a civic consciousness and to encourage the public at large to take an interest in and engage with town planning matters. And as with the SATPHA, the attainment of town planning legislation was a primary T&CPA objective.

The T&CPA achieved its aim to cooperate with similarly aligned groups but in the course of fulfilling that ambition, its broader goals appear to have been adopted and achieved, at least in part, by others. Ultimately then, the history of the South Australian Town and Country Planning Association can be viewed, like 'the kaleidoscope of town planning', as a pattern of rapidly shifting foci and varied, sometimes complex interests that occasionally settled but were invariably shaken by external forces and so took up new forms.

References

1. Robert Thornton, 'Veale, William Charles Douglas (1895-1971)', *Australian dictionary of biography* (Melbourne: Melbourne University Press, 2002), 16, 445-46.
2. J.D. Cheesman to J.D. Storrie, Secretary, RAIA, 17 August 1950. Architecture Museum, Louis Laybourne Smith School of Architecture and Design, University of South Australia (hereafter LLSAM) S209/4/37/20/12-30. W.C.D. Veale, 'Progressive measures in Australia in the field of town planning since the year 1948', 1955, LLSAM S209/4/37/20/16.
3. Director-General, Department of Works to W.T. Haslam, Director of Works, Adelaide, 13 August 1948. National Archives of Australia (hereafter NAA) D156/122.
4. *News*, 5 November 1947.
5. Gavin Walkley, *The Louis Laybourne Smith School of Architecture and Building: a history 1906-1976* (Adelaide: SAIT, 1976).
6. Veale, 'Progressive', 3.
7. *Advertiser*, July 1950.
8. Veale, 'Progressive', 3.
9. *Advertiser*, 12 August 1950.
10. *Advertiser* editorial, 29 January 1953.
11. Andrew Benko and T. Rex Lloyd, *Replanning Our Towns & Countryside* (Adelaide: WEA, 1949).
12. Letters to the editor e.g. *Advertiser*, 28 July 1950, 30 October; 19 November 1952. Editorials e.g. *Advertiser*, 29 January 1953, 25 June 1954; *News*, 22 April, 21 November 1953, 24 June 1954; *Mail*, 31 October 1953; *Sunday Mail*, 14 August 1954.
13. *Advertiser* editorial, 29 January 1953.
14. *Advertiser*, 12 June 1954.
15. No newspaper name (hereafter NNN), 5 December 1953. LLSAM, S209/4/37/20/12-30.
16. Leonie Sandercock, *Property, politics, and urban planning: a history of australian city planning 1890-1990* (New Brunswick, USA: Transaction Publishers, 1990), 2nd edn, 153.
17. NNN, 13, 26 August 1954. LLSAM, S293/16.
18. NNN, 26, 27, 31 August, 4 September, 3, 10 December 1954, 4, 12, 17, 18 November 1955. LLSAM, S293/16.

[19] Veale, 'Progressive', 3.
[20] A.E. Welbourn, *Future town planning administration in South Australia* (Adelaide: Adelaide Division of the Australian Planning Institute, 1962), 21.
[21] NNN, 19 October 1956, LLSAM, S293/16. Alan Hutchings, 'Planning strategies for South Australia: the contribution of Stuart B Hart LFRAPI, State Planner', *Australian Planner*, 32(4), (1995): 199–206.
[22] J.D. Cheesman, handwritten note, 14 August 1957. LLSAM, S209/4/15/9.
[23] NNN, 24 December 1958. LLSAM, S293/16.
[24] *Advertiser*, 28, 30 October 1961.
[25] *Advertiser*, 30 October 1961.
[26] *Advertiser*, 17 October 1963.
[27] Stewart Cockburn, 'Impetus mounts for town plan', [*Advertiser*] 26 November 1964, LLSAM, S293/16.
[28] *Advertiser*, 26 November 1964.
[29] A.E. Simpson, *The national fitness council of South Australia: a history 1939–1976* (Adelaide: Department of Recreation and Sport, 1986), 18–5. D.P. March to Gordon Stephenson, 28 July 1965, State Library of South Australia (SLSA): SRG 299; *Advertiser*, 26 November 1964.
[30] *Advertiser*, 28 August 1963.
[31] Invitation; March to Stephenson, 28 July 1965; March to Sir Frederic J. Osborn, 13 April 1965, SLSA: SRG 299.
[32] NNN, 13 May 1964. LLSAM, S293/16.
[33] Welcome to a meeting, n.d., SLSA: PRG 1366/35/5.
[34] March to Stephenson, 28 July 1965, SLSA: SRG 299; T&CPA, Report for the Year Ending (Report) 30th June, 1965, SLSA: PRG 1366/35/1.
[35] *Advertiser*, 26 November 1964.
[36] *Plan SA*, 1(4), (November 1964); T&CPA, Report 30th June, 1965. March to R.A. Gardner, 4 October 1965, SLSA: SRG 299.
[37] T&CPA, Report 30th June, 1965.
[38] *Advertiser*, 2 July 1964.
[39] Town Planning Committee, *Report on the Metropolitan Area of Adelaide* (Adelaide: Government of South Australia, 1962). *Report on Objections, 8 June 1965*, SLSA: SRG 299.
[40] T&CPA, Report 30th June, 1965; March and K.L. Milne to the Chairman, Festival Hall Site Enquiry Committee, 21 September 1964, SLSA: SRG 229; Letter to the Editor, *Advertiser*, 2 July 1964.
[41] *Plan SA* 4 (November 1964); Membership form, n.d., SLSA: PRG 1366/35/3.

[42] *Plan SA,* 1 and 2 (February and April 1966).
[43] *Planning SA,* 6 (August 1966).
[44] Hon. D.A. Dunstan reported in *Planning SA,* 7 (February/March 1967).
[45] Dunstan, *Planning SA,* 7.
[46] *Planning SA,* 5, 6 (February/March 1979); *Plan SA* 3 (June 1966); 4 (August 1966); *Planning SA,* 2 (April 1966); 8 (April/May 1967); 12 (September/October 1968).
[47] J.W. Warburton, *Sustaining our Heritage: The Civic Trust of South Australia* (Adelaide: The Trust, 1986).
[48] *Planning SA,* 8 (April/May 1967), Supplement.
[49] *Planning SA,* 12 (September/October 1968).
[50] *Planning SA,* 1(2), (September 1964).
[51] Hutchings, 'Planning', 202.
[52] *Planning SA,* 12 (September/October 1968).
[53] D.G. Strahle, Secretary, Natural Environment Committee [T&CPA], 15 April 1968, SLSA: PRG 1366/35/7.
[54] *Planning SA,* 14 (September/October 1969), Supplement; David J. Higbed to Mrs P.K. Beckwith, 16 February 1970, SLSA: PRG 1366/35/7.
[55] c.1972, SLSA: SRG 526.
[56] Strahle, 15 April 1968, SLSA: PRG 1366/35/7; Minutes of Meeting, 4 January 1974, State Records of South Australia (hereafter SRSA): GRG95/1 Box 47.
[57] Letter to the editor, *Advertiser,* 18 November 1969, SRSA: GRG95/1 Box 19.
[58] A short report of activities for the year 1973, SRSA: GRG95/1 Box 47.
[59] *Planning SA,* 14 (September/October 1969), 19 (January/February 1971).
[60] Minutes of Meeting of Council, 5 December 1969, SRSA: GRG95/1 Box 19.
[61] *Planning SA,* 22 (July/August 1971), 28 (July/August 1972), NAA: A446/165.
[62] Letters to the Editor, *Advertiser,* 17 September 1973, 27 March 1974, SRSA: GRG95/1 Box 47.
[63] *Planning SA,* 12 (September/October 1968), 15 (May/June 1970), 20 (March/April 1971), 27 (May/June 1972); Sandercock, *Property,* 170, 174.
[64] *Planning SA,* 18 (November/December 1970); Kerrie Round, conversation with John Coulter, 15 February 2008.
[65] The benefactor was Ken Stirling. See Colin Lawton, 'Stirling, Kenneth George (1935–1973)', *Australian dictionary of biography,* (Melbourne: Melbourne University Press, 2002), 16, 312; *Planning SA,* 56 (February/March 1979).
[66] Minutes of Meeting of Council, 7 August 1970, SRSA: GRG95/1 Box 19.
[67] 'The Great God GNP', *Planning SA,* 17 (September/October 1970).

[68] For example Caldicott called for an enquiry into the SPA's composition, *Advertiser*, 14 July 1970.
[69] Stuart Hart, *The history of the South Australian State Planning Authority 1967-1982* (Adelaide: Government Printer, 1984), 44-47.
[70] *Planning SA*, 50 (June/July[?] 1977).
[71] Minutes of Council Meeting, 23 February 1976, SRSA: GRG95/1 Box 86.
[72] *Planning SA*, 51 (August/September[?] 1977).
[73] *Planning SA*, 61 (February/April 1980).
[74] *Planning SA*, 70 (November 1982).
[75] Minutes of Meeting, 29 June 1982, SLSA: PRG 617/1.
[76] Minutes of Council Meeting, CCSA, 17 February, 18 May 1984, SLSA: PRG 617/3; *Planning SA*, 101 (April 1984), 103, (June 1985[?]).
[77] Minutes of Adjourned AGM, CCSA, 16 December 1983; Minutes of AGM, CCSA, 16 November 1984, SLSA: PRG 617/3.
[78] Minutes of AGM, CCSA, 15 November 1985, SLSA: PRG 1366/36/4 Pt. 3.
[79] *Planning SA*, 106 (November[?] 1985).
[80] Warburton, *Sustaining*, 1.
[81] President's Report – year ended December 1964; March to Council members, 28 April 1965, SLSA: SRG 299.
[82] March to Lance Milne, 9 April 1965, SLSA: SRG 299.
[83] President's Report – year ended December 1964, SLSA: SRG 299.
[84] March to A.D. Hickinbotham, 14 January 1965, SLSA: SRG 299; Minutes of Meeting of Council, 1 September 1966, SRSA: GRG95/1 Box 19.
[85] *Planning SA*, 18 (November/December 1970).
[86] *Advertiser*, 14 September 1973.
[87] www.bisa.asn.au/node/26, accessed 10 November 2008.
[88] *Advertiser*, 4 January 1974.
[89] Warburton, *Sustaining*, 1-6.
[90] *Advertiser*, July 1950.
[91] Federation of Adelaide Metropolitan Residents' Associations (hereafter FAMRA), Annual Report 1972-73, SLSA: SRG 166.
[92] Campbelltown Residents' Association, 1971; Residents' Association of Dulwich, Rose Park and Toorak Gardens, 1972. FAMRA Annual Report 1972-73.
[93] Adelaide Residents' Association, 1972; Greenhill Community Association, 1972; Unley Residents' Society, 1973. FAMRA Annual Report 1972-73.
[94] St Peters Residents' Association, 1971. FAMRA Annual Report 1972-73.

[95] www.ccsa.asn.au/index.php?option=com_content&task=section&id=8&Itemid=143, accessed 8 December 2008.
[96] Hutchings, 'Planning', 205.
[97] Don Hopgood, 'Preface' in Hart, *The history*, v.
[98] *Advertiser*, 26 November 1964; *Planning SA*, 56 (February/March 1979).

8
Visions of the city: town planning and community activism in postwar Perth

Jenny Gregory

By the postwar era numerous flaws had emerged in Western Australia's 1928 town planning legislation that strained the relationship between the state government and the City Council. Underlying this was the emerging dominance of the state as the key player in town planning and the decline of the City's influence. This was made patently obvious when the state government imported Professor Gordon Stephenson to prepare a plan for the metropolitan area in 1955. The plan, however, had deficiencies and not all its consequences were welcomed by the community. Hence a number of single-issue community groups emerged in the 1960s and 1970s to fight against the more controversial elements. While they carried on the tradition of the old TPAWA, it was only after the WA Inc. era of unbridled entrepreneurialism in the 1980s, when developers had been able to manipulate Perth's planning regulations with disastrous results for the amenity of the city, that two more broadly focused community groups formed an informal alliance. They directly mirrored the *modus operandi* of the TPAWA in encouraging public debate over the planning of Perth and, in their determination to create a better city, fought for major changes in the way in which the city was planned.

Postwar town planning and the city

World War II had diverted attention from issues of planning in the city but, in the forward-looking climate of postwar reconstruction, professional interest was again aroused. Harold Boas began to lobby for a regional planning authority for metropolitan Perth and in 1947 the local branch of the Royal Australian Institute of Architects (RAIAWA) set up a special committee to consider reforming the short-lived prewar Town Planning Institute.[1] There was also continuing newspaper debate and public interest was further stimulated by the visits to Perth of the doyen of British planners Sir Patrick Abercrombie in 1948 and the equally influential Sir William Holford in 1951.

In 1951 the McLarty Liberal state government introduced a bill to amend the *Town Planning and Development Act*. David Davidson, the Town Planning Commissioner, was involved in its development but had been seriously ill. The MLA for West Perth and also Perth Lord Mayor Joseph Totterdell, supported the amendments but, believing the Town Planning Board to be 'a dismal failure', was concerned that it was merely an attempt 'to build a superstructure upon a rotten foundation'. He and the City's Town Planning Committee considered that any new town planning authority would have to be 'second to none' before it could be accepted. 'We want to import or obtain the best brains possible'. By inference Davidson was not included in this number. Totterdell was scathing about a draft metropolitan plan that Davidson had prepared, describing it as 'four aerial photographs hung on a wall with a few lines drawn around them'; 'If that is a master plan', he said, 'I will walk from here to Kalgoorlie'. John Tonkin MLA, previously a member of the 1938 Royal Commission and later a Labor premier, wanted the government to engage Abercrombie or Holford to prepare a plan: 'No second rate plan will suit us. We want the best possible plan ... This is a job for an expert'. It seems that, although both Abercrombie and Holford had spoken highly of Davidson's competence, his poor health had had an impact on the framing of the 1951 Bill. It was referred to a Select Committee, later converted into a Royal Commission.[2]

The Commission's report was tabled in the parliament in 1952, just a month after Davidson's death. It recommended that new legislation be developed to abolish the Town Planning Board and set up a new planning authority, with power and finance to deal with the planning needs of the whole state. A highly qualified Chief Planner, working with an Advisory Board, and responsible to the Minister, would direct the authority and have the power to engage consultants as was the practice in Britain.[3]

At the end of 1952, Alastair Hepburn, who had been born and trained in England but had worked as a planner for Brisbane City Council and for Sydney's Cumberland County Council, was appointed Town Planner and Commissioner, and Professor Gordon Stephenson was engaged as Consultant to jointly prepare a plan for the metropolitan area. Stephenson had worked with Abercrombie on the Greater London Plan of 1944, headed up the team that planned its first satellite town Stevenage, and been appointed Professor of Civic Design at the University of Liverpool in 1948.

Although the resulting Stephenson-Hepburn Plan dealt with the whole metropolitan area, the City of Perth was a special focus. At a macro level Stephenson and Hepburn proposed a freeway system to bypass, but also surround, the central area of the city. To achieve this, the wide Mounts Bay on the Swan River at the western entrance to the city centre was filled in for a freeway interchange, amidst great controversy. New parking areas were also created, so that much of city was soon edged with expanses of bitumen. They also proposed that the public transport system be streamlined and modernised and that the railway to the north of the city be reconstructed at a lower level, a long-standing debate in which the old TPAWA had been involved. To solve the city's acute problems they made various recommendations. They suggested a zoning scheme (immediately implemented in a City by-law) to separate industrial, business, civic and cultural areas. In line with this they recommended the consolidation of government offices in several new purpose-built towers, a new City Hall and the demolition of 'antiquated buildings'. They also recommended the establishment of plot ratios. They had no doubt that shopping 'in town' would always be popular and that the city would continue to act as a magnet. Despite their awareness of American trends, they failed to recognise the power of a new counter-force in which the turnover of city stores was decreasing with the success of regional shopping areas.[4] Their plan came into operation in 1963 under the *Metropolitan Region Town Planning Scheme Act*.

Theirs was a modernist vision reflecting the planning ideology of the time, favouring the new over the old, technology over nature, and above all giving the car privileged status. In 1954, of a total metropolitan population of just under 350,000, the inner city housed 29,200 people. This number fell by 60 per cent between 1955 and 1986, while the population of the total metropolitan area grew to 1,050,100. With increased population, increased numbers of cars and an excellent freeway system had come rapid suburbanisation, so that today the metropolitan area stretches for 120 kilometres from north to south along the coast and approximately 30 kilometres from the west coast to the hills in the east. The major features of the Stephenson-Hepburn Plan continue to underpin the planning of metropolitan Perth today even though it was not adopted in its entirety, nor was it wholly successful.

The rise of single-issue community groups

From the 1960s a number of community groups emerged in Perth, in response to the shortcomings of the Stephenson-Hepburn Plan. They were generally single-issue groups formed to deal with a particular issue and then died away once the issue was resolved. If the old TPAWA had still been in existence it may well have been the vehicle to accommodate the issues of planning and transport that arose. Four groups were especially active: the Barracks Defence Council (1961–66), the New Heart for Perth Society (1968–74), the Palace Guards (1973–80) and the Friends of the Railway (1979–83).

Figure 8.1: Barracks Defence Council sticker, c.1966. Source: Courtesy Paul Ritter

The Barracks Defence Council (known as the BDF) was formed to fight Stephenson and Hepburn's proposal to demolish the 1866 convict-built Pensioner Guard Barracks to make way for freeway development and allow Parliament House to provide a more 'fitting climax' to St George's Terrace, the city's most important street (Figure 8.1). The BDF was formed in 1961 as a coalition of the National Trust, the Royal Western Australian Historical Society, the Citizens' Committee for the Defence of Kings Park, the Tree Society, the WA Fellowship of Writers, the Women's Service Guild and the National Council of Women.[5] The issue received huge publicity, but the government went ahead and bulldozed the wings of the building in 1966, leaving only the archway in front of a deep scar that marked the freeway works. Nevertheless, in an historic non-party vote and in response to the campaign mounted by the BDF, in October 1966 the Legislative Assembly rejected the Premier's motion for the removal of the archway.[6] The Barracks Arch still stands today.

The New Heart for Perth Society was formed in response to development proposals associated with investigations into sinking the railway. In 1965 the government commissioned an engineering firm to investigate the feasibility of sinking the railway, which acted as a barrier to the northern expansion of the city. This had been a long-held dream, first proposed as part of a city beautification plan in 1911, and then again in 1929 by the inaugural Town Planning Board, which was keen to use the railway land as a city square.[7] Boas was a great supporter of the proposal and it was also one of the recommendations of the Stephenson-Hepburn Plan. But in 1965 to recoup the high cost it was suggested that the airspace above the railway be leased to developers to build high-rise office blocks.[8] This, however, would block the expansion of Forrest Place, created in the 1920s partly through the lobbying of the TPAWA, as a civic square that was to be the centrepiece of a boulevard running from north to south. In 1968, leading architects and planners founded the New Heart for Perth Society to lobby the government to extend Forrest Place onto the land that would be created above the sunken railway.[9] Costs were too great and the issue gradually faded in the early 1970s.[10] However, after a number of false starts, the plan to sink the railway, first mooted in 1911, was approved in 2009. The massive project that will finally enable northward expansion of the city and potentially provide 'a new heart' for Perth will be funded by Commonwealth and State governments on a 50:50 basis and is expected to be completed by 2012.[11]

The Palace Guards was formed in 1973 to save the Palace Hotel, situated in the heart of the city on St George's Terrace (Figure 8.2). It had had been built in 1895, the heyday of the Western Australian goldrush, and was considered to be one of the last of the High Victorian hotels in Australia and one of the most important of the remaining buildings that evoked the scale and character of prewar St George's Terrace. In 1972 it had been sold to the Commonwealth Bank, which planned to demolish it and build a high-rise office tower. The Palace Guards claiming to represent 23,000 people held a series of protest meetings in collaboration with the National Trust. These culminated in the activist Building Labourers Federation (BLF) imposing a 'green ban' on demolition and national lobbying to save the hotel. Such views were of no consequence to Stephenson, who came out against the preservation of the Palace Hotel: 'A building should have a function if it is to survive. The Palace must continue to be a hotel. Because of the site value ... the Palace cannot remain as it is – a charming but relatively small hotel.'[12] No one should have been surprised by his view. His 1955 plan for Perth recommended cutting a swathe through Perth's 'antiquated buildings'. However the federal government's Hope Committee then investigating the heritage of the nation responded favourably to submissions from the Palace Guards and the BLF, castigating the bank for their plans to demolish the Palace.[13] The bank then sold the hotel to the Bond Corporation in 1978. Entrepreneur Alan Bond, who was later disgraced and gaoled but was one of the key players in 1980s Perth, agreed to save the facade and front rooms of the hotel in return for a bonus plot ratio to enable him to build the 50-storey office tower that stands on the site today.[14] Over seven years of controversy the Palace Guards remained stalwart, but their opposition fell away when compromise seemed the only alternative.

The Friends of the Railway, a subgroup of Friends of the Earth, was formed in 1979 when a government-commissioned study recommended that the twelve-mile rail line between the city centre and the port of Fremantle be replaced by busways, because of the high cost of electrifying the trains. This was in line with Stephenson-Hepburn Plan's emphasis on motor transport and freeways and Sir Charles Court's Liberal/National Party state government, ignoring the oil crisis of the early 1970s, accepted the study. Despite a petition of 120,000 signatures calling on the government to save the Perth-Fremantle line, a newspaper poll showing that 82 per cent of metropolitan voters were against its closure, and protests from local government authorities along its route, it was closed in late 1979. With continued pressure from the Friends of the Railway, the preparation of a number of scientific reports showing the importance of rail over bus transport, and a change of government, the line was reopened in 1983 by the Burke Labor government.[15]

Figure 8.2: St George's Terrace, Perth, 1954. The Palace Hotel is on the left. Source: Frank Hurley Collection, National Library of Australia

Despite the successes of these single-issue groups, two other community organisations have had a much greater impact on Perth's town planning overall and over a longer term. Their remit has been considerably broader, picking up on the ideals of the old TPAWA, albeit with a late-20th-century twist. The right-leaning Civic Affairs Committee of the Perth Chamber of Commerce, which was established in 1967 and tended to be aligned with the Liberal Party, continued to have influence (through various changes in name) until its demise in 2004. The more left-leaning non-politically-aligned City Vision, established in 1987, continues to take an active role in civic affairs.

The Civic Affairs Committee

The Civic Affairs Committee was formed in 1967 because of the Chamber of Commerce's concern with developments in the City Council and the decisions other public authorities were making on various matters that might have a profound effect on the private sector. The extant records of the Committee are patchy.[16] But during the 1970s and 1980s, for example, it was chaired by individuals such as builder and developer Syd Corser, manufacturer R.L. Finch, architect Mervyn Parry and later his architectural partner Ken Rosenthal, realtor Geoff Russell, and Martyn Webb, Foundation Professor of Geography at the University of Western Australia (UWA).[17] Webb was a significant figure throughout the history of the Committee. An Oxford graduate he had arrived in Perth in 1964 at the beginning of the mining boom. Fiercely proactive on a range of issues, including the rights of the individual, and a forceful spokesman, he lobbied government hard on the planning and development of Perth as a state capital. Other members of the Committee represented a wide cross section of informed commercial, professional and academic opinion and included engineers, architects, real estate agents, lawyers, accountants and retailers, all operating at the highest level of their companies.

The Committee was very active in the 1970s, making submissions to inquiries and royal commissions, and meeting with a who's who of planning and development in Perth, including the veteran Harold Boas. Its members were well aware of the Committee's lineage. Its core goal was to maintain a strong and viable city centre. To this end it researched a raft of policies on city parking, the desirability of a city mall, the future of the Barracks Arch, public transport coordination, parking, city council affairs and planning (including zoning by-laws), fountains and city beautification (including the river frontage), a city council hall, the development of a cultural centre, urban land prices and housing policy and the sinking of the railway. The Committee also highlighted public dissatisfaction with the state of town planning procedures, arguing that there was 'widespread and insistent demand for a change from the present situation whereby appeals against planning decisions amount to a judgement on Caesar by Caesar'. Its success in generating public discussion about town planning is indicated by a weekend symposium at UWA held in 1972 to discuss the City's newly released and much delayed planning proposals (Figures 8.3 and 8.4). It was attended by more than 130 delegates drawn from the business community, the professions and academia.[18] The Committee continued to take a very strong public stance when key issues arose, changing its name to reflect these issues so that it became known as the CBD Committee in the late 1980s and 1990s, and then the Capital City Committee until about 2004.

Figure 8.3: At the symposium organised by Professor Martyn Webb and the Civic Affairs Committee at the University of Western Australia, September 1972. Source: WA Chamber of Commerce and Industry

Perth in the 1980s is associated with the activities of 'WA Inc.', the label given to the failings of the Labor governments of those years, particularly under Premier Brian Burke. He and his colleagues attempted to break free of reliance on traditional sources of government revenue by buying into private companies and making financial demands on government trading enterprises. Financial links between big business and the Labor

Figure 8.4: Members of the Civic Affairs Committee after the 1972 symposium at the University of Western Australia. Left to right economist Professor Alex Kerr, architects Bill Fitzhardinge, Michael Fitzhardinge, David Kranz, and others. Source: WA Chamber of Commerce and Industry

Party, including privileges and property deals for favoured entrepreneurs, lay at the heart of many of these activities.[19]

Perth became a battleground of competing interests, with the City Council tussling with developers in order to apply consistent policies to the city's planning, and developers courting both the City Council and the state government. Any semblance of coherent planning policy was destroyed by the activities of WA Inc. in government and allegations of corruption in the Perth City Council. The impact of this climate of rampant entrepreneurialism on the city's development is illustrated by the changes to St George's Terrace in the 1980s, when it became a windswept canyon of concrete, steel and glass, with a dramatically altered scale and only a few remnants to recall the gracious European-style boulevard of earlier years.

In 1987 the Burke Labor government released a new draft State Planning Act. Under the draft act, the state government would gain significantly more power: the State Planning Commission (established in 1985) would be able to override local government town planning schemes and the status of the City's representative on the Commission – the Lord Mayor – was to be reduced from full member to associate member.[20] The City Council was outraged, realising, like other local government authorities, that the attack on the City was part of a drive to centralise planning powers. Voicing a further level of discontent were local residents' groups in Perth. Argued one: 'we are concerned that if an unelected government body were to administer the planning powers currently held by the Perth City Council (PCC) it will remove even further any meaningful influence the city's electors can have on their city'.[21] The issue was seen as a 'clash of the powerhouses' – Parliament House and Council House – and it was in this climate that City Vision, a voluntary group comprised mainly of planners, architects and geographers, emerged in 1987.[22]

The emergence of City Vision

City Vision had far-reaching and visionary aims, for its members sought to develop a city of spirit and vitality – a city for people. Its antecedents were made clear when Stephenson, still considered the guru of Perth's planning in the late 1980s, wrote to City Vision's founder Bill Warnock, 'Many years ago Harold Boas and I talked about re-establishing the defunct Town Planning Association … Nothing came of it. Now you have got going with City Vision, keep going.'[23] In a further letter he wrote 'there ought to be one voluntary association of people keenly interested in planning issues, rather than groups that come and go (e.g. The New Heart for Perth Society … etc).'[24]

Warnock's 'quest for the Good City was a moral pursuit'.[25] An inner city dweller, he was influenced by the writings of Lewis Mumford and Jane Jacobs and the work of architect Richard Rogers and his personal archives show a keen interest in urbanism at an international level. Scottish-born, he had emigrated to Australia with his family in his early teens, gained a BA in English from UWA, and had an extremely successful career in advertising. Retiring in 1975 at the age of only 41, he devoted much of his life to the arts and, until his death in 2001, was passionately involved in City Vision.[26] In 1987 Warnock discussed his concerns about the decline of the city and particularly the loss of inner city population with Ian Alexander, and the two invited like-minded colleagues, mainly architects, town planners, geographers, and planners, to a meeting.[27]

Alexander had long been involved in city planning. Originally a geographer whose master's thesis on Perth was published as *The city centre: patterns and problems,* he began his engagement with the city and its planning in the early 1970s. Even then he was a sharp critic of the City Council, writing that the city was 'bowing to the short term interests of those wishing to use the redevelopment process purely as a vehicle for profit'.[28] This was in the context of a new City Planning Scheme that introduced a new bonus plot scheme, whose unintended consequences were to dramatically alter the face of the city. Perth City Council believed it could control the nature of city development through strict limits to the permissible plot ratio, but it permitted increasingly high-rise buildings to be constructed along St George's Terrace, accentuating the wind tunnel effect of one of the windiest cities in the world.

During his term as a City Councillor between 1982 and 1985, Alexander intimated on a number of occasions that some councillors were corrupt, but after his election to State Parliament in mid-1987, he went public.[29] His allegations resulted in an inquiry which found no evidence of actual corruption but recommended a review of the *Local Government Act* and a reconsideration of the way planning decisions were made in the City of Perth.[30] By the time City Vision came on the scene, Alexander was well known as a radical critic of the status quo.

Ken Adam, the main spokesman for City Vision after Warnock, qualified as an architect in 1964 and went on to study planning in the UK. On his return after several years in the State Public Service he started his own practice. He is the principal author of the Western Australian Residential Design Codes, a Life Fellow of the Planning Institute of Australia, a Fellow of the Royal Australian Institute of Architects, and the recipient of the 2003 Architects Board award for outstanding services to architecture. Outspoken and quixotic he has been a strong advocate for City Vision.

There were 22 founding members of City Vision and its membership has never been more than 30. It has tended to be exclusive (Figure 8.5). Those founding members whose membership continued into the 21st century included Warnock, architects and town planners Ken Adam and Max Poole, architects Geoff Summerhayes and Zdenka Underwood, town planner Verity Allen, and Martyn Webb, whose individualism and passion for the city enabled him to negotiate both the right and left of politics. It has also been a tight knit group and many of its original members are still active. They have run conferences and well-patronised annual dinners and, in collaboration with other groups, have sponsored visiting professionals. In one year, for example, at UWA's annual Summer School, City Vision ran five open forums dealing with central city population, the river foreshore, the pedestrian experience, diversity and traffic, and the structure needed to enable Perth to realise its full 'good city' potential.[31]

City Vision had some early success, claiming responsibility for the establishment of the government's Inner City Taskforce in late 1989. The Taskforce was jointly funded by the Commonwealth Government, the State Department of Planning and Urban Development, Homeswest and the City of Perth. It took submissions from a variety of groups, including City Vision who argued that 'the way you fix crime in the streets is to have people living above shops and the city being used 24 hours a day so you have eyes on the street keeping people safe.'[32] The study area covered the inner-city core and revealed that, although six per cent of Perth people (approximately 70,000) expressed the desire to live in the inner-city area, only 15,000 people actually did.[33]

Figure 8.5: Conviviality marked City Vision gatherings. City Vision members – Diana Warnock, Ken Adam, Verity Allan, and Les and Miriam Styne – at the Mount Street Café. Source: photograph by Bill Warnock, c.1994, courtesy City Vision

The list of City Vision's major campaigns is an inventory of the planning controversies of Perth of the 1980s and 1990s; the Redevelopment of East Perth (1988–c.1996), State Drama Theatre (1988–89), the Emu Brewery site (1988–90), the Swan Brewery Development (1989–91), the establishment of an Inner City Housing Taskforce (1989–92), the Northern Bypass (1989–c.1995), the Cultural Centre (1989–96), the Perth City Foreshore Competition (1990–91), the campaign to save Council House (1994), the Proposal to Sink the Railway (1995), the Western Gateway (1995), the Supreme Court (1996–98), the Northbridge Tunnel and Urban Renewal (1998–99), the Barrack Square development (1998–2000), the Convention Centre development (1999–2000), and Forrest Place walkway (1988–2007) and most recently a revised plan for the Perth

Waterfront (2008). City Vision commented on each of these issues, in some cases developing and submitting detailed plans. Its reputation and the expertise of its members has meant that in most cases its views, although rarely accepted in totality, have been considered by governments and have had an impact on the eventual outcome.

Figure 8.6: The cover of City Vision's Manifesto, 1988. Source: City Vision

When City Vision announced its arrival on the Perth scene with the publication of a 32–page manifesto *New directions for Central Perth* in 1988 (Figure 8.6), it could not be known that one of the key platforms of this small community group would, in coalition with others, result in major changes to the City.[34] They had drafted their manifesto in a climate of intense debate over the planning of the city with accusations of corruption dogging both state government and City Council. It had to be right. Warnock recalled that 'we spent a full year arriving at a set of proposals we could all agree upon. Every thought, every idea, every comma was debated ferociously until we could all nail colours to the mast of our Manifesto.'[35] Its nine objectives, each backed up with a detailed plan, were to restore diversity and vitality to the city, bring residents back into the city, make the city an enjoyable place, day and night, make the city a pleasant, stimulating place to be in, make the city accessible to all people, seek excellence in urban design and preserve heritage, bring together the city and the river, involve people in the future of their city, and establish a planning and development system designed to realise the full potential of Perth.

The response was mixed. Stephenson, who had been sent an early draft, wrote 'we are almost at the twelfth hour ... I hope your Inner City group prospers'.[36] Another wrote, 'Somebody has coordinated a fairly wild group into a pretty sensible answer ... Obviously the way to win is to convince everybody it is all in the City's, and their, best interests to go the way you want to go and not be too confrontationist but to win with honeyed logic'.[37] Several members of the Liberal Opposition, including future premier Richard Court, who had already met with members of City Vision at Warnock's home, wrote 'we share your objectives of creating a Perth which is, to use your words; "enjoyable, pleasant, stimulating, accessible, preserves our heritage, river oriented, diverse, vital and above all a "good city"'.[38] Rod Pether, City Planner at the City of Perth, however, was critical, writing, with awareness of troubled times:

> I fear that in presenting the document the way you have, you may well have alienated people and organizations who may have otherwise been supportive. Our City is a small one and my feeling is that those of us who have concerns about the direction it is taking can be more effective if we approach this matter on a co-operative basis.[39]

But within City Vision's 1988 Manifesto was a call for the establishment of 'a powerful, creative and independent central City Planning Commission'. This became a major platform for City Vision which called on the government to establish a new administrative structure for Perth – 'a joint planning authority involving the state government, the City Council and representative groups with special interest in the capital city' – with City Vision announcing that its proposed structure was 'far more democratic and representative than the present "closed shop" of the Perth City Council, a system that disenfranchises most Western Australians from having any say in the planning of the state's greatest asset, the Capital city'.

Forming a coalition

City Vision joined with the CBD Committee (as the Civic Affairs Committee was now known) and the Western Australian Division of the Australian Institute of Urban Studies (AIUSWA), to form a loose coalition not unlike the old TPAWA in its broadest sense.[40] Initially the CBD Committee had acted alone, making a submission to the state government in March 1988, to argue that as Perth was a capital city it was worthy of 'municipal government reflective of its status', that it was presently disadvantaged because revenues raised in the CBD flowed away from the CBD to suburban dormitory wards of the Council, and that commercial interests were being taxed without adequate representation on Council. Like City Vision it had also argued that planning should be undertaken by a joint City-State body.[41] This was a full-frontal attack on a largely discredited City Council and was a far-reaching initiative.

The commissioning of distinguished Sydney town planner and lawyer, John Mant, by the Burke Labor government to report on its draft town planning legislation, upped the ante.[42] In his report, released in June 1988, Mant was harsh in his criticism of the city; 'Perth lacks the soul and urbanity of great cities. In contrast to the beauty of the city seen from its approaches, the experience from within is disappointing.'[43] Although not going as far as the CBD Committee had proposed, he largely endorsed the proposals made by it and City Vision for a City of Perth Planning Commission, with the proposed Commission to assess any decision to grant bonus plot ratios or to waive standards, and for a reduction in the boundaries of the City of Perth. Predictably the City Council rejected these proposals.[44]

A few months later, in September 1988, the CBD Committee, City Vision, and AIUSWA gained greater traction for their position by holding a forum on the issue. Nearly 60 leading Perth figures who attended the forum supported their call for a Capital City Planning Commission, resolving that the aim should 'to plan a capital city that realises the potential of its geographical setting and the aspirations of the people of Western Australia'. They noted that:

> The 1970s and 1980s have been two decades of growing disaffection with the quality and design and life of central and inner Perth. Numerous commentators – individuals from home and away and community bodies of many kinds, have described the City as spiritless and lifeless, and worse. At the same time the residential population of the inner city has been decimated, its share of metropolitan retail sales has plummeted, and more than fifty buildings listed by the National Trust have been lost forever.[45]

In response to the growing controversy, the City commissioned Peter Waterman and Associates to conduct an inquiry. It was no surprise that it rejected Mant's recommendations.[46] City Vision, however, dismissed the Waterman Report (1991) as 'self-serving and lacking in credibility ... the failure of the present system is staring us all in the face: an almost non-existent inner city population; the 19th-century architectural fabric destroyed; zoning that condemns whole areas of the city to oblivion, and cars ... eating the city.'[47] The CBD Committee supported this stance. The issue impacted on the Lord Mayoral Election of 1991, with one newspaper headline proclaiming that the 'Future of Perth is Key to Election' and pushing the view that 'Perth is dull, lifeless and boring and the interests of all WA people in their capital city are not being met by a council elected by local ratepayers'.[48] The following year the CBD Committee, City Vision and AIUSWA, continued their campaign, launching *Capital city planning for Perth, the capital of Western Australia* (1992) and calling for a strong central planning authority.[49] In a rearguard action, the City invited individuals from each group to participate in a review of the City's Central Area Policy.[50]

But for the City the writing was on the wall. The struggle for control of the planning and land use regulations of the central city is a recurring theme in the history of Perth since World War II. It contains the most valuable property in the state, and powerful business interests constantly lobby both the City and the state to promote their own ends. This struggle has been played out in most of Australia's capital cities. Local government has no legal autonomy. As has occurred in other states, councils can be sacked by the state government and have their decisions overturned by state planning ministers, often on the grounds of the larger economic development needs of the state.[51] There was thus considerable precedent in 1993 when Richard Court's newly elected Liberal/National Party government accepted the recommendations of a report co-authored by David Carr, previously the state's Town Planning Commissioner, to dissolve the Perth City Council and reduce its boundaries.[52] Supporting the proposal was the WA Chamber of Commerce and Industry (as it was now known), City Vision, the Building Owners' and Managers' Association, the Retail Traders' Association and councillors representing the new city, as well as the Liberal government, and the *West Australian* newspaper.[53]

Conclusion

Like the community-based TPAWA before them which lobbied hard and successfully over two decades for the establishment of town planning legislation in WA in 1929, City Vision and the CBD Committee, in its various guises, were successful in lobbying to create a new City of Perth that excluded its suburban wards in 1994. They were not successful, however, in their calls for a Central City Planning Commission. Despite the enactment of a new *Planning and Development Act* in 2005 which consolidated three separate planning acts (the *Western Australian Planning Commission Act 1985*, the *Metropolitan Region Town Planning Scheme Act 1959* and the *Town Planning and Development Act 1928*), the city's governance from a planning perspective is still fragmented.

So what did these two groups achieve? In a number of ways they appear to have followed the modus operandi of the earlier TPAWA – public lectures, forums, mobilising other interest groups, increasing public awareness, creating debate – and, like that community association, their activities eventually resulted in legislative change – on the one hand the 1928 *Town Planning and Development Act* and on the other hand the 1993 *City of Perth Restructuring* Act – though each contained flaws and did not achieve the anticipated results. Like the TPAWA, the CBD Committee gradually faded away. According to Webb, it suffered 'death by a 1000 cuts' as the Chamber of Commerce and Industry refocused its energies away from issues relating to the city.[54] City Vision, however, is still an active lobby group to which the media always runs for a quote on all aspects of city planning.

The activities of both groups are sufficiently recent for members to look back and provide an assessment of their achievements. There is little evidence of the views of members of the CBD Committee, though Webb, one of the major actors within the committee, is still arguing for a Capital City Planning Commission, but his audience and his supporters have diminished. The major actors within City Vision frequently assessed their performance, regarding themselves as 'intellectual provocateurs'. Although Warnock believed that they had failed 'to persuade the community to set up a unitary system of planning for our city', he argued that 'by our networking and media work, City Vision has achieved key things we set out to do to raise the debate about our city'.[55] Adam's view was that 'CV's real credibility and effectiveness stems from its independence and its voluntary nature, having no self-interest barrow to push' and that 'for a small group of people it has had a remarkable influence'.[56] Geoffrey London, Professor of Architecture at UWA and later State

Architect, summed the group up more critically: 'City Vision will be decried by some as an elitist bunch of self-appointed city watchdogs, but this will perhaps be the view of those who have allowed the city to become the subject of serious and concerned criticism'.[57] The final word goes to Max Hipkins, former Director of Planning at the City of Perth (2000–05), involved in both City Vision and the CBC Committee from their earliest days, who has observed, 'What amazes me about Perth is the way a relatively small number of people have linked up and have continually been involved … Don't doubt that a small group of dedicated people can change history'.[58]

References

[1] Neil Foley, *An outline of the evolution of town and regional planning administration in Western Australia: 1927–1995* (Nedlands: self published, 1995).

[2] Quotations from Western Australia Votes and Proceedings, 28 November to 14 December 1951.

[3] Royal Commission on the Town Planning and Development Act Amendment Bill, 1951.

[4] Gordon Stephenson and J. Alastair Hepburn, *Plan for the Metropolitan Region, Perth and Fremantle, Western Australia* (Perth: Government Printing Office, 1955); see also Jenny Gregory, *City of light: a history of Perth since the 1950s* (Perth: City of Perth, 2003), 93–105.

[5] Mrs Ray Oldham, Hon. Secretary BDF, to Bessie Rischbieth, letter, 27 June 1962, Bessie Rischbieth Papers, Battye Library (hereafter BL), MN 634/1, Acc.2552, Item No. 22, 1961–62.

[6] See Gregory, 117–24.

[7] Martyn J. Webb, 'Urban Expansion, town improvement and the beginning of town planning in metropolitan Perth', in *Western landscapes*, ed. Joseph Gentilli (Nedlands: UWA Press, 1979), 359–82.

[8] *West Australian*, 9 February 1966.

[9] *Daily News*, 29 January 1969. Patrick Weir was president of the New Heart for Perth Society, and its other office-bearers were Dr F.J. Roberts, C.V. Malcolm, T.A. Meinck and Mrs E. MacNamara.

[10] New Heart for Perth Society Records, Minutes, 1968–74, BL, MN 1382, MN 4328A, Item No. 7.
[11] For details see 'The Link' at www.epra.wa.gov.au, accessed 15 May 2009.
[12] Gordon Stephenson, *The design of Central Perth: some problems and possible solutions* (Nedlands: UWA Press, 1975) 70.
[13] *West Australian*, 20 April 1974.
[14] See Gregory, 208–14.
[15] Friends of the Earth Papers, 'Friends of the railways', 1979, BL, MN 1035, Acc 3257A, Item No. 61.
[16] Apart from its publications, the records of Committee are limited to Civic Affairs Committee, Correspondence and Circulars file, 1973–74 (including material from 1967–72), Perth Chamber of Commerce, BL, MN882A, Box 205; Perth Chamber of Commerce and Industry, Minutes, 1981–83, BL, COMAP221, COMAP304, Box 2/7. Thanks to the Chamber of Commerce and Industry Western Australia (hereafter WACCI) for permission to access these records.
[17] Founder of Pacesetter Homes, Corser was later a significant benefactor, especially to yachting, and a member of Murdoch University Senate (1978–87). Finch, managing director of chocolate manufacturer Plaistowe & Co, was former chair of the Chamber of Commerce. Russell was from Peet & Co (1894) Ltd.
[18] 'City of Perth draft town planning scheme: proceedings of a symposium held at the Department of Geography, UWA, 22–23 September 1972', Civic Affairs Committee PCC, RAIAWA, AIUSWA.
[19] This eventually led to the Report into WA Inc. Royal Commission, 1992.
[20] *West Australian*, 22 September 1987. The draft act was dropped.
[21] Jan Jermalinski, Secretary/Treasurer of Carlisle Ratepayers and Residents Association, to Bob Pearce, Minister for Planning, letter, 31 December 1987, PCC File, 'Allegations of corruption in council's planning procedures', 1987–90, PCC Depot, Box 3047, File TP1/3.1.
[22] Originally known as Perth Urban Discussion Group, the name was changed to People for Perth and then in 1988 to City Vision (the name is credited to Verity Allen).
[23] Gordon Stephenson to Bill Warnock, letter, 30 August 1988, City Vision Archives (hereafter CV).
[24] Gordon Stephenson to Ken Adams, Letter, 6 September 1988, CV.
[25] Ken Adam, 'A tribute to Bill Warnock', *Western Planner*, 17, 6, 2001.

[26] Diana Warnock, his wife, was a journalist and an activist before her election as Labor Member for Perth (1993–2001).
[27] Bill Warnock, Draft history of City Vision, 1996, CV.
[28] Ian Alexander, *The city centre: patterns and problems* (Nedlands: UWA Press, 1974), 167.
[29] 7.30 Report, ABC TV, transcript dated 29 September 1987. See Ian Alexander, 'City centre planning: for public or private interest?' in *Urban and regional planning in Western Australia*, eds. David Hedgcock and Oren Yiftachel (Perth: Paradigm Press, 1992), 79–92.
[30] *Sunday Times*, 1 November 1987; *West Australian*, 4 and 11 November 1987.
[31] CV, 15 September1988.
[32] 'Window ajar for return of residents', CV.
[33] PCC Minutes, 17 June and 18 November 1991 and 20 July 1992.
[34] City Vision, *New Directions for Central Perth*, Perth, n.d. circa August 1988; revised as *City Vision's Agenda for the Capital City of Perth* in 1993.
[35] Warnock, draft history, CV; City Vision, *New Directions*; and information from Ken Adam and Max Hipkins.
[36] Gordon Stephenson to Bill Warnock, letter, 31 May 1988, CV.
[37] Peter C. Bruechle, Bruechle Gilchrist and Evans Pty Ltd Consulting Chartered Engineers, to Bill Warnock, letter, 30 August 1988, CV.
[38] Barry J. MacKinnon, Leader of the Opposition, to Ken Adam, letter, 7 October 1988, CV.
[39] Rod Pether to Ken Adam, letter, 25 August 1988, CV.
[40] A branch of AIUS was founded in Perth in 1967. Some members of AIUSWA were also members of City Vision and the CBD Committee. Ken Adam and Max Hipkins chaired AIUSWA.
[41] WACCI, 'Perth a Capital City for WA', Submission to the Premier', 1988.
[42] Martyn Webb, interview with author, 2003. Mant had acted as Town Planning Commissioner in Perth in 1985.
[43] John Mant, Summary and Recommendations, 'Planning procedures for Perth's central area', Report to the WA Minister for Planning, Phillips Fox Solicitors and Attorneys, Sydney, 27 June 1988.
[44] PCC Minutes, 15 August 1988.
[45] AIUSWA, WACCI and City Vision, 'Perth: A Capital city planning authority for the capital of WA. A submission to the Premier', September 1990.
[46] Waterman and Associates, 'Future Planning Arrangements for the Central Area: The Position of the Perth City Council', 17 April 1991.

[47] Press release, 1991, CV.
[48] *Sunday Times*, March 1991.
[49] AIUSWA, 'Capital city planning for Perth, the capital of Western Australia', (AIUSWA: East Perth, June 1992).
[50] R.F. Dawson, Town Clerk, City of Perth to Bill Warnock, letter, 5 October 1992.
[51] See Renate Howe, 'Local Government and the Urban Growth Debate', in *Australian Cities: Issues, strategies and policies for urban Australia in the 1990s*, ed. Patrick Troy (Melbourne: Cambridge University Press, 1995), 186; see also Paul Ashton, *The Accidental City: Planning Sydney since 1788* (Sydney: Hale and Iremonger, 1993); J.B. McLoughlin, *Shaping Melbourne's Future: Town planning, the state and civil society* (Melbourne: Cambridge University Press, 1992), 183.
[52] Culminating in the enactment of *City of Perth* Restructuring Act, no. 38 of 1993.
[53] Discussion of the issue can be found in the *West Australian*, October–December 1993.
[54] The Chamber of Commerce amalgamated with the Chamber of Manufacturing in 1984 to become the WA Chamber of Commerce and Industry (WACCI). An early C.E.O. was Colin Barnett, elected Premier of WA in September 2008. West Australian, 24 July 1984 and 2 May 1985.
[55] Bill Warnock, draft speech, reported in *Sunday Times*, 10 December 1995, CV.
[56] Ken Adam, 'City Vision hits back', *Perth News*, 16 December 1992; Ken Adam to Professor Jan Gehl, letter, 16 December 1992, CV.
[57] Geoffrey London, 'Brightening the city', *West Australian*, 3 September 1988.
[58] Max Hipkins, personal communication, 9 February 2003.

9
Democracy in action: public participation in planning in Hobart 1940–65

Stefan Petrow

As noted in an earlier chapter, the first phase of the modern town planning movement in Hobart began in 1915 with the formation of the Southern Tasmanian Town Planning Association (STTPA). This city-wide association incorporated various interest groups, architects and progress associations to coordinate pressure on the City Council for improvements to housing, roads and recreational areas. The STTPA effectively folded in 1926 due to lack of public support and opposition from vested interests. Progress associations remained active to 1939, but concentrated on immediate local improvements and not city-wide planning for the future. After 1945 urban planning in Australia took on a new lease of life as part of broader aspirations for a better postwar society.[1] In Hobart planning was taken up with renewed fervour when progress associations and citizens' groups, in alliance with architects, combined to demand a larger role in the planning process. This chapter will examine the nature of the role of citizens' groups, the planning ideas those groups proposed, and the extent to which they achieved their goals.

Planning, participation and progress associations

The 1940s and 1950s presented governments at the federal and state level with many urban challenges.[2] Some challenges were longstanding such as deteriorating housing, the unregulated expansion of industry, and the preservation of open spaces in and around cities. Other challenges, arising largely from postwar prosperity and accelerated population growth, were new and included urban sprawl, ribbon development, and the demand for more housing and associated infrastructure created by a baby boom and a mass migration program.[3] The decline in the price of cars saw car ownership grow dramatically: cars were the most powerful force changing the face of Australian cities in the 1950s and 1960s.[4]

In Britain, planning after 1945 was underpinned by the idea of progress, which could only occur 'if planning was turned into a democratic process – one that involved all sections of the community and captured their imaginations'.[5] The same idealism suffused the Australian scene and the visits of outstanding British town planners such as Patrick Abercrombie (who visited Hobart and Launceston in late 1948) further heightened expectations of what large-scale metropolitan planning could achieve. Planning enthusiasts argued that a more coordinated approach to metropolitan planning would solve urban problems, but in so doing 'created unrealistic expectations about the ability of planning to achieve radical change'.[6] However, Alexander has argued that Australian metropolitan plans of the early postwar period were 'top-down documents' with little scope for public participation. People had to make 'their voices heard on specific planning issues' in other ways.[7] One mechanism was through local progress associations which demanded that planning become more democratic and inclusive.[8] Although prominent in the improvement and beautification of most Australian suburbs and rural communities from at least the early 20th century, progress associations have received little systematic scholarly attention. Mullins argues that these staunchly middle-class associations significantly contributed to the improvement of household and residential life and urban development in Australia, especially between 1945 and the 1960s.[9]

This chapter reinforces Mullins' claim about the prominent role of progress associations in the postwar period. Although the smallest capital city, Hobart faced similar problems to the other Australian capitals and members of progress associations were consequently active in urban affairs. Citizens banded together because of 'visible shared interests' in ensuring their suburbs had the necessary infrastructure and facilities to forge better lives for their families.[10] After Japan's entry into the war in 1942, progress associations put all their energies into assisting the war effort, but, when the threat receded, resumed their work with renewed and united vigour in the STTPA tradition.[11] In August 1944 the various suburban associations coalesced to form the Council of Hobart Progress Associations (CHPA), hoping to place greater pressure on the City Council.[12] In early 1948 the CHPA persuaded the then town planning conscious City Council to form a Citizen's Advisory Town Planning Committee (CATPC), which would have a representative on the City Councils' Town Planning Committee. The CATPC, a broadly-based community body led by prominent CHPA members, proved to be a vigilant watchdog and key members became powerful advocates of participatory and cooperative planning. Some CATPC members were also elected as aldermen, which strengthened its voice on the City Council. This was a movement of accommodation not confrontation.

The CATPC provided the City Council with ideas on town planning and provided the momentum to sustain public interest in town planning after the brief euphoria for postwar reform. It made various suggestions concerning road alignments that needed widening to avoid bottlenecks, the provision of off-street car parking, port development, the improvement of recreation areas, and the need for coordinated metropolitan planning. By 1958 many but certainly not all of the CATPC's proposals were taken up by the City Council and its push for coordinated planning bore fruit in the establishment of the Southern Metropolitan Master Planning Authority in 1957. Having fulfilled many of its objectives, the CATPC lost momentum and folded in 1958. Its role was taken over by the CHPA. Before examining the work of the CATPC, this chapter begins by providing the background to its formation and the context in which it operated.

The local context

World War II had a great impact on attitudes towards town planning in Tasmania. People became dissatisfied with old ways of doing things and demanded that government deal with the social problems caused by the disregard of housing and planning.[13] Major advances in town planning occurred after housing reformer, businessman and former STTPA member Alderman John Soundy became Lord Mayor of Hobart in 1938.[14] Soundy was aided in his endeavours by the newly-appointed Town Clerk H.J.R. Cole, a keen supporter of town planning. Under Soundy, new powers were acquired to control subdivisions and widen streets. Perhaps Soundy's most important initiative occurred in February 1943 when he set up a Town Planning Committee, comprising one representative of each standing committee of the Council.

The primary function of the Town Planning Committee was to secure a plan of the city. In 1944 the City of Hobart had a population of 54,215 and Soundy wanted a plan for a population of 100,000. He realised that Hobart was 'an old city' and there were numerous topographical 'problems to solve in providing a balanced plan' (Figure 9.1).[15] In 1943 the Town Planning Committee appointed Frederick Charles Cook, City Engineer for Port Melbourne in Victoria, to prepare a town planning scheme.[16] Cook's plan concentrated on the zoning, traffic and recreational needs of the city, but avoided difficult issues such as a Greater Hobart authority that others were calling for and any attempt to estimate the cost of his proposals. Remarkably, Cook also ignored increasingly important issues such as the provision of car parks, community centres and facilities for the young and unwisely minimised the urgency of street widening. Perhaps influenced by his Port Melbourne experience, Cook sanctioned the building of industry on the foreshore, a proposal widely condemned as threatening the tourist industry. Despite its deficiencies, Cook's plan was timely as the State's first major planning legislation, the *Town and Country Planning Act 1944*, was gazetted to be operational in 1945. Based on the English *Town and Country Planning Act 1932*, the

Tasmanian Act strengthened local government responsibility for planning. Councils were required to submit a proposed town planning scheme to the newly-appointed Town and Country Planning Commissioner,

Figure 9.1: Aerial view of central Hobart, c.1944. Source: F.C. Cook, *City of Hobart Plan* (1945)

R.A. McInnis, and, once this scheme was provisionally approved, it remained open for public inspection and objection for three months.

The Hobart City Council intended to use Cook's plan as the basis for its statutory plan under the act. The standing committees of Council would study reactions to Cook's plan from 'all responsible citizens' and then would prepare the official town planning scheme for registration under the act.[17] The Council supplied bound and illustrated copies of the plan to professional bodies (architects, surveyors and engineers) and to progress associations. The few written replies responded favourably towards Cook's plan, but also sent a clear message that a top down approach to planning was unacceptable and could no longer be tolerated. They urged that citizens be involved in future discussion and development of the plan to ensure that public needs were not sacrificed to the demands of vested interests as historically had been the case in Hobart and to ensure that the City Council would put the plan into effect. The engineers and the CHPA wanted a Town Planning Committee composed of technical experts and representatives of government departments, adjoining municipalities and citizen bodies.

Despite receiving generally approving if not enthusiastic comments on Cook's plan, the Hobart City Council lost impetus in preparing a town planning scheme.[18] The Council did not appoint interested and expert residents to its Town Planning Committee and kept its 'actions and attitudes' to planning secret. Work was slow mainly because the Council, claiming not to be able to afford a town planner, had designated the capable but overworked City Engineer J.E. Knott as Planning Officer. This was compounded by the Council's refusal officially to confer with McInnis or to seek his advice. As traffic and parking problems intensified, the public demand for action and representation, voiced through the CHPA and the Institute of Architects, grew louder.[19] As the need to draft a statutory plan became more urgent, the Council, with Town Clerk Cole playing a key role, relented and invited McInnis, the most experienced town planner in the state, to attend meetings of the Town Planning Committee. From his appointment McInnis advocated greater public involvement through town planning committees to advise local government of community needs.[20]

The CHPA also sought representation. It pressed for a conference with Cole and senior municipal officers in July 1946 to discuss 'many subjects affecting municipal administration and the status of progress associations'.[21] CHPA Chairman, John Arthur Turnbull, hoped the conference would 'stimulate public interest in civic problems by a free exchange of views and ideas'.[22] Subjects discussed included providing the CHPA with 'a detailed and comprehensive schedule of works and expenditure' before decisions on works were made and recognising the CHPA as 'a nucleus' of a citizens' Town Planning Committee.[23] The

CHPA finally persuaded Council's Town Planning Committee of the need for such a body and in early 1948 the CHPA accepted Cole's invitation to form a Citizens' Advisory Town Planning Committee (CATPC) and appoint a representative to the City Council's Town Planning Committee.[24] The Citizens' Committee included representatives from the Royal Hobart Regatta Association, the Royal Australian Institute of Architects, the Tasmanian Council of School Parents Association, the National Fitness Council, the Better Homes for Australia Association, the Tasmanian Road Transport Association and suburban progress associations.

Community involvement in planning: the CATPC

Would the appointment of the CATPC be a turning point for community planning in Hobart? Certainly much was expected of it. As one town planning official noted, such 'lively, keen, and knowledgeable groups of citizens' were essential 'to lead, support and sometimes to prod into action Officialdom'.[25] The CATPC hoped to obtain 'a better insight into the difficulties that beset the City Council in its planning' and to develop 'a pronounced feeling of cooperation in the task of completing a plan that will meet present difficulties' based on Cook's recommendations. Drawing on the wide cross section of views of its members, the CATPC hoped, 'as private citizens, to accept our full share of responsibility in the task of planning our City in the future'.[26] If the 'co-operative outlook' and 'essential team spirit' were maintained, the committee was confident it could surmount 'obstacles' in its way. The CATPC was given free use of a room in the Town Hall and the Town Clerk and City Engineer attended meetings in 'an advisory capacity'. Other signs of cooperation included the CATPC agreeing in June 1948 to prepare a civic survey plan to show 'existing use and occupation of all land within the city'.[27] This would be 'an adjunct' to the City Council's final zoning plan.

The CATPC was initially represented on the City Council Town Planning Committee by its Chairman, Major John Arthur Turnbull

(Figure 9.2). Born in East Camberwell, Victoria in 1895, Turnbull joined the Commonwealth Public Service in 1914, enlisted in the First AIF and held positions with the Department of Defence in Brisbane and Melbourne until he was appointed army auditor in Tasmania in 1935.[28] Turnbull was involved in many local bodies, but began his involvement in local affairs as founder and president of the Lenah Valley Progress Association in 1939 and instigated the formation of the CHPA. Turnbull believed that the CATPC had made 'civic history and had opened up unlimited opportunities of civic service'.[29] He was elected a city alderman in 1950 and, resigning as chairman of the CATPC, tried but failed to have even greater influence on shaping planning policy inside the City Council until his defeat at the City Council elections in 1954.[30] He urged his CATPC colleagues to keep working with the City Council to achieve 'the vision splendid' and not be deflected by critics 'whose limited horizon does not permit their gaze to penetrate beyond their own little world of to-day'.

Turnbull was succeeded as chairman and CATPC representative on the City Council Town Planning Committee by K.F. Cowles. When pressure of business forced Cowles to step down, he was replaced in turn by Colin Philp, who had been President of the Tasmanian Chapter of the Royal Australian Institute of Architects in 1945–46 and was the most prominent individual in Hobart to extol the benefits of community planning in the 1940s and 1950s.[31] In 1954 Philp went on a planning tour of North America and England and in 1955 wrote a pamphlet for citizens called *Planning for You*.[32] Planning did not mean regimentation or 'a set of immutable decrees or restrictions', but cooperation in 'a completely democratic manner to serve the best interests of all citizens'. He concluded that the 'right kind of planning will only result if informed and active citizens ... arouse public opinion and assist the planners to make our communities better places for our families, our neighbours and ourselves to live in'.

Figure 9.2: John Arthur Turnbull, community planning advocate.
Source: *Mercury*, 2 January 1967

Philp had a chance to transform the City Council when he became an alderman in 1956. The City Council insisted that he remain the CATPC representative on the City Council Town Planning Committee.[33] This disappointed and puzzled the CATPC, which wanted to replace Philp with its new chairman, another architect, I.G. Anderson, to retain 'the independence of approach to Town Planning problems not always possible when the member concerned had the wider responsibility of an elected civic leader'.[34]

Gradually the influence of the CATPC weakened due to the lack of interest shown by some of its affiliated bodies and attendance at meetings became 'very poor' perhaps because of, as we will see, the new planning 'instrumentalities' that it had suggested be formed.[35] In July 1958 the CATPC realised that interest in it had dwindled and by one vote decided to disband after ten years of active involvement in town planning 'problems and projects' in Hobart.[36] The following sections will discuss some of the specific proposals of the CATPC and the CHPA relating to roads, cars and the waterfront, recreational areas and coordinated planning.

Roads, cars and waterfront

After 1945 the CATPC gave particular attention to the issues arising from the dramatic rise in car ownership, especially after petrol rationing was lifted in 1949, and the concomitant need for better roads to ease congestion and assist traffic flow. In 1949 the CATPC warned that the state government's plans to improve road alignments to Tasmanian cities were not ambitious enough 'to meet future traffic requirements' and would result in bottlenecks.[37] It was satisfied that at 150 feet wide the new northern approach to Hobart, the Brooker Highway, would be adequate, but, in a deputation to the Minister for Lands and Works Eric Reece, criticised the decision to destroy the Risdon Reserve to accommodate the new road.[38] The CATPC was reassured that the road would not 'intersect' the area but would, as it wanted, be raised to 'span it' and that additional land would be purchased so that two separate sports grounds would be built on 'either side of the proposed viaduct'.

The CATPC also raised objections when the southern outlet road was mooted to be built by the Department of Public Works through the lower part of Fitzroy Gardens Reserve.[39] Although conceding that a route through the top of Fitzroy Gardens raised 'technical difficulties', the CATPC thought these should be overcome to stop 'this beautiful park land being destroyed or impaired by an arterial thoroughfare'. After long debate, the CATPC won this argument and most of the area was saved.[40] The CATPC also agitated to stop 'ribbon development' occurring along the main highways and to stop subdivision of land with frontages along highways.[41] It favoured a green belt on both sides of highways with a by-road inside the green belt and received support from McInnis.

Figure 9.3: Congestion in Elizabeth Street, Hobart, looking north.
Source: F.C. Cook, *City of Hobart Plan* (1945)

The CATPC was also interested in inner city street congestion (Figure 9.3) and made numerous recommendations and submissions. For example, it suggested that Davey Street be widened by building a two level road through part of Franklin Square, the city's oldest and most central park, because congestion was intolerable in the area (Figure 9.4).[42] In 1953 CATPC objected to the proposed diagonal road from the corner of Warwick and Elizabeth Streets to Molle and Macquarie Streets because it would create 'many awkward and dangerous intersections'.[43] The CATPC suggested that congestion in North Hobart would be more effectively relieved by extending Murray Street to join Elizabeth Street at the North Hobart Post Office. The City Council sensibly abandoned the diagonal road and decided against the extension of Murray Street on the grounds of expense.

Figure 9.4: Road through Franklin Square. Source: *Lord Mayor of Hobart's Report 1958–60*

When he became an alderman, Philp stressed the problems caused by cars. In July 1956 he warned the City Council Town Planning Committee that 'we have to convince ourselves, as well as the public, that the motor vehicle poses the biggest problem for us in the future and right now'. It was 'a problem we *must* solve if we are to keep Hobart a living, growing, healthy City' and stop 'the inevitable slowing down and strangling of the business of the City'.[44] In 1957, to assist with forward planning, Philp secured the appointment of a planning officer working under the City Engineer.[45] His duties included preparing plans for street alignments and for the development of new areas, including the layout of streets and services and the zoning of land, and maintaining the current draft town plan.

Figure 9.5: Car park fronting Bathurst Street. Source: *Lord Mayor of Hobart's Report 1964–66*

The greater use of cars created a demand for more car parks and the CATPC supported planning for future needs (Figure 9.5). It urged the City Council 'to prohibit the use of property in city areas as timber stacking and timber drying yards' and to buy up existing areas for car parking.[46] In 1955 the City Council installed over 200 parking meters, a first for an Australian city; in 1956 opened its first off-street car park in lower Macquarie Street; and in 1958 zoned four areas near the centre of the city for off-street parking.[47] Newly-built premises would also be required to supply parking spaces.

The CATPC sought to improve traffic flow to and from the waterfront and Philp was appointed the CATPC representative on the Port of Hobart Foreshores Committee to comment on this and other port related issues.[48] The CATPC 'strongly' opposed the proposal to fill in Victoria and Constitution docks for use as parking areas as Cook's plan had recommended and deemed the dock an 'essential' port installation.[49] Opposition was equally strong in 1950 to the Marine Board's proposal to build a fruit inspection shed on the triangle next to Parliament Square. The building would obscure vision in an area where traffic was 'very heavy' and would only increase when nearby Montpelier Retreat was widened.[50] In both cases the CATPC view won out, but Philp lamented that the City Council had 'no control' over any building the Marine Board wanted to build on its land.[51] He supported giving the Council this control to stop the erection of buildings that 'did not conform to accepted standards'. Control was not likely, but the two bodies did devise a joint zoning plan for the waterfront.[52]

Recreational areas

The CATPC vigilantly sought protection of recreational areas for public use. In 1949 Philp's plan to reclaim about six acres of Marieville Esplanade, Sandy Bay attracted notice. The City Council adopted the CATPC proposal to restrict the foreshore to 'aquatic facilities' for the public and stop encroachment by 'sectional interests'.[53] The City Council was less willing to buy properties along the Sandy Bay foreshore to provide open spaces for the public, but agreed to buy 'vacant land where possible as "open windows" to the River'.[54] Other established recreational spots attracted the attention of the CATPC. In 1949 Amy Rowntree, one of a handful of women to contribute to community planning before 1965, suggested a scheme to recondition the tracks and restore signposts on Mount Wellington 'as a greater attraction for tourists'.[55] This was taken up by the City Council, which showed awakened interest in the mountain as a recreational resource. Preserving 'the natural beauty' of areas such as Fern Tree, the suburb adjacent to the mountain, was another CATPC suggestion acknowledged by the Council.[56] The City Council was also urged to acquire the Fort Nelson site on Mount Nelson for its 'scenic, historic, and recreational value' and to keep the CATPC informed about proposed improvements to the Domain, a large area of scenic bushland near the city centre.[57]

Across the Derwent River in Clarence Municipality, the CATPC agitated in 1950 to have the area between Bridge Road and Montagu Bay known as Smelting Works Point 'reserved for public use'.[58] The area had originally been zoned as a shopping area, but McInnis agreed with the CATPC that it was more suitable for a reserve.[59] The issue dragged on and Philp, frustrated at the delay, urged McInnis to stop the area being built over for housing by the Agricultural Bank.[60] This is one of the few instances of the CATPC contributing to the debate over how government departments ignored local government planning schemes when building housing estates. The CATPC showed little interest in the provision of public housing, the most important social issue after 1945, perhaps because its middle-class members did not experience housing and other social problems and the committee was more interested in infrastructure. After a period of 'tremendous growth' in home building, the housing shortage had eased considerably by 1960, but the Housing Department's anti-democratic propensity to build where it liked and to override municipal planning schemes should have concerned community planning bodies more than it did.[61]

Community involvement in planning: the CHPA

In July 1958, after the demise of the CATPC, John Turnbull became the CHPA representative on the City Council Town Planning Committee, but as 'an observer' not a member.[62] This was a considerable reduction in status, but did not stop the CHPA from pursuing similar concerns to the CATPC in roads, the waterfront and recreational areas.

Figure 9.6: The Brooker Highway looking south from Cleary's Gates c.1962. Source: *Lord Mayor of Hobart's Report 1962-64*

In 1957 the demands of 'wise town planning for the future' persuaded the CHPA to start lobbying the City Council for a tunnel to be built under Harrington Street at its intersection with Macquarie Street.[63] Although the improvement would 'eliminate' traffic congestion at this busy intersection, it was considered too costly and was never built. When the cost of the Brooker Highway grew dramatically and the Cosgrove government demanded that the City Council pay for the last part from Cleary's Gates to the central business district, the CHPA supported the view that it was 'a State responsibility' and not a municipal one (Figure 9.6).[64] This prompted Premier Robert Cosgrove to call the CHPA 'stooges' of the City Council, an insult John Turnbull vigorously denied. The government finally built the road to the railway roundabout near Liverpool Street and the Council built the final section to Davey Street after a program of land acquisition.

In 1958 the Marine Board proposed to reclaim about five acres of land at Castray Esplanade to build Numbers 4 and 5 Princes Wharf berths and large goods sheds.[65] A deputation of the CHPA and other associations to the Legislative Council pointed out that the Marine Board proposal would add to the already 'heavy traffic' in the area and would be 'short sighted'. To relieve congestion it was preferable to develop the other side of the port at Macquarie Point, where there was easy access to rail facilities and the new northern outlet road. The deputation also noted the impact on the residents of Battery Point from the noise and fumes and on 'the unique scenic and historical value' of Princes Park and Castray Esplanade. To the dismay of many, Parliament sanctioned the reclamation.[66]

The CHPA also had to be alert for encroachments onto public recreational areas. In 1960 a City Council proposal to alienate about five acres of Mount Wellington for a hotel development threatened to disrupt its 'harmonious relationship' with the CHPA.[67] The sale ran counter to 'the best interests' of Hobart and was soundly defeated in a poll of ratepayers in May, yet the City Council was ready to override that decision by leasing the land for 99 years. This did not alter the CHPA's principled stand against the alienation of 'the people's park land for private profit' and their protest was successful. Turnbull philosophically declared that 'true progress in the city was built on constant striving' and that 'disagreements were part of the effort for progress', but he adhered to his 'policy of constructive thought and co-operative approach'.[68]

Relations with the City Council worsened in 1965 when, for reasons that are unclear, the Council changed its policy on observers and no longer permitted a CHPA representative to attend Town Planning Committee meetings.[69] This must have disappointed Turnbull, who resigned as chairman of the CHPA in 1965. However, he was pleased that their achievements were 'perhaps even greater than envisaged in our initial stages of endeavour'.[70] In the mid-1960s attendance at meetings and interest in suburban progress associations waned, perhaps, as Secretary J.H. Lawler suggested, because 'an affluent community' can be 'somewhat complacent'.[71] Expectations that coordinated planning would solve Greater Hobart's planning problems were also not met and added to disillusionment.

Coordinated planning

The purview of the CATPC was broader than the city of Hobart itself and it led the push for coordinated planning in Greater Hobart. This was a contentious issue and required support from the various local government authorities which had legislative responsibility for planning – the Hobart City Council, the Glenorchy Municipal Council to the north, the Kingborough Municipal Council to the south, and the Clarence Municipal Council on the eastern shore of the River Derwent. Agreement was also required from McInnis as Town and Country Planning Commissioner and government departments and marine boards, which were not bound by planning legislation and ignored municipal planning schemes. Philp told McInnis that he was anxious to get 'planning done, instead of being forever swayed by conflicting interests'.[72] In 1950 the CATPC approved of the Hobart City Council holding a conference with the Clarence, Kingston and Glenorchy municipalities to discuss 'co-operative town planning' on arterial roads, sporting and recreational provision, industrial areas and water supply.[73] In addition to the four councils, nominees of the Hobart Marine Board and of the government became members of the Hobart Joint Planning Advisory Committee. This committee was shortlived because the government and government instrumentalities were opposed to becoming legally bound by the *Town and Country Planning Act*, while Glenorchy was suspicious of possible annexation by the City of Hobart.[74]

The CATPC also grew impatient at the City Council's approach to planning and urged Premier Cosgrove to appoint a planning board for

Greater Hobart with power to bind all councils and the government.[75] McInnis thought the CATPC was 'closely in touch with the planning problems of the City, and their suggestions are worthy of serious consideration'. However, he saw political difficulties in creating a Greater Hobart Council and believed that 'planning must be done and approved by those authorities who must carry it out'. He recommended that the government appoint a Greater Hobart Planning Advisory Committee, with himself as convener and chairman, one councillor and one technical representative each from the four councils, one representative from the Citizen Advisory Committees of each council, one representative from the Department of Public Works, the Transport Commission, the Education Department and the Department of Public Health, and one representative from the professional bodies of engineers, architects and surveyors. Although not suggesting that the committee be given 'statutory authority', McInnis thought giving it 'official status' would enable the committee to receive 'full consideration of its requests' from government departments and councils. Cabinet approved and the new Hobart Metropolitan Planning Committee (HMPC) was formed.

The HMPC held its first meeting on 11 September 1951. Its primary aim was to plan for the metropolitan area as a sub-region to achieve 'the best conditions of living, working and recreation' and to secure 'the implementation of the planning as a framework for statutory Town Planning Schemes'.[76] Although many useful reports were written on subjects like the location of industry, residential development and traffic and transport, the CATPC remained dissatisfied. In July 1952 it urged Premier Cosgrove to appoint a statutory authority with 'complete control over any and all Town and Country Planning Development'.[77] This 'supreme Authority' must be under the direction of Parliament and be 'independent of local preferences when it comes to overall planning and planning policy'. The authority must control land use 'so as to retain natural soil resources to the best advantage' of the community; have power to stop further ribbon development in built-up areas; seek solutions to parking problems; encourage the construction of 'multi-family housing units in a controlled proportion to the total housing program'; and make grants to councils to increase the number of trained personnel engaged in formulating and carrying out town planning investigations and surveys. McInnis again demurred, arguing that the CATPC should give the HMPC 'a fair trial'.[78]

However, Philp, a member of the HMPC, remained critical of the long gap between meetings. In 1953 he thought the HMPC record was 'unsatisfactory' and that if nothing 'worthwhile' was accomplished this would 'seriously affect the public's attitude towards Town Planning generally'.[79] The following year members of the HMPC concluded that their advisory powers were inadequate. In November 1954 Philp chaired a meeting of the general development and implementation subcommittees of the HMPC, which supported a statutory planning authority.[80] This authority should prepare a Master Plan 'for the development of all community needs for the whole Southern Region', including all planning of land use, zoning, and public utilities for a population of 250,000. It would be empowered to commission experts and employ staff or assist in the preparation of the Master Plan, but detailed planning and implementation of the plans would remain the responsibility of municipalities. The full HMPC endorsed the proposal, which in its final form gave equal representation on the authority to the Hobart, Brighton, Clarence, Glenorchy and Kingborough Councils.

In July 1955 representatives of the councils and the implementation subcommittee began to draft a bill for the government, which acquiesced in the wishes of the councils. When finally passed in 1957, the legislation enabled any group of local authorities in a particular area to petition the government to set up a Master Planning Authority and to finance schemes by levying special rates.[81] A Master Planning Authority would be able to issue interim orders to restrict the development of land and to compel landowners to develop their land according to the plan, but with the right of appeal to a magistrate. That the Crown and marine boards were not bound by the legislation was a significant weakness, but Philp hoped that more attention would finally be given to 'our greatest need for co-ordinated development' – 'long range physical and financial planning', which was 'a vital necessity for the preservation of amenities, values and growth'.[82]

The Southern Metropolitan Master Planning Authority held its first meeting in September 1958. Despite losing key staff, experiencing delays in replacing them and dealing with the time-consuming task of mapping and surveying the metropolitan area, the authority drafted and exhibited a Master Plan for public inspection in 1962. The plan contained flaws, such as the absence of a traffic and transportation scheme and simply incorporated much work from existing local planning schemes, which the authority had helped develop.[83] The Hobart City Council was disappointed that the authority had produced not 'a strategic plan in broad outline, with a set of policies in broad scope', but a detailed plan that would be a straight-jacket for the Council and would override the Council's proposals.[84] Ultimately, the Master Plan was withdrawn and the authority struggled on, preparing numerous reports and surveys (some with the help of the CHPA) and sponsoring two transportation studies, before it was disbanded after the Hobart City Council withdrew in 1973.[85] The experiment fell far short of the CATPC's and CHPA's hopes for coordinated planning, but that it was attempted was largely due to their campaigning.[86]

Conclusion

Between 1915 and 1926 STTPA activism did much to improve the provision of parks and reserves in Hobart, but it failed to improve the standard of housing or to secure its major goal of town planning legislation mainly because it was unable to command wide public support. In the postwar period newly-formed city-wide associations took up many of the same issues and public support remained a crucial factor in achieving town planning goals. After 1945 better housing provision was paramount and attracted much government and community attention, but few outside the CATPC took an active interest in planning in Hobart. Both the CATPC and the CHPA often bemoaned their failure to arouse wide public support for urban planning and civic issues more generally.[87]

While these public-spirited urban activists, like the STTPA before them, achieved some gains in areas such as recreational provision and road planning, they also failed to achieve their main goal of a strong central body able to override municipalities. To be sure, the SMMPA was formed, but it lacked what the urban activists like Philp desperately wanted – wide and coercive powers over councils, with representatives of citizens' groups as members and with direct links to the economic and social policy makers in government. It was unsatisfactory for citizens merely to criticise a plan after it had been drawn up: the activists wanted to participate in the act of planning from the outset. Planning in Hobart therefore remained as it had been in the interwar period – an under-resourced, closely guarded and narrowly-conceived local government function preoccupied with development control. The City Engineer conceded in 1962 that he lacked the planning staff to deal with the serious problems arising from the rapid growth of Hobart that community bodies regularly pointed out.[88]

One might be forgiven for concluding that the burst of community engagement after 1945 had not altered planning processes and thinking in fundamental ways. But that conclusion should not detract from what had been achieved by developing closer relations with the City Council. Bodies such as the CATPC and the CHPA forced local and state government to take account of public needs and made some crucial interventions to remind government of its responsibilities to the community in planning for the future. Although less influential than in its first two halcyon decades, the CHPA continues its work into the 21st century.

References

[1] Renate Howe, 'A New Paradigm: Planning and Reconstruction in the 1940s', in *The Australian metropolis: a planning history*, eds. Stephen Hamnett and Robert Freestone (Sydney: Allen and Unwin, 2000), ch.5.

[2] Leonie Sandercock, *Cities for sale: property, politics and urban planning in Australia* (Melbourne: Melbourne University Press, 1977), ch.5.

[3] Howe, 81; Ian Alexander, 'The post-war city' in *The Australian Metropolis*, ch.6.

[4] Graeme Davison, *Car Wars: How the Car Won Our Hearts and Conquered Our Cities* (Sydney: Allen and Unwin, 2004).

[5] Nick Tiratsoo, Junichi Hasegawa, Tony Mason and Takao Matsumura, *Urban Reconstruction in Britain and Japan 1945-1955: dreams, plans and realities* (Luton: University of Luton Press, 2002), 10.

[6] Howe, 87, 92.

[7] Alexander, 102.

[8] A.W. Noakes, *The work of a progress association: how to get what you want! Democracy in action* (Brisbane: The Author, 1948).

[9] Patrick Mullins, 'Progress Associations and Urban Development: The Gold Coast, 1945-1979', *Urban Policy and Research*, 13(2), (June 1995): 67-80.

[10] John Murphy and Belinda Probert, '"Anything for the house": Recollections of Post-war Suburban Dreaming', *Australian Historical Studies*, 36(124), (October 2004): 281.

[11] John A. Turnbull, *Ten Years of Progress: A Story of the Lenah Valley Progress Association* (Hobart: Lenah Valley Progress Association, 1939): 15.

[12] *Mercury*, 10 August 1944.

[13] Stefan Petrow, 'Against the Spirit of Local Government: The Making of Tasmanian Town and Country Planning Legislation', *Australian Journal of Public Administration*, 54(2), (June 1995): 207.

[14] Stefan Petrow, 'A City in Search of a Plan: Hobart, 1945-1962', *Tasmanian Historical Studies*, 5(1), (1995-6): 133.

[15] F.C. Cook, *City of Hobart Plan* (Hobart: Walch, 1945): 9.

[16] Petrow, 'A City in Search of a Plan', 133-39.

[17] Ibid. 138-39.

[18] Ibid. 139-40.

[19] Ibid; Cole to Council of Hobart Progress Associations (hereafter CHPA), 4 April and 18 April 1946, Hobart City Council, Copies of outward

correspondence, MCC 16/8/1/54, Archives Office of Tasmania, Hobart (hereafter AOTH).

[20] *Mercury*, 7 August 1945.

[21] *Mercury*, 26 July 1946.

[22] Ibid.

[23] Ibid.; Cole to City Council officers, 16 July 1946, MCC 16/8/1/54, AOTH.

[24] Hobart City Council, Minutes of City Council Town Planning Committee (hereafter HCCTPC), 21 November 1947, MCC 16/134/1/1, AOTH; Cole to CHPA, 1 December 1947, MCC 16/8/1/54, AOTH; Petrow, A City in Search of a Plan, 139–40.

[25] Neil Abercrombie to CHPA, 15 May 1956, AA 235/1/3, Hobart Citizen's Advisory Town Planning Committee (hereafter CATPC) file, AOTH.

[26] First Annual Report CATPC, Correspondence and papers of Battery Point Progress Association, NS 1479/1/1, AOTH.

[27] Cole to CATPC, 13 May 1948, MCC 16/8/1/54, AOTH.

[28] *Mercury*, 26 November 1970; Turnbull, 15–16.

[29] CATPC, 8 September 1949, AA 235/1/3, AOTH.

[30] CATPC Annual Report to 30 June 1950, AA 235/1/3, AOTH; Stefan Petrow and Alison Alexander, *Growing with Strength: A History of the Hobart City Council 1846–2000* (Hobart: Hobart City Council, 2008): 395.

[31] CATPC, 8 March 1951, AA 235/1/3, AOTH.

[32] Colin E. Philp, *Planning for You* (Hobart: The Author, 1955): pp. 3–4, 8, Town and Country Planning File, Minister for Lands and Works, LSD 270/1/52, AOTH; *Mercury*, 11 September 1954.

[33] HCCTPC, 22 October 1956, 7 February 1957, MCC 16/134/1/3, AOTH.

[34] HCCTPC, 7 February 1957, MCC 16/134/1/3, AOTH.

[35] CATPC Annual Report to 30 June 1953, AA 235/1/3, AOTH; CHPA, 18 April 1957, NS 1284/1/2, AOTH.

[36] HCCTPC, 15 August 1958, MCC 16/134/1/5, AOTH; CHPA, 21 August 1958, NS 1284/1/2, AOTH.

[37] Woodham to McInnis, 19 August 1949, 8 September 1949, AA 235/1/3, AOTH.

[38] CATPC, 10 November 1949, 8 June 1950, 12 June 1952, AA 235/1/3, AOTH.

[39] CATPC, 8 September 1949, Woodham to McInnis, 15 September 1949, AA235/1/3, AOTH.

[40] CHPA Annual Report 1963–64, NS 1284/1/6, AOTH.

[41] Brewster to Premier, 16 September 1950, McInnis to Minister for Lands and Works, 6 October 1950, AA235/1/8, AOTH; HCCTPC, 3 October 1950, MCC 16/134/1/1, AOTH.
[42] CATPC, 10 August 1950, AA 235/1/3, AOTH.
[43] CATPC, 13 August 1953, AA 235/1/3, AOTH.
[44] HCCTPC, 30 July 1956, emphasis in original, MCC 16/134/1/3, AOTH.
[45] HCCTPC, 21 January, 7 February, 5 March, 1957, MCC 16/134/1/3, AOTH.
[46] CATPC, 13 April 1950 and 12 November 1953, AA 235/1/3, AOTH.
[47] HCCTPC, memos. by Knott, 21 March, 2 May 1958, MCC 16/134/1/4, AOTH; Petrow and Alexander, 354-55.
[48] Port of Hobart Foreshores Committee (hereafter PHFC), 1 August 1949, AA235/1/4, AOTH.
[49] CATPC, 9, 23 February 1950, AA 235/1/3, AOTH; HCCTPC, 28 February 1950, MCC 16/134/1/1, AOTH.
[50] HCCTPC, 12 October 1948, MCC 16/134/1/1, AOTH; CATPC, 9 February 1950, AA 235/1/3, AOTH; Audrey Hudspeth, and Lindy Scripps, *Capital Port: A History of the Marine Board of Hobart 1858-1997* (Hobart: Hobart Ports Corporation, 2000): 245.
[51] PHFC, 13 April 1950, AA235/1/4, AOTH.
[52] Petrow 'A City in Search of a Plan', p. 142; Hudspeth and Scripps, 236.
[53] Woodham to Town Clerk, 19 August 1949, NS 1479/1/1, AOTH; HCCTPC, 13 December 1949, MCC 16/134/1/1, AOTH; *Lord Mayor's Report* 1952-54, 32 and 1958-60, 39.
[54] Cole to CATPC, 1 July 1955, MCC 16/8/1/92, AOTH.
[55] CATPC, 8 September 1949 and Annual Report to 30 June 1950, AA 235/1/3, AOTH.
[56] CATPC, 9 November 1950, AA 235/1/3, AOTH.
[57] CATPC, 13 October 1949, AA 235/3, AOTH.
[58] CATPC, 9 November, 14 December 1950, AA 235/1/3, AOTH.
[59] McInnis to Brewster, 28 September 1951, AA 235/1/3, AOTH.
[60] Hobart Metropolitan Planning Committee (hereafter HMPC) minutes, 15 March 1955, AA235/1/6, AOTH.
[61] *Lord Mayor's Report* 1958-60, p. 29; Malcolm Clark, 'Metropolitan Planning in Hobart' in *Spirited Cities: Urban Planning, Traffic and Environmental Management in the Nineties. Essays for Hans Westerman*, ed. Robert Freestone (Sydney: Federation Press, 1993): 182.

⁶² HCCTPC, 5 September 1958, MCC 16/134/1/5, AOTH.
⁶³ CHPA, 21 February 1957, NS 1284/1/2, AOTH; *Mercury*, 23 February 1957.
⁶⁴ HCCTPC, 21 March 1958, MCC 16/134/1/4, AOTH; *Mercury*, 18 July 1958.
⁶⁵ Notes for a deputation to Legislative Council members, NS 1479/1/3, AOTH; Hudspeth and Scripps, 255.
⁶⁶ CHPA, 19 March 1959, NS 1284/1/2, AOTH; CHPA, 19 September 1963, NS1046/1/1, AOTH.
⁶⁷ JPPPT, 1960, vol. 163, paper 43, Local Bills: Hobart Corporation Bill 1960 (No. 74). Report of Standing Committee; Turnbull to Reece, 19 August 1960, Premier's and Chief Secretary's Department General Correspondence, PCS 1/422/134/1/60, AOTH; Petrow and Alexander, 366.
⁶⁸ CHPA, 21 July 1960, NS 1284/1/2, AOTH; CATPC Annual Report 1960–61, NS 1284/1/6, AOTH.
⁶⁹ CHPA Annual Report 1964–65, NS 1284/1/6, AOTH.
⁷⁰ CHPA Annual Report 1964–65, NS 1284/1/6, AOTH; Petrow and Alexander, 415.
⁷¹ CHPA Secretary's Annual Report 1965–66, NS 1284/1/6, AOTH.
⁷² Diary of R.A. McInnis, 14 December 1950.
⁷³ CATPC, 13 April 1950, AA 235/1/3, AOTH.
⁷⁴ Petrow, A City in Search of a Plan, 141.
⁷⁵ CATPC to Premier, 21 February, 7 June 1951, memoranda by McInnis, 21 March, 21 June 1951, Hobart Metropolitan Advisory Committee (hereafter HMAC) AA 235/1/4, AOTH.
⁷⁶ HMPC, 11 September 1951, AA 235/1/4, AOTH.
⁷⁷ CATPC to Cosgrove, 7 July 1952, HMAC, AA 235/1/4, AOTH.
⁷⁸ McInnis to Minister for Lands and Works, 7 August 1952, AA 235/1/4, AOTH.
⁷⁹ CATPC, 12 March 1953, AA 235/1/3, AOTH; RAIA, Tasmanian Chapter, Minute Book, 10 March 1953, RAIA, Hobart.
⁸⁰ HMPC, 2 November 1954, AA235/1/4, AOTH; HCCTPC, 1 March 1955, MCC16/134/1/2; *Mercury*, 9 October 1954.
⁸¹ Petrow, 'A City in Search of a Plan', 144.
⁸² HCCTPC, 7 November 1956, 15 November 1957, MCC 16/134/1/4, AOTH.
⁸³ Petrow, 'A City in Search of a Plan', 146.
⁸⁴ Ibid., 147.
⁸⁵ Ibid.; Clark, 184.
⁸⁶ Clark, 177–85 completely overlooked the CHPA's role.

[87] *Mercury*, 18 July 1958, 6 October 1961.
[88] HCCTPC 10 April 1962, memorandum by City Engineer Peter Crawford, 3 April 1962, MCC 16/134/1/8, AOTH.

10
'Wonderland': planning in a populist Queensland 1931–78

Chris McConville

In Queensland, popular movements for planning had arisen in the 1910s – noble enterprises, driven by hopes for fairness and equality. Bereft of common purpose and popular interest by 1962, the most influential of these organisations, the Queensland Town Planning Association (QTPA), collapsed. In the following decade, with few organisations seeking to combine equity and development through a predictable planning system, it seemed that local communities and property developers had achieved a different sort of unity, this time expressed through their faith in the debased modernism of Queensland's coastal tourist strip. Perhaps in light of this coherence, the regionalism of Queensland and its late modernisation could be identified as responsible for a decline in independent community voices in planning. Queensland's recurrent drift towards increased dependence on tourist urbanisation played a role. At the same time the QTPA in its failure to define a vision distinct from the modernities of the developer, and through its ultimate inability to respond to populist insecurities about property values, cannot entirely evade responsibility for the obstacles that faced community-based planning in 1970s Queensland.

How did popular planning movements lose their way? Why did a once democratic ideal become subsumed under schemes through which town plans could be made for private rather than public good? In responding to such questions this chapter initially revisits the successful shaping of Mackay's town plan. When the QTPA sought to build on this victory in Brisbane (Figure 10.1), it failed; the city's planning was delayed for 30 years and the Association itself disintegrated. A Brisbane Development Association, despite tensions with a chaotic array of localised progress associations, spoke for the community. By 1968 it too faced a municipal regime dismissive of any public consultation about planning. In the rapidly expanding urbanism of coastal Queensland after 1960, planning was even less significant, and community opinion seemed almost entirely interwoven with the fantasies of local property tycoons.

Figure 10.1: Aerial view of Brisbane, 1936. Source: John Oxley Library, State Library of Queensland, 13194

These four events – active community-based planning in Mackay, matched by the struggle for an authoritative community voice in Brisbane, the rise of a assuredly modernist vision under Lord Mayor Clem Jones, and the reformation of community interest in planning in the service of the Gold Coast's property developers and tourism industry – go to the heart of the QTPA's dilemmas. The professionals gathered in the QTPA promoted their own version of a modernised city and assumed that their restrictive sense of community interest could encompass all but the most extreme popular opinion. The journey from Mackay to the Gold Coast via the Clem Jones era in Brisbane demonstrates exactly the opposite. Over time, the modernising dream that struck a chord with Queenslanders was that of the construction and tourism industries and their political acolytes. In the urban space of the Gold Coast, a community voice, as expressed through progress associations, joined the brash chorus reiterating the proclamations of developers rather than town planners.

A provincial triumph: planning Mackay 1931-52

The success of the QTPA in Noosa raised interest in nearby shires. Not for the first time, the Shire of Landsborough sought to mimic Noosa's beachfront developments and set out a planning scheme for King's Beach and nearby streets with their holiday flats and boarding houses.[1] Broad planning goals were destabilised when angry Caloundra ratepayers challenged the elected officials who dared rob them of rights in land use. The shire gave up and withdrew the scheme.[2] Events unfolded differently in a more urbane Mackay (Figure 10.2).[3]

Figure 10.2: Victoria Street, Mackay in the 1930s. Source: Mackay Regional Council Library Service, gmc02270

The city centre of Mackay, Queensland's 'sugaropolis', was slated for rebuilding in conjunction with work on a new port.[4] 'From being a bush town, Mackay jumped overnight into the public eye as a city of the future', proclaimed one local journalist, dazzled by his city of the future's neon lighting and ultra-modern hotels.[5] An agreement to finance the outer harbour works was reached between the city and the state in 1933, subject to a vote in favour by Mackay citizens. Work on the harbour had begun in 1934 and the new port, the deepest in Queensland, was open to shipping in 1939.[6]

Even before port work got underway, Mackay residents had taken up the cause of town planning, led by a youthful civic identity, Ian Wood (Figure 10.3). Wood won a place on the Mackay Council in 1927 and was mayor for twelve years, initially as the youngest in Australia. Moving from local politics to the national stage, as a Queensland senator, Wood tirelessly promoted bicycling (during his years in Mackay almost half the local workforce commuted by bicycle and in the national capital he was dubbed 'The Bicycling Senator') and sat on a Senate Committee which reviewed the development of Canberra.[7] Wood also pioneered regional aviation, had interests in resort building on Lindeman Island and promoted national parks. At a local government conference in Brisbane in 1932 he had long discussions with both Charles Chuter and R.A. McInnis, before returning north convinced that 'the Home Secretary's Department is apparently out to encourage town planning and commends our efforts'.[8] Within a few months the Council had appointed McInnis to draw up a plan for the city and adopted a QTPA proposal for a citizen's committee.[9] Work it seemed had already commenced on Wood's favoured street plantings and concrete public buildings.[10] By December that year McInnis presented invoices for final payment claiming that the plan was complete, even though to some critics the advisory committee appeared to have had little real involvement. To others town planning remained a useless fad, as a Mr M.A. McColl complained in the local paper: 'it is quite easy for some people to spend other people's money, but I can assure the "Town Planners" and the "Knights of the Garden Plot Order" that they should know that there is no money to burn on such unnecessary "show window" stunts at the present time'.[11]

Figure 10.3: Ian Wood, Mayor of Mackay (1930–33, 1943–52, 1967–70). Source: John Oxley Library, State Library of Queensland, 185372

State parliamentarians were also wary of localised planning. Debate on Mackay's town plan became entangled with disputes over the independence that Charles Chuter had ensured for the Brisbane City Council in 1925.[12] McInnis' town plan finally passed into law in 1941 before being amended by the architect Karl Langer in 1952.[13]

The slow death of the town planning association 1951-62

McInnis and others in the town planning movement had envisioned the Mackay town plan with is special legislative backing as a model for the entire state. In fact the impetus brought to planning by the coastal tourism industry seemed to enhance the prospects for localised, community-driven planning. In retrospect, the Mackay plan seemed more like a dignified epitaph for the popular movement in town planning. Once both progressive and influential, the QTPA found itself marginalised in Brisbane and more or less defunct in the state's regional localities by 1940, even though one of its shining lights now occupied the post of city planner for Brisbane. R.A. McInnis had lobbied hard for the QTPA during the 1920s. After at least one failed application to become Brisbane planner he finally won that role in the 1930s, with a specific brief to complete Brisbane's town plan. McInnis pursued this single-mindedly – to the extent that he turned his back on the QTPA's long-standing goal of public participation in the process.[14]

Doggedly throughout the 1930s, the QTPA sought a say in any city plan.[15] McInnis now sided with his new employers rather than his former colleagues and dismissed QTPA proposals. In 1938 for example the QTPA wrote to McInnis suggesting a local plan for inner-city Spring Hill, so as to avoid 'slum conditions'. McInnis ridiculed the suggestion of his one-time colleagues as a 'waste of time', observing that:

> re-planning would entail the resumption of land and houses, the demolition of buildings and, in many cases, of roads; the re-surveying into larger allotments and wider roads which would result in less properties than there are at present; then finally the reconstruction of houses and roads. Such an undertaking cannot be made to pay for itself, and is not warranted.[16]

After a trip north, en route to taking up a wartime role in Darwin, and passing comment on the zoning possibilities of Townsville, McInnis returned to Brisbane in 1944 where he affirmed his faith in a minimalist town plan and his disdain for direct public input.[17] In an address to the Rotary Club of Brisbane in 1944, McInnis explained that only 30 objections to his plan were submitted. The public had categorically accepted his goals. The plan he insisted ought now become law and unalterable. And whereas the QTPA argued for a board to oversee planning he was certain that planning control was best 'vested' in a singular City Planner.[18] In 1951, with McInnis' plan still not passed into law, Brisbane's Lord Mayor J.C. Chandler suggested that the city needed no 'hard and fast' town plan but one with minimal interventions.[19]

Indeed the banner for the town planner's ideal of the garden city was now carried in Queensland by agrarian associations and state officialdom. Queensland state governments had organised small farmers into cooperatives with marketing control in the interwar years.[20] When the Oxford economist Colin Clark replaced J.B. Brigden as government statistician he was already a supporter of village settlement schemes such as those promoted by B.A. Santamaria and his Roman Catholic communitarians. Clark's vision for the state, shared by Labor Premiers Ned Hanlon and Vince Gair, was consistent in many ways with a decentralising garden city program, of populating an 'empty' Queensland.[21] In a dream with many echoes in recent Queensland history, Clark proposed that population rather than investment drove productivity.[22] And agrarians like Clark rather than modernising planners like McInnis, had the ear of state cabinet.

As these agrarian cooperatives and their supportive civil servants assumed much of the influence previously wielded by men like Charles Chuter, the QTPA could no longer present itself as the standard-bearer for garden city principles. In a series of unsuccessful reformations the QTPA failed to reach out to the professions or public.[23] The Association lapsed in 1951 but meetings in 1953–54 suggested to acting secretary T. Lowther, that transport problems would attract new membership.[24] In 1957 members drew up a constitution and changed the Association's name to the Queensland Town and Country Planning Association

(QTPCA) – something of a peculiar transition since it no longer had any presence in country Queensland, nor indeed precious little beyond inner Brisbane. Instead of hastening a revival in the Association, the change of name heralded its collapse.

By 1961 the Association had to give up on meeting after meeting, as members turned away to the professional Australian Planning Institute (API).[25] The meeting for May lapsed for want of a quorum.[26] The meeting in June proceeded but was 'not well attended'. The July meeting was abandoned and the few who attended wondered if there was sufficient interest in planning in Queensland for both the API and the QTPCA to exist in tandem. The September meeting also lapsed, the October meeting failed to garner a quorum, and with the annual general meeting now three months overdue any further meeting was delayed until after the release of the new Brisbane town plan.[27] By the following year the Association was still trying to decide its direction with members looking back wistfully on what they now regarded as an illustrious era during the interwar years, when the old QTPA had a paid secretariat, subsidy and support from government and the governor as patron. By 1962 the Association had not held a successful meeting for twelve months. In an indication that time and relevance had passed the Association by, one of the last acts of the QTCPA was to congratulate two of its members on becoming grandfathers.

Progress and development 1952–75

The decline of the QTCPA was matched by a rise in the ebullience of localised ratepayers' and progress associations, joined eventually by a central city rather than suburbanised body, the Brisbane Development Association.[28] Not all such groups automatically objected to planning. In 1946 the Pinkenba association noted 'the thoughtful planning behind your [the city council's] scheme', and at the same time voiced fears for recreational space.[29] The Wavell Heights Progress Association hoped that the town plan would allow their suburb 'to progress along modern lines' and asked for strict controls over shops and residential areas so as to protect a planned green belt.³⁰

Figure 10.4: Roma Street Markets, Brisbane, late 1930s. Source: John Oxley Library, State Library of Queensland, 33763

Nonetheless, as the postwar consensus on civic duties and reconstruction faded, progress associations were emboldened in challenges to municipal power. Forming local 'Fight Funds' in 1951, these associations joined in an aggressive, occasionally menacing, defence of the rights of individual property holders or in appeals for upgraded local services.³¹ Eventually they came to see zoning proposals as the fundamental threat to their suburban securities.

Once Brisbane's zoning proposals were publicised in 1944, progress associations in the north-eastern suburbs combined to fight against industrial zones.³² Having set themselves deliberately outside the electoral process such groups could do little other than resort to the crudest and most aggressive of confrontational politics. Progress associations routinely demanded that the city council listen to them, often insisting that their elected representatives could not act without such consultation.[33] As the issue of a Brisbane town plan resurfaced once more in 1957–58 a new body, the Brisbane Development Association (BDA) sought to set itself apart from the irrationalities which warped so many outbursts from progress associations.[34]

The BDA had come into existence as an umbrella association to bring a reasoned if critical voice to discussions of the Brisbane town plan. It deliberately saw itself as representing business and professional interests rather than those of suburban householders with much of its focus on the city centre.[35] One of its longest running campaigns, for example, was to open up the western entrances to the city centre by removal of the Roma Street markets (Figure 10.4). Through good relations with the city and state, rather than strident antagonism, the BDA hoped to ensure proper planning. As one BDA publication made clear:

> As a body BDA can do nothing really definite in gaining better results but by diplomatic and friendly co-operation … the BDA was not formed with any desire to, or intention of, attacking existing elected bodies but rather to co-operate with them and support progressive elements in the interests of civic progress.[36]

The BDA understood well that a Brisbanite could only be prompted to take an interest in planning once a crisis loomed. Nevertheless, the organisation intended to raise community interest in strategic planning rather than waste energy in short-term battles over rates or rubbish.[37]

In a drive for new members in 1964, it was explained that 'the BDA feels that, by world standards, Brisbane is a backward city, and the public should be brought to a full realisation of this fact'. Ascribing backwardness to Queenslanders was probably not the best way to garner widespread support, but still the BDA continued to appeal for 'the strongest possible financial support from citizens'.[38] An interest in planning may well have been stirred but without the necessary support, financial or otherwise, flowing to the BDA. BDA President Tom Cross went on in the following year to decry the proliferation of progress and other associations with an interest in planning to the extent that Brisbane's progress was 'being partly bogged down by a growing number of commercial and community organisations'. Cross proposed a one-day seminar bringing all groups together as a prelude to 'resolute action on a joint basis' and provision of a sound financial platform for campaigns.[39]

Figure 10.5: Clem Jones, Brisbane Lord Mayor, 1967. Source: Brisbane City Council Library Services, Brisbane Images

The BDA, as a popular voice in planning, did encounter many obstacles, yet managed to survive to become critical to public interest in planning the 21st century city. Yet in the 1960s, with a charismatic and confident mayor reshaping Brisbane, it had to abandon at least some if its desire to work cooperatively with municipal authority.

If the BDA struggled to shore up its role as sole voice of the community in planning matters, the QTCPA meanwhile was offered one final opportunity for influence in the City of Brisbane. One of its members, Clem Jones, had won pre-selection as the Australian Labor Party (ALP) candidate for mayor and on winning the mayoral race in 1961 invited the QTCPA to a meeting at city hall. Predictably enough, the Association's key officials were unable to attend. Nonetheless Clem Jones carried some of the Association's interest in modernity and motorised traffic management into city hall, at the same time demonstrating somewhat less interest in the QTCPA's concern for public participation in planning. In the long run perhaps the QTCPA, even had it retained a broad membership, may have had little influence with the man lauded as Mr Brisbane.

It is now hard to find critical comment about Clem Jones, the multimillionaire who shaped Brisbane between 1961 and 1975 (Figure 10.5). Most residents of Brisbane seem content with the comments made at Jones' state funeral in 2007, where he was praised for initiating the vibrant and cosmopolitan Brisbane of the 21st century.[40] That the modernism of Jones' dreams might not necessarily have provided the perfect platform for vibrancy and cosmopolitanism seemed to elude mayoral eulogists. In fact two years before Jones first donned mayoral robes, Queensland's centenary celebrations identified Brisbane's premodernity as its redeeming quality. W.J. Hudson, writing in *The Courier Mail* noted that Brisbane was 'still more countrified than urban ... perhaps closer to being what is regarded as "really" Australian'.[41] No doubt many Brisbanites did come speedily to share Mr Brisbane's modernist aspirations. At the same time his increasingly independent style aroused plenty of criticism during his fifteen years as mayor. Jones spoke often to the suburban masses in the press and on radio. He took up their highly localised problems of neighbourhood rubbish collection or street lighting with alacrity. Parks, sports grounds and new roadways around Brisbane only existed because of his energy and single-mindedness. He reshaped Brisbane whilst maintaining, along with his town clerk J.C. Slaughter, a tight control over planning decisions.

If any concern about Clem Jones' Brisbane survives it is to be found in regret at his closure of tramlines (Figure 10.6). Jones had promised completion of the long-awaited town plan with an emphasis on modernity – in the form of city office towers, a freeway system and suburbanised and modernist recreation centres. The city centre of Brisbane would be converted to a high-rise commercial heart and he noted: 'it is absurd to have a main city street in a city of more than half a million people with a large number of two and three storey buildings in it'.[42] And yet it was his love of motorised transport and his desire to rid the city of its trams which gave rise to Brisbane's first really popular planning movement, as residents and unionists joined together to save them.[43] Whilst the tram network was not closed down until 1968 Brisbane had already, and despite objections from within Jones' party, taken trams off four lines by 1963.[44] By 1966 Jones had fallen out with some trade unionists and members of his own party over the tram closures.[45]

Clem Jones' determination to rid the city of trams was no doubt bolstered by independent advice from traffic consultants. Along with other Australian planning authorities, Brisbane had commissioned the American company Wilbur Smith and Associates to prepare a plan for transportation. In 1965, Brisbane considered removal of all fixed rail transport, freeways through the city and buses in place of trams. The Brisbane Tramways Union responded with threats to boycott aldermanic committees formed to study the Wilbur Smith scheme (an ineffectual threat as it turned out since such committees carried little weight).[46] Several key community groups were pushing in any case an alternative although still fundamentally modernist plan for Brisbane known as 'The Bligh Plan' (after its author, architect Arthur Bligh) which centred on the redevelopment of the Roma Street markets.[47] By 1966 local ratepayers' groups revived in several areas, sometimes to urge the city to start building the Wilbur Smith freeways, but more often alive to the prospects which the transportation study held out for declines in suburban amenity.[48] Jones did delay work on several of the planned motorways, but at the same time moved to rid the city of trams, with buses taking over on several routes.[49] One account of these events noted that the decision to cut trams from four city routes was taken without a vote in council (council was actually in recess).[50]

In 1966 the state government had set up the Bennett Commission to inquire into the Brisbane City Council's land dealings and the Brisbane Development Association, emboldened it seems by the commission, branded the city's planning administration as 'despotic'.[51] By the following year it appeared that public criticism of the city's planning had widened markedly, with the BDA criticising the spread of flats and apartments, the basis they saw for a new 'slum' problem in the inner city.[52]

Not much of this opposition would have bothered Clem Jones. His view of objectors to plans was that professional planners ought to be able to by-pass them. As he remarked on one occasion:

> The satisfied citizen plays very little part in establishing the overall relationships between the administrators of local government and the people. It is the dis-satisfied citizen who determines this … in local government, there must quite obviously be many people who are frustrated, or denied something in the interests of the community, and these people naturally react unfavourably and blame, as they call it, the Council. It never occurs to any individual who has not been able to do just as he wishes, that the reason is that it would have had a detrimental effect on the community at large.[53]

Ultimately, Mr Brisbane's reputation as a successful urban reformer was ensured by the body least admired amongst Queenslanders of the 1970s, the ALP government in Canberra. When Gough Whitlam's urban affairs minister Tom Uren withdrew federal funding for Brisbane's freeways, whilst providing loans for sewerage works and public transport, Jones' plan of a motorised city was undermined, and his reputation as a progressive urbanist cemented.[54] Until halted by Uren, Brisbane City

Council had planned to drive motorways across the river and through suburbs like New Farm and Paddington – locales emblematic of Brisbane's supposed cosmopolitan vitality.

Figure 10.6: Trams in Adelaide Street, Brisbane, 1955. Source: John Oxley Library, State Library of Queensland, 82051

Mr Brisbane, charismatic, ready to listen, aware of local concerns but happy to deflate the expectations of organised planning groups and local progress groups, whilst determined about his own modernisation plan, remains a pivotal figure in Queensland's planning history. And yet towards the end, his career demonstrated some of the central contradictions surrounding popular movements in town planning. Even as he departed City Hall, his planning staff were dealing with nearly 30,000 objections to a revised town plan and the city had to create a new department separating the almost insurmountable problems of traffic planning from other aspects of urban strategy.

With the retirement of Clem Jones, the last vestiges of the QTPCA's influence disappeared. Always in thrall to car enthusiasts, the old QTPA would have found much to their liking in Jones' transport proposals.

Keen for zoning and slum demolition, his modernist projections for the inner city would also have pleased them. They would equally have been unsettled by the increasingly authoritarian style of planning in Brisbane and by the sidelining of community voices. But then the QTPA had its own limited view of 'the community', envisioning this vague entity as composed entirely of like-minded and professionally trained men. And whilst they might well have seen themselves as a class above the raucous progress associations of suburban Zillmere and Banyo or colourful backroom deal-makers in trade unions and local government, over the years, they had repeatedly drawn back from any direct challenge to private property rights.

With the QTCPA now defunct, local ALP branches, trade unionists and community groups, often backed by city aldermen had formed new resident action groups to oppose freeway plans during Jones' last years as mayor. Instead of manicured sports grounds (typified by the Brisbane Cricket Ground, the 'Gabba', where Jones personally kept tight surveillance over wickets and grass cover), these local groups were demanding respect for native plants and clean creeks. And rather than accept the demolition of the old, that prerequisite for an all-conquering modernity, they sought conservation of Brisbane's ramshackle form, especially of its once maligned 'higgeldy piggledly' stilt housing. The QTPA's combination of a faith in motorised modernity, with the citizenry's right to a say in planning, could no longer be maintained by the 1970s. Jones appeared as the last in a long line of influential members of the QTPA. Like Tom Price and Ian Wood before him he was bent on radical refashioning of Queensland's urban space. Like Ronald McInnis and others he wanted a motorised city. He shared Ray Nowland's faith in modernity and Archbishop Duhig's desire for sewers. Mr Brisbane, like others who ascended from QTPA meetings into city hall, eventually ran up against formally organised groups, which with all their false starts, stridency and incongruities, still sought to protect localised community from the wildest dreams of modernist town planning.

Wonderland: the Gold Coast 1964-78

Perhaps Jones had little choice but to adopt an autocratic style. Brisbane people may have accepted and indeed gloried in his destruction of their 'countrified' township and grown proud of the crude modernity with which it was overlain. But Jones, unlike interwar town planning advocates, faced a Country Party state government, whose members drew their power base from agrarian cooperatives and who remained suspicious of planning and of the city itself. Whilst in the removal of the Roma Street markets to Rocklea, these agrarians may have been defeated by city-based pressure groups amongst them the BDA, when it came to planning matters, they more often than not were able to find sympathetic listeners in state government. As Premier Frank Nicklin observed:

> Town planning is in itself a profession ... the average man on the street knows very little about it, although in the end it is for the public benefit. It is born of an idea generally within a local community and is passed on to the planner. From this point problems emerge ... Chief among these are land resumptions, either partial or whole, which will incommode those whose homes or access thereto may be removed in the consummation of the plan.[55]

In these somewhat stiff sentences, Nicklin, whose political base lay in agrarian cooperatives in the Near North (Sunshine) Coast hinterland, articulated the fundamental problem of planning in Queensland. Planning may well have originated in the community, and town plans may well have been drawn up for long-term communal benefit but town planners, like other professionals, could easily stand apart from this community of property holders. It ought come as no surprise then to find planning and planners besieged in the site of the most untrammelled land capitalism – the Gold Coast (Figure 10.7).

Figure 10.7: Surfers Paradise, 1951. Surfers Paradise Hotel is in the foreground at the intersection of the Pacific Highway and what is now Cavill Avenue. Source: John Oxley Library, State Library of Queensland, 68707

In that light the recent Crime and Misconduct Commission's (CMC) inquiry into the Gold Coast City Council makes for interesting reading. In 2004, the CMC reported on possible irregularities in Gold Coast City Council elections. More in amazement than dismay the commissioners remarked:

> There were occasions during this inquiry when an ordinary observer could have been forgiven for thinking that they had fallen through a hole, not just into a foreign country, but into a Wonderland where all the usual notions of reasonableness and honesty were reversed.[56]

In many ways the 'usual notions' of planning over almost a century had been reversed. Once community organisations abandoned the founding goals of equitable town planning, local government could easily follow. Much of local land-use planning, and not just on the Gold Coast, did become a Wonderland.

One historian of the Gold Coast lauded the anti-planning spirit of the city thus: 'many planners who consider themselves to be judges of taste and style find the Coast disgusting, a living example of what happens when the masses are actually allowed to dominate the political and planning system'.[57] From this vantage point then, the shared interests between the development industry and community concerns were united in antagonism towards professional planning. The Gold Coast's progress associations provided the forum for enunciating this common ground.

Interestingly the Gold Coast was chosen by Patrick Mullins as the site for perhaps the only thorough analysis of Australian progress associations. In his review, Mullins considered the development of progress associations on the Gold Coast between 1949 and 1975 in a relatively benign light.[58] He saw them in terms defined by Manuel Castells as urban social movements, driven by a sense of equity and democracy and defying an oppressively bureaucratic planning system. This may be true if we look at progress associations in a statistical framework of issues, the methodology chosen by Mullins. Yet on the Gold Coast the drive of progress associations and their allies in many localised chambers of commerce was not so much for equitable distribution of resources, but to garner as much as possible for their own shopping strip or beachfront.

These Gold Coast progress associations were according to their most enthusiastic interpreter 'natural antagonists of government', none more so than the Surfers Paradise Progress Association. Alexander McRobbie the proud chronicler of the Surfers Paradise Progress Association traces the origins of this august body to the 1920s when it campaigned for the name of a nondescript beach to be changed to Surfers Paradise.[59] Once reformed in the 1960s the Association according to McRobbie 'attracted every resident of vigour'.[60] Stern constitutions were indeed essential, since the association included one legendary Gold Coast hostess, famous for her three-day parties. Charismatic publican and entrepreneur Bernie Elsey was another Progress Association stalwart, lauded widely for his imaginative tourism ventures, amongst them the fire-breathing Tiki Idol and his regular weekend pyjama parties at the Beachcomber Hotel (to one of which he invited the visiting evangelist Billy Graham).[61] Elsey also dreamt up Surfers Paradise's unique contribution to transport planning – the meter maid – in reaction to the state government's closure of local railway connections and the arrival of parking meters and parking fines on the free-and-easy Gold Coast.[62]

By the 1980s, according to McRobbie, the association was but a 'shadow of its once crusading self'.[63] Perhaps it had simply taken on some of the mundane tasks of other progress associations. For between 1960 and 1980 it fought to get rid of telephone poles and fix footpaths along the Gold Coast. It resisted town planning controls and imaginatively proposed a mall for Cavill Avenue. These forays were interspersed with meetings, at which according to McRobbie 'splinter groups, attempted coups, takeovers, resignations, writs, counter-writs, punch-ups and threats were routine'.[64] This was not the sort of environment in which the straight-laced and self-improving members of the QTPCA would have felt at home.

Gold Coast chambers of commerce often joined with progress associations in promoting one or other of the embryonic town centres along the coastal strip. As well as making certain that their rivals gained no special concessions in street plantings or car parking, the views of chambers of commerce on urban development consisted in large part of a desire to beautify tourist areas – as in their appeal on the northern approaches to Surfers Paradise, which were described as desolate and needing replacement by 'swaying palm trees and masses of tropical shrubs', a view endorsed by Russell Hinze, Queensland's planning supremo and Gold Coast hinterland MLA, who expressed his very great concern about aesthetic values in planning.[65]

New environmental groups as Mullins noted did emerge during the 1970s. One of the more influential at the end of the decade was the Gold Coast Protection League which proposed a height limit for Gold Coast apartments.[66] A United Council of Progress Associations went even further and wanted to restrict tourist development to a three-storey height limit.[67] It was in this context that the state government closed down the Gold Coast City Council and installed administrators in 1978. In subsequent years administration was renewed, sacking proposed and a town plan created. On the fringes of the popular movement in town planning an underlying racism surfaced; the planning controls so bitterly rejected in the 1960s seemed now a suitable response to Japanese property purchases further north at Yeppoon and along the coastal strip.[68] 'When Japs own coastal land there will be nothing to prevent them from bringing in illegal migrants at night in boats', warned one correspondent to the local press.[69]

So in some ways the Gold Coast did demonstrate failings in town planning, and the superiority (at least for white Queenslanders) of a city shaped almost entirely by a free market in land. But for all its popular vitality, the Gold Coast exposes incongruities in defining progress associations as authentic and efficient expressions of popular will. Rather, and in this they were like the interwar QTPA, they fell at least for a time, under the sway of the development and tourism industries. Where municipal councillors and planners sought to resist this influence they faced the prospect of council closures and their planning powers exercised by an often unsympathetic state minister.

Conclusion

Planners on the Gold Coast did eventually bring the more erratic of their citizenry into some consensus about the need for controls and regularity. The Gold Coast City Council has made strenuous efforts to upgrade design standards. But Queensland's popular movements for planning always threaten to destabilise orderly procedure. Opportunities for community-based planning were clearly encapsulated in Mackay, just as the delay in approval for Mackay's interwar planning venture displays the reluctance of state parliamentarians to allow too great an independence for local municipalities. And even in Mackay, planning depended as much on the possibilities for expanded tourism and major development projects as on localised community interest. In the failure of Brisbane to secure zoning over several decades and through Clem Jones' role as a city-building mayor, we can see both the attractions of a modernised city and the declining community voice in planning. Battles to save trams and to prevent freeways as much as earlier fights over zoning, point to the possibilities of an anti-modernist popular movement. The Gold Coast and its colourful developers and progress association activists, however, remind us of the brittleness in any popular planning movement. For in Surfers Paradise, progress associations had their greatest influence only once aligned with tourism and property development.

By the 1970s, under the admirably immense reach of Local Government Minister Russell Hinze, even McInnis' cherished zoning patterns were easily and frequently dispensed with through ministerial re-zonings. In the kleptocratic political styles of Queensland between 1968 and 1978, orderly urban planning, with structured and formalised community involvement, seemed all too often irrelevant. Not all of this absence can be blamed on a small clique of developers and their parliamentary cronies. Queensland's regionalism favoured local planning schemes, as can be seen in Mackay and its agrarian cooperatives remained open to some planning ideals. The QTPA remained instead intent on shaping Brisbane rather than the bush or coast. In the city, its rearguard of influential membership preferred a modernising order to any enlarged if less regimented public involvement.

The QTPA had enjoyed political support and state finance in the 1920s, because town planning promised greater equity in both rural and urban life. Once the QTPA openly lent support to private property owners in their resistance to planned controls on land use, and once prominent members emphasised the wonders of a modernised rather than equitable city and favoured professional rather than popular opinion, the Association was easily marginalised. With the advantages it had possessed in the 1920s, the QTPA ought to have better resolved tensions between its several aims, especially those surrounding modernising urban space and democratic planning procedures. In its failure and by 1962, irrelevance as an entity, it helped prepare the ground for that curious conjoining of an often artificial populism with the debased modernism typical of Queensland in the late 20th century. In the state's new urban regions, those old dilemmas of sustaining democratic ideals and equitable use of space, in a planning process dominated by tourism and intensive development, are yet to be comprehensively addressed.

References

[1] Nambour *Chronicle*, 21 February 1930.
[2] Nambour *Chronicle*, 16 August 1936.
[3] Queensland Government Intelligence and Tourist Bureau, *Mackay District* (Brisbane: Queensland Government Printer, 1929), 2nd edn, 9–11.
[4] Department of Harbours and Marine Queensland, *Harbours and Marine: Port and Harbour Development in Queensland from 1824 to 1985* (Brisbane: Queensland Government Printer, 1986), 293–94, 562–65; Queensland Government Tourist Bureau, *Mackay and Whitsunday*, (Brisbane: Queensland Government Printer, 1930), 4.
[5] Mackay *Topical Review*, 12 December 1936.
[6] *Mackay Outer Harbour Official Souvenir* (Mackay: Mackay Printing and Publishing, 1939).
[7] Mackay-Blair Athol Railway League, *Mackay-Blair Athol Illustrated Record* (Mackay: Mackay Printing and Publishing, 1946).
[8] *Mackay Outer Harbour Official Souvenir*.
[9] Mackay *Daily Mercury*, 10 September 1932.
[10] City of Mackay Centenary edition, Mackay *Daily Mercury*, 6 April 1962, 26; Mackay *Daily Mercury*, 10 December 1932; Mackay *Daily Mercury*, 27 January 1933.
[11] Mackay *Daily Mercury*, 30 January 1933.
[12] See for example *Queensland Parliamentary Debates*, CLXVI.
[13] City of Mackay Centenary Edition, *Daily Mercury*, 6 April 1962, 46.
[14] The first meeting of the council's zoning committee held in February 1935; *Courier Mail*, 26 February 1935.

[15] QTPA to Town Clerk, Brisbane City Council, 4 December 1936. Home Secretary, General Correspondence regarding the Second Australian Town Planning Conference, series 17996, Queensland State Archives.
[16] McInnis to J. Cavanagh, QTPA President, 27 June 1938, Brisbane City Council Archives.
[17] McInnis Diary, University of Queensland Archives.
[18] *Daily Telegraph*, 11 December 1944.
[19] Discussions reported in *Courier Mail* throughout 1951.
[20] Diana Shogren, 'The creation of the committee of direction of fruit marketing', *Queensland Heritage*, 2(5), (1971): 31–38.
[21] Colin Clark, *Visions for Australia* (Canberra 1951).
[22] Chilla Bulbeck, 'Colin Clark and the greening of Queensland: The influence of a senior public servant on Queensland economic development, 1938 to 1952', *Australian Journal of Politics and History*, 33(1), (April 2008): 7–18.
[23] Like others interested in planning the Association seemed ignorant of the presence in their midst of one of the most celebrated of planning theorists – Constantine Doxiadis, who left his cabinet post in Greece to grow tomatoes in Queensland. But then most Queensland radicals were not aware that Alexander Kerensky the leader of the Russian Revolution had fled to Clayfield and holidayed at Surfers Paradise.
[24] *Daily Telegraph*, 14 August 1954.
[25] *Planner*, 10(4), (1970): 6–7.
[26] 'Association Notes', *Planner*, 1(2), (March 1961): 3.
[27] *Planner*, 8 September 1961, 6–10 November 1961, 7.
[28] A.W. Noakes. *The work of a progress association: how to get what you want! Democracy in action* (Brisbane: Rallings and Rallings, 1948).
[29] R. James for Pinkenba District Progress Association to City Architect City Hall, 13 November 1946, Brisbane City Council Archives (W 46725).
[30] J.W. Peachey, Secretary Wavell Heights Progress Association, to Town Clerk Brisbane, 17 November 1945 (W 29009), City of Brisbane Archives.
[31] Editorial, *Contact: The Monthly Newsletter of the Everton Park and Bunyaville Improvement Association*, 1 (September 1951), 1.
[32] 'They want to have their say', *Courier Mail*, 23 March 1959.
[33] *Banyo Improvement Association Newsletter* (16 March 1959); *Zillmere Progress Association News* (19 March 1959).
[34] L.A. Suggars, 'Story of B.D.A Growth'. *Brisbane Development Association Progress Report 1972*. (Brisbane: BDA, 1972): 2–3.

[35] Brisbane Development Association, *Constitution of the Brisbane Development Association* (Brisbane: BDA, 1957).
[36] Brisbane Development Association, 'Citizenship and the Brisbane Development Association', *A Better Brisbane*, 1(3), (June 1961): 1–3.
[37] C. Faragher, *Third Annual Report of the Brisbane Development Association for the Year 1959/60* (Brisbane: Brisbane Development Association, 1960), 1.
[38] 'Help us to enrol more.' *A Better Brisbane*, 3(1), (January 1964): 3.
[39] 'Work together for progress', *A Better Brisbane*, 4(2), (May 1965): 1.
[40] *Australian*, 17 December 2007.
[41] *Courier Mail*, 19 March 1959.
[42] *Courier Mail*, 8 July 1961.
[43] Bill McCormack, 'Fair for all policy', *Brisbane Bus and Tram Union Bulletin*, 2 (1968), and *Courier Mail*, 25 June 1968, 26 June 1968.
[44] See Bill McCormack, 'Fair for all policy', *Brisbane Bus and Tram Union Bulletin*, 2 (1968): 2; *Courier Mail* 25 June 1968; Howard Clark and David Keenan, *Brisbane tramways: the last decade* (Sans Souci NSW: Transit Press, 1977).
[45] Clark and Keenan; K.N. Toms, *Urban government, politics and planning: a study of the administration of the Brisbane town plan* (Brisbane: Queensland Regional Group of the Royal Institute of Public Administration, 1973).
[46] Bill McCormack, 'Fair for all policy', *Brisbane Bus and Tram Union Newsletter*, 2 (1968): 2.
[47] Chris McConville, 'Buying food for Brisbane: the market problem, 1884–2005', unpublished paper (University of the Sunshine Coast, 2007).
[48] Peter F. Moses, 'Trams for Australian Cities, with particular reference to Brisbane' (Master of Urban and Regional Planning Thesis, University of Queensland, 1977); *National Times*, 25 September 1972.
[49] Moses: 82.
[50] Ibid.
[51] *Courier Mail*, 5 October 1966.
[52] See generally, *A Better Brisbane*.
[53] Clem Jones, 'The Governance of a Great City and Its Problems', *Address to the Royal Institute of Public Administration*, Canberra, 26 September 1963.
[54] Clem Jones, *Brisbane, a beautiful city* (Brisbane: Brisbane City Council, 1973).
[55] Frank Nicklin, 'Planning for the Future in Queensland', *Australian Planning Institute Journal*, 2(8), (January 1964): 240.

[56] Crime and Misconduct Commission Queensland, *Influence and integrity in local government: a CMC inquiry. Inquiry into the 2004 Gold Coast City Council Election,* (Brisbane: Crime and Misconduct Commission, 2004), foreword, ii.

[57] Michael Jones, *A sunny place for shady people: the real Gold Coast story* (Sydney: Allen and Unwin, 1986), 147–48.

[58] Patrick Mullins, 'Progress associations and urban development: The Gold Coast, 1945-79, *Urban Policy and Research,* 13(2), (1995): 67–80.

[59] Alexander McRobbie, *The real Surfers Paradise* (Surfers Paradise: Pan News, 1988).

[60] McRobbie, 289.

[61] Amongst the many press investigations into the pyjama party craze, see *Courier Mail,* 7 March 1959.

[62] See Meter Maids web: www.metermaids.com/history.htm, accessed January 2008.

[63] McRobbie, 289.

[64] Ibid.

[65] Gold Coast *Bulletin*, 29 June 1978; J.H. Andrews, 'Some aspects of administration of the City of Gold Coast', *Australian Journal of Public Administration*, 38(4), (1979): 383–90; A.C. Worthington and B.E. Dollery, 'An analysis of recent trends in Australian local government', *International Journal of Public Sector Management*, 15(6), (2002): 496–515.

[66] Gold Coast *Bulletin*, 30 June 1978.

[67] Gold Coast *Bulletin*, 29 June 1978.

[68] Gold Coast *Bulletin*, 28 May 1988; 3 June 1988, *Courier Mail*, 27 May 1988.

[69] Gold Coast *Bulletin*, 2 May 1978.

11
A new planning landscape for professional and community action in Sydney 1935–67

Robert Freestone and Margaret Park

By the mid-1930s Sydney had evolved beyond the city which the founders of the Town Planning Association of New South Wales (TPANSW) surveyed on the eve of World War I (Figure 11.1). Sydney became Australia's first metropolis with over one million people in the 1920s as its population effectively doubled from 630,000 on track to 1.5 million by 1947.[1] The physical form, functioning and image of the city had been transformed by the opening of the Harbour Bridge in 1932, the development of a central city underground railway, and the electrification of the suburban network which complemented an extensive tram network serving mostly the inner city.[2] But after a decade of prosperity the shadow of economic depression had again highlighted the problem of slums as well as the looming problem of considerable unplanned speculative subdivision and uncontrolled ribbon development. The lack of open space in both inner working class communities and new suburban estates similarly signalled a continuing dilatory approach to town planning.

While the city had undergone a metamorphosis, the TPANSW had not significantly changed. Its basic organisational structure and *modus operandi* remained remarkably constant from its formation in 1913 throughout the interwar period. Its standing in the professional community and in government circles guaranteed its place at the table of topical planning debates. The more eminent and well-known members were often on the invitation list to offer expert advice and to bear witness to the unfolding development of the city and the issues being thrown up. In

September 1934, the TPANSW celebrated its 21st birthday. Whilst toasting the Association's health, probably over a luncheon or dinner as habit dictated, the members patted each other on the back for the good work achieved. This reassured them of their place in the city's history: 'The Association has brought about something of a renaissance of interest in Town Planning and Civic Development generally'.[3] But from here, as this chapter recounts, it was virtually all downhill decade by decade.

Figure 11.1: Sydney's Central Business District, 1948. Source: *Report on the Planning Scheme for the County of Cumberland 1948*

From an amateur to a professional planning movement

To be sure, the culture of planning in Sydney did not seem radically different from the 1910s when the TPANSW was founded. There were few professional planners, and planning practice was mainly a sideline for interested architects, engineers and surveyors such as Norman Weekes. The sole professional planning job in the metropolitan area was the City of Sydney Council's Town Planning Assistant position filled from 1938 by Dugald McKenzie McLachlan.[4] The organisation of planning did not reflect the great changes in Sydney's physical and social fabric. The Town Planning Advisory Board – an initiative of the reforming *Local Government Act 1919* – had lapsed. Proclamation of residential districts under this Act continued apace in upper class suburbs to provide a rudimentary form of land use zoning but there was still no comprehensive town planning legislation.[5] Successive state governments had failed miserably on this score and dreams of consolidating local councils into a Greater Sydney federation never came to fruition.[6] Planning in action meant mainly the incremental implementation of the recommendations of the 1909 Royal Commission into the City of Sydney and its Environs by the state government and the Sydney City Council.[7]

From the early 1930s discourses on planning began to perceptibly shift. A greater sense of urgency was evident in the built environment professions concerned with continuing piecemeal actions outside of the framework of comprehensive functional plans for either the central city or the region. Bolder ideas were informed by best practice overseas, particularly from Britain and the United States. The new leader to emerge in Sydney through this time was Alfred John Brown (1893–1976). New Zealand-born, like Charles Reade before him, he had a similar compelling grasp of the broader possibilities of planning.[8] He had trained as an architect and worked as chief assistant architect and planner at Welwyn Garden City, England in the early 1920s. In 1931 he became the Vernon

Memorial Lecturer in Town Planning at Sydney University, with John Sulman one of his sponsors. Brown was committed to progressive ideals, community education and raising technical standards, as reflected in numerous articles in *The Sydney Morning Herald* and technical journals, eventually culminating in the first definitive Australian textbook on the subject co-authored with Howard Sherrard in 1951.[9]

In July 1933 Brown assumed presidency of the TPANSW. Undoubtedly uppermost on his agenda was both the reform of that body and instigating decisive action by government. His tenure was short-lived and he resigned in acrimonious circumstances on 31 May 1934. One explanation was a dispute with the Institute of Architects over the latter's Martin Place design competition won by Sydney University's Professor Leslie Wilkinson.[10] But Brown later explained his decision on the grounds that 'many of its leading members were out of step with planning theory and practice. Many of the professional members walked out with me'.[11]

The first gestures toward professionalisation had actually originated within the TPANSW itself. As early as 1929, President Dr J.S. Purdy had suggested that either a branch of the British Town Planning Institute or an Australian Town Planning Institute should be established. He believed that the Association's membership could be merged into the new institute. A committee was appointed to investigate drafting a constitution for 'further consideration' and within a month it reported that formation of a NSW Town Planning Institute was timely.[12] Brown's action a few years later proved far more decisive. He believed that the new institute was 'the outcome of a long-felt need by a group of professional men who realised that town and country planning was so broad in its ramifications that it required the closest collaboration between members of the three professions'.[13]

The Institute's inaugural meeting was held on 25 September 1934. At this meeting, Professor Leslie Wilkinson, the then president of the NSW Chapter of the Royal Australian Institute of Architects, moved the motion to 'constitute the institute' wherein a provisional committee was formed and Brown was elected its chairman.[14]

A 15-member council was assembled with equal representation from architects, surveyors and engineers. Walter Burley Griffin was elected a councillor, the sole link to the original executive of the TPANSW in 1913. Its first meeting was held on 13 November 1934 and Brown was officially elected president of the new Town and Country Planning Institute of Australia (TCPIA).[15] The Institute was incorporated under the *Companies Act* in 1947 with a list of over 20 objectives of which the principal one was advancement of 'the study and practice of town and country planning and of kindred arts and sciences'. At the outset, to achieve its goals in this regard, the Institute committed itself to instigate town planning courses, examinations and diplomas.[16]

This was a decisive moment in moves toward a more professional foundation for planning in Sydney, signalling a restlessness to strive beyond general propaganda and ad hoc improvement advice. The TPANSW lost its last vestiges of professional support as the TCPIA quickly gathered credibility by assembling a strong professional membership which included planners, architects and engineers, similar to the original make-up of the early TPANSW.[17] Leslie Wilkinson suggested that a proper reply to anyone asking 'who is a town planner?' would be the reply: 'A member of the Town and Country Planning Institute'.[18]

Triggered by Brown's resignation, in August 1934 Bertram Ford became the ninth, longest-serving and last president of the TPANSW. The formation of the TCPIA was seen by Ford as a direct assault on the integrity and longevity of the TPANSW. 'There was no room for more than one body to direct matters relating to town planning', he protested, 'the new organisation was in direct opposition to the Town Planning Association, which for 21 years had been regarded as the official body'.[19] Other members were more accommodating but Ford remained obstinate and believed the Institute was a direct competitor. He was right.

The late 1930s

The narrative of the TPANSW from this point essentially becomes Ford's story (Figure 11.2). By the 1950s and 1960s rarely is any other member mentioned publicly. Born in 1880, Bertram Willoughby Ford trained as an architect, beginning a career in 1905 noteworthy for his eclectic designs of small banks in rural NSW.[20] He was a member of the Institute of Architects when the TPANSW formed and attended some of its earliest public lectures but became unfinancial in the Great Depression.[21] The first formal mention of his link to town planning in an official capacity is in 1922 when he was listed as a founding member of a new progress association calling itself the Manly Town Planning Association.[22] It was not until 1931 that he appeared on the council of the TPANSW and took on the role of honorary secretary. Indeed, he had only just resigned this position owing to 'private business interests' when pitchforked into the presidency.[23] Ford was an individual of mottled interests and callings. From 1925 to 1931 he also worked as a sports journalist with *The Sydney Morning Herald* and followed the lawn tennis circuit.[24] His public interest preoccupations ranged miscellaneously from basic wage increases and their effect on the building trade, painting the Sydney Harbour Bridge in 'old gold', and abolition of the upper house of parliament to feeding 'hungry kookas'.[25] At heart he held a deeply conservative stance which limited and skewed his reading of the issues. His political affiliation was the United Australia Party, a forerunner of today's Liberal Party on the political right.[26]

Figure 11.2: Bertram Ford, President of the Town Planning Association from 1936–37. Source: *Truth*, 6 February 1949. Courtesy Mitchell Library

Under Ford's leadership, the Association's activities in the late 1930s continued in similar vein to previous decades through protestations in the media, deputations to government, and occasional planning advice, albeit on a much less visible membership base. Table 11.1 provides a representative sample of actual and proposed deputations obtained from available sources. Recurring issues included replanning Macquarie Street, extending Martin Place, the future of Circular Quay, contesting alienation of parklands (particularly showpieces like Sydney's Domain), and more ambivalently, the need for general planning legislation. There was some continuing involvement in the life of local communities, in some ways through roles comparable to a local progress or community association. Invitations occasionally arrived from local councils seeking support, such as one from Illawarra Shire Council for assistance with a beautification scheme for Port Kembla. Several members led by Ford and the veteran Henry Halloran visited the area to prepare yet another plan with little evidence of implementation.[27] In November 1938 Ford and A.H. Edmonds travelled to Armidale and Uralla to speak on the benefits of town planning and advise on general planning needs with Ford also producing a plan for revitalisation of the Armidale Hospital grounds. A letter of thanks from local Country Party member D.H. Drummond intimated that while their work was 'excellent' and 'comprehensive in its sweep', he could only hope that the councils would have the means to implement their general recommendations.[28]

The major focus remained with central Sydney. The desire to improve Sydney's main thoroughfares was a constant preoccupation, and the Association was frequently at odds with Sydney City Council over bread and butter town planning problems. Ford and his colleagues emphatically spoke out for the northward extension of Elizabeth Street between Hunter and Bent Streets.[29] Talk of widening and extending Elizabeth Street had been on the City Council's agenda since 1902 when it was listed as one of the city's 'danger spots'.[30] The widening of Elizabeth Street southward from Hunter Street in 1935 at a cost of £1,000,000 was criticised as a partial solution that only created a 'dead end'.[31] Ford wrote to the Lord Mayor expressing his Association's 'serious concerns' regarding Council's proposal to 'substitute a square at the junction of Elizabeth and Hunter Streets for the proposed extensions of the former Street'.[32] The Association felt that a better location for a long-desired public square for central Sydney would be the eastern end of Martin Place when extended to Macquarie Street (Figure 11.3). Ford continued agitation for a civic square with a vision embracing a new Parliament House, a one-way traffic route, ornamental balustrades, shrubs and a memorial statue to King George V.[33] Some observers acknowledged the Association's role in extending Martin Place[34] but funding constraints eventually scuttled any grandiose plans for a civic space.[35]

Table 11.1: A select list of TPANSW Deputations 1935–57

Year	Issue	Representation
1935	Bilgola Quarry: TPANSW protested the quarry and associated workers' camp at Bilgola on Sydney's northern beaches	Premier
1935	Milsons Point, North Sydney: TPANSW, PPM and McMahons Point/Lavender Bay Progress Association protested the lease of the former Dorman Long construction site to an amusement park [Luna Park]	Assistant Minister for Lands
1935	Naval Oil Tanks at Chowder Bay: Dr Bean of the PPM sought TPANSW's representation**	Minister for Defence
1935	Elizabeth Street Extensions and widening. TPANSW voiced concerns over funds expended by City Council resulting in a new city 'bottle neck'*	Lord Mayor and Sydney City Council Works Committee
1936	Elizabeth Street Extensions: TPANSW along with Circular Quay Association and others called for a extension to corner of Bent and Phillips Streets with a square at eastern end of Martin Place	Lord Mayor
1936	Mt Tomah 'The Jungle' Reservation: TPANSW agreed to assist the PPM in its deputation to preserve Mt Tomah as a natural forest as heritage	Minister for Lands
1936	City improvements public meeting held by TPANSW discussed Macquarie and Elizabeth Streets*	Civic Reform Party – Sydney City Council
1936	Martin Place Square and Elizabeth Street extension: TPANSW sought Government contribution and public funds to proceed with proposal by the Association*	Deputy Premier
1937	Elizabeth Street Extension: Premier had promised to receive a deputation from TPANSW but permission was refused*	Premier

Year	Issue	Representation
1937	Macquarie Street replanning: objected strongly to proposals by Macquarie Street Replanning Committee; government refused to hear views of TPANSW*	Premier
1938	Chinamans Beach, Middle Harbour: protested against proposed land subdivision	Minister for Lands
1938	Circular Quay delays: Circular Quay Association introduced by City Council Lord Mayor and others including TPANSW call for a conference before plans finalised	Premier
1938	Elizabeth Street Extension: members led by Bertram Ford met with City Council to discuss failure to extend the street and construct a square at Hunter Street instead	Lord Mayor – Sydney City Council and Minister for Transport
1938	Martin Place Square: urged government to reserve from sale portion of land of 25 feet in depth in Martin Place between Phillip and Macquarie Streets	Minister for Social Services (on behalf of Premier)
1941	Manly Reservoir: requested Water Board to reconnect the 'disused Manly dam' with the metropolitan water supply	Premier
1955	Overhead pedestrian bridge: promoted bridge over Parramatta Road at Sydney University; TPANSW sought meeting with Government, Police and University Senate*	Minister for Transport, Commissioner of Police and Sydney University Senate
1957	Sydney's GPO Clock Tower: TPANSW frustrated by lack of government response approached Dr H.V. Evatt to introduce legislation to reinstate the tower*	Federal Opposition Leader

* Proposed deputation resolved at meeting – no evidence if deputation proceeded
** No reference to support being lent to Parks and Playground Movement (PPM) on this issue from sources available
Main Sources: TPANSW *Annual Reports*, Sydney City Archives, *Harmony* and *Sydney Morning Herald*.

Figure 11.3: Proposed remodelling of Martin Place at Macquarie Street, late 1930s. Source: *Building,* November 1950

Circular Quay was another city hotspot to attract the Association's attention over many years. Even by the late 1930s the fate of the overhead railway and roadway at Circular Quay remained undecided nearly a decade after the opening of the Sydney Harbour Bridge. The state government had for years promised to complete this crucial link within the city's transport network overhauled by TPANSW member J.J.C. Bradfield, but lacked the resources or perhaps the political will to proceed.[36] In 1938 a government-appointed Circular Quay Advisory Committee headed by Sir John Butters called for public submissions and the TPANSW responded quickly with a submission. By this time the Association had bonded with the Circular Quay Association and a combined effort resulted in a 21-point proposal, mostly focused on traffic circulation, streetscapes, building setbacks, and landscaping.[37]

By not constructing the railway station – the basic element in the plan – the underground system was under great strain according to the president of the Circular Quay Association, E.A. Buttenshaw. His request for a conference of groups and individuals concerned with the advancement of the replanning of the Quay and its environs fell on deaf ears. A deputation to Premier Stevens in May 1938 led by the Lord Mayor, Alderman Nock, was assured that 'a conference of the bodies interested would be called'.[38] Nothing eventuated and the Quay Association protested vehemently in the press when the government approved works without further public consultation. With proposals estimated to cost £5,000,000, the Butters Plan in 1939 similarly drew the ire of the TPANSW. Ford accused the government and city council of producing a design not worthy to adorn Sydney's 'front door'. He insisted that 'it was not too late for the state government to invite competitive designs from architects for a station building in keeping with the dignity of the city'.[39] The TPANSW and the Circular Quay Association contended that in spite of public meetings, consultation and deliberations, after ten long years the area was still in chaos, shaped by delays and insufficient funds. But by the end of 1939, Australia was at war and Circular Quay replanning would be put on hold for another two decades.[40]

Another ongoing issue was the enactment of effective town planning legislation. In the 26th annual report of the Association published just before the start of World War II, Bertram Ford emphasised that chaos would reign without the enactment of a town planning bill. Such legislation was needed to take proper control of development and also to stop the financial waste which the community had to bear due to vacillating politicians causing postponements, indecision and delays.[41] However, the leadership for this reform by the late 1930s had shifted to the TCPIA. In January 1939 their outgoing president stated that unless members 'lead in the advocacy of the passing of suitable town-planning legislation in New South Wales' it would never be achieved.[42] By mid-year the TCPIA in conjunction with the Parks and Playground Movement (PPM) initiated a conference of sympathetic bodies to urge the government to enact the legislation. Representatives from the TPANSW were invited by the PPM to attend, probably via the hand of its former ally, C.E.W. Bean. Ford reported that 'full agreement had been reached on the principles to be adopted in the proposed new bill for consideration of Parliament'.[43] The conference agreed upon several important technical points: the importance of a new bill covering 'town and country planning', the composition of a decision-making authority, the inclusion of regional planning, and provision for compensation and betterment procedures.[44] These deliberations took place in the months prior to the beginning of the war. The timing could not have been worse and once again the illusive legislation was put on hold, this time until planning became an unavoidable catchcry in postwar reconstruction talks.

The 1940s

Through the war years the TPANSW battled on, offering solicited or speculative suggestions for small-scale planning projects to councils and other civic organisations (Figure 11.4). Bertram Ford and another member G. Rosten Lee were signatories to a variety of proposals including a plan for the renewal of residential areas and improvements to recreational spaces at Campbelltown;[45] proposed civic centre at Bankstown (Figure 11.5); a new park at Chinamans Beach, Middle Harbour;[46] a community centre complex at Collaroy for the Collaroy Community League (Figure 11.6); and replanning of the approaches to Penrith Railway Station.[47] Although industrious and displaying an interest in civic design under-represented in professional discourse, the reality was that by the beginning of World War II, the credibility and clout of the TPANSW had been severely eroded.

The Association's dealings with the Sydney City Council and the state government were now not only reduced in number but frequently strained. A request to hold a public meeting in the Sydney Town Hall regarding the Association's concern with the Martin Place extensions cost blow-out and the Elizabeth Street extension was refused. A notation on one of the Association's publicity flyers promoting a public meeting encapsulates the Council's views of the Association by that time: in handwriting a distinct 'Rot' is written in the margins.[48] While earlier deputations evidenced some respect in the corridors of power, later attempts were more often refused. Disheartened and disappointed, the TPANSW withdrew into itself to profess an increasingly idiosyncratic and occasionally cantankerous parochialism.

This declining status and public profile came just as the official landscape of planning was being transformed into something akin to the goals of the Association's founders. The war marked a watershed as it dawned on politicians at all levels of government that the methodical organisation which underpinned the successful military effort should be applied to a raft of peacetime needs. Postwar reconstruction ideology highlighted not only the importance of proper housing for returned soldiers but correction and prevention of broader urban ills. While architects, surveyors and engineers reactivated interest in planning discourse within their own professions in the 1940s, the need for a new integrative and coordinative discipline was acknowledged. Trained planners had to lead the way.

Figure 11.4: Wartime meeting in a bomb shelter, 1941. Source: *Annual Report of the Town Planning Association of New South Wales*, 1940–41

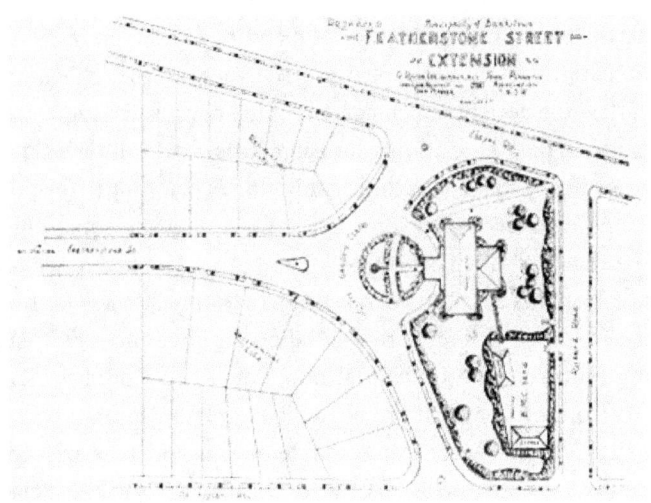

Figure 11.5: Proposed civic centre at Bankstown, 1941. Source: *Annual Report of the Town Planning Association of New South Wales*, 1940–41

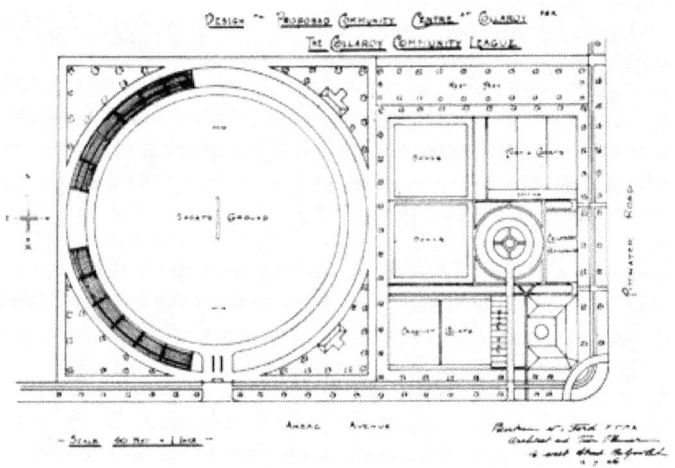

Figure 11.6: Proposed community centre at Collaroy, 1946. Source: *Annual Report of the Town Planning Association of New South Wales*, 1944–46

In NSW the breakthrough passage of planning legislation in 1945 enabling preparation of statutory planning schemes was the critical catalyst that sparked the decisive advancement of the new profession.[49]

Incredibly, the Association's annual reports provide little insight into the extraordinary changes in the organisation of planning in the postwar period, opting to record a diverse array of seemingly personal causes. It could be that Bertram Ford was piqued by his and the Association's exclusion from the corridors of power. In his annual review for the year ending 1946, he revealingly protested the state government's 'insult' in omitting him from the influential new Town and Country Planning Advisory Committee which provided high level ministerial advice from 1945 to 1963.[50] The larger frame of reference is a further shift toward politically conservative positions. The overall flavour of the Association's annual reports trend to the same anti-socialist line instigated by founders George and Florence Taylor many years earlier.[51] That NSW was under a left-of-centre Labor government from 1941 to 1965 obviously did not help Ford's feeling of alienation.

In 1943 Ford had written to Prime Minister John Curtin suggesting he look towards his own state of Western Australia and direct all states to do good deeds in planning and housing. Ignoring the actual controversy being sparked in Perth, Ford highlighted the 'invaluable work' done there by its town planning commissioner and former TPANSW president David Davidson. He believed it was timely for all Australians to have the best possible housing at the most affordable price.[52] Voicing concern about housing shortages in a postwar world, the TPANSW devoted several pages to this issue in its 1942–43 annual report. But at the end of the war, Ford's bipartisan commitment to the postwar political consensus, which established a foundation for planning and housing legislation, had evaporated. He reverted to barbs, childish stories and poetry to express his disappointment and outrage at the work of the Commonwealth Housing Commission, widely considered a landmark in national urban policy, as a 'communistic' operation.[53]

Larger contemporary questions of town planning of the kind which A.J. Brown sought to promote in his brief presidency were frequently ignored. The TPANSW's stance on two of the most significant planning institutions of the 1940s was highly problematic and akin to anti-planning. From its formation through to the early 1940s, the Association had promoted town planning legislation for NSW. In 1935 Bertram Ford felt that 'our goal is in sight',[54] yet another decade passed before assent of the *Local Government (Town and Country Planning) Amendment Act*.[55] But he railed against the government for not including the Association in the deliberations leading up to the drafting of the bill. He spoke disdainfully of the Premier and the Minister for Local Government for refusing 'to meet us or to hear our representations in connection with it', and far from welcoming the legislation, he decried it as 'a cynical betrayal of a great movement'.[56]

Similarly, Ford was troubled by the formation of Sydney's pioneering metropolitan strategic planning authority – the Cumberland County Council (CCC). Ford was initially sceptical about what it could achieve without the technical expertise and knowledge of town planners.[57] But when it produced its landmark metropolitan blueprint in 1948, he aligned the TPANSW with real estate and other critics in blasting it as an expensive, heavy-handed and unsound plan that would stifle development.[58] Life member Florence Taylor weighed in with similar sentiments: it encompassed 'all the idealistic considerations' associated with modern town planning but threatened 'possessions and property ... without any regard for goodwill or sentiment'.[59]

The 1950s and 1960s

By the early 1950s the TPANSW had completed a metamorphosis into a reactionary organisation more often than not standing against planning rather than representing a constructively critical and informed independent voice. In 1949 Chief County Planner Sidney Luker observed that 'This Association is discredited in the eyes of most professional planners in this state, in spite of the fact that many years ago it had a membership of prominent professional men'.[60] Nigel Ashton, a senior planner in the Department of Local Government's Town Planning Branch in the 1940s and 1950s and Chairman of the State Planning Authority of NSW from 1964 to 1974 was more blunt: 'We more or less poo-poohed them'.[61]

As a virtual one-man band by the late 1950s, Bertram Ford's style was eccentric and emboldened. Under his pen, the tone and content of the Association's annual reports became erratic and often bizarre, alternating between gushing prose, tortured angst and sheer anger.[62] Like all presidents before him, a self-assured and confident Ford was blunt and to the point when it came to offering an opinion, but opinions were about all the TPANSW had to offer by the 1950s.

Ford became regularly outspoken in his criticism of government expenditure, and from that standpoint was occasionally sought out by the media for his views on specific aspects of city improvement. There was no shortage of targets: the Sydney Opera House,[63] the Cahill Expressway,[64] and general waste and inefficiency, especially in regard to planning schemes. Following the report of a study tour made by a delegation of City of Sydney councillors to North America, Ford declared in the press that it was 'utterly stupid' and full of 'fatuous findings'.[65]

While the Association often spoke out against loss of open space, it was not overly concerned about demolition of historic buildings in the interests of progress. When the National Trust protested the state government's demolition of historic St Malo in suburban Hunters Hill in the late 1950s, Ford's position was that the Trust 'should pay attention to more worthy matters'.[66] In his final report, Ford presented thoughts on topics as disparate as increased fares on the Manly Ferry to a claim that the Association was instrumental in the lifting of Olympic champion Dawn Fraser's overseas swimming ban. Criticising the state government for failing to listen to his ministrations, Ford also announced that it was time for the Association to 'go it alone' in tackling the rising toll of human life in road accidents. He named his crusade 'Knights of the Road' with his knights to pursue various principles like assisting pedestrians across the road.[67]

Nearing the end of its lifespan there was one quirky and final issue in which the Association appeared to have had some positive influence: the reinstatement of the clock tower on Sydney's General Post Office (GPO). This had been deconstructed at the start of World War II as a potential target risk in an air raid. The Commonwealth Government (which ran postal and communications services) removed the tower and placed it, stone by stone, along with the clock and bells, into storage for the duration of the war with a promise of restoration when it was over.[68]

Sydneysiders endeavoured to hold the government to its promise. Ford was early off the mark to declare his interest. His annual report in late 1946 reported 'representations to the Post-Master General' and a guarantee of imminent reinstatement.[69] But nothing eventuated year after year. Why the delay? Had the disassembled structure been misplaced; was it beyond repair and re-erection; was it aesthetically displeasing considering changing attitudes towards architectural features; was it considered structurally unsound; or too much of a financial burden? Various explanations were canvassed as Ford and others agitated for its return to the city skyline.

Letters to the Prime Minister, federal members of parliament, and repeated pleas published in the press carried little weight until 1960 at which time the 'Sydney Spectator' section of *The Sydney Morning Herald* appealed to the 'old Sydney-Melbourne city rivalry' and chided Sydney politicians 'to stand up for their own city in Federal Cabinet ... If a similar Melbourne landmark had been removed in 1942, it would have been back long ago'. By this time the City of Sydney Council had jumped on board in favour of the tower's restoration with a qualification that if that scenario was not possible, it would request a 'new tower'.[70]

Ford dispatched at least eight telegrams to Prime Minister R.G. Menzies who, according to Ford, initially guaranteed the tower would be back in place in 1953.[71] The saga finally came to an end in April 1962 when

Figure 11.7: Bertram Ford in the Sydney Domain. He is addressing a public meeting demanding restoration of Sydney's GPO clock and tower, 1954. Source: *Annual Report of the Town Planning Association of New South Wales*, 1947–62

Menzies declared 'I am happy to tell my Sydney friends that although it is said you cannot put the clock back, we are prepared to do so with all reasonable speed'. Contracts were signed and the work began a year later. By Anzac Day 1964, the clock tower's chimes rang out for the dawn service at the Martin Place Cenotaph.[72] In his final annual report, Ford jubilantly pronounced that this culmination of years of hard work on the part of the Association was its 'supreme effort' and 'finest hour'. Wider issues of town planning had been forgotten; an image of him standing on a soap box preaching to a few stray souls on a free speech Sunday in the Sydney Domain is a telling metaphor of a marginalised association which had once helped shape the city's modern town planning agenda (Figure 11.7).

The new competing climate for environmental reform

The formation of the pioneering Town and Country Planning Institute of New South Wales in 1934 was a decisive event in the steady decline of the TPANSW's influence. In 1951 the NSW organisation federated with similar bodies in two other states to constitute the Australian Planning Institute (now, Planning Institute of Australia) as the peak professional body nationally.[73] Had the Association been better established to offer a truly informed and independent stance on planning issues, it may have entered an influential new era.

The formation of the CCC in 1945 meant that Sydney led the nation in having a statutory planning organisation with a local government constituency which could attend to local concerns. Arguably this was a significant reason why there was not the same planning activism in the 1950s and early 1960s as in other states.[74] Nevertheless, concerns with its activities and those of the state government over issues of land acquisition developed from the outset.[75] By the early 1960s, with the TPANSW nowhere to be seen, new organisations were mooted to work for more vision and less government regulation in development matters.[76]

A major factor which saw the TPANSW's relative significance continuously erode was the rise of other non-government organisations pursuing specific issues sliced from the broad portfolio inherited from the early years. Such rival and indeed spin-off bodies progressively diminished the TPANSW's role as a community voice in broadly environmental matters. While the TPANSW stuck to its guns, clearly it was not a lone voice instructing fellow citizens on the virtues of town planning. Other organisations worked to secure healthier housing, ensure family welfare, and protect and conserve historic buildings. For example, on social justice issues and the family at home, the Progressive Housewives' Association commenced its operations in 1946. Within a few years it became the New Housewives Association and thereafter the

Union of Australian Women. Such associations advocated that the home and all its comforts were an essential aspect of 'everyday life and proper organisation'. Wartime circumstances particularly galvanised its concerns and the more obvious shortages of food and housing were high on a 'declaration of war' list.[77]

Countless local progress associations throughout Sydney and its suburbs also made their presence heard by appealing to local councils for support in their protestations and urgings for civic improvements and new amenities. In a rare show of organisational initiative, the TPANSW engineered formal affiliations with some of these parochial associations to arrest thinning membership and declining financial support including the Guildford Progress Association, the Noise Abatement Society, the Austinmer Progress and Ratepayers' Association, the Pennant Hills Citizens' Association, and the Kogarah Bay Progress Association. Little resulted from these partnerships.[78]

Arising from the need to provide protection for 'the natural charms of the Municipality', the Tree Lovers' Civic League of Ku-ring-gai formed in 1927 at the home of Mrs Annie Wyatt. This organisation was initially dedicated to the distribution of seeds and planting trees.[79] By the late 1930s, Mrs Wyatt and her colleagues extended their interest beyond trees to the destruction of Sydney's historic buildings then under threat from redevelopment. This desecration paved the way for the founding of the National Trust in 1947 which soon became the most credible voice for conservation issues in planning in the 1950s.[80]

The TPANSW's critique of metropolitan planning was mainly ideological and was less substantive than the activities of more localised and specialised protest groups. An early example was opposition to the proposed oil refinery at Kurnell at the entrance to Botany Bay. This significant protest provided some indication of the environmental coalitions to come. Member groups of the Kurnell Oil Refinery Protest Committee included the Forestry Advisory Committee, Wildlife Preservation Society, Mountain Trails Club of NSW, National Parks and

Primitive Areas Council, Federation of Bushwalkers, Sydney Bush Walkers, Tree Lovers Civic League, Progressive Housewives Association, and the NSW Womens Justice Association.[81]

From the late 1960s resident action groups sprang up wherever planning and redevelopment endangered amenity, flora and fauna, and urban character.[82] Such groups constituted a new form of informed and activist environmental protest vastly different from the ideological rhetoric of the latter-day TPANSW. Professional bodies were slower to show dissent but Milo Dunphy's Environment Subcommittee of the Royal Australian Institute of Architects led the way from 1963.[83] In the same decade, a new Civic Design Society at the University of NSW marked a renaissance in community concern for better urban design.[84]

In 1958, an interested citizen wrote to *The Sydney Morning Herald* alarmed at the poor state of town planning in Sydney. He raised concerns about 'lack of depth in professional organisations' plus 'apathy on the part of the general public – businessmen and educational bodies alike'. He pleaded for change and offered a solution – revive the existing town planning association 'which has been fading into oblivion for years'.[85] Several years later in the twilight of that oblivion in his final report Bertram Ford looked to the future as he mourned the deaths of many of his planning colleagues. He expressed the will to 'hand the torch to those who follow, but right now there is much to be done, and most of us are good for at least another 20 years or so'.[86] It was not to be. On 15 September 1967, Ford died of cardiac failure at the age of 87. No further meetings of the Town Planning Association took place as honorary secretary R.M. Duncan, the last remaining member, closed the books. Few in the mainstream planning profession, community action or government would have even known of its passing. Warren Halloran, one of the last vice-presidents, cannot today remember Ford or even the Association, surmising that his status was bestowed by his father Henry who died in 1953.[87]

Conclusion

When Bertram Ford assumed leadership of the TPANSW from the mid-1930s, deep ambivalences were already apparent in its social mission. There was an historical mandate to spread the word and elevate community understanding as to planning's desirability. But this guise was largely eschewed for the role of a polite protest group, contesting government's action when considered not in the public interest. Yet while the Association sought change for the better through creative public policy, it was hamstrung by a 'small government' philosophy which further undermined the capacity for any transformative change. Town planning was a fine goal when it stood for visions such as suburban parkland, community centres and civic design. It proved more problematical when it infringed on private property rights and business profits. This never seemed to bother the Taylors in an earlier era of advocacy, but it severely incapacitated the TPANSW in the second half of its existence.

Although a singular achievement in surviving for over half a century, the Association never fundamentally altered its ways of doing things. There was no name change or even discussion about the name it held from 1913. Despite the fact that there were changes in membership and leadership, there were no significant constitutional or directional changes throughout its life. It inevitably failed to keep pace with the evolution of planning theory and practice. As the world changed, the TPANSW remained static and hence was sidelined more and more in planning matters in Sydney. To view its records and hear the Association's repeated laments and its unchanging methodical approach to its organisation and operations offers one explanation for its being out of step with the planning community. Its response to failure was, surprisingly, continuity. In effect, it atrophied away from a genuine social movement capable of external reinvigoration towards a small private club and then into a personal hobbyhorse.[88] It was an inglorious demise for a once vigorous voluntary association which had helped shape the city's modern town planning agenda in the 1910s.

In the history of postwar planning in Sydney, the activities of the TPANSW ultimately constitute an intriguing sidebar. This should be a story of pioneering community involvement in the planning process but is derailed by conservative political ideology and personal eccentricity. The real machinations and contestations of major planning narratives of metropolitan and central city planning, housing and urban development lay elsewhere.[89] The Association had led the way in community agitation over planning issues decades earlier. The one resilient trend accompanying its protracted and sad decline into the 1960s was the revolution happening around it in the rise of new forms of environmental activism.

References

[1] Peter Spearritt, *Sydney's century* (Sydney, University of New South Wales Press, 2000), 32.
[2] Peter Spearritt, *The Sydney Harbour Bridge: a life* (Sydney: UNSW Press, 2007).
[3] *Building* (12 September 1934): 61.
[4] Paul Ashton, *The accidental city: planning Sydney since 1788* (Sydney: Hale and Iremonger, 1993), 61.
[5] Helen Proudfoot, 'Milestones in planning history: residential district proclamations in Ku-ring-gai', *Australian Planner*, 30(1), (March 1992): 25–28.
[6] F.A. Larcombe, *The advancement of local government in New South Wales 1906 to the present* (Sydney: Sydney University Press in association with Local Government Association of New South Wales and Shire Association of New South Wales, 1978).
[7] Denis Winston, *Sydney's great experiment: the progress of the Cumberland County Plan* (Sydney: Angus and Robertson, 1957).
[8] Leonie Sandercock, *Cities for sale: property, politics and urban planning in Australia* (Melbourne: Melbourne University Press, 1975), 89, 92.
[9] A.J. Brown and H.M. Sherrard, *Town and country planning* (Melbourne: Melbourne University Press, 1951).
[10] Town Planning Association of New South Wales (hereafter TPANSW), *Annual Reports*, 1944–46, 12–14.
[11] Alfred John Brown, CV, c.1975. Courtesy the late Howard Sherrard.
[12] *Commonwealth Home* (1 July 1929):18; *Commonwealth Home* (1 August 1929): 13.

[13] *Sydney Morning Herald*, 10 August 1934, 11.
[14] *Sydney Morning Herald*, 26 September 1934, 18.
[15] *Sydney Morning Herald*, 15 November 1934, 5b.
[16] *Sydney Morning Herald*, 10 August 1934,11; 26 September 1934, 18.
[17] Robert Freestone and Margaret Park, 'From progressivism to conservatism: the decline of the Town Planning Association of New South Wales in the 1930s', *Journal of Australian Studies*, 33 (September 2009): 344–45.
[18] Leslie Wilkinson, 'Presidential Address, 19th AGM of the Town and Country Planning Institute of New South Wales', *The Shire and Municipal Record*, (28 February 1945): 305.
[19] *Sydney Morning Herald*, 10 August 1934, 11.
[20] Brad Vale, 'Bank of New South Wales Branches in rural and regional centres of NSW' (Masters of Heritage Conservation thesis, University of Sydney, 2004), 119.
[21] Information courtesy Anne Higham, Royal Australian Institute of Architects (NSW), March 2008.
[22] *Building* (April 1922): 54.
[23] TPANSW, *Annual Report* (August 1934), 7.
[24] *Principal women of the Empire: Australia and New Zealand*, vol. 1 (London: Mitre Press, 1940), 49.
[25] References from *Sydney Morning Herald* articles and letters to the editor in Fairfax Archives Online, 1955–90.
[26] *Principal women of the Empire*, 49.
[27] TPANSW, *Annual Report* (1936), 7 and (1937), 7.
[28] TPANSW, *Annual Report* (1939), 6–8.
[29] *Guardian*, 15 February 1935; *Guardian*, 8 November 1935.
[30] *Town Clerk Annual Report*, 1932: 95, Sydney City Council Archives.
[31] TPANSW, *Annual Report* (13 August 1936), 4.
[32] Minutes of City Planning and Improvement Committee, 3808/30, 23 March 1938: 15, Sydney City Council Archives.
[33] *Sydney Morning Herald*, 27 August 1936, 10.
[34] *Building*, 12 December 1934, 116.
[35] *Sydney Morning Herald*, 4 October, 1934, 109.
[36] TPANSW, *Annual Report* (1936), 7.
[37] TPANSW, *Annual Report* (1937), 6–7.
[38] *Sydney Morning Herald*, 17 September 1938, 13.
[39] *Sydney Morning Herald*, 25 January 1939, 19.

⁴⁰ Spearritt, *Sydney's Century*, 135.
⁴¹ TPANSW, *Annual Report* (1939), 3.
⁴² *Sydney Morning Herald*, 28 January 1935, 18.
⁴³ TPANSW, *Annual Report* (1939): 10.
⁴⁴ Report of Town Planning Conference, received by C.E.W. Bean on 1 July 1939, report dated 14 June 1939, C.E.W. Bean Private Papers, 1929-79. Australian War Memorial.
⁴⁵ TPANSW, *Annual Reports* (1942-43): 4.
⁴⁶ TPANSW, *Annual Reports* (1944-46), 7, 9.
⁴⁷ TPANSW, *Annual Reports* (1944-46), 10.
⁴⁸ Martin Place Extension File, Item 2485/36, Sydney City Council Archives.
⁴⁹ Winston, 33.
⁵⁰ J.H. Shaw, 'The N.S.W. Town and Country Advisory Committee', *Australian Planning Institute Journal*, 3(1), (1964): 22-24.
⁵¹ Robert Freestone and Bronwyn Hanna, *Florence Taylors hats: designing, building and editing Sydney* (Sydney: Halstead Press, 2008).
⁵² Town Planning - Correspondence 1937-48, Series 9816 Control 1943/183, 1943, National Archives of Australia.
⁵³ 'A communistic commission'; 'The Bungaloathesome home'; and 'Alice in Blunderland' in TPANSW, *Annual Report*, (1944-46), 8-12.
⁵⁴ TPANSW, *Annual Report* (1936), 3.
⁵⁵ Winston, 33.
⁵⁶ TPANSW, *Annual Report* (1944-46), 3-5.
⁵⁷ TPANSW, *Annual Report* (1944-46), 6.
⁵⁸ Bertram W. Ford, 'Letter to the Editor', *Sydney Morning Herald*, 1 November 1949, 7.
⁵⁹ 'Industry: A Plea for Factory Consideration', *Building* (November 1949): 81-86.
⁶⁰ Sidney Luker to Harold Boas, 1 November 1949, Boas Papers, 881A/19, J.S. Battye Library of West Australian History.
⁶¹ Nigel Ashton, Interview by Robert Freestone and Peggy James, Sydney, January 2008.
⁶² TPANSW, *Annual Report* (1939), 3-5.
⁶³ TPANSW, *49th Annual Review* (1947-62), 14.
⁶⁴ 'Planning the Domain roadway', *Sydney Morning Herald*, 19 February 1959, 2.
⁶⁵ 'Traffic Report Called 'Stupid'', *Sydney Morning Herald*, 3 February 1955, 7.
⁶⁶ '£200,000 to divert expressway, states minister', *Sydney Morning Herald*, 17 September 1959, 11.

[67] TPANSW, *49th Annual Review*, 10.
[68] Peter Bridges and Robin Appleton, *The city's centrepiece: the history of the Sydney G.P.O.* (Sydney: Hale & Iremonger, 1988), 84.
[69] TPANSW, *Annual Reports* (1944–46): 17.
[70] 'A Clock Tower and a Cabinet' in *Sydney Morning Herald*, 1 June 1960, 3; 'Council Suggests a New G.P.O. Tower', *Sydney Morning Herald*, 1 June 1960, 6.
[71] 'Fashions in buildings, too', *Sydney Morning Herald*, 30 October 1961, 3.
[72] Bridges and Appleton, 92.
[73] Bruce Wright, *Expectations of a better world* (Canberra: Royal Australian Planning Institute, 2001), 8.
[74] Nigel Ashton, Interview, January 2008.
[75] Lesley Johnson, 'Feral suburbia: Western Sydney and "the problem of urban sprawl"', in Helen Grace, Ghassan Hage, Lesley Johnson, Julie Langsworth and Michael Symonds, *Home/world: space, community and marginality in Sydney's west* (Sydney: Pluto Press, 1997), 31–65.
[76] 'The business man takes a hand', *Australian Journal of Social Issues*, 1(1), (1961): 26–29.
[77] Lesley Johnson and Justine Lloyd, *Sentenced to everyday life: feminism and the housewife* (London: Berg, 2004). See also Judith Smart, 'The politics of consumption: the Housewives' Association in south-eastern Australia before 1950', *Journal of Women's History*, 18 (2006): 13–39.
[78] TPANSW, *Annual Report* (1927): 2 and Parks and Playground Movement, *Circular*, 6 September 1939.
[79] I.F. Wyatt, *Ours in trust: a personal history of the National Trust of Australia (NSW)* (Sydney: National Trust, 1987), 5.
[80] Wyatt, *Ours in trust*, 21.
[81] Guy Moore Papers, Letter from KORPC to Premier, 29 August 1952 in MSS 6237(8), Mitchell Library, SLNSW. Our thanks to Peggy James for this reference.
[82] Zula Nittim, 'The coalition of Resident Action Groups', in *Twentieth century Sydney: studies in urban and social* history, ed. Jill Roe (Sydney: Hale and Iremonger, 1980), 231–47.
[83] Peter Meredith, *Myles and Milo* (Sydney: Allen and Unwin, 1999).
[84] Paul-Alan Johnson, and Susan Lorne-Johnson, 'Elias Duek-Cohen', in *FBE Interviews*, (Sydney, University of NSW, 2007).
[85] 'Planning Sydney's development', *Sydney Morning Herald*, 25 November 1958, 2.

[86] TPANSW, *49th Annual Review*, 10.
[87] Warren Halloran, Interview with Robert Freestone, Huskisson, January 2008.
[88] Sidney Tarrow, *Power in movement: social movements and contentious politics* (New York: Cambridge University Press, 1998).
[89] John Toon and Jonathan Falk, eds, *Sydney: planning or politics. Town planning for Sydney Region since 1945* (Sydney: Planning Research Centre, University of Sydney, 2003).

12
Dreams come true? Town planning ideals and realities in postwar Melbourne

Susan Reidy and Andrew May

In 1941 the Town Planning Association of Victoria became the Town and Country Planning Association of Victoria (TCPA). From its foundation in late 1914 as the Victorian Town Planning and Parks Association, the TCPA has maintained a durable role as the mouthpiece of town planning idealism in Victoria. While it would prove to be a resilient organisation – indeed the only Australian town planning association to survive into the 21st century – its activities and effectiveness might be measured against the development of more formal town planning legislation and practices, particularly in the postwar period. While popular with the press and community groups alike, its efficacy at influencing public decision-making and in consistently representing itself as a powerful and focused lobby group has been both a strength and a weakness.

From the 1960s, successive generations of community and professional interest groups donned the dependable mantle of what was by then a well-established and venerable organisation, and lay claim to an authoritative voice in public debate. The Association thus gave status and kudos to each new wave of urban agitators, although the targets of its campaigns were not always listening. While the fluidity of membership and amalgam of social and political persuasion left it vulnerable to the whim of individual reform agendas, it also ensured that the TCPA played and continues to play a role as an independent platform in urban debate in Victoria. This chapter will follow the successive fortunes of the TCPA in the decades following the effective institutionalisation of town planning through legislation in 1944.

'Overall planning': the 1940s

Up until World War II, the Association's tenets of town planning had followed closely those of interest in 1914 when the Association was formed. But from 1940 it is possible to see a shift in the meaning of town planning and a change in emphasis captured by the renaming of the Association to the TCPA. Issues in the 1940s included street systems, traffic, the architectural appearance of buildings, the 'continued occupation' of parklands by the Commonwealth Government and the military beyond their presence during World War II, airport facilities, ribbon development, the optimum size of cities, building regulations, and specific details such as a proposed road tunnel under the Yarra River. Off the agenda were playgrounds, agricultural belts and any references to the 'garden city'. The strongest interest was the push for 'overall planning'. At the TCPA's 1941 Annual Meeting, the architect Frank Heath (and TCPA Honorary Secretary from 1936 to 1948) gave a speech on his involvement with the development of a new plan for the regional town of Swan Hill, in which he articulated this vision:

> Town Planning aims to bring order into the town's physical development – to bring the government ... and its citizens together in preparing for present and future needs. Its main purpose is to mould and co-ordinate the artificial processes of growth in harmony with natural conditions. The town as the most dominant factor in civilisation, calls upon its designer to recognise its fundamental relationships as a complete being, and not as an aggregation of disparate units.[1]

Such a vision was expressed through new ideas for urban planning. One of the most dominant was the civic centre, which was now at the heart of postwar reconstruction. The TCPA began the decade with a strong call for a civic centre for Melbourne 'worthy of the city' and proposed that instead of spending £40,000 fixing the Royal Exhibition Building ('a waste of money' the Association claimed), a new civic centre could be developed.[2] The TCPA noted:

> It is now generally recognized that every town, whether small or large, should contain a large open space set as centrally as possible in the town, whereon should be erected the Town Hall, Municipal offices, and all other meeting rooms and offices for the various municipal activities and services connected with the town. Such a place should act as a focal point for civic life.[3]

By the early 1940s the TCPA had a strong contingent of organisational members, including representatives from the Municipal Association (whose offices it used for its meetings),[4] the Melbourne and Metropolitan Board of Works (MMBW), the Railways Commissioners, the Country Roads Board, and the State Rivers and Water Supply Commission. A number of TCPA members also held positions in these authorities.

Although the TCPA's 1941–42 Annual Report remarked that 'war conditions' had 'curtailed' its activities (which saw the number of Council meetings fall to just two or three a year), its level of activity in the 1940s may also have been affected by Sir James Barrett's increasing age. He resisted an attempt to have him step down in 1939.[5] In 1940 the Council had established a smaller Executive Committee, which, in theory, met every two months. Its effect was to disable the Council, which hardly met at all for years. Meetings for general members were supposed to be held quarterly during this time, but in 1942 this idea was abandoned.[6] The Executive kept things going, but its minutes reflect a reluctance to make decisions. It may be that this extra layer of bureaucracy had a somewhat stultifying effect and perhaps makes clear the seriousness which the organisation attached to finding a figurehead president following Barrett's death.[7]

After a lengthy process, the TCPA in 1943 affiliated with the British Town and Country Planning Association and adapted the latter's constitution for its own use. The constitution required some adjustment to reflect Australia's three-level system of government (in contrast to Britain's two levels) and so allow municipal members to sit on the TCPA Council. Nevertheless, the constitution still managed to reflect a distinctive Englishness and used British terms such as 'village' and 'small holdings'. Its objects were:

- to promote Town and Country Planning and Civic Design and the practice of the Arts and Sciences applied thereto

- to advise on and promote Garden Cities, Garden Towns and Garden Villages, and, in special cases, Garden Suburbs

- to promote housing and sanitation and social amenities connected therewith

- to further the provision of open spaces, allotments and small holdings

- to collect and disseminate information, to educate public opinion and to influence and promote legislation or public or private action as to the above subjects.[8]

With the passing of the Victorian government's *Town and Country Planning Act* in 1944, the TCPA's emphasis shifted to advocacy for a town and country planning board to administer the new legislation. This was achieved in 1946 when J.S. Gawler, a TCPA member, became the new board's first chairman. It is perhaps surprising that the Association did not strongly maintain its connections with local government, given that local councils now had some town planning powers under the new legislation. Even so, it continued to work at increasing membership. New members in 1944 included Sir William Angliss and Sir Keith Murdoch, along with several organisations – Australian Consolidated Industries, Broken Hill Pty Ltd, Equity Trustees Company, General Motors-Holden, the Health Inspectors Association, Hume Pipe Company, and the Myer

Emporium among them. These connections reflect Melbourne's status in these decades as Australia's pre-eminent business and financial centre.

In some instances, the TCPA became momentarily interested in a particular issue or event. In 1944 it discussed the site for a new Melbourne arts and cultural centre. It turned out that TCPA Council members Keith Murdoch and Percy Everett (the Government Architect) were on the site committee alongside Association Secretary Frank Heath as the nominated TCPA representative.[9] In 1944, Heath was also appointed as convenor of the Commonwealth Ministry of Postwar Reconstruction's Town Planning Committee.[10] The TCPA also participated in preparations for British town planner Sir Patrick Abercrombie's Australian lecture tour in 1948. From time to time the Association was approached by organisations – such as the Commonwealth Housing Commission in 1944 – to provide town planning information.[11]

Support for national parks continued to occupy the TCPA. At the beginning of the decade it had shown its interest in the natural landscape and areas of 'unusual scenic beauty' by declaring that only by reserving these 'is it possible to give absolute protection to the natural fauna, flora and natural phenomena in an endeavour to preserve for future generations sections of our country with the scenery and wild life as they were when the early pioneers first saw them.'[12] In 1944 this philosophy led to the Association's National Parks Section initiating an extensive survey on the condition of national parks in Victoria using worldwide comparisons, which resulted in one of the TCPA's most popular publications, *National Parks in Victoria*, published in 1949. The 38-page booklet, containing a folded map of Victoria inside the back cover, was sold through tourist bureaus throughout the state, and in 1950 the Association successfully sought funding from the Victorian Premier for a reprint. Not only did the booklet promote the TCPA's advocacy of national parks, it made a profit (Figure 12.1).

Figure 12.1: Cover of the TCPA's most successful publication, *National Parks Victoria Australia*, 1949

Despite the Association's activities, the enactment of town planning legislation in 1944 had a dampening effect on the TCPA. It now had to deal with a field of endeavour that had become, in effect, institutionalised. When a Planning Institute of Australia was proposed, the TCPA at first misunderstood its purpose, thinking it would be a rival organisation; it took some time until it understood the new organisation would be a representative body for a new breed of planning professionals.[13] The TCPA found itself responding to government plans and regulations instead of initiating debate or fighting at the frontline of urban development. In 1945 and 1946 the Committee tended to have long discussions over several meetings that resulted in no action. Moreover, once the *Town and Country Planning Act* had been passed, municipal councils began to resign their TCPA membership (in 1945, for example, Northcote and Essendon, then Ballarat and Fitzroy), suggesting that the new legislation obviated their need for Association membership. The Association undoubtedly contributed to these resignations by closing its Council meetings to municipal members from the beginning of 1945.[14]

In May 1945 Sir James Barrett died. He had remained a dominating influence and a persistent presence. The TCPA's annual report for 1944–45 recorded his achievements, but incorrectly documented his connection with the Association as beginning after his service in World War I, effectively forgetting his status as a founding member and first president.[15] A new president was needed, and the Council searched for a figurehead and approached TCPA member Sir Keith Murdoch, newspaper publisher and chairman of the Trustees of the National Gallery of Victoria, who accepted. But Murdoch's poor health prevented him from playing an active role or attending meetings. For this reason he attempted to resign in 1947, but was persuaded to continue. His failure to attend the 1948 annual meeting prompted him to resign again, and the Council reluctantly accepted. Architect Leslie Perrott Snr chaired the Council until a new president could be found.[16] This would take nearly two years. A number of figurehead-types were approached (businessman Sir Thomas Nettlefold, and new Melbourne Lord Mayor James Disney included) without success.[17]

In 1947 the TCPA undertook to lobby the state government for a central coordinating authority to manage metropolitan planning, and began a lengthy process of gathering other organisations together (representing, for example, architects, engineers and surveyors institutes, the Building Industry Congress, and the Royal Automobile Club of Victoria) to send a delegation to the Premier. In the same year it received a bequest of £100 from James Barrett's estate. Council discussions during the next three years sought ideas about how this might be used as a memorial to

Barrett, rejecting one suggestion for an 'essay competition' for secondary school students.[18]

Perrott was an energetic chair of the Publications Subcommittee, and one of its first publications was *Town planning or muddle*, printed mid-1947 at the same time as Perrott was suggesting a booklet on traffic 'bottlenecks', although the latter would prove too costly.[19] While the Association had published occasionally before World War II, from the 1940s its publication record is impressive, from time to time perhaps reflecting the promotional and publishing interests of members with an eye for publicity, such as Perrott and, later, Robin Boyd and Robert Gardner. The subjects of these various publications reflect the town planning issues which were engaging the TCPA in each decade (Table 12.1).

Table 12.1: Publications by the TCPA 1942–87

1942	F. Oswald Barnett, 'National reconstruction and housing: address by F. Oswald Barnett', eight-page pamphlet of address given at TCPA annual meeting, December 1942.
1942	Brian Fitzpatrick, 'War and decentralization', 12-page reprint of speech and questions from the audience, TCPA meeting, Melbourne, May 1942.
1943	James Barrett, 'The future of Australia's population', eight-page pamphlet, Melbourne.
1944	TCPA and Frank Heath, *Living in your community*, Melbourne.
1945	James Barrett, Frank Heath and others, *Let us plan*, Melbourne.
1946	K.N.E. Bradfield, 'Airport design in relation to town planning: address at a General Meeting of the Town and Country Planning Association, Victoria, on 27th March, 1946', six-page pamphlet, Melbourne.
1946	P.S. Robinson, 'Master plan for the City of Melbourne', eight-page pamphlet of address given at 8 November 1946 TCPA meeting at Melbourne Town Hall.
1947	TCPA, *Town planning or muddle?*, Melbourne.*

1949	TCPA National Parks Committee, *National Parks Victoria Australia*, Melbourne.
1955	RA Gardner and NB O'Connor, *Ring road*, Melbourne.
1959	TCPA, *Estate development*, Melbourne.
1960	FM Corrigon, *A Report on Victoria's Coastline and Foreshore*, Melbourne.
1964–71	*Plan News Review*, magazine, Melbourne.
1967	TCPA, *The future planning of Melbourne: a summary of reports presented to the Minister for Local Government*, Melbourne.
1969	TCPA, Report on the Melbourne and Metropolitan Board of Works 'Residential planning standards', Melbourne.
1969	TCPA and the Australian Planning Institute (Victorian Division), *Conservation and Development: Who Said You Can't Have Both: Report of Proceedings of a Seminar*, Melbourne.
1969	TCPA Housing and Redevelopment Committee, *Policy on housing*, Hawthorn.
1969	TCPA, 'Policy on Housing May 1969', pamphlet, Melbourne.
1969–72	Ruth Crow and Maurice Crow, *Plan for Melbourne*, Communist Party of Australia Victorian State Committee with TCPA, Melbourne.
1974	Alan A. Parker and Robert McAlpine, 'Essential: a pedestrian city centre', four-page pamphlet, Nunawading.
197?	TCPA, 'Analysis of M.C.C. "Mixed use areas study"', TCPA report, Melbourne.
1971	TCPA Transport Subcommittee, *Melbourne transportation: statement of principles forming the basis of the Association's six point transport policy*, Nunawading.
1971	TCPA, *water pollution policies for industry: papers as presented by speakers at the seminar held on Thursday April 29, 1971*, Melbourne.
1973–91	*Space: Town and Country Planning Association Victoria*, magazine, Melbourne.
1987	Jenny Barnett and Rosemary Baker, *Standing up for your local environment: an action guide*, TCPA with Conservation Council of Victoria, North Melbourne.

* This publication is undated, but TCPA Minutes for 16 May 1947 record that it went to the printers that month, and its printing was recorded in the Minutes for 18 July 1947.

The *Town and Country Planning Act 1944* had empowered (though not required) municipalities to introduce planning schemes. While the remainder of the decade saw a growth in awareness about the need to address planning issues in an holistic way, the Town and Country Planning Board which had been appointed under the legislation to review local planning schemes was seen to be inadequate for the task. The 1940s ended with the government revising town planning legislation through the *Town and Country Planning (Metropolitan Area) Act*, which required the MMBW to prepare a comprehensive planning scheme for Melbourne. One of the first things it would do was define Melbourne as a metropolitan area incorporating a radius of 15 miles from the city's central Post Office, plus Dandenong, Frankston and Ringwood.[20]

Future development: the 1950s

After the interregnum occasioned by Murdoch's vacation of the presidency, in late 1949 Perrott suggested the architect, Professor Brian Lewis of the University of Melbourne for the role (Figure 12.2). Lewis accepted, chaired his first Council meeting on 21 April 1950 and was officially elected at the annual meeting on 5 November 1950. Lewis would prove to be a conscientious president. He abolished the Executive Committee, reinstated the Council and took the Association into a decade of considerable activity. One of Lewis' first actions was to propose and get agreement to use Barrett's bequest to fund a medal and annual award to recognise 'the best contribution annually towards town planning in Victoria'.[21] It took a while to agree on a medal design but on 14 October 1952 at an afternoon tea in Melbourne University's Professorial Board Room, the Governor of Victoria Sir Dallas Brooks, presented Frank Heath with the first Sir James Barrett Memorial Medal.[22] It continued to be awarded at a dinner or luncheon nearly every year until the late 1990s, including to (and despite the terms of the award) Los Angeles planner Charles B. Bennett in 1952.[23] Heath was also the recipient of the Association's first life membership (in 1950), an honour bestowed on only a handful of other individuals including Leslie Perrott Snr, Keith MacKay, Noel O'Connor, Saxil Tuxen and Ruth Crow. The Association's Secretary from 1951 to 1964 was the journalist, publicist, printer and promoter of Melbourne (he founded the city's Moomba Festival), Robert Gardner (1916–2002). He also served as Secretary from 1968 to 1970 and was President from 1972 to 1975 (Figure 12.3).

New topics of interest and examination in the 1950s included finding a site for the Melbourne Olympic Games and a call to develop a large public park on a site on the western side of Melbourne's central business district, an area that was still known at the time as the West Melbourne Swamp.[24] Old issues that never seemed to go away included slum abolition and park alienation (such as opposing the use of parkland for car parking in 1952).[25]

Despite the formation of the Victorian National Parks Association in 1952, the TCPA maintained its own National Parks Section, lobbying as it always had done for the creation and preservation of new state reserves. In 1950 the government's State Development Committee used the TCPA book *National Parks in Victoria* as evidence in its examination of the national park question.[26] The creation of the National Parks Authority under the *National Parks Act* in 1956 effectively completed the TCPA's persuading work. Its focus would subsequently shift to specific issues, such as advocacy for protection of the Upper Yarra Valley.

For what was perhaps its first direct educational activity, the TCPA ran a successful town planning course for the Council of Adult Education in 1952 with 36 enthusiasts enrolled. It also attempted to get a magazine started, but this proved too complex until the 1960s.[27] In the early 1950s the TCPA also sought to revive connections to municipalities and community groups; it made a list of 96 'active' progress associations, for which it created a special category of membership and wrote to every one of them.[28]

Figure 12.2: Professor Brian Lewis, 1966. Source: State Library of Victoria, Image hp001714, Courtesy of The Herald & Weekly Times Pty Ltd

By the 1950s, 'town planning' had become 'planning' and 'future development' was the catch-cry. Henry Bolte's election as Victorian premier in 1955 put an end to a period of political instability which had seen ten governments rise and fall since the 1944 town planning legislation, and a consequent lack of achievement in town planning advancement.[29] The 1954 publication of the MMBW's *Melbourne and metropolitan planning scheme*, and the government's call for responses to it, provided the TCPA with plenty of opportunity to put its views. It was an early advocate for an over-arching planning body but also warned that it shouldn't be responsible for 'every detail of municipal administration'.[30]

Lewis stepped down as president at the beginning of 1954, as his academic work took him overseas. He suggested the leading retailer Kenneth Myer, who took up the role from February 1954. At first Myer attended meetings regularly, but by mid-1955 his attendance was sporadic, with Lewis (now back in Melbourne) and one of the vice-presidents, Noel O'Connor filling in. Despite this, Myer remained president until May 1958, when O'Connor took over.

Figure 12.3: Robert Gardner. Source: Report on proceedings of the seminar held at Monash University on 26, February, 1972 on the Melbourne and Metropolitan Board of Works report 'Planning policies for the Melbourne metropolitan region'

The cheapest part of development: the 1960s

In this decade, the Association once again had the Victorian Governor as its patron (this time Sir Rohan Delacombe) and the prominent Melbourne architect and social commentator Robin Boyd briefly on its Council.[31] It seemed as vigorous and relevant as it had ever been. Issues of concern in this decade included multi-storied building, unplanned development and still the lack of an 'overall plan … Surely planning is the cheapest part of development', the Association claimed.[32] It supported the MMBW's call for freeways and ring roads (Figure 12.4). Consistent with some of the most enduring concerns of the TCPA were reminders that slum abolition and inner area development were still on the agenda.

In 1964 the TCPA began publication of a magazine, *Plan News Review* (renamed *Space* in 1973) which ran until 1991. It was published until the early 1980s as a commercial proposition, taking advertising (Humes Pipes, an earlier member of the Association, advertised regularly), and selling initially for two shillings an issue with annual subscriptions available. In 1965 and 1966 it was a vehicle for the Association's advocacy of issues, for example, to 'make planning compulsory' and 'put the coastline under planning control'.[33] From 1967 the pages reflect a shift to the provision of information for its professional readership. Preservation of the Yarra Valley became a significant concern for the TCPA from the 1960s and it devoted a complete issue of *Plan News Review* to it in 1967.[34]

Figure 12.4: Elevated view of Jolimont looking towards Melbourne, with proposed ring road indicated, 1963. Source: State Library of Victoria, Image hp004515, Courtesy of The Herald & Weekly Times Pty Ltd

By 1968, the TCPA's membership had dropped to 60, but despite this, at the end of the decade it ran an all-day seminar on the topic, 'Conservation and development – who says you can't have both?', at the Camberwell Civic Centre, attended by 300 people and opened by the Minister for Local Government, Rupert Hamer. It then published the 50-page proceedings for two dollars a copy; it sold out and in 1970 was reprinted.[35]

Figure 12.5: Ruth Crow at Palm Sunday rally, Carlton Gardens, 19 March 1989. Source: John Brant Ellis collection, University of Melbourne Archives, UMA/I/689

Noteworthy members of the TCPA Council through this period included the social and political activists Maurie and Ruth Crow (Figure 12.5), joint recipients of the James Barrett Memorial Medal in 1971 for objections to the Metropolitan and Regional Planning Scheme. Their book of the time, *Plan for Melbourne*, was a collaborative publication between the Communist Party and the TCPA, possibly the Association's most radical moment. Ruth Crow was further awarded a TCPA life membership in 1997 for what she referred to as her 'toil at the grass roots of urban action'.[36] It also reflected her dedication in preserving a large part of the TCPA's organisational records within the Crow Collection.[37]

The decades after the 1950s had also seen the Association continue in its drive to reconnect with progress associations, which were regarded as a potential source of members. The TCPA ran a campaign that involved writing to over 120 suburban progress associations, offering to provide guest speakers. In the 1920s the TCPA had forged strong relations with these bodies that represented local interests, seeing them as both worthy of support and as groups for educating. But from the early 1930s, the relationship had died and requests from progress association for a guest speaker were invariably refused. At a time when the body had a high public profile, and it was concerned with 'big' issues like town planning legislation, housing and reserves, perhaps it deemed that broader public alliances were not necessary.

But the emerging urban activism of the 1960s created opportunities for the TCPA to refashion itself as being relevant to informing a new era of debate about urban issues such as freeway construction, heritage, and housing provision. Conversely, and perhaps more pertinently, inner-urban action groups saw the chance to use the elite status of the TCPA as something of a Trojan Horse with which to launch their radical ideas about urban reform into mainstream debate. This was a new generation of community activists, and the 'alienation of residents from local government was a significant factor in the formation of new associations'.[38] As former TCPA member Renate Howe recalls, the Association served to galvanise the concerns of inner-city residents in their campaigns against public authorities such as the Housing Commission of Victoria, the Country Roads Board and the MMBW:

> But it did have a fairly elitist image, I think. In a way that was transformed somewhat in that period, but it certainly also helped some of those who were involved in the resident associations at that time to get a wider acknowledgement, as the TCPA conjured up a certain status, so the residents' ideas in a sense were able to get some credibility through the TCPA name.[39]

Members of the Fitzroy, Carlton and North Melbourne residents' associations were able to refashion the Association in their own image, using its name in the community, and in so doing rejuvenating the TCPA's activities and relevance as an activist organisation that could be a catalyst for new ideas and which could develop new approaches to planning in Melbourne. Old approaches which stressed land use planning were now refreshed with new ideas 'about how communities might work ... certainly they were very ahead of their time in terms of environmental issues'.[40] The influence of this new breed of activism was soon felt; members were encouraged to see that municipal governments were appointing professionally qualified planners with a very different approach to local planning.

Fed up with ideals: the 1970s and 1980s

Not surprisingly given the tenor of the time, the 1970s proved to be the Association's most interventionist since the 1920s. It had hinted at this in 1968, stating in *Plan News Review* 'we are fed up with contemplating ideals of planning and pleasantly reporting on its sundry successes'.[41] A membership drive saw numbers jump to 540 in 1971 and the Association was making money from its functions and publications.[42]

In reverse of its support for freeways and road development in the 1960s, by the mid-1970s, the TCPA had become pro-public transport and anti-roads and by the 1980s was actively promoting bicycle paths. In mid-1971 it published the findings of a transport study, rejecting aspects of the 1969 Metropolitan Transportation Committee's report, which had proposed over 300 miles of new freeways and over a hundred miles of new arterial roads. The TCPA's opposition to the overwhelming scale of the plan reflected a populist groundswell on the issue, as the 'community was becoming more sophisticated and informed about planning and traffic engineering.'[43] In 1973 it was deeply involved with Melbourne's anti-freeway campaign (Figure 12.6) and it published its own policy, claiming that it was the 'first organisation to question the recommendations made in the Melbourne Transportation Plan'.⁴⁴ As immigration and postwar suburban growth swelled the population, manufacturing industries and housing stock of Melbourne's now sprawling suburbs, the TCPA was invigorated in its attention to a raft of urban issues.⁴⁵

Figure 12.6: F19 freeway protest, 30 April 1977. Source: John Brant Ellis collection, University of Melbourne Archives, UMA/I/330

From 1973, *Space* ran to 20 pages, had a full colour cover and was published commercially with a staff of nine. It gave the TCPA confidence to express its opinions on pollution, conservation, transportation planning, pedestrian malls, waste disposal, zoning, land prices, population growth, the state of the Gippsland lakes and the national estate. Connections with politicians whom it saw as friends were cultivated, such as federal Labor politicians Tom Uren and Gough Whitlam (Figure 12.7), but the TCPA had a complex relationship with State Liberal politician Rupert Hamer, who shifted from friend to foe depending on his government role; in 1977 the TCPA attacked the Liberal government for potentially ruining planning in Victoria.[46] Even before he won government, Gough Whitlam had been invited to the 1970 TCPA annual dinner at the Victoria Hotel, where he spoke on pollution to a crowd of over 300.[47] Whitlam gave the Association's first R.A. Gardner Oration in October 1976 and in the same year the Barrett Medal was awarded to the Australian prominent Government 1972–75 (accepted at the presentation by Gough Whitlam, by this time Leader of the Opposition).

By the mid-1970s the big issue was threats to the built character of inner suburbs, partly because of the impact of the Eastern Freeway. Carlton and North Melbourne residents' groups became active and many of their members joined the TCPA as protest over the potential sweeping away of the inner urban lifestyle. In 1977 their annual reports were incorporated into the *Space* newsletter, and Margaret Nicholls began her service as the TCPA's first female president (to 1980). Wal Currie remained the last of the old guard on the Council. In 1977 the Association initiated the Certificate of Planning Achievement, awarding it firstly to Dr Miles Lewis for 'outstanding work on streetscape planning and preservation', but it would not sustain the award.[48]

By the 1980s the TCPA's membership reflected a high level of participation from people involved in planning education, its meetings were being held at Melbourne University or Swinburne Institute of Technology, and the publication of *Space* was partially supported by the Footscray Institute of Technology. Leslie Perrott's architectural firm paid for administrative support.[49] However, membership had fallen to 115. *Space* was no longer a public magazine, but was reconstituted into a member newsletter and published only four times per year. Town planning issues in this decade included nature conservation, Victoria's heritage plan, dual occupancy, urban planning education, and municipal restructuring. The Association continued to prepare submissions to relevant bodies on most of these issues. In 1989 it devoted two issues of *Space* to climate change (the 'greenhouse effect').[50]

Figure 12.7: South Australian Premier Don Dunstan (left) and federal Labor Minister Jim Cairns (right) from cover of the TCPAV's 1974 Annual Report

Sustainability: the 1990s and 2000s

After *Space* ceased publication in 1991, the TCPA slipped into a period of declining membership and inactivity, perhaps because of a perception that many of its long-standing objectives had been achieved through changes to planning legislation and practice. At one point in the decade its membership fell to only six. Just as resident association groups had reinvented the TCPA in earlier periods, it was probably saved from extinction by the arrival of a group from the Public Transport Users Association. One of them, Ray Walford, became President and introduced Brian Lewis' son, architectural academic Miles Lewis to the TCPA. As Ray Walford, who is still an active member, recalls:

> Once again, there was another group moving in and pushing an agenda, or using the TCPA logo as it were to push an agenda, and I think this time that wasn't totally welcomed by those who had been keeping the TCPA going in the intervening years. However, I did speak at the meeting at the South Melbourne Town Hall where the Charter for Planning was launched ... and there was a feeling that there was a need for a new approach to planning.[51]

The development of the *Charter for planning* arose from growing concerns in the mid-1990s about planning, sustainability and other issues associated with living in Melbourne under the Kennett Liberal state government that surfaced in particular at a Planning Crisis Conference held at the South Melbourne Town Hall in June 1996. According to Lewis, the Charter attempted 'to make explicit all the formerly unwritten assumptions about accountability, fairness, etc in planning' at a time when these were 'under challenge'.[52] Published in 1997 after a well-organised period of consultation over its contents (with input from organisations such as the National Trust, the People's Committee for Melbourne, and the Save Albert Park Group), the *Charter for planning* articulated a set of planning goals, ethics, principles and policies (Table 12.2). The Association intended the Charter to be used 'by amenity groups, professional associations and government bodies, and would have a real effect upon planning practice and procedures'.[53] The Charter was designed to help planners do their work ethically and as a template to help them take everything necessary into account. It bears a deliberate resemblance to other such guidelines and principles of the period, such as ICOMOS' Burra Charter on best practice conservation procedures.

Table 12.2: Outline of the Town and Country Planning Association's 'Charter for planning' (1997)

---

1. PLANNING GOALS

1.1 Efficiency

Planning policy must seek efficiency, in the sense of returning the greatest possible good to the community, to the extent that this may be consistent with ecological sustainability and other agreed objectives.

1.2 Social equity

Planning policy must aim to give all members of the community equal access to benefits and facilities, to the extent that this is practicable and consistent with their own desires and capacities.

1.3 Ecological sustainability

Ecological sustainability must be a primary criterion for the establishment of planning policy.

1.4 Quality of life

Planning policy must aim to provide quality of life through social interaction, variety of experience, cultural depth and aesthetic satisfaction.

1.5 Amenity

Planning policy must aim to maximise the amenity enjoyed by the relevant property owners and occupiers, neighbours, and the community at large.

1.6 Conservation of nature

Planning policy must protect natural assets including parkland, rural land, coasts, creeks, rivers, wetlands, flora and fauna.

1.7 Conservation of cultural significance

Planning policy must ensure the conservation of the cultural significance of all places.

1.8 Quality of design

Planning policy must foster good landscape, urban and architectural design.

2. PLANNING ETHICS

2.1 Common interest

Planning must serve the common interest.

2.2 Property equity

The planning process must treat owners and occupiers of land in an equitable manner. The planning process must give equal weight to the interests of current and future generations.

2.3 Consistency

Changes of planning philosophy or direction must occur in an evolutionary rather than a revolutionary manner. Individual planning decisions must be made on a consistent and, so far as practicable, a predictable basis.

2.4 Public input and accountability

The planning process must be responsive to the needs and views of the community. It must provide for public participation and be open to the scrutiny of the community at all stages.

2.5 Barriers to participation

Individuals or groups must not be prevented by technical, administrative or financial barriers from exercising their legitimate roles in the planning process.

2.6 Transparency

The reasons for planning decisions, the evidence upon which they are based, and the principles applied, must be readily accessible to the public in an easily comprehensible form.

2.7 Freedom from political interference

Planning administration must be independent of political interference except where policy decisions are superimposed at the behest of democratic government, or in cases of genuine emergency.

2.8 Overriding commitments

Planning decisions must honour national and international commitments, consistent with this charter.

2.9 Compensation for demonstrable loss

Planning decisions must not curtail or remove the existing rights of owners or occupiers without compensation.

2.10 Unearned gains

Planning decisions which accord development rights to property owners should include a levy which captures the unearned increment and returns it to the community.

2.11 Amenity

Planning decisions must give due recognition to the amenity enjoyed by the relevant property owners and occupiers, neighbours, and the community at large.

3. PLANNING PRINCIPLES

3.1 Legislation

Planning legislation must provide an effective and democratic mechanism for the management of all changes in land use, consistent with the goals of this charter.

3.2 Policy development

Planning policies should be framed at a state level, having regard to all applicable national policies, treaty obligations, and related state policies already in existence, and these policies should be developed at a regional and a local level.

3.3 The development of plans

The purpose of a plan is to provide a just and effective mechanism by which policy objectives are implemented in relation to specific local conditions.

3.4 Objective assessment

Where any social, environmental or material effect is likely to result, the decision itself, and all professional assessments relied upon, must be made by bodies independent of the proponent, user or developer. The process must also allow for public input.

3.5 Information rights

A planning proposal must be properly notified to those who may be affected; adequate information about it must be readily available; and sufficient time must be provided for response.

3.6 The appeal process

The appeal process must enable any interested party to be satisfied that planning decisions are made in accordance with the principles of this charter.

3.7 Environmental and social impact assessment

The environmental or social effect of a planning policy or action must be evaluated before a decision is taken. Where the effect may be significant, the evaluation must take the form of a comprehensive and objective environmental and social impact assessment.

3.8 Government intervention

Government intervention in the decision-making process may occur under only two conditions. The first is where the actions of other authorities or parties threaten to delay, frustrate or bias planning decisions, in which case the intervention must be challengeable at law. The second is where government is willing to offer mediation, financial or other assistance which may help to resolve an issue without disadvantage to the principal parties.

3.9 Financial assessment

The financial consequences of acquiring or rezoning land, using or developing public property, or other such planning decisions, must be the subject of competent, independent and publicly accessible assessment as the basis for any financial compensation, assistance, betterment tax, levy or similar transaction which may ensue.

3.10 Public assets

Public assets should be disposed of, radically altered or committed to new functions only when not required by the community concerned, and with due recompense to that community.

4. PLANNING POLICIES

4.1 Environmental standards

Environmental standards must be defined and enforced objectively, for the good of the community at large, in the present and in the long term.

4.2 Targets

Targets must be set for the achievement of economic, environmental and social objectives.

4.3 Performance standards

The administration and regulation of land use must be based so far as is practicable upon performance standards which take into account the real effects of the use in terms of economic, environmental and social impacts, and of amenity, where these can be measured. Where these effects cannot be reliably measured, standards and rules based upon precautionary principles should be applied.

4.4 Conservation and rehabilitation of natural areas

Planning policy must seek to conserve and rehabilitate natural areas.

4.5 Containment of urban spread

Planning must seek to control the spread of urban development onto rural land, and more especially to land of high economic, natural or cultural value.

4.6 Minimisation of travel
Land uses should be arranged to minimise the need for travel, particularly by environmentally inefficient forms of transport.

4.7 Integration of land use and transport
Land use and development must be integrated with the necessary systems of transport for people and goods, and on the basis that these systems must be in turn compatible with the ecological and other principles identified above.

4.8 Maintenance of open space
Planning must proceed upon the basis that urban areas are provided with appropriate and sufficient open space for the provision of light and ventilation, psychological relief, aesthetic enjoyment, recreation, nature conservation and other community requirements.

4.9 Long term strategy planning
Planning decisions must accord with the objectives of long term strategy plans.

Revised and adopted by the Committee of the Town and Country Planning Association, 1 September 1997, in accordance with the recommendations of the delegated working group.

By 1997, TCPA membership had increased enough to allow it to organise five working groups (transport, Agenda 21, strategic planning, parklands, and urban fringe).[54] A concern for sustainable city development emerged in 1998, linked to the development of the state government's *Good design guide for medium density housing* which was intended to constrain sprawl and the associated infrastructure costs. The Save our Suburbs movement formed from a coalition of concerned suburban residents as a result. A persistent view throughout this period was that freeways and road building dominated planning, and this saw the Association call for the closer integration of transport planning (including cycling) with urban development. Other issues of interest to the TCPA through the 1990s included defending the public realm (linked to 'Hands off our parks'), locality issues such as efforts by Friends of Merri Creek to protect native grasslands, the lack of consultation about the decision to hold the Formula One Grand Prix races in Albert Park, and support for 'green wedges' as non-urban zones within the metropolitan area.

In the new millennium the TCPA's attention turned to pedestrians as a group neglected by planners, and it increased its support for cycling, walking and public transport. It consistently provided feedback to government across a range of planning issues and documents, including ResCode (2001), the Inner-West Integrated Transport Strategy, the state government's Greenhouse Strategy, the federal government's National Transport Plan (2002), dredging in Port Phillip Bay (2005), the Melbourne 2030 metropolitan plan, and the Eddington rail proposals (2008). New president Ray Walford set out a new agenda for the Association, although there are still many echoes of its enduring concerns with low-income housing, density, trees, multi-unit developments, and park nibbling (the latter due to concern over plans for the Commonwealth Games' athletes village in Royal Park).

Conclusion

It would be fair to say that the TCPA became smaller and less vocal as it entered the new century with a low public profile. After the release of the Victorian government's new Transport Plan in 2008, the media looked to organisations such as the Planning Institute and Public Transport Users' Association for comment – such bodies have taken over this public profile task that used to belong to the TCPA. Other organisations that increasingly rivalled the Association for membership now included the Women's Planning Network; Save Our Suburbs; the Public Transport Users Association; Bicycle Victoria; single issue groups such as Unchain St Kilda, Save Albert Park, and Plug the Pipe (a campaign to stop the government's north-south water pipeline); and the rise of 'friends groups', such as Friends of the Merri Creek, which provide community participation as well as keeping a watchful eye on local issues. Many of these groups are connected through the Victorian Environment Friends Network.

Now, after nearly a century of lobbying on town planning and related issues, the TCPA sees its primary purpose – within its role a non-profit and non-party political public organisation – as the advocacy of 'environmental planning of land use for ecological sustainability via effective strategic planning frameworks'.[55] A transformed bureaucratic mechanism which saw the Victorian Civil and Appeals Tribunal created in 1998 – through the amalgamation of 15 separate tribunals and boards – to adjudicate planning disputes, now means it is much more difficult for non-government organisations and community groups to determine where their influence can lie. While Renate Howe might rightly note that Sir James Barrett 'would have turned in his grave to see what has happened to many of Melbourne's city and suburban parks', she still concedes the advantage of the TCPA as an independent platform, 'outside the system', with 'the capacity to be able to be a conduit for some of that dissatisfaction, or new ideas'. At worst, this can be a dispiriting exercise of putting out spot fires, or attending 'interminable meetings, in which nothing much [is] achieved'.[56] But while admitting that seeing both sides of the development coin can at times be paralysing, current member Ray Walford also sees the advantage of a broad-brush organisation that can avoid the NIMBY taint:

> We look at the way Melbourne is developing in a very broad way and so, we don't have any vested interests, and we don't come from a particular viewpoint associated either with a particular location or with, say, an industry, say with the development industry or with resident groups or whatever. So, we've got a very general focus, and I think that would give us some credibility as being impartial.[57]

The Victorian Town and Country Planning Association transformed over the course of over 90 years of activism, from an elite and prestigious lobby group under the guidance of Sir James Barrett, to a 'little rump'[58] of obsessed enthusiasts who doubted that the Planning Minister 'even knows we exist'.[59] Yet it has managed to continue as an advocate for responsible planning, making its voice heard through submissions to government and instrumentalities, and making these available to the public via its website. As each dominating membership group – the middle-class philanthropists, then local government bureaucrats, architects, and planning educators – had done with it, the engineers, always members, and the planners, have quietly continued to mind the store.

References

[1] Town and Country Planning Association of Victoria (hereafter TCPA), Report of Annual Meeting 1941, 9, University of Melbourne Archives, 93/7, Box 1.
[2] TCPA Annual Report, 1939–40, 4. The Royal Exhibition Building is now a World Heritage site.
[3] TCPA, Annual Report, 1939–40, 4.
[4] TCPA, Report of Annual Meeting 1941.
[5] TCPA, Annual Report 1939.
[6] TCPA, Executive Minutes 6 March 1942, State Library of Victoria.
[7] See TCPA, Annual Report 1945 for example; in the same year the Committee could not decide whether to send a speaker to fulfil a request from the Garfield Progress Association.
[8] TCPA, Executive Minutes 29 April 1943.
[9] Interim Report, Committee to Consider A Site for a New Art or Cultural Centre, October 1944, TCPA papers, University of Melbourne Archives, Box 3.
[10] TCPA, Annual Report 1943–44.
[11] TCPA, Minutes 8 February 1944.
[12] TCPA Report of Annual Meeting 1941.
[13] TCPA, Minutes 24 October 1944.
[14] TCPA, Minutes 19 January 1945 and 3 May 1945.
[15] TCPA, Annual Report 1944–45.
[16] TCPA, Minutes 14 May 1948.
[17] TCPA, Minutes 18 June and 10 September 1948; 17 February and 3 March 1949.
[18] TCPA, Council Minutes 28 February 1947.
[19] TCPA, Minutes 16 May 1947 and 3 March 1949.
[20] Tony Dingle and Carolyn Rasmussen, *Vital Connections: Melbourne and its Board of Works 1891–1991* (Melbourne: McPhee Gribble, 1991), 231–35.
[21] TCPA, Minutes 14 July 1950.
[22] TCPA Minutes 16 October 1952.

[23] TCPA Annual Report 1964–65, 5–6.
[24] TCPA, Minutes 17 April 1952.
[25] TCPA, Minutes 20 February 1952.
[26] TCPA, Minutes 20 September 1951.
[27] TCPA, Minutes, for example, 20 April 1951.
[28] TCPA. Minutes 16 October 1952.
[29] Leonie Sandercock, *Cities for sale: property, politics and urban planning in Australia* (Melbourne: Melbourne University Press, 1975), 147–48.
[30] TCPA, Minutes October 1951.
[31] TCPA, Annual Report 1964–65.
[32] TCPA, Annual Report 1964–65, 1–2.
[33] *Plan News Review* (February/March, 1965).
[34] *Plan News Review* (April/June 1967).
[35] *Plan News Review* (December/January 1969–70): 3, and October 1970.
[36] Ruth Crow, letter to TCPA President Miles Lewis, 7 September 1997.
[37] These TCPA records are now housed in the State Library of Victoria.
[38] Renate Howe, 'The spirit of Melbourne: 1960s urban activism in inner-city Melbourne', in *Go! Melbourne: Melbourne in the sixties* eds. Seamus O'Hanlon and Tanja Luckins (Melbourne: c.2005), 219.
[39] Transcript, Renate Howe Oral History Interview, 11 February 2009, by Susan Reidy.
[40] Renate Howe Interview.
[41] *Plan News Review* (September 1968): 3, and (November 1968).
[42] TCPA, Annual Report 1971.
[43] Dingle and Rasmussen, 317.
[44] *Plan News Review* (February 1973): 3.
[45] Tony Dingle, '"Gloria Soame": the spread of suburbia in post-war Australia', in *Changing suburbs: foundation, form and function* eds. Richard Harris and Peter Larkham (London: Spon, 1999), 187–201.
[46] *Space*, supplement (April/September 1977).
[47] TCPA, Annual Report 1970, 7.
[48] *Space* (January/March 1979): 6.
[49] *Space* (June 1986).
[50] *Space* (June and September 1989).
[51] Transcript, Ray Walford Oral History Interview, 11 March 2009, by Susan Reidy.
[52] Miles Lewis, *Suburban backlash: the battle for the world's most liveable city* (Melbourne: Bloomings Books, 1999), 186.

[53] Letter from Miles Lewis, President TCPA, to the Deputy Leader of the Opposition, Demetri Dollis, 27 June 1996. Courtesy Miles Lewis.
[54] TCPA, Organisation Chart 1997.
[55] Town and Country Planning Association, 'Submission to the Victorian Government's Needs Assessment Study for an east-west transport link across inner Melbourne', submitted to Victorian Department of Transport, May 2007.
[56] Transcript, Miles Lewis Oral History Interview, 25 February 2009, by Susan Reidy.
[57] Ray Walford Interview.
[58] Miles Lewis Interview.
[59] Ray Walford Interview.

Conclusion

Mixed fortunes, broadening agendas, and changing times

Robert Freestone

Town planning associations provide an illuminating lens for comprehending the development of urban planning in modern Australia. Reformist rather than radical in orientation, and from time to time even reactionary in their politics, they are not consistently the insurgent forces for progressive community change beloved by planning theorists.[1] They are nonetheless relatively unacknowledged actors in Australian planning history whose stories tell of the fundamental importance of community contributions in shaping the emerging discourse of city planning in the early 20th century.

At crucial formative stages in the evolution of Australian planning practice, town planning associations provided a means for civil society to productively communicate concerns and priorities to government officials and politicians and were thus important agents in promoting early pathways to community wellbeing in Australian cities. In time they were partly victims of their own success as the role which they envisaged for planning in society was largely accommodated by government. As this occurred, their own independent agendas tugged against the mainstream and in most states there was an historic transformation of their own roles from supporter to critic of the state. In this revisionist guise, they helped pave the way for many more organisations bringing new insurgent agendas to fresh urban challenges, albeit continuing the vital role of the community in both shaping and critiquing city planning policies and programs.

Any voluntary body confronts success or failure mediated by the calibre of its leadership, its administrative organisation, and its ability to liaise, negotiate and cooperate with similar bodies and the powers-that-be. Durability requires not only a realistic pursuit of a consistent vision but the ability to change, re-organise and respond to challenging and changing internal and external forces. One framework to generalise the Australian experience of town planning associations is to draw from studies of the political efficacy of pressure and interest groups. Abbott distils this to the successful integration of robust internal authority and strong external legitimacy.[2]

High internal authority relates to key factors in representativeness and competitiveness: membership attraction, effective decision-making, and solidarity of member actions.[3] A key factor is effective leadership to suit the times and attract and offer incentives to a committed membership, secure sustainable funding, and build alliances. The obligation is to successfully negotiate the 'organisational maintenance' required by changed circumstances and challenges, a capacity factor evident across the lifetime of a body like the Regional Plan Association of New York founded in 1929.[4] For the Australian town planning associations, activism was undoubtedly a function of champions within the organisation. They enjoyed their highest profile with the strong leadership of organiser-proselytisers. In Sydney it was the founders journalist-publishers George and Florence Taylor, both articled as architects earlier in their careers, allied to the presidency of John Sulman for over a decade. In Perth, the continuity of the presidential tenure of William Saw, a state civil servant in land administration, was crucial along with partnerships he forged with respected individuals like architect Harold Boas and local government figure William Bold. Lawyer Henry Uffindell held the reins in Adelaide for the greater part of the first town planning association's life. In Brisbane in the early 1920s it was Ronald McInnis and in Hobart

Rudolph Koch. In Melbourne the pre-World War II colossus was Sir James Barrett, then architect Frank Heath in the 1940s, and from the 1950s Robert Gardner, a journalist and public relations expert.

External legitimacy is primarily derived from the changing social milieu of planning – most broadly through cycles of war, reconstruction, cyclical economic health and social change[5] – prevailing public opinion and social attitudes, and what Dalton has called the 'political opportunity structure' within which environmental interest groups like the town planning associations worked.[6] State and local politics created shifting climates of enthusiasm for advocates of planning reform. Progressive left-of-centre Labor governments tended to offer a more receptive or at least less hostile institutional setting. But the correlation is far from perfect. Other political allegiances and conditions, notably those periods of consensus forged by conditions of war and economic crisis, also created windows of opportunity to influence public and political opinion. This illustrates a process known as 'bureaucratic accommodation' whereby groups can be incorporated into decision-making structures and gain some degree of 'insider' status, albeit in the process potentially annulling their independent voice. There were periods when the town planning associations became 'insider' groups at the peak of their influence, being recognised by government as legitimate spokespersons for particular interests to engage in public and informal dialogue.[7] This appears to have been the situation in Sydney in the 1910s, Adelaide and Perth in the 1920s, Melbourne in the 1940s, and, not always for the better, in latter-day Queensland.

Internal authority and external legitimacy tended to move in concert, but they have also diverged on occasions. An instance would be Melbourne in the 1920s where a well-organised town planning association struggled for influence with a government which had established its own planning machinery in the form of an official Town Planning Commission headed by the city's influential Lord Mayor Frank Stapley who espoused a far more pragmatic business-minded planning philosophy compared to the green belt-and-playgrounds ideas of Barrett.[8] Similarly, the Queensland Association, despite moving in a more conservative direction, was effectively marginalised in the 1920s by the political leadership of the new Brisbane City Council, the major success story of the 'greater city' movement for local government consolidation in Australia. The toehold which associations could secure was ultimately dependent on the oscillating reform and institutional cultures of the different capital cities. Adapting Marion Orr's perspective from contemporary community organisations, each city constituted a unique local 'ecology of civic engagement' wherein the various associations had varied success at different intervals in developing effective connections with the key institutional players.[9] The chapters of this book have recounted those instances where the efforts of voluntary advocates were most closely aligned with political priorities.

If real success could spell the death knell for a town planning association as the goals which it most directly stood for were achieved, the rise of other organisations seen as more representative of planning practitioners was even more challenging. Despite a base of community membership, the early associations assumed the role of de facto professional bodies. They were a recognised inter-professional forum for architects, surveyors and engineers interested in planning. But they could not sustain that role because it set up a conflict with the 'amateur' arm of the planning movement that had sundry and localised interests which were not necessarily mainstream planning concerns. Moreover, the professionals themselves were restless to move from propaganda to practice. In Perth, Harold Boas who had been the first secretary of the association there in 1916 personally led the charge to found a Town Planning Institute of WA in 1931.[10] In Sydney in 1934, Alfred Brown resigned as President of the NSW Association to assume the same title at the new Town and Country Planning Institute. An embittered Bertram Ford complained that the TPANSW has been 'the official body' for 21 years and there was only room for one.[11] Other state based professional bodies were formed in Melbourne in 1944 and in Adelaide in 1947.

In August 1951 extant state entities were folded into a national Planning Institute of Australia.[12] This had major implications for the surviving town planning associations because of the Institute's assumption of their historic general mission for promoting planning. They would have to carve out a different position of watchdog. With planning broadly accepted by the community as a necessary element of the modern state apparatus, their focus could be as guardians of best practice without fear or favour. The experiences of the postwar successor bodies were mixed. The NSW body pursued an idiosyncratic agenda completely marginalised from most trained planners. The bodies which largely took over from their prewar predecessors in Hobart (The Council of Hobart Progress Associations and the spin-off Citizens' Advisory Town Planning Committee) and Perth (the Civic Affairs Committee and City Vision) carved out more responsible platforms. A new Town and Country Planning Association in Adelaide (1964–85), unconnected with the prewar body, played a key role in the orchestration of public scrutiny of government planning initiatives from the 1960s and helped provide a crucial platform for the advancement of the green agenda. By contrast, the Queensland Town and Country Planning Association (1957–61) failed to secure an independent mandate and as it faded members were urged to join the professional body. Again, the Victorian Town and Country Planning Association negotiated the new climate most tenaciously. Moving away from the older model of local authority affiliates, new constituencies of concerned citizens and academics were forged firstly in the 1970s around emergent issues of heritage, urban renewal, transport and community, and again in the 1990s around local government reform, sustainability and pedestrians.

The other organisational challenge for town planning associations evident even before World War II came from groups with more specialised objectives. The associations were initially empowered by the various improvement associations, debating societies, nationalistic groups, and environmental bodies which came together on the common ground of town planning. However, over time these affiliations tended to dissolve or fracture. For example, led by prominent journalist and war historian C.E.W. Bean, the Parks and Playground Movement in NSW spun off from the Town Planning Association of NSW in the 1930s. The traditional propaganda mission of the associations was also outmoded in the postwar landscape by the institutionalisation of planning. With calls for more public participation and an ever-widening set of targets defined by the things which planners both did and did not do, the relevance of the old omnibus style of organisation was eroded by the formation of new bodies. Unshackling themselves from an oftentimes constricting if not disastrous modernist planning agenda forged in the 1920s, new groups pursued ever more specialised and usually sophisticated environmental agendas: civic design, environmental quality, coastal protection, pollution, public transport, bicycles, and a myriad of resident action causes.

Remarkably, the Town and Country Planning Association in Melbourne has managed to survive into this new era by periodically reinventing itself to sit alongside a plethora of community and environmental organisations concerned not so much with inventing planning, the goal of the 1910s, so much as confronting and re-imagining it. In other capital cities, while the town planning associations are long gone, their model of independent community-based organisations pursuing multi-faceted reform agendas promoting the ameliorative power of good planning can still be traced into other organisations such as City Vision in Perth, the Council of Hobart Progress Associations, and the Brisbane Development Association.

None of these bodies matches the prototypical Town and Country Planning Association in the United Kingdom in its ongoing contributions to contemporary urban policy debate and planning reform.[13] But the equivalent Australian bodies had different origins and were not underpinned by the same deep-seated and enduring commitment to both social justice and sustainable development originating in the garden city movement. The origins, agendas and vigour of the Australian town planning associations were contingent on different historical circumstances. Their grand mission of promoting town planning as almost a panacea for urban ills now seems old-fashioned. A national professional institute has largely assumed the role of representing the interests of both planning and planners while community and environmental groups have directed their energies to concerns in which planning seems to be as much the problem as the solution. The notion of resuscitating a town planning association movement is chimerical with its historic task of campaigning for effective planning now expressed in many different ways. But amid the fractured interests which presently dominate urban planning and development debates in Australian cities, the value of a strong, balanced and independent voice for an informed and engaged community remains valid.

References

[1] Leonie Sandercock (ed.) *Making the invisible visible: a multicultural planning history* (Berkeley: University of California Press, 1998).

[2] Keith Abbott, *Pressure groups and the Australian Federal Parliament* (Canberra: Australian Government Publishing Service, 1996).

[3] Philip Lowe and Jane Goyde, *Environmental groups in politics* (London: Allen and Unwin, 1983).

[4] F.B. Hays, *Community leadership: the Regional Plan Association of New York* (New York: Columbia University Press, 1965).

[5] Stuart Macintyre, *A concise history of Australia* (Melbourne: Cambridge University Press, 2000).

[6] Russel J. Dalton, *The green rainbow* (New Haven: Yale University Press, 1994).

[7] W. Grant, 'Pressure politics: the changing world of pressure groups', *Parliamentary Affairs*, 57 (2004): 408–19.

[8] Robert Freestone, *Model communities: the Garden City movement in Australia* (Melbourne: Thomas Nelson, 1989), 210–11.

[9] Marion Orr, 'Community organizing and the changing ecology of civic engagement', in her *Transforming the city: community organizing and the challenge of political change* (Lawrence: University Press of Kansas, 2007), 3.
[10] Robert Freestone, 'WA's first planning institute', *Australian Planner*, 20(3), (1982): 138-39.
[11] *Sydney Morning Herald*, 10 August 1934, 11.
[12] Bruce Wright, *Expectations of a better world* (Canberra: Planning Institute of Australia, 2001).
[13] Dennis Hardy, *1899-1999: The TCPA's first hundred years, and the next ...* (London: Town and Country Planning Association, 1999).

Index

Abercrombie, Sir Patrick, 6, 204–05, 236–37, 261, 346
Aborigines, 110
Adam, Ken, 248, 255
Adelaide (SA), 19, 42, 120–21, 124, 142, 206–07, 209, 212, 222
Adelaide City Council, 122–23, 127, 132, 134, 137, 141, 212
Adelaide Gas Pipeline Looping Project, 225
Adelaide Hills, 212, 217–19
Adelaide Street (Brisbane), *301*
Adelaide Town Hall, 135
Advertiser (Adelaide), 207, 209, 218, 221, 227
Advisory boards and committee, 2, 17, 241, *see also* town planning associations; New South Wales, 39, 317, 323, 328, 334–5; Queensland, 74, 80, 82, 290, 299; South Australia, 121, 127, 133, 154, 206–11, 216–17, 221, 223–26; Tasmania, 162, 165, 263–68, 271–72, 274, 279, 276–78; Victoria, 93, 96, 352, 358, 362; Western Australia, 184, 186, 188–89, 191–94, 236, 2239, 242, 252–56

Albert Park (Melbourne), 367–68
Alexander, Ian, 247, 261
Alexander, S.B., 178
Allen, Verity, 248, *249*
Anderson, E., 32
Anderson, I.G., 268
Angliss, Sir William, 345
architects and architecture, 4, 15, 29, 31, 39, 41, 72, 75, 105–06, 113, 124–25, 129, 133, 138, 151, 155, 157, 168, 178, 193, 204, 209, 211, 213, 227, 240, 243, 255, 260, 264, 278, 315, 317, 324, 326, 370, 376
Architectural and Building Journal of Queensland, 17–18
Argus (Melbourne), 91, 95
Armidale (NSW), 320
Ashton, Nigel, 330
Atkinson, Dr, 178
Australasian Town Planning Tour, 65, 91, 95–97, 99–100, 123–24, 142, 149, 176
Australian Conservation Foundation, 218, 220
Australian Council for the New Urbanism, 6
Australian Forestry League, 38, 140

381

Australian Institute of Urban Studies, 6, 252–53
Australian Municipal Journal, 111–12
Australian Natives Association, 121, 157
Australian Planning Institute (API), *see* Planning Institute of Australia/Royal Australian Planning Institute/Town and Country Planning Institute (NSW)
Australian Town Planning Conferences and Exhibitions; 1917 Adelaide, 5, 42, 73, 75, 104–05, 128–32, 138, 155; 1918 Brisbane, 5, 42, 64, 68–70, 72, 74–77, 82, 105–06, 132; 1919 Ballarat, 107
Australian Urban History/Planning History Conference 1991 (Sydney), 6

Badger Creek (VIC), 111
Baillie, William, 161
Ballarat (VIC), 105, 107
Bankstown (Sydney), 325, *327*
Barker, V.W.O., 151
Barnett, F. Oswald, 5, 113
Barracks Arch (Perth), 239, 243
Barracks Defence Council, 238–9
Barrett, Dr Edith, 95, 99
Barrett, Sir James, 20, 91, *92*, 92–96, 98–105, 107–11, 114, 344, 348–49, 351, 356, 360, 369, 375–76, *see also* Sir James Barrett Memorial Medal
Barton, E.C., 65–66, 72, 76
Barwell, Henry, 131, 133–34, 139–40
Bathurst Street (Hobart), *272*
Battery Point (Hobart), 157, 162, 276
Bean, C.E.W., 38, 101, 321, 324, 378
Beaver, H.P., 132
Bennett, Charles B., 351
Bennett Commission, 300
beautification, 14, 17, 29, 50, 59, 111, 162–64, 166, 168, 184, 195, 240, 243, 261, 319, *see also* city beautiful/civic improvements/parks and gardens
Bedford, Josephine, *68–69*
Beirne, T.C., 80
Bellerive (Hobart), 157
Bendigo (VIC), 105
Benko, Andrew, 206
Berry, Dean W., 204
Berry, Professor Richard, 99
bicycles, 227, 290, 358, 368, 378; Bicycle Institute of South Australia, 227
Bicycle Victoria, 368
Black, Alfred Barham, 125
Blackburn, Maurice, 99

Blakeway, A.J., 133–4
Bligh, Arthur, 299
Boas, Harold, 175–78, 181, 186–87, 189, 191–94, 235, 240, 243, 246, 374, 376
Boelke, Dr Grace, 32, 35, 48, 50, 54
Bold, William E. 5, 16, 19, 95, *174*–76, 178, 181, 185–86, 189, 191–94, 374
Bolte, Henry, 353
Booth, Dr Mary, 32–33, 54
Boyd, Robin, 349, 354
Bradfield, J.J.C., 32–33, 41, 323
Breakfast Creek (Brisbane), 66–67
Brigden, J.B., 293
Brisbane (QLD), 64, 74, 78–79, *288*, 292, 294, 298–99, 301
Brisbane City Council, 78, 82, 296, 376, *see also* Greater Brisbane City Council
Brisbane Development Association, 288, 294, 296–97, 300, 303, 378
Brockman, Fred, 178
Brooker Highway (Hobart), 269, *275*
Brooks, Sir Dallas, 351
Brown, Alfred J., 6, 34, 58, 315–17, 329, 376
Builders Labourers Federation, 240–1

Builder (The) Incorporating Town Planning & Local Government Journal (Adelaide), 136–37
Building (Sydney), 17, 29, 35, 42–43, 57, 64
building activity, 29, 65, 77, 168, 263, 274, 290, 318, *see also* town planning – regulations
Building Better Cities (Commonwealth program), 6
Building Owners' and Managers' Association, 254
Bulcock, R.A., 75
Bulletin, 39
Burke, Brian, 241, 244
Burke, T.M., 84
Burnham, Daniel, 181, 195
Burt, W.O., 5
bushland, 191, 274
businessmen, 15–16, 44, 79, 124, 148, 152, 164, 167–68, 210, 335
Buttenshaw, E.A., 323
Butters, Sir John (Sydney), 323–24

Cadbury, William, 160
Cahill Expressway (Sydney), 330
Cairns, Jim, *361*
Caldicott, Ron, 218, 220–23, 227
Caloundra (QLD), 289
Camberwell (Melbourne), 103

383

Campbelltown (Sydney), 325
Canberra (ACT), 6, 41, 44, 290, 300, *see also* federal capital
capitalism, 7, 303
cars and car parking, 84, 212, 237–38, 243, 253, 261–63, 269, 271–73, 279, 301, 306, 352, *see also* town planning – transport
Carlton (Melbourne), 104, 356
Carr, David, 254
Castells, Manuel, 305
Castray Esplanade (Hobart), 163
Cavanagh, J.J., 79
Cavanagh, Michael, 178
cemeteries, 166
Central Business District (CBD), *28*, 50, 191, 244, 275, *314*, 352
Central Business District (CBD) Committee/Capital City Committee, 244, 252–53, 256
Chamber of Manufacturers (QLD), 82
Chambers of Commerce; Queensland, 82, 305–6; South Australia, 210, 216; Tasmania, 157; Western Australia, 178, 242, 254–5
Chandler, J.C., 293
Charter for Planning (Melbourne), 362
Cheesman, Jack, 204
Chelsea Progress Association, 103

children's playgrounds, 11, 13–14, 19, 38, 68, 76, 93, 95, 99, 102, 104, 107, 126, 129, 136–38, 148–51, 157, 165–67, 173–74, 180, 184, 187, 343, 376, *see also* Parks and Playground Movement/ parks and reserves
Child Welfare Association, 157
Children's Playground Association, 68, 167
Chinamans Beach (Sydney), 325
Chronicle (Nambour), 83
Chuter, Charles, 72, *73*, 74, 77–78, 81–83, 85–86, 290–91, 293
Circular Quay (Sydney), 319, 323–24
Circular Quay Advisory Committee, 323–24
citizens and citizenship, 1–3, 34, 36, 72, 93, 111, 121–22, 142, 153, 195, 203, 206, 209–10, 226, 229, 239, 260–62, 264–68, 281, 300, 302, 307, 334, 377, *see also* participatory democracy/ progress associations/ resident action groups
Citizens' Advisory Town Planning Committee (CATPC), 262, 266–69, 272–74, 280–81, 377, *see also* town planning associations

Citizens' Committee for the Defence of Kings Park, 239
City Beach (Perth), 178, 185
City Endowment Lands Estate (Perth), 181, 185
city beautiful movement, 120, 148, 176, 184–85, 192
city planning, *see also* town planning/urban planning; Canada, 93, 187; Europe, 31, 65, 93, 124, 176, 185, 189, 245; India, 93, 187; New Zealand, 188; United Kingdom, 3–4, 7–8, 13–14, 18, 20, 43, 95–96, 112–13, 135, 186, 204, 210, 236, 261, 316, 344–46, 378; United States, 4, 8, 13, 80, 93, 176, 189, 238, 315
City Vision, 242, 246–56, 377–78
Civic Affairs Committee, 244, 377
civic centres, 17, 41–42, 84, 112, 175, 185, 325, *327*, 343–44, 356
civic design, 68, 237, 325, 335–36, 345, 378
Civic Design Society, 335
civic improvement, 4, 11, 14, 17, 27–29, 40–41, 45, 50, 55, 58, 91, 100, 104, 107, 120, 124–26, 130, 142–43, 149, 156–57, 163, 166, 168, 176, 180, 185, 187, 191, 210, 260–62, 274–75, 330, 334

Civic Trust, 214, 227–28
Clamp, J. Burcham, 31
Claremont (Hobart), 160
Clark, Colin, 293
Clonston, J.H., 125
Coalition of Resident Acton Groups, 6, *see also* resident action
Cohen, Lewis, 124
Cole, H.J.R., 263, 265
Collaroy (Sydney), 325, *327*
Collaroy Community League, 325
Collingwood, (Melbourne), *108–9*
Colonel Light Gardens (Adelaide), 135
Commonwealth government *see* federal government
Commonwealth Home, 17, 42
Commonwealth Housing Commission, 5, 328, 346
Commonwealth Ministry for Post-War Reconstruction, 346
communism, 75, 177, 328, 356
community planning *see* neighbourhood units, urban planning
competitions; design, 5, 13, 37, 249, 316, *see also* civic design/federal capital
essay, 40, 349

Concord (Sydney), 45
conferences, symposiums and exhibitions, 5, 6, 11–12, 16, 39, 41–43, 51, 68, 95, 127, 129, 183–84, 189, 192, 204–05, 207, 209–11, 213–16, 224, 243–44, 248, 253, 265, 277, 290, 324–25, 355–56, 362, *see also* Australian Town Planning Conferences and Exhibitions
Connolly, J.D., 178
Conrad, Albert Selmar, 125, 130
conservation, 7, 14, 56, 100, 216–28, 302, 334, 355, 359–60, 362
Conservation Council of South Australia, 220, 224–25, 228
conservatism, 16, 29, 36–37, 57, 112, 150, 156, 176, 318, 328, 337, 376
Construction (Sydney), 17
construction, 84, 168, 185, 289, 357, *see* building activity
Cook, Frederick Charles, 263–64, 266
Cook, Roland, 33
Co-operatives Estates Ltd. (Hobart), 160
Co-partnership housing *see* housing
Coorong National Park (SA), 225

Coronation Park (Brisbane), 78–9
Corrigan, Col J.J., 84–85
Corser, Syd, 243
Cosgrove, Robert, 275, 277–8
Coulter, Dr John, 215, 218, 220, 225, 227
Council of Hobart Progress Associations (CHPA), 262, 265–67, 269, 275, 280–81, 377–78, *see also* town planning associations
Country Roads Board, 111, 344, 357
Courier Mail (Brisbane), 298
Court, Sir Charles, 241
Court, Richard, 251, 254
Cowan, Edith, 179, 181
Cowdery, W.D., 32
Cowles, K.F., 267
crime, 150, 223, 248, 304
Cross, Tom, 296–97
Crow, Maurice, 350, 356
Crow, Ruth, 350, 352, 356
Culburra Beach (Nowra, NSW), 44
Cumberland (VIC), 111
Cumberland County Council (Sydney), 6, 237, 329, 333
Currumbin (QLD), 78
Currie, Wal, 360
Curtin, John, 328

Daceyville Garden Suburb (Sydney), 38
Daily Herald (Adelaide), 127
Daily Post (Hobart), 150, 164
Dalkeith Estate (Perth), 178
Dandenong (Melbourne), 351
Dandenong Police Paddock, 110
Darling Downs (QLD), 70
Darra (QLD), 70
Davey Street (Hobart), 270
Davidge, William, 5, 14, 46, 65, 76, 95–96, 113, 123–24, 149, 159
Davidson, David L., 33, 49, *190*, 192–94, 236, 328
Day, Harold Chalkan, 206
democracy, 305, 309, *see also* participatory democracy
depressions, 5, 21, 29, 57, 113–14, 175, 190, 192, 195, 313, 318
Department (Commonwealth) of Urban and Regional Development (DURD), 6
deputations, 17; NSW, 38, 45–50, 319, 321–6; Queensland, 78–80; South Australia, 121, 133–34, 137–39, 206, 210–11; Tasmania, 269, 276; Western Australia, 186–88, 206
Derwent River (Hobart), 153–54, 162, 274

design competitions, *see* competitions
development, 1–2, 15, 18–19, 27–29, 35–36, 38, 58, 80, 91, 94–95, 111–12, 120, 135, 142, 150, 157, 159, 165, 185–86, 188–89, 191, 203, 206, 209–10, 212–13, 216, 219, 225, 227, 239, 243, 245, 247, 249, 251, 261–62, 269, 272, 276, 278–81, 287–90, 294–300, 306–09, 313–14, 324, 329, 333–35, 337, 343, 351–56, 367–69, 379, *see also* town planning
development associations, 84, *see also* progress associations
Disney, James, 348
Dobson D. Bennet, 33
Domain; Hobart, 162, 165, 274; Sydney, 319, 332
Downes, R.H.B., 178
Drummond, D.H., 320
Dual Club, 140
Duhig, Archbishop James, 74, 77, 302
Dunphy, Milo, 335,
Dunstan, Don, 211, 214–15, 226, *361*

Eagle Farm, Pinkenba (Brisbane), 77
Earle, John, 153

Earle, William J., 78–9
economic conditions, 112, 192, *see also* depressions
Edmonds, A.H., 320
Eggleston, Frederic William, 99
Electoral Reform Society, 142
electricity, 183, 211–12
Electrolytic Zinc Company, 154
Elizabeth Street (Hobart), *270*
Elizabeth Street (Sydney), 320, 325
Ellery, Torrington George,104–05, *122*, 125, 137, 141
Elsey, Bernie, 305–6
engineers, 4–5, 13, 15, 29, 66, 69, 72, 76–77, 105, 113, 133, 178, 181, 193, 211, 243, 264–65, 278, 315, 317, 326, 348, 370, 376
environment, 7–8, 11, 35, 93–95, 122, 127, 140, 211, 216–25, 227, 229, 306, 360, 365, 368, *see also* conservation/town planning – environmental/water conservation; climate change, 20, 360; green agenda, 35, 377; greenhouse effect, 360, 368
eugenics, 42, 100–1
Everett, Percy, 346
expressways *see* freeways/town planning – transport

federal capital, 5, 8, 13, 27–29, 30, 178, *see also* Canberra (ACT)
federal government, 7, 29, 185–86, 204, 221, 225, 241, 248, 300, 331, 343, 346
Federation, 13, 27, 121, 140, 148
Federation of Bushwalkers, 335
Ferguson, W.I., 85
ferries *see* town planning – transport
Field Naturalists Club, 110
Finch, R.L., 243
Fisher, Betty, 225
Fisherman's Bend (Melbourne), 111
Fitzgerald, John D., 16, 28, 31–32, 35–36, 38–39, 42, 51, 56, 59
Fitzroy (Melbourne), 101
Fitzroy Gardens Reserve (Hobart), 269
Flannagan, H. D., 153–54, 159
flat development, 29, 112, 289, 300, *see also* building activity, housing and residential development
Floreat Park (Perth), 178
Footscray Institute of Technology, 360
Forbes, W.J., 178

Ford, Bertram W., 20, 33–34, 58, 317–18, *319*–20, 324–25, 328–*32*, 335–36, 376
foreshores, 104, 111, 248–49, 263, 272–73
Forest Advisory Committee, 334
Forest League, 110
Forrest, Sir John, 175–76
Forrest Place (Perth), 186
Fortitude Valley (Brisbane)
Fowler, Thomas, 154
Franklin, J.T.178
Franklin Square (Hobart), *163*, 270–*71*
Frankston (Melbourne), 351
freeways, 228, 237–39, 241, 299–300, 302, 308, 330, 354, 357–60, 367, *see also* town planning – transport
Friends of the Railway, 238, 241
Fremantle (WA), 184, 241
Fuller, Henry Ernest, 125

Gair, Vince, 293
garden cities, 3, 5, 7–8, 14, 65, 78, 93, 96, 103, 123–24, 135, 345
Garden Cities and Town Planning Association (UK), 5, 14, 96, 103, 123
garden suburbs, 8, 28, 30, 38, 43, 78, 84, 107, 131, 135–36, 139, 150, 152–54, 160, 345, *see also* Daceyville Garden Suburb/Mitcham Garden Suburb
Gardner, Robert, 349, 352, *354*, 360, 375
Gawler, J.S., 345
Geelong (VIC), 105, 111
General Post Office (Sydney), 331–2
Giblin, L.F., 153
Glenlyon Estate (Brisbane), 84
Glenorchy (Hobart), 157
Glenorchy Municipal Council, 162
Gliddon, E.H., 178
goldrush, 174–75, 240
Gold Coast (QLD), 288–89, 303–09
Gold Coast City Council, 307
Gold Coast Protection League, 306
Golf Links (Hobart), 157
Gough, C.O., 83
Grassby, Al, 220–1
Greater London Plan, 237
greater cities movement, 77, 86, 141, 153, 156–57, 162, 175, 207, 263, 277–78, 376, *see also* metropolitan planning; Greater Brisbane City Council, 64–65, 77, 79–80, 82; Greater Perth Council, 95; Greater Sydney, 38, 315; Greater Toowoomba Council, 70

Greater Hobart Planning Advisory Committee, 278
green bans, 2, 6, 240
green belts and wedges, 68, 109, 126, 186, 269, 295, 368, 376
Greig, Dr Jean, 95, 99, 110
Griffin, Marion Mahony, 35, 41
Griffin, Walter Burley, 5, 13, 29, 31, 35, 38, 41, 51, 317
Griffiths, John, 95
Griffiths, Walter Scott, 32, 34, 136
Guildford Progress Association, 334
Grundy, E.B., 125
Guy, J.A., 158

Haberfield (Sydney), 30
Hall, David, 36
Halloran, Henry F., 32–33, 44, 58, 319, 335
Halley, Dr Ida Gertrude, 125–*26*, 129, 131, 138, 141
Hamer, Rupert, 356, 359
Hanlon, Ned, 293
Hardwick, W.B., 178
Hart, Stuart, 208, 229
Hawken, R.W.H., 77
Hawkins, J.B., 190
Hawthorn (Melbourne), 103
Hayes, John, 164
Health Society, 56
Heath, Frank, 5, 343, 346, 349, 351, 375

Heidelberg (Melbourne), 103
height of buildings, 65, 77, 79, *see also* high rise development
Herald (Melbourne), 103
heritage, 110, 216, 241, 251, 357, 360, 377, *see also* conservation
Hepburn, Alastair, 237–41
Hickinbotham, Alan, 226
Higbed, David, *219*, 220, 223–24, 227
high rise development, 240, 247, 299, *see also* development, flat development, height of buildings
Hinze, Russell, 306, 308
Hipkins, Max, 256
Hoardings, 74, 125, 180, 185, 225
Hobart (TAS), 148–49, 151, 153–54, 158, 167, 260, *264*
Hobart City Council, 148, 150, 159, 162–63, 165–66, 168, 264–65, 268, 271–72, 276, 280
Hobart Development League, 167
Hobart Metropolitan Planning Committee (HMPC), 278–9
Hobart Rotary Club, 167
Holden, Henry J., 125, 140
Holford, William, 236
Home and Garden Beautiful, 93

Hooton, Ettie, 179
Hope, Percy, 177–8
Hope Committee (Inquiry into the National Estate), 241
Hopetoun Gardens (Melbourne), 103
Hornabrook, Annie, 141–2
Hornabrook, Canon Charles, 121, 124–25, 141
housing, 5, 7–8, 13, 16–17, 28–29, 31, 38, 43, 65, 71–76, 81, 86, 91, 94–97, 99, 103–04, 106, 111–13, 121, 124, 127–28, 135–36, 148–54, 157, 159–62, 168–69, 206, 209, 212, 228, 243, 249, 260–61, 263, 274, 279–81, 302, 326, 328, 333–34, 337, 345–46, 357, 359, 367–68, *see also* slum clearance
Housing Investigation and Slum Abolition Board, 113
Housing Commission of Victoria, 112, 357
Howard, Ebenezer, 3, 17
Howe, Renate, 357, 369
Huggan, John (J.B.), 99–*100*, 102–03
Huxham, John, *71*–74, 81, 84
Hyde Park (Sydney), *41*–42

immigration, 101, 154, 220, 307, 359

Imperial Health Conference (London, UK), 95
industrial development, 70, 71, 75–77, 112, 152–54, 167, 185, 191, 207, 210, 222, 237, 277, 295, 359
Irvine, Professor Robert, 31–32, 38–39, 43, 51
Isaacs, Isaac, 132
Ithaca (Brisbane), 68

James, Rev. J. Ernest, 121, 125, 141
Jenkinson, C.M., 65
Johnstone, Gilbert, 160, 163, 166
Jolly, William Alfred, 80
Jones, Clem, 288–89, *297*–303, 308
Jones, G. Sydney, 29, 31–32, 39
Joyner, Ethel, 179, *180*, 184

Kelly, Col T.H., 32
Kemsley, A.N., 207
Kew (Melbourne), 103
Kindergarten Union, 179, 184
King, Hannibal, 81
Klem, Carl, 175, 177–78, 185–87, 189, *190*–92
Knott, J.E., 265
Koch, Rudolph, 149, *151*–52, 155–56, 158, 161, 167–68, 375
Kogarah Bay Progress Association, 334

Kurnell Oil Refinery Protest Committee, 334

Lambert, William, 50
land-use *see* town planning – land-use/zoning
Lang, Jack, 57
Langer, Karl, 291
Langham, W.H., 142-3
Launceston (TAS), 149, 154
Lawler, J.H., 277
Leach, Dr John, 99
League of Loyal Women, 141
lectures, 5, 6, 14, 16, 27, 38-39, 50-57, 59, 65-66, 77, 80, 91, 93, 96-97, 103, 108, 120-21, 123-24, 129, 149, 151, 153, 173, 176, 181, 192, 204, 213-18, 255, 316, 318, 346
Lee, G. Rosten, 325
Lee, Walter Henry, 153-5
Legislation, 4, 8, 13, 15, 17, 19-21, 36, 43, 188; New South Wales, 5, 38, 59, 315, 319, 324-25, 328-29; Queensland, 77; South Australia, 5, 120-21, 124, 126-27, 133-36, 138-39, 142-43, 203, 206, 209, 211-13, 218, 223, 225, 227-9; Tasmania, 5, 148-49, 151, 153-61, 169, 263, 277, 279-80
Victoria, 5, 96, 103-05, 107, 111-13, 342-43, 345, 347-48, 351, 353, 357, 361; Western Australia, 5, 20, 173, 180, 186-87, 193-95, 235-36, 252, 254-55
Lenah Valley Progress Association, 267
Letchworth (UK), 93
Lewis, Professor Brian, 351, *353*-54, 361
Lewis, J., 125
Lewis, Dr Miles, 360-62
Liberal League of Western Australia, 176-77
Light, William, 120, 122-23, 132, 135-36, 207
Light Journal of Town Planning and Housing (Adelaide), 17, 135-36, 142
Lindeman Island (QLD), 290
Lipscombe, L.J., 162-64, 166
Lloyd, M.L., 178
Lloyd, Rex, 206
Lobbying, 35, 45, 59, 77, 91, 96, 98, 111-12, 134, 184, 216, 235, 240, 254-55, 275, 342, 348, 352, 369, *see also* deputations
local government, 7, 17, 20-21, 376; New South Wales, 28, 36, 315, 325, 328-29, 333; Queensland, 66, 70, 72-75, 81, 84, 300, 302, 304; South Australia, 132, 137, 141-42, 168, 206, 211, 216, 223, 227; Tasmania, 148, 157, 159,

161–62, 264–65, 267, 274, 277, 279, 281; Victoria, 103, 111, 113, 345, 348, 350, 357–58, 360, 370; Western Australia, 175, 178–79, 181, 183–85, 188–89, 191–93, 241–43, 246–47, 254
Local Government Engineers' Association (NSW), 55–56
Local Government Women's Association, 142
London, Geoffrey, 255–6
Long, Charles Richard, 99
Longmore, Lydia, 129, *130*–31, 138, 141
Lord, Richard David, 165
Lowther, T., 293
Luker, Sidney, 329
Lyons, Joseph, 158

McColl, M.A., 290
McInnes, Ronald A., 67, 76–77, 80, 84, 264–65, 269, 274, 277–79, 290–93, 302, 308, 374,
MacKay, Keith, 352
Mackay (QLD), 287–88, *289*, 290–92, 307
McKenzie, J.A., 157–58, 168
McLachlan, Dugald McKenzie, 315
McNamara, Francis, 131
McPhee, J.C., 156, 158, 167
Macquarie Street (Sydney), 319

McRobbie, Alexander, 305–6
Manly Town Planning Association, 318
Mant, John, 252–3
March, Don P., 210
Maroochy Shire (QLD), 83–4
Marshall, P.D., 160, 165
Martin Place (Sydney), 316, 319–20, *323*
Master Builders' Association; New South Wales, 56; Queensland, 82; Tasmania, 156
Mawson, Thomas, 181
Mayo, Dr Helen, 141
Meagher, Richard James, 166
media, 13, 17, 39, 56, 95, 109, 150, 168, 204, 206–07, 255, 319, 330, 368
Melbourne (VIC), 94, 101–02, 107, 109–10, 113–14, 189, 346, 351–52, *355*, 358–59, 362, 368–69
Melbourne City Council, 105, 107, 109
Melbourne Cricket Ground, 109
Melbourne Metropolitan Planning Scheme, 6
Melbourne Town Hall, 97–8
Menzies, R.G., 331
Mercury (Hobart), 149–50, 153
Metropolitan Adelaide Transportation Study, 221

Metropolitan Board of Works (Melbourne), 106, 344, 351, 353–54, 357
Metropolitan Local Government Association, 188
metropolitan planning, 6, 35, 77–78, 81, 107, 112, 141, 188, 193, 208, 210, 235, 247, 261–62, 277–78, 280, 329, 334, 348, 351, 368, see also town planning
Metropolitan Town Planning Commission (Melbourne), 5, 91, 107–09, 111, 114, 162
Metropolitan Town Planning Commission (Perth), 188–90
Metropolitan Transportation Committee (Melbourne), 358
Middle Harbour (Sydney), 325
Minimum Allotment, Anti-Slum and Housing Crusade Committee (MAASHCC), 96, 99, 102
Mitcham Garden Suburb, 131, 135–36, see also Colonel Light Gardens
Mitchell, Sir James, 187–88
modernism, 2–4, 18, 21–22, 27, 29, 35, 70, 75–76, 94, 100–01, 121, 135, 142, 191, 238, 260, 287–89, 294–95, 298–99, 301–03, 308–09, 329, 332, 336, 373, 377–78
Moonah (Hobart), 157

Morialta Residents' Association, 228
Morrell, James, 5
Mount Lawley No 3 Estate (Perth), 178
Mount Lofty Ranges Association, 216–18
Mount Nelson (Hobart), 161, 273
Mount Tambourine (QLD), 80
Mount Wellington (Hobart), 273, 276
Mullins, Patrick, 305
Mumford, Lewis, 246
Municipal Association of Victoria, 94, 344
Municipal Journal, 95
Murdoch, Sir Keith, 345–46, 348, 351
Murdoch, Thomas, 164
Murray Street (Hobart), 270
Myer, Kenneth, 353–4

Nambour (QLD), 83–4
Nambour Development Association, 84
Nambour Progress Association, 83
Nangle, James, 32, 39
Nathan, Sir Matthew, 73
National Capital Development Commission, 6, see also Canberra and federal capital

National Council of Women, 99, 141, 179, 209–10, 239
National Fitness Council, 210, 224
National Parks and Primitive Areas Council, 334–35
National Parks Association, 99–100, 102, 105, 108, 110–11, *see also* Victorian National Parks Association
national parks, 15, 70, 92, 99, 111, 114, 222, 225, 290, 334, 346–47, 352, *see also* parks and reserves
National Trust
New South Wales, 5, 330, 334; South Australia, 216; Victoria, 111, 362; Western Australia, 239–40, 253
nationalism, 13, 101, 140
Nelson (Hobart), 157
Nelson, W.A., 178
Nettlefold, Sir Thomas S., 165, 348
Neville, Sir Ralph, 96
New Farm (Brisbane), 67, 301
New Heart for Perth Society, 238–40
New Housewives Association, 333, *see also* Progressive Housewives Association/Union of Australian Women
New Town (Hobart), 157

New Town Bay, 153, 162
Newcastle Betterment Board, 55
Newlands Estate (Hobart), 160
Nicholls, Margaret, 360
Nicklin, Frank, 303
NIMBYism, 1, 369
Noise Abatement Society, 49, 334
Nock, Norman, 324
Noosa (QLD), 84–85, 289
North Hobart, 157, 270
North Terrace (Adelaide), 137
North-West Bay (TAS), 154
Nowland, Ray, 80, 302
Nunn, G.M., 178

O'Connor, Noel, 352, 354
Olympic Games (Melbourne), 352
open space, 4, 13, 17, 28, 38, 68, 93–95, 102–03, 121–22, 126–27, 155, 161, 164–66, 182, 191, 210, 213, 260, 273, 294, 313, 330, 344–45, *see also* parks and reserves

Packard, J.H., 136–38
Paddington (Brisbane), 301
Palace Guards, 238, 240
Palace Hotel, 240–41
Parents and Teachers Association, 179, 184
parkland *see* parks and reserves

Parks and Playground Movement (PPM), 38, 322, 324, 378, *see also* children's playgrounds/parks and reserves
parks and reserves, 13, 38, 40, 45, 65–68, 75–76, 91, 93, 95, 99, 102–04, 108–11, 121, 124, 126, 138, 148–51, 157, 162–68, 173, 180–82, 184, 187, 207, 223, 227–28, 280, 298, 319, 336, 343, 352, 357, 367, 369, *see also* national parks
Parks Land League, 126
Parks Victoria, 110
Parry, Mervyn, 243
Pearson, Arthur, 96, 99
pedestrians, 37, 50, 84, 184, 248, 331, 359, 368, 377
Pennant Hills Citizens' Association, 334
Permanent Road Congresses International Association, 94
Perrott, Leslie (Snr), 348–49, 351–52, 360
Perth (WA), 6, 19, 175, 184, 235, 247, 249, 252
Perth City Council, 175, 181, 184–86, 188–89, 191, 242, 245–47, 251–52
Perth City Foreshore Competition, 249
Perth Town Hall, 178
Pether, Rod, 251

Philp, Colin, 267–68, 271–74, 277, 279–81
Phillips, Morris Mondle, 99
Pinkenba Association, 294
Plan SA, 221
Plan News Review (Melbourne), 18, 355, 358
Planner (Brisbane), 18
Planning SA, 221, 224, 226
planners *see* town planners
Planning Institute of Australia, 7, 18, 210, 294, 333, 347, 368, 377, *see also* Town and Country Planning Institute (NSW)/Royal Australian Planning Institute
Playford, Thomas, 206–7
Poetry Society, 140
politics, 1, 4, 15–16, 20–21, 72–73, 112, 114, 120–21, 139–40, 142–43, 150–51, 154–55, 176–77, 194–95, 290, 295, 318, 323–24, 326, 328, 337, 342, 353, 356, 359, 373–76, *see also* political parties
political parties, *see also* politics; New South Wales, 318, 320; Queensland, 70–71, 73, 298–99, 303, 305, 308; South Australia, 139, 141, 228; Tasmania, 150–51, 153, 158–59; Victoria, 112, 356, 369;

Western Australia, 177, 239–42, 244, 254
Poole, George Temple, 178–79, 187
Poole, Max, 248
population, 6–7, 10, 13–14, 36, 65, 75, 109–10, 112, 120, 150–51, 154–55, 158–59, 174, 189, 207–08, 220–21, 223, 238, 247–48, 253, 260, 263, 274, 279, 293, 313, 343, 349, 359
Port Kembla (NSW), 319–20
postwar reconstruction, 2, 7, 325, 343, *see also* wars
poverty, 70, 141, 161, 223, *see also* social conditions
Price, T.A., 69–71, 78, 82, 302
Prince of Wales Bay (TAS), 153
Princes Wharf (Hobart), 163–64, 276
Princes Wharf Improvement Association, 164
progress associations, 10, 19, 56, 83, 103, 110, 156–57, 167–68, 260–02, 264–67, 277, 288–89, 294–96, 302, 305–08, 318, 334, 352, 357, 377–78
Progressive Housewives Association, 333, 335, *see also* New Housewives Association
progressivism, 20, 29, 60, 100–01, 114, 210, 276, 292, 296–97, 316
property developers, 287–88, *see also* development
Property Owners Protection Association, 82
property ownership, 3, 16, 65, 80, 82, 137, 148, 156, 159, 169, 295, 303
public participation, 1–3, 209–11, 226–27, 229, 239, 260–61, 264–65, 292, 298, 307, 360, 368, 377–78
publications, 16–18, 39, 42–44, 56, 107, 135, 206, 267, 346–47, 349–45, 355–56, 358, 360
publicity and propaganda, 9, 17, 27, 29, 39–41, 108, 135, 180–81, 191, 227, 239, 317, 325, 349, 376, 378,
Purdy, Dr J.S., 32–33, 40, 316

Queenborough (Hobart), 157
Queensland Workers Dwelling Board, 74

racism, 100–01, 307, *see also* eugenics
Railway Square (Sydney), 50
railways, 175, 184, 186, 191–92, 239–40, 323, 325, *see also* transport
Raw, J.T., 99

Rea, Frank, 178
Reade, Charles, 5, 14, 19, 38, 65, 73–74, 95–98, 113, *123*–24, 127–29, 131–34, 138, 140, 149, 151, 153–55, 159, 176, 178, 203, 315
real estate, 82, 85, 243, 329, *see also* property ownership
Real Estate Institute
Queensland, 82
South Australia, 213
redevelopment *see* development/civic improvement
Reece, Eric, 269
regional planning *see* town planning – regional
Register (Adelaide), 125, 127–28, 138
Reid, Reg E., 32
resident action, 2, 6, 226, 302, 335, 360 369, 378,
residential development, 6, 36, 50, 104, 112, 121, 126, 184, 191, 228, 248, 278, 295, 315, 325, *see also* development, flat development, housing
resumptions, 292, 303
Retail Traders' Association, 254
ribbon development, 111, 260, 269, 278, 313, 343
Richards, H.C., 137
Rigby, Edward, 99, 105, 110
Ringwood (Melbourne), 351

Rischbieth, Bessie, 179, *180*–81, 184, 187
Risdon Reserve (Hobart), 269
Risdon Road (Hobart), 157
Ritter, Paul, 211
roads *see* town planning – transport
Robinson, R.T., 178
Rockhampton, 74, 82–3
Rofe, T.E., 33
Rogers, Richard, 246
Rolls, John, 225
Roma Street Markets (Brisbane), *295*–96, 299, 303
Rosebery (Sydney), 41
Rosenthal, Sir Charles, 32–3
Rosenthal, Ken, 243
Rosetta (Hobart), 162
Rossi, Daisy, 179
Rowntree, Amy, 273
Royal Automobile Club of Queensland, 67, 80
Royal Automobile Club of Victoria, 348
Royal Australian Institute of Architects (RAIA), 204, 214, 236, 248, 266–67, 316, 335
Royal Australian Planning Institute (RAPI), 6–7, *see also* Planning Institute of Australia/Town and Country Planning Institute (NSW); Australian Planning Institute, 6, 18, 210, 294, 316, 333

Royal Commissions, 175, 194, 236
Royal Commission into the Improvement of the City of Sydney and Its Suburbs (1909), 28–29, 41, 315
Royal Exhibition Building (Melbourne), 344
Royal Victorian Institute of Architects, 106
Royal Western Australian Historical Society, 239
Rundle Street (Adelaide), 219
Russell, Geoff, 243
Russell, Hugh McDiarmid, 66
Russell, Percy, 95
Ryan, T.J., 72, 74–75
Ryan, Victor, 121, 129, 131, 138

Salamanca Place (Hobart), 163
Salon (The), 39–40
Salter, Miss, 32
Sandercock, Leonie, 6, 112
Sanders, James D., 178
Sandy Bay (Hobart), 161, 273
Santamaria, B.A., 293
Save Our Suburbs, 6, 367–68, *see also* suburbs
Saw, Dr Athelstan, 176
Saw, William, 19, 175–76, 178, 182, 184, 187–90, 192, 374
Sawyer, Geoffrey, 32

schools and school children, 39–40, 127, 129, 184, 349
sewerage *see* town planning – public health and sanitation
Shaw, W.B., 178
Sherrard, Howard, 6, 316
shops and shopping, 37, 85, 167, 192, 219, 237–38, 243, 248, 274, 295, 305
Sibly, John, 224–25, 227
Simpson, Albert, 123, 210, 224
Sir James Barrett Memorial Medal, 351, 356, 360, *see also* Barrett, Sir James
Slaughter, J.C., 298
slum clearance, 4, 13, 35, 91, 112, 149, 158, 160–61, 184, 215, 313, *see also* housing
Small, Arthur J., 33–34, 36, 45, 57
Smeaton, Thomas, 125
Smith, Wilbur (and Associates), 299
Smythe, Dr John, 99
social class, 15, 34, 36, 68, 70, 77, 96, 100–01, 111–14, 127, 149, 159, 261, 274, 313, 315, 370
social reform, 20, 38, 51, 57, 91, 101, 113–14, 121, 150, 162, 179, *see also* town planning – reform/urban reform
socialism, 64, 70, 72, 75, 175

soldier settlement, 75, *see also* War Service Homes and Wars
Soundy, John, 263
South Australian Conservation Newsletter/Bulletin, 216, 222
South Australian Institute of Architects, 124–5
South Australian Institute of Surveyors, 127, 133, 137, 139
South Hobart, 157
South Melbourne, 104
South Melbourne Town Hall, 362
Southern Metropolitan Master Planning Authority (Hobart), 262, 280
Sowden, William, 125–27, 138, 140
Space (Melbourne), 18, 355, 359–61
Spain, Lt Col Alfred, 31–33, 58
Springbrook Plateau (QLD), 78, 80
Sprott, Dr Gregory, 165
St David's Park (Hobart), *165*–66
St George's Terrace (Perth), 175, 185–86, 239–40, *242*, 247
St Malo (Hunters Hill, Sydney), 330
Stannage, Tom, 194
Stanton, Richard, 30, 32
Stapley, Frank, 16, 104–07, 110, 375
state government, 7–8, 16–17, 56, 373, 375; New South Wales, 28–29, 36–38, 43, 45–49, 56–57, 313, 315, 319, 321–24, 328–30, 333; Queensland, 64, 70, 72–73, 84, 293–94, 300, 303, 305–07; South Australia, 121, 126–27, 129, 133–34, 139–40, 153–60, 203–04, 206–08, 219, 227–29, 377; Tasmania, 153–59, 168–69, 260, 263, 269, 275–81; Victoria, 20, 93, 107, 110–13, 345, 348, 351–53, 360, 362, 368, 370; Western Australia, 20, 173–76, 178–80, 182–83, 185, 188, 190–91, 195, 206, 219, 235–37, 239–41, 244–52, 254
state planning authorities; New South Wales, 36, 329–30; Queensland, 292, 308–09; South Australia, 206, 212–13, 223–24, 227–28; Tasmania, 150, 262, 279–80; Victoria, 112; Western Australia, 235–36, 252, 254,
State Planning Commission (WA), 246
Stead, David G., 33, 34, 58, 60
Steffanoni, L., 178

Stephen, Justice Milner, 32–34, 39
Stephens, John, 120
Stephenson, Professor Gordon, 235, 237–41, 246, 251
Stephenson-Hepburn Plan, 237–241
Stevens, Bertram, 324
Stewart, Bruce, 155, 163
Stirling, Harriet, 141
Stowe, Major F. Ernest, 31
Strahle, David, 216, 222
street barrows, 37
street lighting, 183, 184, 298, *see also* electricity
street widening, 13, 29, 50, 79, 165, 174, 185–86, 207, 262–63, 270, 320, *see also* town planning – transport
Streeton, Arthur, 110
Stretton, Hugh, 6
Styne, Les and Miriam, *249*
subdivisions, 13, 79, 95, 107, 134, 155, 157, 160–61, 180–82, 190, 203, 208, 216, 218, 221, 263, 269, 313
suburbs, 2, 8, 28, 35, 38, 41, 65, 70, 78, 91, 93, 95, 97, 101, 104, 111–12, 121–22, 126–27, 130, 134, 139, 142, 156, 160–61, 167, 178, 187, 191, 204, 221, 228, 238, 252, 254, 261, 294–95, 299, 301, 313, 334, 336, 359, 367, 369, *see also* garden suburbs
Sulman, John Sir, 5, 13, 29, 31–33, 35–37, 39, 41, 43, 50–51, 55, 56–58, 66, 181, 316, 374
Summerhayes, Geoff, 248
Sunshine Coast (QLD), 303
Surfers Paradise (QLD), *304–06*, 308
Surfers Paradise Progress Association, 305
surveyors, 5, 13, 15, 29, 44, 72, 77, 96, 99, 105, 113, 123, 127, 133–34, 136–39, 168, 176–78, 182, 193, 204, 264, 278, 315, 326, 348, 376
Sutton, C.R., 206
Swan Hill (VIC), 343
Swan River (WA), 174, 179, 185, 237
Swan River Improvement Scheme, 185
Swinburne Institute of Technology, 360
Sydney (NSW), 27, *28*–29, 313–*14*, 315, 320, 324, 334–35, 337, 374–75
Sydney Bush Walkers, 335
Sydney City Council, 37, 50, 320, 325
Sydney Harbour Bridge, 41, 318, 323

401

Sydney Morning Herald, 31, 316, 318, 331, 335
Sydney Opera House, 330
Sydney Region Outline Plan, 6
Sydney Regional Plan Convention, 58
Sydney Town Hall, 31, 41, 325
Symons, F.W., 205–06

Tait, J.M., 190
Taylor, Sir Allen, 39
Taylor, Florence M., 17, 29, 33, 35, 37–38, 40, 42, 51, 56–58, 138, 328–29, 336, 374
Taylor, George A., 5, 13, 17, 29–*30*, 31–32, 35, 37–43, 45, 51, 57–58, 60, 138, 178, 328, 336, 374
Theodore, Ted, 74
Thomas, Right Rev. Dr Nutter, 125
Thynne, A.W., 83
Tomkinson, Amy, 125, 131, 141–42
Tomlinson, Professor A., 178
Tompkins, H.W., 99
Tonkin, David, 228–29
Tonkin, John, 236
Toowoomba (QLD), 70
tourism, 100, 121, 140, 149, 163, 166–67, 228, 263, 273, 287–89, 292, 305–09
Town and Country Planning Advisory Committee, 328
Town and Country Planning Institute of Australia (NSW), 5, 58, 317, 324, 333, 376, *see also* Planning Institute of Australia/Royal Australian Planning Institute
town planners, 2, 45, 65, 68, 71, 75, 79, 85, 142, 149, 159, 185, 188, 208, 211, 213, 227, 236, 240, 246–48, 251, 261, 267, 289, 291, 293, 300, 303, 305, 307, 315, 317, 326, 329, 358, 362, 368, 370, 377–79
town planning, 1–3, 19, 27, 29–30, 36, 42, 51, 56, 154, 290, 301–02, 328, 373, 375, 379, *see also* city planning/urban planning; anti-planning, 20, 305, 329; community, 4, 101, 210, 267, 287, 313, 319, 358; education, public, 14, 39, 55, 59, 77, 92, 93, 129, 135, 210, 316; environmental, 1–3, 7–8, 14, 21, 35, 43–44, 65, 101, 112–13, 120, 140, 149, 166, 168–69, 215, 218–19, 221–25, 306, 333–35, 337, 358, 367–69, 375, 378–79; alienation and encroachments, 13, 38, 91, 109, 65, 95, 109, 273, 276, 352; institutional, 7, 193, 343, 347, 378; landscape, 17, 148, 166, 227, 326; land-use, 8, 64, 78, 208, 221, 304, 315, 358,

369, *see also* zoning; professional planners, 21, 193, 204–05, 211, 315–17, 326, 328, 347, 360, 376; public health and sanitation, 4, 13–14, 28, 51, 68, 70, 76–77, 81–82, 85, 95, 141, 157–58, 174, 178, 278, 300, 345; reform, 13–14, 16, 20, 27, 72, 101–02, 112–13, 120–21, 127–28, 136, 138, 156, 375–78; regional, 279, 308, 325, 343; religious influences, 74, 121, 141, 293; streetscape, 37, 59, 323, 360; transport, 7, 9, 28, 29, 35, 37, 67–68, 75–80, 86, 94–95, 97, 103–04, 107, *108*–09, 111–12, 148–49, 158–59, 161–62, 175, 180, 182, 183, 184–86, *187*, 191–92, 206–07, 221–23, 228, 237– 43, 248, 262–63, 265, 269–73, 275–76, 292–93, *298–301*, 306, 308, 313, 320, 323, 330, 343–44, 354–55, 357–59, 361, 367–68, 377–78

Town Planning Advisory Board (NSW), 59, 315;

Town Planning and Housing (Sydney), 17, 43, 135

town planning associations, 2–4, 8, 10–14, 16–22, 342, 374, 376, 378–79, *see also* advisory boards and committees;

(United Kingdom) Town and Country Planning Association, 3, 18, 378; (New South Wales) Town Planning Association of New South Wales (TPANSW), 9, 13, 20, 27, 31–34, 36, 40, 59, 101, 138, 313–14, 317–20, 324–26, 331–34, 336–37, 376–37, *see also* town planning associations; (Queensland) Town Planning Association (QTPA)/Queensland Town and Country Planning Association (QTCPA), 9, 64, 66, 72, 76, 78–79, 84, 86, 287–90, 292–94, 297–98, 301, 302, 308–09, 376–77; (South Australia) South Australian Town Planning and Improvement Society (SATPIS)/South Australian Town Planning and Housing Association (SATPHA)/ Town and Country Planning Association (T&CPA), 9–10, 120, 125–29, 139–43, 203, 210–13, 216, 224–29; (Tasmania) Southern Tasmanian Town Planning Association (STTPA)/ Southern Tasmanian Town and Central Progress Association (STTCPA), 10, 148–49, 151,

403

154–55, 160–61, 166, 168, 260, 280, 377; (Victoria) Town Planning and Parks Association of Victoria (VTPPA)/Town Planning Association of Victoria (TPAV)/Town and Country Planning Association (TCPA), 9, 20, 91, 95, 98, 102–05, 107–10, 114, 342–46, 351–52, 362–70, 377–78; (Western Australia) Town Planning Association of Western Australian (TPAWA), 10, 173, 176, 178, 184–89, 192–93, 195, 235, 237, 254–55

town planning associations membership; New South Wales, 15–16, 27, 29, 32–34, 36, 44, 51–55, 58–59, 313, 319, 336; Queensland, 72; South Australia, 16, 125, 127, 137, 210–11, 224–25; Tasmania, 153, 156; Victoria, 99, 105, 110–11, 113, 344–46, 348, 352, 355–58, 360–62, 367; Western Australia, 178–79, 193, 248–50 (City Vision)

Town Planning Board (NSW), 36

Town Planning Board (TAS), 154

Town Planning Board (WA), 190–93, 236, 240

Town Planning Commission (QLD), 67

Town Planning Company of Australia, 41

Town Planning Institute of South Australia, 204–07

Town Planning Institute of Western Australia, 193, 236

town planning movement, 13, 18–19, 21–22, 58–59, 64, 70, 157, 292

trade unions, 76, 140, 299, 302

traffic *see* town planning – transport

trams, 104, *108*–09, 182–84, 299, *see also* town planning – transport

Tree Lovers' Civic League of Ku-ring-gai, 334–35

Tree Society, 239

trees and tree planting, 44, 56, 59, 65, 77, 109, 111, 148, 163, 167, 173, 183–84, 191, 228, 334, 368

Trousselot, H.E., 167

Troy, Patrick, 6

Turnbull, John Arthur, 265–67, *268*, 274–76

Tuxen, Saxil, 99, 111, 352

Uffindell, Henry, 125, 127–29, 130–32, 134, 136–37, 140, 374
Underwood, Zdenka, 248
Union of Australian Women, 334, *see also* Progressive Housewives Association and New Housewives Association
University of Adelaide, 206
University of Melbourne, 96, 360
University of New South Wales, 6, 335
University of Sydney, 5, 6, 39, 56
University of Western Australia, 244
Unley Corporation, 121, 127
Uralla (NSW), 320
urban development *see* civic improvements/development
urban planning, 1, 4, 112, 281, 308, 343, 360, 373, 379, *see also* city planning/town planning
urban reform, 4, 8, 15, 21, 27, 28, 73, 91, 157, 175, 300, 357, 376, *see also* social reform/town planning – reform
urban renewal *see* slum clearance
Uren, Tom, 300, 359

Vacuum Oil Company, 166
Vaughan, Crawford, 125
Vaughan, Hon J.H., 125, 139–40
Veale, William C.D., 204–06
Vernon, Walter Liberty, 31, 56, 315
Vernon Memorial Lectures, 5, 56, 315–16
Victoria Park Station Estate (Perth), 178
Victoria Square (Adelaide), *208*
Victorian National Parks Association, 352, *see also* National Parks Association
Vincent, R.P., 178

WA Fellowship of Writers, 239
WA Inc., 235, 244–45
Walford, Ray, 361, 368–69
Walker, J.D., 33–34
Walkley, Gavin, 204
Wallis, F.S., 125
Wapping (Hobart), *160*–61, 165, 168
war memorials, 50, 80
War Service Homes, 159
Warburton, Jim, 213, 227
Ward, W., 125
Warnock, Bill, 246–48, 250–51, 255
Warnock, Diana, *249*
wars, 5, 375, *see also* postwar reconstruction; Vietnam, 2, 6
World War I (and post-WWI), 5, 8, 13–14, 16, 55, 70, 76,

405

102, 104, 114, 123, 125, 153–55, 159, 168, 177, 313; interwar years, 19, 28, 75, 132, 168, 177, 185, 204, 236, 281, 292–94, 303, 307, 313, 343, 349, 375, 377

World War II (and post-WWII), 2–3, 5, 7, 8, 14, 19–21, 27, 154, 168, 177, 191, 203–04, 235, 254, 260–63, 280, 295, 324–26, 328, 331, 334, 337, 342–44, 346, 359, 377–78

water conservation, 56, 216, *see also* conservation/environment

water supply, 70, 81–82, 95, 174, 221, 277, 344, *see also* town planning – public health and sanitation

Waterhouse, E.G., 33–34

Waterman, Peter, 253

Wattle League, 110

Wavell Heights Progress Association, 294

Webb, G.A., 125

Webb, Professor Martyn, 243–44, 248, 255

Weekes, Norman, 33, 315

Wells, Col R.M.S., 32–33

Welwyn Garden City, 181, 315

West Australian, 181, 185, 254

West Hobart (TAS), 157, 162

West Park Lands (South and East Park Lands), 129, 135, 138

West Terrace Children's Playground, *131*

Weyba Bridge (Noosa), 85

Whitlam, Gough, 300, 359–60

Wildlife Preservation Society, 334

Wilkinson, Professor Leslie, 316–17

Wilkinson, William, 125

Williamson, William, 39

Williams-Ellis, Clough, 204

Wilson, R.M., 85

Winston, Denis, 205–06, 228

women, 14–15, 35, 42, 56, 68–69, 99, 124–25, 141–42, 157, 179, 184, 187, 209–10, 239, 273, 334–35, 368

Women's Service Guilds, 179, 187, 239

Women's Non-Party Political Association, 141

Wood, Dr A.T., 95

Wood, Ian, 290–*91*, 302

Worker's Political League, 153

Wright, A.R.L., 178

Wyatt, Annie, 334

Wyperfeld (VIC), 111

Yarra Park and River (Melbourne), 103–04, 109, 343

Yarra Valley, 352, 355

Yelland, S.E., 125
Yeppoon (QLD), 307
Young, A.H., (Jeanne), 125
Young, Frank W., 121

zoning, 76–79, 82, 86, 91, 107, 111–12, 157, 192–93, 228, 237, 243, 253, 263, 266, 272–73, 279, 292, 295, 302, 308, 315, 359, *see also* town planning – land-use

www.ingramcontent.com/pod-product-compliance
Lightning Source LLC
Chambersburg PA
CBHW071809230426
43670CB00013B/2405